FLANNERY O'CONNOR, HERMIT NOVELIST

RICHARD GIANNONE

Flannery O'Connor,
Hermit Novelist

UNIVERSITY OF ILLINOIS PRESS

URBANA AND CHICAGO

*Publication of this book was supported by a grant
from Fordham University.*

Library of Congress Cataloging-in-Publication Data
Giannone, Richard.
Flannery O'Connor, hermit novelist / Richard Giannone.
p.   cm.
Includes bibliographical references and index.
ISBN 0-252-02528-8
1. O'Connor, Flannery—Religion.
2. Christianity and literature—United States—History—
20th century. 3. Christian fiction, American—History and
criticism. 4. Monastic and religious life in literature.
5. Spiritual life in literature. 6. Asceticism in literature.
7. Solitude in literature. 8. Hermits in literature.
9. Deserts in literature. 10. Desert Fathers. I. Title.
PS3565.C57Z6794   2000
813'.54—dc21   99-6653
CIP

C 5 4 3 2 1

To Frank D'Andrea and Joseph Sendry

The journey is long, and the way dry and barren, that must be traveled to attain the fount of water, the land of promise.

—Statutes of the Carthusian Order 1.4.1.

Contents

Acknowledgments

DURING THE YEARS of work on this book, I have accumulated a number of debts. My thanks first go to Fordham University for the two faculty fellowships that gave me the time to develop and complete the manuscript. When I initially tested my ideas with other scholars, their positive response heartened me about the importance of the study. Portions of this work have appeared earlier, in different form, in *Christianity and Literature, Flannery O'Connor: New Perspectives* (published by the University of Georgia Press), *Literature and Belief,* and *Religion and Literature.* I am grateful to the editors of these journals and the Georgia collection of essays for permission to reprint the essays.

Here I should like to acknowledge, in particular, Emily Rogers, acquisitions editor at the University of Illinois Press, whose interest in the project helped to give it life. The manuscript found other friends in two readers for the University of Illinois Press. By his sensitive evaluation of the argument as a whole, Arthur Kinney helped me to improve this study. Again, John Desmond meticulously read the typescript, and I have profited greatly from his insights and suggestions for changes. Over a number of years, the community of Cistercian monks at St. Joseph's Abbey in Spencer, Massachusetts, has provided me with a place of rest and silence in which to share in their life and think about some fundamental issues. Finally, many colleagues and friends have enthusiastically supported my research. For their encouragement and help, I would like to express my appreciation to J. Robert Baker, Gary Ciuba, Mary Erler, Rose Adrienne Gallo, Eve Keller, Edward John Mullaney, Joyce Rowe, Philip Sicker, Joseph Wholey, and Margaret Smith Wholey.

All of this generosity from so many people and all the assistance rendered while writing this book have brought home to me one of the central teachings of the desert. For the ancient hermits, their quest for God in solitude was inextricably bound to their concern for others. The same attention to personal ties animates the life and work of Flannery O'Connor. Those human bonds have held my work together, for friendship lies at the heart of my pursuits and obligations. The dedication of this book to Frank D'Andrea and Joseph Sendry expresses a debt that I have felt to two friends for their decades of unfailing loyalty and guidance.

Abbreviations

CW   *Flannery O'Connor: Collected Works.* Ed. Sally Fitzgerald. New York: Library of America, 1988.

HB   *The Habit of Being: Letters of Flannery O'Connor.* Ed. Sally Fitzgerald. New York: Farrar, 1979.

Lives   *The Lives of the Desert Fathers.* Trans. Norman Russell. London: Mowbray, 1980.

MM   *Mystery and Manners: Occasional Prose,* by Flannery O'Connor. Ed. Sally and Robert Fitzgerald. New York: Farrar, 1969.

Sayings *The Sayings of the Desert Fathers. The Alphabetical Collection.* Rev. ed. Trans. Benedicta Ward. Kalamazoo, Mich.: Cistercian, 1984.

Note: Throughout the text, the first number in parenthetical citations to patristic works, including those listed above, indicates the section, paragraph, or saying; the second, bracketed number indicates the page. For some works, including the *Lives* and *Sayings,* the subject's or speaker's name is also given. In the case of Cassian's *Conferences,* the conference number is indicated by a roman numeral.

FLANNERY O'CONNOR, HERMIT NOVELIST

1 *The Hermit Novelist*

Be solitary, be silent, and be at peace.
—Arsenius, *The Sayings of the Desert Fathers*

Lord, I'm glad I'm a hermit novelist.
—Flannery O'Connor, *The Habit of Being*

THIS BOOK STUDIES the importance of desert life and ascetic
spirituality in Flannery O'Connor's fiction. O'Connor's use of this tradition takes us back to late antiquity. About four centuries after Christ, the
founding father Anthony the Great and a number of men and women were
dissatisfied with the accepted way of Christian life in Greco-Roman culture and withdrew from society to live as hermits alone or in small groups
in the nearby desert and mountain crags of Egypt, Syria, and Palestine.
Hermit comes from the Greek *eremos*, meaning desert. The story of the
desert was one of the most lasting creations of the ancient world. It was
and remains in the history of spiritual quest a legend of a harsh reality
and a glorious ideal.

The aim of the first Christian hermits was simple: to find their true
selves that could bring them close to God. The means the hermits em-
ployed to reach divine intimacy was correspondingly austere. They fought
evil in themselves through rigorous self-scrutiny to clear away the sin
that separated them from God. The pitfalls and defeats along with the
victories experienced in this inner combat yielded insights that have been
for centuries the rich source of spiritual renewal. The practice of these
spiritual warriors reached Flannery O'Connor, who wrote to a friend on
16 March 1960: "Those desert fathers interest me very much" (*HB* 382).

O'Connor's interest in the desert monastics—which did not ebb even as she discovered other subjects, topical and theological—flowers in the course of her artistic development. She found a wisdom in the desert fathers (*abbas*)and mothers (*ammas*) that stirred her imagination with possibilities for replenishing our century, the era of T. S. Eliot's waste land and John Barth's artistic exhaustion.

The devastations of the age may be right for solitaries. O'Connor certainly is not the only recent American novelist to tap the roots of asceticism for an antidote to the ills of our time. Others have perceived the desert and have come on their own emphases in its vastness. Two rigorous moralists who share O'Connor's concerns, Walker Percy and Don DeLillo (Desmond, *Crossroads* 126–34), stand out as bringing the desert tradition newly minted into the final decades of the twentieth century. In Percy's first published novel, *The Moviegoer* (1961), Binx Bolling discovers in the sawdust of his life the power of self-denial and withdrawal to restore some wholeness within himself. With hope arising from catastrophe, Lancelot Andrewes Lamar in Percy's *Lancelot* (1977) asserts that "everything will go back to the desert" (32). He should know. His life is one long, barren tract, running from the depravity of his society that leads to confinement in the Institute for Aberrant Behavior and out into the solitude awaiting him. With the guidance of Father John, a self-abnegating priest, Lancelot makes his way by means of confession to the hope of a new life alone in the Blue Ridge Mountains with, perhaps, love. *The Thanatos Syndrome* (1987) sums up Percy's career by going all the way back to the practice of the primitive monastics as embodied in Father Rinaldo Smith. Smith truly fathers those around him in the lessons of renunciation. Amid the death-dealing of modern science and politics, Smith's selflessness shows the way to renewal. In the end, Father Smith cares for the dry bones of persons dying of HIV. With his death and that of his charges before him, Father Smith lives out a simple honesty and active ministry that revive love.

Don DeLillo depicts the ruins blighting the end of the century. His desert is one of waste and excess. The sources of this refuse are the media—driven by consumerism, greed, terrorism, technology—and the cult of personality. These forces create a capitalist junkyard that is the setting for all of DeLillo's narratives. To protect himself, the rock-star hero Bucky Wunderlick in *Great Jones Street* (1973) goes into deep seclusion. Isolation shields him from a demanding public and gives him power. The noise in *White Noise* (1985) is a cacophony of loud, harsh, discordant sounds. The din signals death and rumbles throughout an interminable consumption of goods and information. The racket invades family life to envelop its members in an aura of data-generating terror but offering neither understanding nor wisdom. The babel inevitably affects how one thinks and feels. It clogs the mind of Jack Gladney, a professor of Hitler studies, and creates a metaphysical excess that allows him to intellectualize Hitler and separate genocide from Gladney's writing. Through this uncontrollable moral jumble, DeLillo issues a call starkly to pare down the conceptual falsities and frustrating appetites caused by the marketing of desire. DeLillo's recent *Underworld* (1997) is an imposing work about a massive accumulation of waste that demands a drastic ascesis in the culture to check and cleanse the noxious profusion. The task falls to Nick Shay, a waste manager. He must makes sense and order of the detritus of civilization. Like the desert elders in their rocky crags, Shay must sift through the world's mess to recover the inherent mystery of creation.

O'Connor's treatment of the desert is even more comprehensive. Personal, biblical, and aesthetic forces undergird O'Connor's evolving sympathy with the spiritual experiment of the ancient Christian East. With these biographical and typological sources as continual points of reference, this study undertakes a reexamination of O'Connor's fiction. Its aim will be to trace the development of her treatment of the desert as she brings self-denial to bear on the urgencies of twentieth-century American life. That reapplication of desert spirituality is perhaps the allure and magnificence of O'Connor's fiction. Many writers have explored the "under-consciousness" that D. H. Lawrence in *Studies in Classic American Literature* (1923) calls "devilish" (83); a number of artists also have portrayed the solitude and empty spaces of America; and some even have described the desert we carry within; but only Flannery O'Connor has shown how encountering the devil in this inner emptiness opens life up to fullness in God. Through O'Connor's record of her protagonists' anguish and triumphs, the whole of an ancient wisdom, simultaneously theoretical and practical, has been transmitted, giving modern fiction new life.

My account begins with a consideration of O'Connor's life and sensibility that disposed her to ascetic spirituality. The second chapter shows how the ancient ascetic search unfolds in *Wise Blood* (1952), O'Connor's first novel. In this ambitious chapter, my aim is dual: to lay out the complexities of ascetic life by examining the solitary's struggle within the contexts of both late antiquity and contemporary experience. My understanding of *Wise Blood* as the Ur-text of O'Connor's asceticism accounts for the length of this section. The study then distinguishes among the various desert calls summoning her characters to solitude in *A Good Man Is Hard to Find and Other Stories* (1955), her first collection of short fiction. As O'Connor takes her protagonists into deeper zones of renunciation in *The Violent Bear It Away* (1960) and *Everything That Rises Must Converge* (1965), new ascetic topics come to the fore; accordingly, I take up with finer precision these special aspects of desert practice. These include *acedia* (bitterness leading to a hatred of life), *catanyxis* (stabbing the heart), *penthos* (tears and mourning), compunction, and friendship. Appropriately, the book sums up matters with a profile of the *geron* or the old man, a lifetime preoccupation for O'Connor, who is for her—as for the desert mothers and fathers—the person of maturity recognized for his spiritual gifts. The discussion proceeds chronologically.

In tracing the ascetic patterns of O'Connor's art, *Flannery O'Connor, Hermit Novelist* departs from the usual scholarly text in several ways. In the first place, while the discussion takes into account the few studies that mention O'Connor's solitary life and medically enforced asceticism, the book does not go into the nearly forty books and two thousand articles on O'Connor simply for the sake of inclusion or quibbling. My practice is to focus sharply on the spiritual issue at hand. Accordingly, I emphasize the ancient materials because these are the most relevant to the argument and least known to O'Connor scholars. In the interest of reaching a general audience, I have avoided trendy academic jargon to make my writing as clear and readable as I can for all readers. Anything that makes it difficult for those not in the "guild" to read this book defeats my purpose. I seek, finally, to go beyond the objective marshaling of facts and erudition. Along with the analyses, I wish to express a personal reflection that brings to life the striking inner worlds of O'Connor's writing.

I hope to do justice, in this way, to the range of O'Connor's artistic craftsmanship in the course of gauging her spiritual exploration of our age. The study draws heavily on *The Sayings of the Desert Fathers* and *The Lives of the Desert Fathers*, the principal records of their unusual experiment. Through the *Sayings*, the *Lives*, and allied texts, O'Connor discovered how to guide her fictional solitaries to start life afresh and, despite their unbelief, come close to God. Readers of this study will also find John Cassian's *Conferences*, the fifth-century pioneering commentary on desert spirituality, helpful in putting alien desert asceticism into a modern psychological perspective. The affinity linking O'Connor's sensibility with Cassian's exploration of early Christian monasticism runs deep and wide— just how extensively will be clear in the chapters on O'Connor's short stories. Should we need further support of their kinship, we will find it confirmed from a reciprocal direction by Columba Stewart, a monk writing about a monk in *Cassian the Monk* (1998). Stewart finds O'Connor sufficiently insightful about ascetic life to use her remarks on renunciation, grace, and purity (*HB* 126) as an authoritative modern way into these ancient eremitic concepts as taught by Cassian (Stewart 42).

Within O'Connor's attention to the qualities of inner life, we can sense a prescient concern for the crisis unfolding in the outer world. As we enter the twenty-first century, the need for guidance to deal with the evil that makes us dominate and destroy others in unprecedented numbers has become increasingly compelling. In his 1995 study of cultural responses to evil, *The Death of Satan: How Americans Have Lost the Sense of Evil*, Andrew Delbanco argues that a "gulf has opened up in our culture between the visibility of evil and the intellectual resources available for coping with it" (3). The point is well emphasized. Wallace Stevens, from whom Delbanco's title comes, and others have observed the moral deficit. During this most brutal of centuries, horrors such as death camps, nuclear explosions, napalm, smart bombs, and ethnic cleansings have far outstripped our responses to these monstrous events. The wide gap between the evil act and our awareness or understanding of it has made room for the archtrickster to pull off one of his finest stunts yet: Satan has vanished. He has slipped out of his many traditional guises into thin air, permeating the moral atmosphere we breathe. Barbarity and sin have been so institutionalized that they are no longer identified as evil but rather have been assimilated into the expected hum and buzz—the white noise—of everyday life to become policies of various governments, sources of financial profit, and amusements on the evening news. Looking back on the American past, Delbanco sees by contrast in Puritan culture a time when the "devil was an incandescent presence in most people's lives, a symbol and explanation for both the cruelties one received and those perpetrated upon others" (4). After tracing the nineteenth-century negotiations (liberal individualism, Marxism, and psychoanalysis) leading to our present "crisis of incompetence" (3), Delbanco calls for a recovery of our sense of sin and personal responsibility that will bridge the chasm between evil and our comprehension of it and thereby smoke the devil out of hiding.

Delbanco's project, reset within a Christian perspective, would have been instantly endorsed by Flannery O'Connor. Early on, she detected the way the time-spirit was moving. In fact, immediately following World War II, when the United States was flush with righteous triumphalism and global prestige, she sounded the alarm about the modern world, which she found experiencing "a dark night of the soul" (*HB* 100). The dark night she saw not only eclipsed decency but disabled the soul's discernment of evil. From her first published story in 1946 to her posthumous volume of 1965—from the war's aftermath to the advent of the civil rights movement and feminism—she sought to revive our sense of evil to bring us to God. She struggled persistently to give the devil his due against "an audience which does not believe in evil, or better, in the reality of a personal devil, in principalities and in powers" (*HB* 357). In failing to recognize evil, modern readers, O'Connor shrewdly understood, also lose sight of good. "My audience are the people who think God is dead" (*HB* 92). It is no exaggeration to claim that O'Connor waged a one-woman war against the age's moral blindness. She knew that to have a sense of sin, one must first see it for what it is.

Writing to John Hawkes on 20 November 1959 and apprehensive about the misreading of her forthcoming novel *The Violent Bear It Away* (1960), in which the devil repeatedly tries to finesse his own disappearance, O'Connor states: "I want to be certain that the Devil gets identified as the Devil and not simply taken for this or that psychological tendency" (*HB* 360). None of the disavowals of evil fogging the mind of our time blurs her perception. "My Devil has a name, a history and a definite plan," she declares in her famous correction of Hawkes's mistaking his Manichean devil for her biblical adversary. O'Connor proceeds: "His name is Lucifer, he's a fallen angel, his sin is pride, and his aim is the destruction of the Divine plan" (*HB* 456). Satan's ascendancy is tangible to O'Connor. "If you live today you breathe in nihilism," she states to "A," who has been identified as Betty Hester. In her correspondence, occasional prose, and fiction, O'Connor aims to name evil, put a face on it, and teach her audience "the necessity of fighting it" (*HB* 97). In the course of helping us wage war against the devil and make moral sense of our lives, O'Connor has given us in her writing a spiritual record of modern America at mid-century (which is something of a fault line in our history) that abuts on the disintegrating segments of our millennial consciousness.

Simply put, learning to discern and combating Satan constitute the essential dramas of O'Connor's fiction. The way in which she has her characters fight the good fight, however, is not through critical inquiry, political debate, or social activism. Laudable and effective as these strategies might be for others, they are not in the least her affair. With typical self-humor, at once disarming and edgy, that reveals important truths about herself, O'Connor writes to her friend Maryat Lee: "Lord, I'm glad I'm a hermit novelist" (*HB* 227). The term "hermit novelist" places O'Connor firmly in the tradition of fourth-century spirituality; and it is by living out the radical simplicity of eremitical solitude and ascesis (training and discipline) that her characters grapple with their demons. Ascetic withdrawal, past or present, is more than a means of expressing social distance. Ascesis equips O'Connor's solitaries with self-criticism, prayer, and humility. Though these austere weapons hardly seem adequate against death camps and racial hatred, this ordnance from the soul's armory embodies nothing less transformative than the Gospels' redemptive power. Moreover, far from being solely a spiritual effort, this battle fully engages the physical body. The protagonist's whole physical structure and substance are swept into this momentous inner struggle; the body, the fragile token of humanness, in this engagement comes to bear the awesome help of God in the war against Satan. Strangely, divine aid in this fight against the demons comes violently and with unexpected pain for the spiritual combatant. God's interfering presence shocks and penetrates the very blood and sinews of the solitary warrior.

From their huts and caves, the ancient desert-dwellers saw the late Roman Empire rife with evil and developed ways of facing it out. O'Connor had an equally clear perspective on and concern for the world in which she lived. Although she lived and wrote in the Georgia backwoods, O'Connor grasped the horrors of our time, and she boldly took them on. War (both hot and cold), concentration camps, racism, terrorism, mass murder, infanticide, suicide, economic oppression, exile, sexism, and sheer human loneliness make up the historical and existential context of her art. And there are, lest we ignore and incite them anew, the masses roaming the planet raging at their insignificance. O'Connor was even more daring (as of course her spiritual ally in the Kentucky cloister, Thomas Merton, was during the same period) in reviving the strange, still voice of the fourth-century desert mothers and fathers as a response to the rampant evil of our century. O'Connor may have been miles away from the action and crippled by disease, but she strode across our era as if it were her front porch. Here, amid the sheltering pines of her Georgia hermitage, all the sinful power relations of the larger world play themselves out. Her sanctuary remains in her fiction the moral measure of her vast spiritual adventures. Once accepted as the condition of her life and felt through in her art, the desert life of solitude and warfare provides the ideal against which O'Connor would henceforth judge the heartrending dissensions of the society around her.

When Flannery O'Connor called herself "a hermit novelist" in the letter of 28 June 1957 to Maryat Lee, who was pursuing a writing career in New York at the time, O'Connor was referring specifically to being cut off from that larger world where her intellectual and artistic affinities might have taken her. But the word *hermit* over time acquired greater suitability to describe O'Connor than the initial context could indicate.

In the condition of her life, as with the nature of her art, O'Connor's faith made all the difference, for belief in God opened up the spiritual possibilities of her seclusion in backwoods Georgia. From all the biographical facts that we have, thanks to Sally Fitzgerald, we can see that O'Connor also became a hermit in the religious sense of the word. Her inner needs were answered in Scripture and patristic writings, which O'Connor read not merely for interest but for use. She practiced what contemplatives call *lectio divina*, which is the classical way of reading and listening to sacred texts as if in conversation with Christ. Her library and reviews also tell us that she grew in isolation as a woman of faith through prayerful reading. Nourished by a desire to draw close to God and to have a prayer life, her inner development inevitably affected her artistic practice; and, as a consequence of this influence, O'Connor finally became a hermit novelist in her integrating with her stories and novels the anguish and wisdom of the desert-dwellers' inner search for God. The result is a fiction that probes the warring life of the soul. At a time such as now when power more than inner truth preoccupies us, and when, as a crisis technician in DeLillo's *White Noise* tells the hero, "'you are the sum total of your data'" (141), O'Connor gives readers accounts, modern and yet ancient, of the uncommon renunciative adventure through the arid wastes of solitude and across the human body.

The life of solitude, in sum, was essential for Flannery O'Connor's vocation as an artist. She thrived in isolation from the larger literary world. From December 1950 until her death in August 1964, the productive period of her career, O'Connor lived on her mother's dairy farm of 1,500 acres, affectionately dubbed the Andalusian Cow Plantation (*HB* 576), four miles outside Milledgeville, the antebellum capital of Georgia. Contact with the larger world was limited. "I live on a farm and don't see many people," O'Connor explained to "A" on 2 August 1955 (*HB* 91). Every two or three years, she might have gotten to see a movie (*HB* 248). For contemporary readers who channel-surf disasters and whose attachment to cyberspace provides instant and multiple intimacies through electronic mail, web sites, and facsimiles, life off Highway 441 North must seem incomprehensibly disconnected. A telephone line was not run out to the farm until 27 July 1956 (*HB* 167); a portable television arrived as a gift only in 1961 (*HB* 435). There were trips to Atlanta, ninety miles away, to colleges and universities for talks, and to Europe for a grudging pilgrimage in the spring of 1958; but the patch of dairy farm encompassing 500 acres of fields and 1,000 acres of woods in the far corner of Baldwin County, lying "four miles out with the birds and the bees and the prospect" (*HB* 278), was O'Connor's place of work.

Fruitful as it was for her in the long run, rural Georgia was not O'Connor's place of choice. Her intention was to live elsewhere, as far away from the South as New York and its environs, for a while at least to test the literary waters. As Joyce had to leave Ireland to know it, O'Connor felt the need to distance herself from "the dear old dirty Southland" (*HB* 266) to write about it. Sickness, however, changed her plans. A life-threatening flare-up of lupus in late 1950 yanked O'Connor back to a "very muddy and manurey" outpost (*HB* 226) on Route 441 heading north toward Eatonton (*HB* 205), home of Joel Chandler Harris's Uncle Remus. When faced with a future in the backwoods, she feared for her creative life. Even though she needed her mother's supportive care because on arrival she "was nearly dead with lupus" (*HB* 448), as she admitted eleven years later in 1961, O'Connor had to be "roped and tied and resigned the way it is necessary to be resigned to death" (*HB* 224) and "borne home on a stretcher, all out helpless" (*HB* 495) before she would submit to being hauled back to a farmstead that could be reached only by "bus or buzzard" (*HB* 77). O'Connor naturally wanted to be with other young writers and talented people with whom she could grow as a literary artist. In Georgia, she would be a displaced person. And so she was. O'Connor was forced to be a solitary against her will.

With her great achievement before us, we can now see that O'Connor's being *une solitaire malgré elle* remanded to "the Georgia wilderness" (*HB* 77) released her genius in ways that she could not have anticipated. The fourteen years in the desert/wilderness were a personal and artistic exodus for her. In time, O'Connor came to see reclusion not with resistance and anger but with gratitude and humility. From a hospital bed on 19 June 1964, six weeks before her death on 3 August 1964, O'Connor wrote to a friend who was emotionally close to her in illness: "but home is home" (*HB* 585). Home means "peaceful days & nights" (*HB* 583), affording the deepest comfort and rest. The exile that seemed at first dreadful turned out to be a godsend. Compelled by writing, exhausted from illness, O'Connor found somewhere to be quiet, genuine, and refreshed. To be sure, O'Connor's change of heart came at great emotional cost, but she paid the price and did acknowledge that her refuge of necessity became her sacred space of growth. Far from being "the end of any creation, any writing, any WORK from me," O'Connor reassures Mary-at Lee, who was facing the same prospect of return to the southern hinterlands, that reclusion "was only the beginning" (*HB* 224)—the slow, painful beginning of an all-too-brief yet amazing creative endeavor.

The desert mothers and fathers understand the interior bearings of the new starting point to which the homecomer, by choice or fate, is brought. "Humility," says Abba Alonius, a desert father, "is the land where God wants us to go and offer sacrifice" (Merton, *Wisdom* 83 [53]). O'Connor describes to "A" the medical condition that brought her to this place of oblation. "I have never been anywhere but sick," she writes on 28 June 1956 (*HB* 163). Sue Walker has followed O'Connor into "the country of sickness" and has cogently explained how lupus yields very particular figures in O'Connor's art and shapes her idea of grace (33–58). Again, set within the desert tradition, O'Connor's geography of lupus reconfigures Abba Alonius's land of humility within the ancient world of reclusive solitude: "In a sense sickness is a place, more instructive than a long trip to Europe, and it's always a place where there's no company, where nobody can follow" (*HB* 163). Between the desire for physical and artistic freedom and the constraints of chronic illness yawns the unbridgeable abyss of O'Connor's personal passion and cross. There, family and friends cannot follow. There, from that essential distance, O'Connor creates a fiction that plunges the reader into an incredible closeness. This closeness itself begets another distance as it calls from her solitude to that of another.

As with the desert elders, the trial of solitude was for O'Connor the trial of will. Her bitter resistance turned into acceptance of confinement. Surrender by surrender, O'Connor became, despite herself, a monk in the original meaning of solitary (Greek feminine *monaché*). Though she read from *A Short Breviary*, O'Connor did not undergo monastic training; her spiritual regimen was her rich scholarship, raising peafowl, and daily writing. This private discipline fostered self-scrutiny, which for the Christian involves cultivating within oneself the disposition that led Jesus to his death. Fourteen years in the land of humility worked their obediential lesson on O'Connor. She learned how to fight self-sorrow and defeat with a prayerfulness that converted affliction into acceptance, achievement into gratitude. "I work from such a basis of poverty that everything I do is a miracle to me" she writes to "A" (*HB* 127). Life, in the land to which God called O'Connor, forged in her the spiritually crucial habit of humility, the virtue that Abba Anthony understands to be mighty enough to get one through "the snares that the enemy spreads out over the world" (*Sayings*, Anthony the Great 7 [2]).

Humility has for O'Connor another power that it had for the desert teachers. As with the solitaries, place for O'Connor becomes a form of knowledge. Recalling in a letter to "A" (16 December 1955) the now-celebrated evening with Mary McCarthy, O'Connor said to the group: "St. Catherine of Siena had called self-knowledge a 'cell,' and that she, an unlettered woman, had remained in it literally for three years and had emerged to change the politics of Italy. The first product of self-knowledge was humility" (*HB* 125). The metaphors and frankness of O'Connor's remarks have the aphoristic ring of desert wisdom. An ear attuned to the ancient sayings can hear the assured calm voice from the ancient sandy wastes in these phrases. The same grounded utterance reverberates throughout O'Connor's writing. In fact, the spirit of desert simplicity and integrity comes so alive in her letters that we might very well call them *The Sayings of a Hermit Novelist*, for the genius of O'Connor's correspondence is to speak directly from practical experience that issues from her love of people, God, and creation. This is the essence of *The Sayings of the Fathers* (*Apophthegmata Patrum*). The great-hearted warmth that informs the *Sayings* comes through especially in O'Connor's letters to "A," in which she writes openly from one solitude to another. To have given so much time and thought to this particular set of letters, as well as letters to other correspondents, O'Connor must have valued friendship as much as or more than ambition.

Several readers have commented on how O'Connor's cell proved to be a source of full life and important art. Robert Fitzgerald, in his introduction to O'Connor's posthumous collection *Everything That Rises Must Converge*, is the first to raise the issue of asceticism. It is for him a stylistic discipline of the strictest observance. "She would be sardonic over the word *ascesis*," Fitzgerald observes, "but it seems to me a good one for the peculiar discipline of the O'Connor style. How much has been refrained from, and how much else has been cut and thrown away, in order that the bald narrative sentences should present just what they present and in just this order!" (xxxii). The cool disapproval of the word *ascesis* that Fitzgerald attributes to O'Connor would lie not in the self-denial implied by ascetic practice or the spareness it accounts for in her style. Rather, what would trouble O'Connor are the personal moral claims that ascesis might convey. Self-promotion or even a hint of heroicizing her sheltered life or bodily suffering are far removed from her deep-seated humility and simple dignity.

While O'Connor would have her back turned firmly on any attention to her personal life, she would probably see the validity of Frederick Asals's textually based argument that the "bond between suffering and triumph" in the short stories and novels systematically asserts O'Connor's "native asceticism" (226). As Asals sees it, this pervasive need for self-denial drives O'Connor's imagination toward sacramental expressions of her prophetic temperament. That imperative, for Robert Brinkmeyer, moves less toward self-mortification and more toward creating "ascetic oppositions" (180), technical interactions between southern and

Catholic affinities as well as tensions between cenobitic (communal) and eremitic (solitary) forces. Mortification carries deeper meaning for Ralph Wood. In *The Comedy of Redemption,* Wood puts the issue of self-denial into an Augustinian frame to argue that O'Connor offers indirect confessions of the shadow selves that she might have been and fights against becoming. Alterity in her fiction gives O'Connor a way to fight negativity in her life and in the brutal and racist culture around her. Leaving aside theoretical interests, Kathleen Spaltro, in "When We Dead Awaken: Flannery O'Connor's Debt to Lupus," focuses on O'Connor's disease—both its morbidity and mortality. Spaltro argues that O'Connor owes her achievement to her disease and makes the case through Pierre Teilhard de Chardin's belief that matter can be spiritualized and thereby lead the way to perfection. Spaltro's insight rings true. Teilhard's repeated, unsentimental attention to human pain as part of divine providence does support O'Connor's need to find God's will in her disease. Spaltro applies this Teilhardian theology of pain to O'Connor's narrative manner to redefine O'Connor's grotesque as a challenge to readers to accept in themselves suffering and deformity. By these lights, ascesis takes the shape of a disciplined consciousness.

In scouting the trail into the place where no one can follow, each of these readers illumines a segment of the ascetic path in O'Connor's life and writing. Fitzgerald traces the purifying force back through a stylistic stripping away of verbal inessentials. For Asals, that paring down of language guides the reader through the characters' systematic forfeiture of their private wills to the will of God. The inner stripping away of personal desires results from an external intervention, which O'Connor calls the "action of grace on a character who is not very willing to support it." O'Connor, after Augustine, calls this change "conversion," which she insists "all good stories are about" (*HB* 275). The Augustinian character of O'Connor's conversions for Wood derives from the renunciatory force prompting the *Confessions.* The effort behind all endeavor for Teilhard is "one of extreme self-denial and altruism" (28). By these diverse routes— not straight Roman roads but winding Georgia dirt roads and craggy Near Eastern footpaths—we are led back to the tracks navigated by O'Connor and her fictive hermits making their way in the unbounded landscape of natural and spiritual life.

The bodily weakness that kept O'Connor confined "between the house and the chicken yard" (*HB* 290–91) forced her into the displacement that the ancient hermits chose for themselves. But whether voluntary or involuntary, solitude brings one to confront physical limits and infirmities. Solitude in the desert is life on the edge, where physical needs are acute and bare survival is subject to harsh contingencies. The restriction of human frailty was the basis of desert spirituality and could not help but influence all the choices and actions of these self-styled displaced persons. The hermits not only accepted but intensified the way to holiness through their physical limitations. They set out to control the body. By disciplining the body, the solitaries sought to integrate their physical needs into their spiritual aspiration. "The body prospers in the measure in which the soul is weakened," says Abba Daniel, "and the soul prospers in the measure in which the body is weakened" (*Sayings*, Daniel 4 [52]). Weakening the body has to do with overcoming its powerful temptations, the control of which fortifies the spirit. The ascetic objective implies no hatred of the body, no sense that the body is an inconsequential appendage to the human person that can or should be discarded.

Far from disparaging or trying to rid themselves of the body, as the Reformation and many historians have argued, the hermits exalted the body as integral to the great search for human wholeness in God. The body was the mentor of the soul (Brown, *Body* 224–26). By dominating their bodies, the hermits were free to resist the nagging physical passions that violated their search for holiness. Such a constructive respect for the body sustained them in their unsparing discipline. The mastery gained over the body could reach into the soul and tame the will. Control of the will was crucial. Since Adam, the human will has had the propensity to choose its private good over that good that is set by God's law. The idolatry of the self-will is a formidable barrier to inner growth. "The will of man is a brass wall between him and God and a stone of stumbling," says Abba Poemen, and it must be renounced to be overcome (*Sayings*, Poemen 54 [174]). To control the body means to teach the human will how to choose God's will.

Moderating the body's innate processes was exacting for the desert mothers and fathers. Sickness and desolation frequently challenged both the solitaries' efforts to control their will and their faith. In its perpetual exposure to the extreme deprivation that exaggerated the ache of basic physical needs, desert life ineluctably centered on the insoluble bond between the body and belief, disease and liberty. Unlike the Manicheans of their time—and entirely like O'Connor in our time—the hermits believed that the matter and spirit are one. The elders' unitive understanding of human nature yielded lessons that speak directly to O'Connor. Having been tested by illness and having taken on bodily mortifications to turn their will toward God, the primitive monastics could teach O'Connor how to convert her unbidden dislocation and disease into human growth. The way of the desert mothers and fathers was to persevere in a kind of open expectation, without anxiety, without forcing a conclusion. It was nothing more. This entrusting of her being to God became O'Connor's way and expressed her most personal bond of faith in Christ.

Concern for the body eventually requires taking into account its natural end, death. In this century—during which over 200 millions have been killed in wars and death camps—mortality has assumed in art the position of topical determination. "Death," O'Connor writes in her preface to *A Memoir of Mary Ann*, "is the theme of much modern literature"(*MM* 223). O'Connor's writing shares in this moral preoccupation, but it does so with a crucial difference. For those seeking God, death carries the supernatural importance of divine union. Accordingly, the hermits made death the focus of their practice because death is the entrance to the fulfillment of their search. The modern mind, ruled as it is by the denial of death, would regard such a fixed attention as morbid; but the *Sayings* and the *Lives* evince a realism and radical openness about death that hearten rather than depress. "Always keep your death in mind and do not forget the eternal judgement," says the soft-spoken Abba Evagrius, "then there will be no fault in your soul" (*Sayings*, Evagrius 4 [64]). Inasmuch as the confrontation exposes the ultimate consequence of every choice, mindfulness of death can harrow the will. To be aware that sin can eternally separate one from God is, then, a way to uproot the deepest tentacles of self-will grasping personal desire. Remembering judgment day fosters the inner perfection the hermits sought, for the future end discloses the ultimateness in the present moment. The discipline brought about by this focus is glacial in progression, seismic in outcome. What happens is that the ascetic effort gradually brings every aspect of life into alignment with the relationship to God that is central to the desert pursuit. Contemplating one's mortality brings a felt strength. Looking at death through faith spans a boundless desert horizon that firmly embraces the here and now, as do so many of the sayings. "A man who keeps death before his eyes will at all times overcome his cowardice" (Merton, *Wisdom* 138 [76]), says an elder, who effectively accounts for the quiet, life-affirming stamina perceptible to anyone acquainted with the modern hospice.

That clear-eyed moral courage before death pervades O'Connor's fiction and letters. The lives of O'Connor's solitaries are perhaps rightly to be considered as an anticipation of death—or, rather, of the life that is born from death. For the ancient desert-dwellers and O'Connor, the death of the body, while being a brutal tearing away from the known physical world, is freedom from the claims that hold us in bondage, most of all from the chain of disordered love of oneself. Love and freedom are intricately bound up with death for O'Connor, not only in her fiction but also in her life. As captivity in the Georgia backwoods was imposed on O'Connor, death also was thrust early and poignantly before her eyes. It came with her father's protracted illness. Edward Francis O'Connor Jr. became sick with lupus in 1937, when Flannery O'Connor was twelve; he died of the wasting disease on 1 February 1941, when she was sixteen. During her teenage years, O'Connor, who was close to her father, could not help but wrestle with his progressive physical debilities and death as the central forces in her life. O'Connor's sense of loss unfolds in several ways. One measure of her mourning was that she rarely spoke of her father; but her attachment to him, like her disturbing political (Schaub 116–36) and religious (Wood, "Flannery O'Connor" 1–21) views, takes expressive form in her art. There is, for instance, her canonical story of the old man, always a father, always dying alone in exile. Again, the confrontation with disease, dying, and death permeates her fiction in as many different forms as there are stories. Coming on death can be premature; it can be delayed, anticipated, or unexpected; but staring at death for O'Connor is inescapable and holds the position of dramatic resolution forcing final self-judgment.

Whenever this encounter with death occurs, it is for O'Connor instructive. Surely, her father showed her day by day how to live with lupus and how one dies of lupus, the disease she inherited from him. O'Connor's letters repeatedly strike the note of her knowing what is in store for her and "about what to expect" from cortisone (*HB* 572) or the latest opportunistic ailment that comes with a compromised immune system. If the course of lupus was clear to O'Connor from seeing her father decline over four years, then the challenge of sickness was meeting it with dignity; the mystery of illness was finding meaning in the body's suffering. O'Connor's father, I venture to say, taught her how to rise to the demands of illness and pierce the shroud covering death. And yet her sensitivity to impermanence lies deeper than any single experience. Sally Fitzgerald, who speaks with authority and from a familiarity with O'Connor's unpublished early journals, sees her sense of human transience as characterological: "I think she became acquainted with the night, as Robert Frost puts it, at an early age. She knew that life was fragile. We all know this theoretically, but we're allowed to forget it much of the time. She wasn't" (15). O'Connor, in turn, has helped others to confront death. A recently published homage to O'Connor written by Joseph Torchia just before he died of AIDS in 1996 poignantly testifies to the spiritual power of her writing. As he makes a pilgrimage to Milledgeville, Torchia in the solitude of his disease transforms the hermit novelist's experience with suffering into a prayerful and deep journey to an understanding of his own pain (81–102).

The crises of O'Connor's life are the donnée of her fiction. Death teaches O'Connor's protagonists (especially through their bodies) the hard lessons about their destiny, lessons that they seek to evade. Nowhere is this reluctant confrontation more forcefully presented than in *The Violent Bear It Away*, which replicates the biographical circumstance of a teenager dealing with the death of the elder whom he loved and who spiritually fathered him. O'Connor's 1960 novel is only one example of forging her personal experience with the desert precept to keep death before one's eyes into a position of structural determination. Within this complex of forces, O'Connor finds fresh verbal forms to vivify her grief, her struggle with her body, and their combined place "in a larger framework" than her own "personal problems" (*HB* 377). She writes the sorrow and the strangeness of her inner desert world. What is most conspicuous in O'Connor's fiction of the desert are wrenched bodies: a twisted face; a boy's floating corpse; a boy hanging from a rafter; a lady coiled in a puddle of blood; a woman impaled; a man wrapped in barbed wire; a girl evangelist's twisted legs; a hermaphrodite; a raped teenage male; a crushed backbone; a comatose woman; an old man tortured in stocks; cracked skulls; crumpled corpses. These and similar anatomical fragments are the "afflictions you can't get rid of and have to bear" (*HB* 509). Each can be understood as exemplifying an aspect of the ascetic discipline of the body that can sink down to teach the will.

How the character's will learns the lesson of abandonment to God's will depends on how each bears suffering and the isolation attending death. Endurance in turn depends on how one sees these mangled parts fitting into the whole of reality and where one sees the struggle ending. For O'Connor herself, it takes a relapsing of illness and faltering of artistic determination to put things together. On 28 June 1956, six years into her seclusion, O'Connor writes to "A" that she, "like everybody else," learned "the hard way and only in the last years as a result of . . . sickness and success." The hard way is the desert way, which intersects the isolation of vanity brought about by success; and the hermit novelist, acclaimed yet alone, comes out in this candid letter in the same spiritual place inhabited by the anonymous hermits and with their unsparing verbal precision that cleaves to the bone. "Sickness before death is a very appropriate thing and I think those who don't have it miss one of God's mercies" (*HB* 163). Benevolence lies in the way that sickness can teach the heart to let go, to put oneself in divine hands.

We will take stock of those mercies, hard or tender, when looking at the fiction; but what is needed now is to adjust our ear to the harmony between O'Connor's voice and the desert tonality she echoes in her statement concerning the spiritual benefit of sickness before death. Another good example of this agreement comes from one of the great desert women, Amma Theodora. "A Christian discussing the body with a Manichean expressed himself in these words," says Amma Theodora. "'Give the body discipline and you will see that the body is for him who made it'" (*Sayings*, Theodora 4 [83]). Theodora speaks directly to O'Connor's presentation of the body as sacramental and conveys her critical power in a rejoinder to the very Manicheanism that O'Connor finds besetting our age. Theodora's saying strikes but one major note among the harmonious echoes of desert utterance in O'Connor's writing. Even the plain sense of Theodora's saying illustrates how much O'Connor shares with the early ascetics. Her fiction will show how disciplining the body strips away the gaudy—and usually demeaning—cultural wrappings to reveal the dignity of the body conferred at its source.

The theme of discipline recurs in O'Connor's appraisal of the moral needs of the modern age. The self-marketing beat writers of the late 1950s who were making a splash when O'Connor began to write, for example, laid claims to spiritual aspirations that O'Connor did not accept because their lives and art were, in her eyes, self-indulgent and sprawling. O'Connor's entire response to the beats in a 21 June 1959 letter to T. R. Spivey seems to have desert life as an implied referent for inner quest. The context of O'Connor's quiet teaching lends itself to imaginative rescripting of a desert tableau. Like Francis Marion Tarwater envisioning his great-uncle reclining on a desert slope in Palestine, we can conjure up ourselves as novices sitting at the foot of the hermit novelist on her front porch as she comments discreetly on the "ill-directed good" in the beat artists. "They seem to know a good many of the right things to run away from, but to lack any necessary discipline," says Amma Flannery. In her thinking, God, not rebellion against society alone, provides holiness. Their abandonment "to all sensual satisfactions" makes them "false mystics." The beats may "call themselves holy but holiness costs and so far as I can see they pay nothing." The price in the ascetic economy is self-will bent away from private desire toward submission to God. The way, O'Connor makes plain, is "to practice self-denial" (*HB* 336–37), which makes one receptive to divine grace.

Self-denial is negative in word only for O'Connor. For her, at the heart of renunciation lies charity. In linking ascesis to concern for others, the hermit novelist reaffirms the essential aim of desert solitude. Above all, the hermits are fathers and mothers of love. "Our life and our death is with our neighbour," says Anthony. "If we gain our brother, we have gained God" (*Sayings*, Anthony the Great 9 [3]). Anthony's living for, if not always with, his brother and sister sets the goal of desert life. The marks of charity in their sandy abode are receiving visitors, caring for the sick, burying the dead, not judging others so as not to hurt them, and bearing the sins of the world oneself—good works that readers will recognize as pivotal in O'Connor's narratives. Both in her writing and patristic texts, the biblical commandment to love underlies the call to put charity into action. Part of the warfare against Satan is waged against self-interest. The solitary fights to love.

Reading the *Sayings* and the *Lives* makes one aware that being men and women for others is a struggle. No polite phrases, no gushing sentiments, no smooth sales talk soften the hard demands of charity as understood by the elders. They know that the private will resists Jesus' example of laying down his life for others. There is a desert story of the brethren discussing charity that must have taken too abstract and cozy a direction, because a challenge abruptly intrudes on the group's conference. Abba Joseph asks: "Do we really know what charity is?" To provide the lesson that Abba Joseph believes the brethren need to know, he tells of a brother who came to see Abba Agathon, "who greeted him [the brother] and did not let him go until he had taken with him a small knife which he had" (*Sayings*, Agathon 25 [24]). The vignette condenses the antecedent action to a spare and somewhat cryptic minimum, but the teaching is clear, if vexing. Agathon receives the brother in love and sends him away with love in his hand in the form of a knife, an instrument that cuts. Love cuts and wounds.

Agathon's knife has passed into the nimble hands of O'Connor. She, in turn, with Agathon's stern wisdom, places it in the hands of her searchers so that they too may know the cut of love. Single-edged or double-edged, the blade slashes a path through Georgia and Tennessee and usually ends up, on one occasion in the form of a bull's horn, in the heart of her characters. That a sharp-pointed blade should be the instrument of love may make sense to the hermits, but it has confused modern readers who are shocked to see the violent woundings it has caused in O'Connor's fiction. In one of her explanations of violence in her writing, O'Connor uses an ascetic model to show the positive link between suffering and living for others. Again she is writing to T. R. Spivey; the context is the general misunderstanding of the title *The Violent Bear It Away*. O'Connor says that readers who mistake the phrase for a passage from the Old

Testament miss the fact that the words are Jesus' and that Jesus is speaking of love. O'Connor speaks with Agathon's voice and to the same ignorance, citing the biblical exemplar of renunciation that both revere. "That this is the violence of love, of giving more than the law demands, of an asceticism like John the Baptist's, but in the face of which even John is less than the least in the kingdom—all this is overlooked." Tellingly, what focused O'Connor's attention on Matthew 11:12 and revealed its spiritual depth was that "it was one of the Eastern fathers' favorite passages" (*HB* 382). The enthusiasm of those early masters of the East sparks O'Connor's preferences.

O'Connor's words about the wounds of love and self-denial take on added poignancy if we consider that they were written in spring 1960, when her bones were softening from taking steroids for ten years to control her lupus. Soft hips mean persistent pain (*HB* 440). But her decaying body directs her attention and will outward toward the world. Abba Motius's words are helpful in following O'Connor's compassionate turn of mind. "For this is humility: to see yourself to be the same as the rest" (*Sayings*, Motius 1 [148]). This is O'Connor. She sees in her personal condition how life in the contemporary desert presents endless demands to develop the charity that endures violent woundings. No matter how merciless the blows of hatred, anger, and oppression, no matter how scorched the earth is by the sirocco of nihilism, O'Connor shows her readers a way through "the modern, sick, unbelieving world." She points to the ascetic love that gives "more than the law demands" (*HB* 382). Charity, "however foolish" (*HB* 434), comes before self; and O'Connor declares with the radical simplicity informing the *Sayings* that "charity is beyond reason, and that God can be known through charity" (*HB* 480). Such a way of knowing God arises from the wounds of love, which are an almost unbearable shattering that rives away all that is not secured in the divine.

The desert and its arduous life are so inextricably a part of O'Connor's thinking that they are the terms of her defining charity. A life for others is the sandy terrain in human form. As there is a geography of lupus, there is for O'Connor a topography of love. "Charity is hard and endures," she explains to Cecil Dawkins (*HB* 308). And with a sanity that reins in the excesses in asceticism, O'Connor (in a letter to "A," who shared an interest in the desert) comments on "positive charity as opposed to flagellation and the hairshirt. It's harder and more wearing on the nerves and availeth more" (*CW* 1096). Charity, in O'Connor's fullest understanding of ascetic practice, is the way to know God. By responding in love, rather than through self-mortification, to those around them, the solitaries realize the spirit of God in themselves.

This realization demands a vigilance that is on guard against evil even in slumber. Every Tuesday night during monastic Compline, the last office of the liturgical day, there sounds a call to watchfulness before the community retires. Immediately after a brief calling on God for a blessing, the exhortation unadorned by chant fills the air. The urging comes from 1 Peter 5:8–9. "Discipline yourselves, keep alert. Like a roaring lion your adversary the devil prowls around, looking for someone to devour." And so, into the darkness go the monks to sleep with prayers of inner vigilance against the hungry beast. The early hermits knew the peril well, for lions were numerous in biblical Palestine. The desert mothers and fathers lived close to the rapacious predator and built their lives to ward off the growling menace.

From her stated intention to give the devil his due, we know that O'Connor also heard and heeded warnings about the fatal attacker. In fact, having since about 1950 said Prime in the morning and sometimes Compline at night (*HB* 159), O'Connor was familiar enough with the first letter of Peter to marry its words with her own language in a 22 June 1961 letter to John Hawkes. Among the "hierarchy of devils" that O'Connor is explaining to Hawkes, she singles out "the devil who goes about like a roaring lion seeking whom he may devour" (*HB* 443). The Georgia wilderness had no lions; but polecats and other ravenous creatures, such as the Ku Kluxers of the Invisible Empire and its prideful dragon, did lie in ambush in the pines and gullies. O'Connor took seriously the command to be on the lookout day and night for lurking adversaries. Vigilance is the first step for the ancient hermits; warfare is their next, decisive, and constant undertaking. As we read time and again in her letters and essays, O'Connor—like her desert predecessors—declared war against evil. O'Connor's alliance with the hermits in actively fighting Satan points toward the source of her originality that baffles many contemporary readers. Those eerie voices and weird visages that materialize in O'Connor's world and confound her audience would be commonplace to the fourth-century person. A few words about the place of the demonic in the hermits' world will help prepare us for O'Connor's recommissioning those unearthly forces now dismissed as superstitions in her modern narratives. First of all, the culture of late antiquity taught people to believe in the demonic. "Beware of what you have in your heart and your spirit," said Abba Elias, "knowing that the demons put ideas into you so as to corrupt your soul by making it think of that which is not right, in order to turn your spirit from the consideration of your sins and of God" (*Sayings,* Elias 4 [71]). The belief in demons was part of all the prevailing religions. Jew, Christian, and Gnostic understood that evil forces worked against humankind. The Jew and Christian recognized that demons were waging war against God. The Christian hermits further believed that the demons were personal enemies who were scheming to thwart their quest for holiness. Demons swarmed the desert and would burst into the hermits' cells.

The attack was sudden and tumultuous. It drew the desert mothers and fathers into hand-to-hand combat with the devil. Abba Poemen explains the immediacy of demonic belligerence: "I say this about myself: I am thrown into the place where Satan is thrown" (*Sayings*, Poemen 171 [190]). Close quarters do not guarantee success for the demons, but their tactics make up with guile what they lack in certainty. Abba Matoes gives us an idea of how the fiend stalks his prey: "Satan does not know by what passion the soul can be overcome. He sows, but without knowing if he will reap, sometimes thoughts of fornication, sometimes thoughts of slander, and similarly for the other passions. He supplies nourishment to the passion which he sees the soul is slipping towards" (*Sayings*, Matoes 4 [143]). In fine, Satan seeks out and attacks our particular weakness. Abba Matoes's warning about the devil's gambits richly condenses an elaborate psychology of satanic thought flows—*logismoi* in Greek—that the elders recognized as circulating in themselves. There is subtlety to the elders' understanding of how supernatural spirits invade our bodies from the outside and jostle for a place in our own personality. Comparable insights into their operation emerge from O'Connor's narratives. The nuances of O'Connor's demonology are fleshed out in her modern recapturing of the same demonic currents of thought. Her boldest and sustained plumbing of Satan's strategies for seizing the human soul appears in *The Violent Bear It Away*.

For the solitaries to grapple with these sly gambits, they had to develop the ability to discern the ways in which the demons work their way into the human heart. Such clarity about the subtlest insinuations of temptation and evil is difficult on several counts. To begin with, it is in the nature of the demonic to mar the victim's vision. Moreover, discernment involves tracking one's own disordered emotions, which is difficult indeed, since the human mind favors its own perceptions. Always eager to gratify, the demons make a specialty of trafficking in the illusions cherished by the mind. And so the demons utilize endless guises, many of them bizarre, to take over the hermits' thoughts and emotions. "The often graphic and cartoonlike imagery of these demons" in the *Sayings*, explains Douglas Burton-Christie in his superb study of the desert quest for holiness, "belies the clear sense among the monks that the real drama of the demonic was psychological" (193). No one is better than Peter

Brown in transcribing ancient modes of experience into their modern equivalents. For Brown, the demonic "was sensed as an extension of the self. A relationship with the demons involved something more intimate than attack from the outside: to 'be tried by demons' meant passing through a stage in growth of awareness of the lower frontiers of the personality." Brown's explanation of those edges of consciousness brings the ancient idea of the demonic close to O'Connor's notions of the grotesque or the human condition without grace. "The demonic stood not merely for all that was hostile *to* man; the demons summed up all that was anomalous and incomplete *in* man" (*Making* 90). Such a person, for O'Connor, is one without grace. The desert-dwellers knew full well that the demons were entangled with their personal desire. "Our own wills become the demons," says Poemen with a ruthless honesty that brooks no equivocation (*Sayings*, Poemen 67 [176]).

O'Connor shows herself equally aware of the fact that, while demons are vital presences, the most malevolent responses come from within the person. By bringing her characters to confront their demons, as all do in the end, O'Connor forces them to look at the worst vices within themselves. We will see that the contemporary trial by demons in O'Connor's fiction is at once a tribulation and an opportunity. If demons make us aware of our irregularities and deficiencies—as Brown provocatively explains the clash—for O'Connor, that new consciousness can lead to spiritual advancement. "I measure God by everything that I am not," O'Connor says to "A." "I begin with that" (*HB* 430). Taking stock of imperfections is an auspicious starting point in the spiritual struggle. Part of giving the devil his due in O'Connor's fiction involves the characters owning up their deficiencies, the most conspicuous lacking of which is goodness. Since a good man or woman is hard to find, this acknowledgment of fault enforces a ruthless admission of sinfulness.

A good measure of O'Connor's confidence in writing about the devil comes from her reading of Thomas Aquinas. The *Summa Theologiæ* provides "a hillbilly Thomist" (*HB* 81), as O'Connor calls herself, with philosophical support for the spiritual affinities she has with the desert mothers and fathers. Thomas offers a scheme that endows the diabolical trickster with a solidity he cannot make evaporate and that firmly locates the fiend in God's order of creation. Whereas the Manichean mind throughout history holds the force of evil to be equal to the force of good, Thomas asserts that the devil does not occupy a world of his own but is part of the universe made by God and sustained by God's tolerance. Thomas, it bears noting, is not preoccupied with Satan, as are the hermits and O'Connor. He discusses the devil in the *Summa Theologiæ* at the very end of his first of three sections, in a part that concerns the existence and control of God over creation. To tuck away the devil here (6 [158–59]) amounts to a put-down of the prestige of the satanic ego. Devils are a minor if formidable component of the structure of the Thomistic whole. Thomas enumerates the roles of creatures in descending order of power: angels, devils, fate or heavenly bodies, and humankind.

In the Thomistic hierarchy, the devils test humans through the satanic knowledge of deception and ruin to cast them into sin with Satan. Satan's lackeys can instigate but cannot force people to sin. Freedom of human will remains Thomas's overriding theme. "God allows the devil to try men's souls and vex their bodies," Thomas states, but Christ's suffering prepares a remedy by which people can protect themselves from the "enemy's assaults and avoid the ruin of eternal death" (14 [529–30]). Thomas systematically explains the relation among demons, human will, and the Cross as the axis of his redemptive theology; and these contending forces are the coordinates of the spiritual quest for the hermits and O'Connor.

If the eyes of the medieval church doctor sharpen O'Connor's vision of the devil's role in the cosmic order, it is the heart of the primitive desert-dweller that sustains the hermit novelist of Milledgeville in the war she declared on Satan. The mothers and fathers show O'Connor how a woman of war is a woman of prayer. Two features of desert prayer bear in a particular way on this study of O'Connor, each involving strife. One is the struggle to have a prayer life at all; the other is the effectiveness of prayer as a weapon against evil. Prayer was not something the ancient solitaries practiced now and then; prayer was their life. They sought to live out Paul's urging "to pray without ceasing" (1 Thessalonians 5:17). The Pauline counsel recurs in the *Sayings.* "The true monk should have prayer and psalmody continually in his heart," says Abba Epiphanius (*Sayings,* Epiphanius 3 [57]). The rule carried with it a good measure of practical understanding, for the hermits, who were preeminently realists, knew from experience that ceaseless prayer was hard to achieve. When they wanted to pray, their enemies—their demons—wanted to prevent them, because the adversaries knew that only by turning the ascetics from prayer could they hinder the quest to God. Never given to underestimating either the devil or what it takes to resist his wiles, the elders admitted that "prayer is warfare to the last breath" (*Sayings,* Agathon 9 [22]). Prayer demanded persistence against great odds.

O'Connor appreciated the stubbornness required for prayer because she shared the hermits' trust in it and was honest about her limitations when it came to worship. "The only force I believe in is prayer," O'Connor writes to "A" on 6 September 1955, "and it is a force I apply with more doggedness than attention" (*HB* 100). O'Connor does cite several prayers in her letters and fiction, but she really does not have much to say about prayer, the only force she believes in. Nor do the desert elders. For all the prominence of prayer in the lives of O'Connor and the hermits, it requires little talk. Taciturnity on the subject of prayer, like struggle, may be a sign of life. Prayer is a matter of doing. Desert life is prayer life. The making of the day is worship of God. With O'Connor, there is another propensity causing her relative silence. Besides her innate reticence to talk about her private habits, O'Connor distrusts "pious phrases, particularly when they issue from my mouth" (*HB* 92–93). Her activities take their meaning from her faith in God, and she relies on her art to communicate that trust to readers; but when it comes to her personally approaching God, O'Connor expresses a healthy sense of inadequacy. "My prayers are unfeeling but habitual," she writes to Maryat Lee on 19 May 1957, "not to say dogged" (*HB* 220). Returning to her letter of 2 August 1955 to "A" in which O'Connor openly discusses her faith, we can see that O'Connor's tenacity has a desert freshness of its own: "And all I can say about my love of God, is, Lord, help me in my lack of it" (*HB* 92). O'Connor's disclaimer is a prayer, the simple, flat petition found in the *Sayings*.

There is nothing overspiritualized about prayer for O'Connor. Nor is there anything trivial about prayer. The "vapid Catholicism" (*HB* 139) that promotes novenas and sentimental pieties bordering on superstition and that converts the Roman Catholic Church into the Elks Club offends her sense of faith as serious and demanding. Spoony hearts offer their spoony homage. Prayer, however, works the other way. Opening the heart to God fights against any such infantilism by revealing the dark powers in the depths of one's soul. Brought to see those recesses, the person is made to feel the responsibility of having personally sinned and is not allowed the mere self-excusing admission of being a sinner. These facts overwhelm and terrify the ego. Prayer is like the desert in stripping away defenses; there is no hiding out from oneself or God. As deceptions of one's virtue and uniqueness give way, there is the chance of finding God in the range and depth of God's indwelling.

These comments are, of course, my extensions of O'Connor's spare remarks; and they are intended to stir some anticipatory excitement with hints of what lies ahead in the poetics of solitude that distinguishes her fiction. O'Connor, when speaking for herself, expresses a plain sense of prayer: it encourages spiritual maturity and integrates the human person. Integrity is paramount. When she warmly counsels Roslyn Barnes—a student from O'Connor's undergraduate college who also went on to study at the State University of Iowa—about becoming a Catholic, O'Connor states that "study can prepare your mind but prayer and the Mass can prepare your whole personality" (*HB* 422). Prayer, by these lights, is not a matter of mouthing set words but of disposition, of the entire person's being alive to God. Small wonder, then, that in responding to Cecil Dawkins's plan to read Thomas Aquinas, O'Connor warns that clearing up the vexations of life and faith "is done by study but more by prayer" (*HB* 308).

O'Connor's emphasis on the power of prayer to integrate the human person is most important for understanding her fiction because prayer addresses both personal and cultural needs for wholeness in our fractured, dark times. Without using so many words, but through the heart's deep and secret longing, O'Connor's searchers find that the Spirit of God steals into the hard and stony places made arid by the bitterness of life. Prayer is the truest path to reform that her lonely and broken characters can take up. From the Georgia wilderness, in her wry anchoritic voice, she called on the members of her church, which in America was then an immigrant church, to get beyond apologetics and develop an informed and responsible inner life. On the matter of prayer, as with other issues, O'Connor is a spiritual essentialist who points the way to maturity through the inner life. In advance of and alongside Vatican II (1962–65), she conducted in print and by example an *aggiornamento* that brought her readers and her faith into vital confrontation with the modern world, which in a sense became her hermitage. From that most parochial corner of Baldwin County, O'Connor envisioned a religious pluralism that her church had not embraced for centuries. With the desert teachers who held, "If you have a heart, you can be saved" (*Sayings*, Pambo 10 [197]), O'Connor believed that God is for all. No one is beyond the Cross. Narcissists, two-bit tyrants, and murderers win the heart of God. Desperate cries of dereliction by unloved searchers who believe themselves unlovable reach God's ear. That capacious faith gives her writing its distinctive relevance to this century that has witnessed the killing of over 200 million people in violences a list of which cannot express the evil and suffering of what they seek to represent.

To keep the record straight, O'Connor makes it clear that, when it comes to personal sin, she knows "all about the garden variety, pride, gluttony, envy and sloth." She minces no words: "I am not a mystic and I do not lead a holy life" (*HB* 92). Nor did she want her soul tampered with by admirers. Anonymity as to her personal habits suited her and worked in favor of the classical submergence of self into art that O'Connor sought. Her achievement inevitably has catalyzed public interest in her life—and with good reason. After all, a woman of great talent who cultivated an inner life against great odds is, at the very least, an anomaly. She was an unmarried Catholic woman in the rural, fundamentalist South; a hermit novelist; and a hillbilly Thomist who read theology and philosophy and wrote about violence and God and faith. Surely, such a life presents itself to the modern world as a problem and even as a scandal. The paradox of her life manifests the paradox of the ancient solitaries. The long struggle of the elders thrived on improbability. Out of the most austere forms of self-abnegation there arose extravagant material and emotional generosity toward others. Amid rigorous privation, the hermits felt grateful for an abundant life. The harshness of the desert brought about great tenderness. All these surprises repeat themselves in O'Connor's life and work.

Keeping in mind her disavowals of leading a holy life while remembering that holy people invariably deny their virtue, we cannot help wondering how she spent her days. How does a woman coping with chronic illness develop her art and faith in isolation and do it so well? The picture that emerges of the scrappy hermit novelist is one of her patiently refining her work, intermittently and doggedly paying attention to formal prayer, sleuthing out the devil, receiving occasional visitors, and joyfully tending nine Muscovy ducks, a bantam hen, a moth-eaten, one-eyed swan, and assorted peafowl. These activities are all of a piece, an unhurried order to sustain creativity where it might easily perish. "Routine is a condition of survival" (*HB* 465), she advises "A." A survivor O'Connor was, and routine she developed. Although her daily rounds obviously varied over fourteen years according to her strength and commitments, a glance at some habits on some days will give an idea of what life in the Georgia hermitage was like (page numbers in parentheses refer to *HB*):

—rises as the first chicken cackles (438);
—says morning prayers from the Mass (572);
—says Prime every day from *A Short Breviary* (159);
—writes in the morning with a fresh mind (205);
—works every morning when able to (156);
—writes two hours a day without interference in bedroom; wants a studio (242);
—works only one hour a day during last year (577);
—says prayer to Saint Raphael every day (590);
—exhausted every afternoon (398);
—paints in afternoon (376);

—3:30 at home (205);

—receives visitors on front porch (447);

—sundown is bedtime (159);

—sometimes says Compline from *A Short Breviary* (159);

—reads Thomas Aquinas twenty minutes before sleeping (93);

—9:00 retires to bed "and am always glad to get there" (236);

—says Rosary at night during terminal hospital stay (582).

One need be neither religious nor sympathetic to asceticism to follow the humanizing rhythm of such a day. Work and leisure, solitude and sociability, struggle and ease, renunciation and celebration, reflection and activity, fatigue and convalescence all flow smoothly in a poetry of their own. Days so centered in work continuous with love of God pass with great rapidity, all too fleeting as they turned out for O'Connor, who died at thirty-nine.

There are many ways to appreciate such a routine, but perhaps the clearest way is briefly to historicize O'Connor's moment and set her pace against the tempo of the postwar American world from which she lived apart. After years of wartime restraint, the 1950s and the early 1960s were frenzied. The era, born in violence and quaking in more violence, was moved by convulsive aftershocks. There were the tremors of fragmenting nations, the loss of roots on a global scale in nature and in the home, the tidal waves of racism, the breaking fault of sexism, the nuclear degradation of people, air, water, and land that emitted the particles of hopelessness and nihilism in a spiritual fallout. By way of home entertainment, there were political witch-hunts on television. The arrogance and vulgar disregard of truth in the name of patriotism epitomized by Joseph McCarthy's chairing the House Committee on Un-American Activities did not self-destruct until the spring of 1954. Against all of this, O'Connor's life in the Georgia desert, while sharing in the displacement, loneliness, and affliction of the time, was harmonious, productive, and self-giving. Hers was a practical and simple life, and it was sane.

If prayer is a "conversation between God and the soul," a dialogue in which "God's word has the initiative" and we are "listeners" (14–15), as Hans Urs von Balthasar eloquently explains prayer, then O'Connor's way of living aspired to the condition of prayer. God's word, as O'Connor was fully aware, was the founding call of her life. As "the mind serves best when it's anchored in the word of God," as O'Connor tells "A" (*HB* 134), so also do the hands and feet and ears work best when fixed in service to God. Prayer makes a totality of one's being. O'Connor's listening to the divine initiative became an active response. She answered God's word not by periodic and dramatic peak experiences but at her typewriter and galley proofs and by the unremarkable quotidian give-and-take of hospitality and friendship. The truest religious activities for her are those in which religion is least emphasized. They occurred as she sat on the porch exhilarated by the sight of a peacock lifting his tail to unfurl a map of the cosmos and raising his high voice in cheer for an invisible parade. She was deeply pleased when she got a story just right. Receiving and answering mail were eventful. In fact, she put so much of her best self in the ordinary courtesy of correspondence that her letters comprise an achievement independent of her fiction, a manifesto of inner life for our time.

From O'Connor's center of gladness for and gratitude to God's word, she finds meaning in the scourge of lupus. Affliction remains affliction but fits into the moral accommodation opened up by her faith. "We are all rather blessed in our deprivations," O'Connor assures "A" on 11 August 1956, "if we let ourselves be" (*HB* 169). O'Connor was spiritually strong enough to let herself receive divine favor. She said *yes* to *yes*. She accepted cultural and physical loss, renouncing her expectations to rejoice in whatever she got. Abandonment to divine providence made her body, like her art, a prayer. Without a trace of condescension or standing in a pulpit to us tell us how to bind the modern wounds of alienation and guilt, O'Connor shows the age the way to integrity by living and writing a life in which body and spirit, work and faith, the moment and the timeless are all one. Her art, in unison with her life, yields an important desert lesson: that much can come from little. O'Connor's short stories and novels are like the Georgia pines, purifying the atmosphere by their presence. In this replenishing way, O'Connor speaks well for the country we live in. For all our arrogance and acquisitive excess, here in O'Connor's fiction and letters is proof that Americans can be modest and prayerfully self-giving as well.

A final introductory word: the intention of this chapter is to establish O'Connor's interest in the desert mothers and fathers of late antiquity and to show her share in the life and practice of eremitic spirituality. If O'Connor went to Augustine, Thomas Aquinas, and Pierre Teilhard for ideas, she looked to the hermits for ways of living wisely. The hermits were not intellectuals. They left no original ideas about human nature. Nor were they theologians. Argument and apologetics never enter their sayings. The issues that slowly seep up from the late antique desert into the modern wilderness of O'Connor's world are protest, warfare, ascesis, surrender, prayer, and paradise. The elders' physical and

spiritual survival was so basic that it left no room for theological techni-
calities and abstract niceties. Their search for God was too direct to allow ideas about God to intervene with that felt urgency. Mostly what
comes through is how much they know about human nature because they
realize how little they know about God. Proving or arguing was overtak-
en by sheer believing. They were shy, deeply silent persons not disposed
to speeches on the divine presence or to subtle exegesis on the herme-
neutics of Scripture.

What the hermits cared about was gritty, like the sand on which they
struggled. They sought to survive, to overcome sin, to develop purity of
heart, and to have direct communion with God that would open them
to the way of salvation. Striving to be saved did not mean securing a place
with God in the peace that begins on the other side of the grave. The
hermits understood that every moment of time reaches into eternity and
that our essential and central fulfillment was to seek God in the here and
now and among neighbors. Solitude sensitized the hermits to the ways
in which the eternal intersects with daily life. The human heart was the
center of their task. Charity pervades their spare sayings and hard lives.
Practicality, as is expected for people living on an ungiving land, governs
their ways. They are very much centered, as we now say, in vital matters such as food, the body, endurance, and prayer. For all the extraordi-
nariness of their desert heroics, it is their ordinariness that accomplishes life. Their feats of humility and sanity recommended the mothers and
fathers to O'Connor. As with O'Connor, God mattered to the hermits,
and they subordinated every struggle to the battle of deepening their bond
with God. They knew how to live humanly. Obedience to authority took
a far inferior place to the necessity of love. The fruit of their lives is wisdom. No wonder O'Connor declares plainly: "Those desert fathers interest me very much." They show her how an awareness of the eternal anchors one firmly from pitching in the storm, a stability and repose that
she believes our turbulent century sorely needs.

Flannery O'Connor's affinity with the primitive Christian hermits,
I believe, throws new light on her art. At the heart of its affirmations,
desert spirituality posits a world in which the most hidden vibrations of
thought and choice bear on and can change the world without. O'Connor's spiritual poetics brings these modulations to light by dispelling the
darkness shrouding the empty places in which her lonely searchers live
to reveal a transformational space where solitude and warfare against
demons prepare her embattled sojourners for an encounter with God. As
their struggle unfolds, the desert perspective brings into view secret,

modern solitaries whose inner qualities have been obscured. To see what has been too little seen in Flannery O'Connor's art, we must turn to the novels and stories. In following O'Connor's narratives, we will take the themes of interior aspiration out of the crowded and confused lives of her seekers and, with the ancient hermits, watch them bud into new, unexpected growths in the broad light of the desert.

2 Hazel Motes and the Desert Tradition

> If you have a heart, you can be saved.
> —Pambo, *The Sayings of the Desert Fathers*
>
> Then the eyes of the blind shall be opened,
> and the ears of the deaf unstopped . . . ;
> For waters shall break forth in the wilderness,
> and streams in the desert.
> —Isaiah 35:5–6

NOT LONG AFTER the end of World War II in 1945, residents of Taulkinham, Tennessee, in Flannery O'Connor's *Wise Blood* (1952) have in their midst a man of twenty-two facing out—in the direst possible way—the consequences of his family history, war experience, and beliefs. The man is Hazel Motes, a veteran who believes in nothing and is the hero of O'Connor's first novel. Were the townspeople to observe Motes on one particular day, they would see him walk three hours from the outskirts back into town, stop at a supply store to buy a bucket and quicklime, and, on reaching the boardinghouse where he lives, go up to his room to pour the lime solution into his eyes. Motes's self-blinding presents itself as a mere preliminary to a new life of complete denial and self-injury. Motes takes to mortification as a bird sets out into the air—and on a comparable wing of freedom. An onlooker might understandably see this flight as an attempted release from the strictures of Motes's body, for his determined abstinence easily overrides ordinary human physical satisfactions. Sexual desire quickly gets stamped out. Reversing the usual fee-for-pleasure relationship, Motes pays money to a pestering young woman to leave him alone. Smaller enjoyments and vices offer no resistance to his abnegation. He neither uses tobacco nor drinks whiskey. In his economy of refusal, money is superfluous. After paying rent, he throws bills and change into the trash. Voluntary poverty purchases whatever Motes needs. Nourishment is not one of his requirements. Motes soon curbs his taste for food to the point at which he loses flesh. To sharpen his grip on any remaining appetite and resistance, Motes wraps three strands of barbed wire around his chest. This tight restraint on his frail body allows the blind searcher to forge ahead on a lonely journey he has been undertaking for some time.

The hairshirt of twisted metal apparently does not cut deep enough to get Motes to the destination he has in mind. Wherever that place is, he needs ceaselessly to push forward to get there. Weak and blind as he is, Motes develops the habit of taking walks, first around his room and then outdoors with a cane, as he totters five or six blocks, circling the house. All he seems to know is that by harnessing every sinew he has, he will move onward. He uses his body as fuel for perpetual motion to some indefinite objective, for a deliverance he cannot make clear. His final effort to subdue his body conspicuously challenges the bounds of natural life. To cross those borders, he searches out the added velocity of winter winds to propel him there. With reverence or fascinated horror, depending on their sensibilities, onlookers could follow this man to the frontiers of his desire. To do so, they would have to pay close attention to Motes for nearly three cold days as he limps, wracked by influenza and in rock-lined shoes, through icy rain until he reaches a drainage ditch at a peripheral abandoned construction site where two policemen find him. The policemen are under orders to take the spindling back to town, but the blind man lying in the trench is digging his way in the opposite direction. "'I want to go on where I'm going'" (*CW* 131), he tells the officers. They respond by clubbing the defiant stray unconscious, and he dies in the squad car on the way back to his rooming house. The blow is superfluous. The derelict's punishing will already has made a shell of his mortal remains. In that chiseled frame, Motes achieves a body and fate as spare as the strict aloneness that he sought. However bereft and stricken, he is always maneuvering onward, never finding rest.

The outcome of Hazel Motes's struggle brings together the spiritual and cultural forces that underlie the essential drama of O'Connor's fiction. In working out of the conflicts leading up to this convergence, O'Connor outlines in a broad pattern the tensions and terms of the spiritual solitude shaping her characters' lives. Through Motes's body, O'Connor conveys the abiding modern notions of the human person and of society, which are implied through Motes's renunciations. His desiccated corpse pictures what the majority of individuals have made of their lives. At the same time, Motes's mortification wields the harsh surgery that is for him the only remedy for his predicament.

Clearly, Motes has deep inner needs that his society does not answer. His ebbing toward the remote construction site and adjacent inner zones of dilapidation marks his rejection of social engagement as a condition for gaining whatever he seeks. Although O'Connor values Motes's way of life enough to refer three times in her note to the novel's second edition in 1962 to her hero's actions as expressing his "integrity" (*CW* 1265), ordinary citizens of Taulkinham would more likely agree with Motes's landlady, Mrs. Flood, that Motes's habits push him off the deep end of respectability. His denial of money, sustenance, and comfort strikes at Mrs. Flood's idea of life's meaning; and his embracing of pain defies her understanding. Grateful that she is neither religious nor morbid, Mrs. Flood would simply kill herself if she felt bad. Her wisdom of easy destruction of life sums up the world's ethos, as epitomized in the slaughter and displacement of more than fifty million people in the war that has just ended. The moral atmosphere that Mrs. Flood and the rest of society breathe inspires a preference for extinction over a consent to suffer. Mrs. Flood, a decent woman, best gauges the vast distance that Motes has traveled from the social world when she haughtily imagines that he "might as well be one of them monks" doing whatever those creatures do "in a monkery" (*CW* 123). By her reckoning, Motes is a "mad man" (*CW* 124). Monastic life represents all that is antithetical to social fulfillment and therefore embodies all that proper upstanding people like Mrs. Flood would never take on themselves.

Although Mrs. Flood's sense of the worthwhile life comes from passively accepting the tenets of what she believes to be "the real world" (*CW* 123), she is not ignorant of the shadowed underside covered up by conformity to sentimental maxims. On the contrary, her heart intuits certain concealed truths, for she shares in the grief of her dark, war-torn times. "She had had," she admits to herself, "a hard life." Widowed when her husband was killed in an airplane crash, Mrs. Flood sets out to avoid aloneness and grief and, in doing so, settles for a life "without pain and without pleasure" (*CW* 130), a life devoid of any satisfying connection with others. Instead of risking the kindliness that might bring her close to others, Mrs. Flood adopts a pragmatic individualism to cope with the demanding toil of widowhood. Money gives her the sense of worth that the social realm withholds from her. Not being religious or morbid compensates her for the delight that she does not feel. And her overall stance of resentment over being cheated of human warmth and purpose in her hometown allows the landlady to handle guilt and isolation. Should painful feelings overwhelm her defenses, as they threaten to, Mrs. Flood has in reserve the culturally sanctioned solution of killing herself. The guiding materialism and nihilism of the age, then, reconcile Mrs. Flood to the anguish they create in her.

Mrs. Flood's distress is real, and so too is her yearning. When her guard is down and her hand is not held out for money, the landlady can be affecting. In such an off moment, one of the shrewd landlady's grievances expresses the inhospitable condition in which all the characters in *Wise Blood* must find meaning for their lives. Her remark comes as an aside to rationalize her generosity in proposing marriage to the ravaged Motes as he is about to embark on a three-day fast that is continuous with a death march. She is trying to keep him from going out into the bad weather: "'The world,'" Mrs. Flood says, "'is an empty place'" (*CW* 128). The statement is partly a taunt, partly a dare, and entirely accurate; Motes's spectral crossing into the winter waste is his response to her plea. Mrs. Flood may not be religious, and self-sorrow may prompt her concern for Motes; but on this climactic occasion, she utters a spiritual truth about the moral condition of life in the modern century. In fact, at the end of the novel, we see a reflective side of her that can be easily passed over, a vulnerable side that fears have brought her to develop selfishness and detachment as a psychological overlay. At heart, Mrs. Flood is benevolent and akin to Motes. Both are solitaries; both struggle against desolation and ruin. Their world is an empty place, a desert. Whereas geology characterizes a desert as a region with less than ten inches per year of rainfall and with sparse vegetation, common usage and the Bible take a desert to be a deserted place or wilderness. Rain, an icy and slashing downpour, does fall on Taulkinham, just as rain falls on a desert; but the rain cannot be trusted to make the land arable or human life fruitful in Taulkinham. Through everyday language, Mrs. Flood's "empty place" carries the original scriptural denotation of desert as a waste and an empty or trackless place, the holy ground where the human meets the divine. Her words express with moving simplicity the anxiety and bewilderment humans feel when inhabiting the desert.

Mrs. Flood's personal experience of the world as a desert radiates out to historical and cultural implications that impinge on Hazel Motes's search in *Wise Blood*. Since the word *desert* comes up repeatedly and in many different ways in this study, it is valuable at this point—when the figure of the empty place first arises in this discussion of O'Connor's fiction—to consider some of the rich and provocative connotations surrounding *desert*. Part of the history of the desert is the history of the word's recurrent usefulness to vivify human dispossession. The desert readily lends itself as a trope of humankind's anxiety about a menacing environment. Although Native Americans, especially the nomadic hunter-gatherers, related to our rolling hills and great plains as a harmonious part of themselves, the same America to white Europeans settlers was a desert. Colonizers and their westering successors confronted an alien nature that had to be made kind and merciful. To look on America's vastness as a desert promoted the notion of European newcomers civilizing an untamed world. Barrenness invited subjugation of the desert and made the conquest of the land a heroic undertaking. This self-justifying view comes at a price, and we are still paying it. Seeing America as a desert brought along the feeling of not being at home, of being alone, in America. Estrangement goes with the American landscape. We have redescribed the physical immensity with our own sense of immigration and dispossession. The "empty spaces" that Robert Frost sees between stars lie adjacent to his "own desert places" that are "so much nearer home" in his native world north of Boston (296).

As the word *desert* evolved among the British colonists, the quality of emptiness overtook the quality of aridity as the distinctive feature of the desert. Arriving in the seventeenth century in New England, which is by no means dry or sandy, the English could describe their planting the seed of new life, in the words of the Puritan divine Cotton Mather, "in a squalid, horrid American Desert" (Williams 108). Centuries of Judeo-Christian thinking are behind Mather's attitude and language. When William Bradford disembarked from the *Mayflower* in 1620, he set foot in a "hideous and desolate wilderness" (qtd. in Nash 23n.62). It did not take long for Bradford's identification of the desert/wilderness to seize the American imagination since that link was already solidified in the Bible they knew well. Hawthorne, a writer O'Connor admired, was one of many artists to draw on the attitude toward the desert in America. The forest outside Boston in *The Scarlet Letter* is "the moral wilderness" (132) that is "never subjugated by human law" (146) and in which the outcast Hester Prynne wanders freely beyond the confines of the incarcerating Puritan code. Such selective observations necessarily leave out a multitude of important things about the desert, but these connections do provide a new way of thinking about how the American wilderness spreads out to include Mrs. Flood's empty place. The desert is freighted with geographical, subjective, and literary meanings, all of which O'Connor incorporates into her writing.

The physical desert is sufficiently varied and complex to the degree that defining the desert is a problem. Setting limits does not solve the problem, because the concept of the desert precludes restrictions. Add to the difficulty of setting conclusive boundaries the dimension of fear and mystery that the desert elicits in its inhabitants and explorers, and the task of fixing the boundaries of the desert is vexed with indeterminacy. The upshot of this perplexity is that, to consider the desert at all, one must simply allow the word *desert* to define itself in the context at hand. Therein lies the desert's spiritual richness. Given the tendency of the desert to be a state of mind as well as a physical locale, we can take as desert those places that people call desert. And there are many ways of naming the sandy waste. In this study, the physical nature of the desert is important but remains subordinate to what the characters think and feel the desert is. Since the desert is both a topographical entity and an individual experiential matter, the desert is sometimes no desert at all (at least in a scientific sense).

The Taulkinham, Tennessee, of *Wise Blood* illustrates how a place comes to be known as a desert. Certainly, O'Connor's city and its environs do not have the high degree of exposed rock and soil of the Humboldt Desert, the Great Salt Lake Desert, or the deserts of the Colorado Plateau. On the contrary, rain drenches Taulkinham; moss hangs over the trees. Nevertheless, Mrs. Flood's hometown is stark and fearfully lonely. Because she relates to her native environment through victimized desperation, the entire world takes on the antagonism of an empty place. To grasp the interior significance of the topography in O'Connor's fiction, we need to read her writing as Mrs. Flood responds to her world—through its hardship and what sets the landlady apart from others. It is Mrs. Flood's construing Motes through her inner desolation that indicates what O'Connor's hero is all about. Mrs. Flood tries to understand what makes Motes tick by thinking of him as a monk, which is her way of accounting for what is most offensive and most intriguing about her self-mutilating tenant. Her outrage leads to a truth about him. Without knowing it—and surely without consecrating his life by vow or belief—the nihilistic Motes becomes a monk-solitary in the root meaning of *monachos* (solitary). *Monos* in Greek means alone. Motes is isolated, held firmly by the inexorable limitations of his own aloneness. The gory punishments by which he plumbs his isolation affronts Mrs. Flood's civic mindedness. "'It's not natural,'" she declares, "'it's something that people have quit doing—like boiling in oil or being a saint or walling up cats'" (*CW* 127). In trying to pry into Motes's mind and chart his inward course of retreat from society, Mrs. Flood brings us far beyond those gothic walled-up cats and unreformed European monasteries that insult her sensibility. She takes us to the very origin of renunciatory life in the late third and the fourth centuries in Egypt, when Christian men and women fled to the desert. The motive in late antiquity was spiritual unity or holiness (Mrs. Flood's "'being a saint'"), and that need for integrity also drives Hazel Motes, O'Connor's solitary without a cowl or a god, into his chosen disengagement. The figure that baffles Mrs. Flood and startles readers of *Wise Blood* is that of an ancient desert renouncer who has stumbled unexpectedly from fourth-century Egypt into twentieth-century America, and he has brought with him in his dry bones and parched soul the desert in human form.

To understand O'Connor's aim in introducing into modern fiction this extreme venture of Christian asceticism, we need to glimpse the person who initiated the bizarre experiment in late antiquity. As mentioned in the previous chapter, the pioneer is Saint Anthony the Abbot—hereafter called Anthony—the first of the Egyptian fathers of the desert. Anthony's inspiring example was known to O'Connor and preoccupied at least one of her characters. It is the life of Anthony that the retiring Thomas in O'Connor's "The Comforts of Home" (1960) explicitly cites as an example of reckless immoderation in severing all social ties, which caused devils to assail the saint. True enough, by retreating from the comforts of home to the desert, Anthony entered the terrain occupied by demons, who did plague him. Anthony knew, however, that his search for holiness entailed making himself a stranger to the social world and required that he wage war against evil. An outline of Anthony's call to the desert and his response will open up the path that Hazel Motes, O'Connor's first fully developed renouncer, takes to his fate.

One day in church, Anthony heard the Gospel command him to "go, sell what you own, and give the money to the poor, and you will have treasure in heaven; then come, follow me" (Mark 10:21); and he obeyed. He willingly took drastic steps to find spiritual satisfaction. After settling his estate, Anthony returned to live in solitude for fifteen years on the edge of his Nile village. Although old hermits in the neighborhood gave Anthony the initial example of living in reclusion, Anthony soon put his own sharp personal stamp on eremitic life. He stripped himself of all inessentials; and, in doing so, Anthony broke the established frame to become a model for others. He lived on bare physical necessities and with very limited human contact. Withdrawal became more than social distance. It fostered severe self-discipline and a wrestling with evil that gave Christians a fresh form of witness at a time when martyrdom had ceased to be required after Constantine the Great in 312 A.D. ended the persecutions by making Christianity the official state religion. Desert solitude became the new heroicism.

From Athanasius's biography *The Life of Anthony* (written between 356 and 362 A.D.), we learn that rugged solitude developed in the legendary Anthony particular vulnerabilities and resources. Isolation inevitably brought terror as physical survival and moral stability were challenged constantly. Satan attacked Anthony by various temptations. Since he was twenty-two when he fled to the desert, we can imagine what trials a young man met. Anthony's most formidable demons, as we would expect and as confirmed by Athanasius, were those of fornication and willfulness, which Anthony was ready to fight with body and spirit. The strengths he brought were self-scrutiny and a commitment to draw close to God. From his consciousness of purpose, there developed—alongside physical deprivation—a psychology of solitude. He kept his body "under subjection" (7 [36]) not merely for the sake of depriving himself but to foster inner control of his passions that might otherwise invite demonic attention. In the course of his discipline, Anthony kept his spiritual arsenal in full preparedness. His strongest weapon was humility. The weaker he was before God, the stronger he stood before himself and Satan. Humility overcame principalities and powers. After many years of eking out daily needs in the desert, years of strict obedience to the divine will that involved fighting the devil, Anthony died in 356 A.D., ready for whatever was willed for him next.

Anthony's example kindled a desire for holiness in others. During the fourth century, numerous women and men abandoned civilized life to inhabit the deserts of Egypt, Palestine, Arabia, and Persia. The effect of Anthony's life resonated not only through Roman society but also down through the centuries in those with a taste for the exploits of holy men and women. The appeal of asceticism crossed cultural and political lines. As the solitaries challenged the bounds of natural life on flinty soil, they became extremists extending life into mystery. For political activists, the ascetics were models for pushing law into reform, guides for the legendary mid-fifth-century Simeon perched on his pillar and precursors of 1960s civil rights fighters chained at the barricades and fasting in prison cells.

Not unexpectedly, immoderate yearning in a vast parched land produced excess, for the desire to live beyond time while still in the human body begot a discipline that rivaled the exaggerations of the harsh terrain. Inhuman austerities and squalor also marked the pursuit of spiritual liberty, but freedom remained the overriding purpose. The athletics were secondary. In the words of Peter Brown, here "was a grouping of self-styled 'displaced persons,' who claimed to have started life afresh" (*World* 98). Chosen spiritual displacement was the fourth-century answer to Christianity's first-century call to a new beginning. Once again, a new start in the inner world hastened the end of an old political order. Eremitic austerity disturbed and altered the official Greco-Roman world. The public response then was one of fright tinged with admiration; and to this day, asceticism has inspired invective, outrage, and reverence.

O'Connor combines all three reactions in Mrs. Flood; and at the end of the novel, Mrs. Flood's ambivalent awe effects a startling shift in the way she sees Hazel Motes. This change takes the landlady far beyond the social norms of judgment to dispatch her as a fellow-traveler in darkness with Motes. Her last attempt to understand Motes occurs as he lies dead before her. Her next step into his presence demands a leap of imagination. She must shut her eyes. As the Lord "sets the prisoners free" and "opens the eyes of the blind" (Psalm 146:8), so the Lord frees the closed mind of Mrs. Flood. With her heart yearning for some human connection, she forms an image of the dead Motes drifting into a distant point of light. By recombining elements from Christmas cards that she has seen with intuitions of her eremitic tenant's wandering, Mrs. Flood reaches a center where many important motifs in *Wise Blood* converge. The bright point in her picture is the star over Bethlehem in Palestine.

Mrs. Flood is too xenophobic ever to leave Tennessee on her own. But O'Connor habitually sends her homebodies afar to learn about themselves. The excursions are sometimes actual, as with Motes's distant combat tour, and frequently visionary, as for Mrs. Flood. In the case of Mrs. Flood, O'Connor sees to it that the insular woman has the benefit of an inner pilgrimage that introduces her to a way out of cramped turmoil. The journey opens out to the desert—not any desert, but the locale that O'Connor in "The Displaced Person" calls her characters' "true country." The capital of those "tremendous frontiers" (*CW* 305) is Palestine. For geographical and economic necessities, especially those that created trade routes, and for theological reasons, Palestine in ancient times was considered as the place where order was established. Palestine was the navel from which flowed hope to the ends of the world (Isaiah 2:2–3; Micah 4:1–2). The drift of Hazel Motes's practice carries Mrs. Flood beyond her empty place across wide waters to the center of the earth. This inward current also takes readers to the center of O'Connor's writing. She relied for her faith and work on the biblical tradition that emerged from this holy land. She never visited Palestine (and never expressed a desire to); but the Palestine of O'Connor's mind is ever the point of light from which illumination proceeds.

The great physical fact about the country of the Bible is its deserts. The scriptural region spans the eastern Mediterranean coastal plains and the Western Arabian Desert. The climates in the area run to extremes of snow and heat. There are richly varied features of highlands, plateaus, steppes, and canyons over the terrain, but deserts and semideserts make up much of this small portion of the Fertile Cresent. (All of biblical Palestine is smaller than Massachusetts.) The desert powerfully enters the Islamic, Hebrew, and Christian records of the believing communities of Palestine. Their Scriptures are parched by the desert. It is likewise with Flannery O'Connor's texts. Her stories and novels—chronicling nihilists, murderers, and impious revilers grappling with their disordered passions and world and then with the absolute—are always seared by the energy of the desert. The biblical representation of the sun-bitten desert and of the ferocious wilderness establishes the basis for Anthony's postbiblical experiment in holiness that leads directly into O'Connor's modern adaptation of the desert tradition.

Desert ascesis in *Wise Blood* arises in response to life among the ruins of World War II. The disgust and dread that had erupted when Germany invaded Poland in September 1939 grew into a force of terror over many years and around the world. That tide of horror left more than fifty million humans dead and gathered momentum long after the surrender of Japan in August 1945. The world seemed to have given itself over to be raped and defiled by organized slaughter. People and nations were systematically annihilated. Rapacity and injustice inexorably invaded the human spirit. The question that pressed urgently was whether or not there was life left that transcended cruelty and war.

Though not struck directly by bombs, postwar America experienced massive spiritual dislocations. The effects of these prevailing upheavals, O'Connor felt, were presciently described in Carl Jung's *Modern Man in Search of a Soul* (1933) more than a decade earlier. Jung writes: "The man whom we can with justice call 'modern' is solitary." There is a patrician tone in the Swiss psychologist's linking of modernity with solitude. He has in mind not the ordinary person but one who is removed from "the mass of men." This archetype of high spiritual rank stands upon a peak, or at "the very edge of the world, leaving behind him all that has been discarded and outgrown, and acknowledging that he stands before a void out of which all things may grow" (197). Specialist in lower social and intellectual status that O'Connor makes of herself, she sees universal truth in Jung's observation and in *Wise Blood* democratizes the painful sense of being cut off from other people. Not only Mrs. Flood, whose life was shattered by the war disaster that killed her husband, but all the characters in the book are citizens of her empty place, gazers into Jung's void. Backwoods people and urbanites alike are estranged from one another and from their physical surroundings. There is no embracing, no one is safely held; there is only one moment of touching (which I will take up later) in all of *Wise Blood.* Loneliness is in the water everyone drinks.

Desolation, so immediately present in human experience, has lost its capacity to affect people. Try as he might, the religious huckster Onnie Jay Holy is unable to work the crowd he draws one evening outside a movie theater with the subject of human misery. He makes his pitch four different ways with the question: "'Do you know what it's like not to have a friend in the world?'" (*CW* 84, 85, 86). Lonesomeness is all too familiar to this crowd. Each time Holy asks, the audience becomes more cynical. Eventually, the spokesperson of the group announces that not having a friend is "'no worsen havinum that would put a knife in your back when you wasn't looking'" (*CW* 84). In the Hobbesian world of Taulkinham, friendlessness is preferable to the treachery that goodwill toward others sometimes brings about. The promoter of amicability, Holy, can only remind his "'friends'" (*CW* 86) of their predicament. Fatalism prevents them from showing any concern for others.

If not held in bondage—as is Mrs. Leora Watts, who in her massive availability is trapped in "the friendliest bed in town!" (*CW* 16) the characters are in pursuit of the latest tactic that fails to relieve their isolation. Most commonly, they try to allay their inner confusion by manipulating others, which pushes the characters further apart from one another and the world. Motes feels the separation and starkly confronts the townspeople with the loss brought about by their defeat: "'Where is there a place for you to be? No place,'" he calls out from the pulpit of his car. Motes challenges the trickle of illusion fed people leaving the Odeon Theater to acknowledge their shadow world. Human persons, for Motes, are exiles everywhere—and forever. His proclamation offers no hope for redressing solitariness, displacement, and guilt in the exterior world: "'Nothing outside you can give you any place'" (*CW* 93). The grim tidings of O'Connor's nihilist searcher sum up the moral atmosphere that she finds "full of the poison of the modern world" (*HB* 403). And yet if Motes is taken at his word, as O'Connor finally has him take himself, then the nihilist's desperation fully faced out leads to unexpected truths. If nothing outside can put one in substantial relation to life, there remains the possibility that something inside can locate the person in a meaningful order. But first one must find and believe in an inner world. That is Motes's task.

To remove the virulence destroying Motes, O'Connor sends him to the desert for detoxification. In doing so, O'Connor puts Motes on a path to discover something inside himself. Without a clear sense of what is happening, Motes participates in the ascetic revival that was the counterlegacy left by World War II, a renewal catalyzed by Thomas Merton's autobiography *The Seven Storey Mountain* (1948), which burst Trappist monasteries with new entrants to a point of rapid expansion. For Motes, the desert is the ground of tribulation that the desert has always been. That trial is inseparable from O'Connor's narrative technique. "It has always seemed necessary to me," she writes on 8 December 1955 to "A," "to throw the weight of circumstance against the character I favor. The friends of God suffer" (*HB* 120–21). If adversity is a sign of O'Connor's favor, then she must cherish Hazel Motes. And so she does, calling him "a kind of saint" (*HB* 89) on one occasion and on another referring to him as "a Protestant saint" (*CW* 919). For her holy nihilist with the least tractable will, O'Connor finds the appropriate counterforce in the overmastering hardship of the desert. It is not a metaphorical desert that O'Connor pits against Motes. He experiences the *midbar*, blighted with grisly denizens and terror, of the Hebrew Scriptures and the *eremos*, stripped of consolation, of the Gospels. Nothing less than this combined ferocity described in sacred texts will do. Not satisfied that one desert tries Motes, O'Connor sends him to a second. This deeper terrible land is in the Middle East, where the asceticism of the desert mothers and fathers first took hold. The Palestine of O'Connor's faith becomes Motes's Palestine of fact.

We learn of Motes's desert experience when the narrator details Motes's military career after being drafted. "The army sent him halfway around the world and forgot him. He was wounded and they remembered him long enough to take the shrapnel out of his chest—they said they took it out but they never showed it to him and he felt it still in there, rusted, and poisoning him—and then they sent him to another desert and forgot him again" (*CW* 12). The narrator here speaks from that part of Motes that wants to obliterate from his memory four years of conscription, war, the desert where he was shot, and the other desert where he was sent to recuperate from the wounding; and so the recollection neglects military and geographical particulars. The generality of the references encourages readers to pass over the two deserts as incidental facts, but we are fortunate that Marcus Smith has pursued his curiosity about the historical background of Motes's sketchy army past. In "Another Desert: Hazel Motes's Missing Years," Smith has speculatively filled in historical facts that are valuable for understanding Motes's desert trial.

North Africa, Smith explains, was the site of crucial desert battles during World War II. The American and British commands on 8 November 1942 launched a surprise attack called Operation Torch against the Germans in French North Africa. The desert campaign in Algeria and Morocco lasted eight months and brought heavy losses on both sides. Smith numbers Hazel Motes among the 70,000 Allied casualties. (There were also 350,000 Axis soldiers killed, wounded, or captured.) The American wounded were sent to various hospitals in North Africa and the Middle East. Palestine was one such place to which the injured were sent for recovery; there were convalescent centers in and around Jerusalem for American soldiers. Arguing from a scriptural sensitivity that accords with O'Connor's poetry of ideas, Smith proposes Palestine as Motes's "other desert" (56), which in turn anticipates the star over Bethlehem that Mrs. Flood associates with his final destination at the end of the novel. Smith's resourceful thinking squares with the spiritual bent of O'Connor's sensibility and confirms John Desmond's argument in *Risen Sons: Flannery O'Connor's Vision of History* that O'Connor assimilates historical fact into eschatological overview.

If O'Connor is ambiguous about the desert halfway around the world where Motes gets shot and about the second desert where he goes to convalesce, she is definite about Motes's purpose while he is stranded on alien sand: "He had all the time he could want to study his soul in and assure himself that it was not there" (*CW* 12). This spiritual self-examination amounts to a solemn profession to contemplate his inner abyss. Motes is Abba Anthony in reverse. Whereas Anthony embraced the desert and felt permeated by its spiritual energy and believed himself capable of contacting God, Motes, banished to a strange waste against his will, denies his inner being and struggles to get as far away from God as he can. The battlefield for both soldiers is the soul. As Anthony battles against his demons and Satan, Motes fights God by trying to burn out any traces of his interior world. Motes wages a solitary war within the global war. In effect, Motes extends the conflagration of the army's Operation Torch that scarred his body by turning the fire inward against himself. Unlike the political hostilities, however, Motes's inner battle is a truceless war.

Motes conducts his interior offensive with ceaseless vigor. His mind emits a burning stream of inferences with the annihilating force of a flamethrower. The eruption devours any speculation about ultimates. If Motes has no soul, then he has no sin. If he does not sin, then Jesus did not die on the Cross to redeem him. If Jesus did not save him, then Jesus did not rise again. If Jesus had stayed dead, then Jesus was a liar about saving people. If Jesus was a liar, then Motes does not owe Jesus or his nonexistent father anything. Since nothing is true, nothing matters.

Motes is logical, and he is positivistic. He will not simply take the word of his fellow soldiers or the governmental authorities that he has no soul. Furthermore, warring nations by their technological holocausts may degrade and destroy human and planetary life on the conviction that nothing has value, but Motes must verify for himself that existence has no purpose. As Jae-Nam Han argues, Motes, like the countercultural theologians of his era, must be sure that God is dead (117–20). To gain this certainty, he must comprehend his nihilism in the very tendons of his body. O'Connor's use of the word "integrity" (*CW* 1265) captures this traumatized soldier's undivided effort to get rid of God from his mind so that he can be certain that "'there's only one truth and that is that there's no truth'" (*CW* 93).

Contradiction inheres in Motes's nature and inner conflict. He declares that there is no truth and that there is no soul, and yet he freely puts his faith in the credibility of his own nature and soulless existence. What we have in Motes the protesting saint is blind unbelief, the counterpart to the paradox of blind faith. Should he be open to questioning, which he never is, one would ask Motes: How is it possible to prove an absence, the absence of the soul? The soul, at least in the Christian teaching in which Motes was raised, is a principle of being, a source of life, and not an entity that exists on its own as a completed thing to be verified. But then to reason with Motes is to miss the contrariety of his nature and the ardor O'Connor values in him. His actions spring from the depth of his inner life that demonstrates in its turmoil that Motes has in full measure the soul he sets out to deny.

Large intellectual statements are irrelevant to Motes's search. He never really knows what he wants. He only knows what he does not want or believe, and so he is propelled by defiance, not reflection, to the challenge at hand. Pondering whether or not humankind has a soul is his way of abstracting a basic yearning he cannot grasp and so cannot face out. One outcome of his convalescent days in the Middle Eastern desert is that for the moment, at least, he can put a name on an aspect of his desire. Confident that he has resisted the army's attempt to convert him to evil and that he has resisted Jesus' effort to catch him, Motes is ready to leave the desert. Unaware of the benefit of being a stranger in a barren land, Motes takes with him a valuable lesson. The desert instructs him in exile: "The misery he had was a longing for home; it had nothing to do with Jesus." Discharge from military service settles his inner commotion: "All he wanted was to get back to Eastrod, Tennessee" (*CW* 13). Motes is wrong about his home waiting to receive him in Eastrod, Tennessee, which will instead turn him out, and he is wrong about Jesus, who has everything to do with his wretchedness; but Motes correctly interprets his distress as a desire for a resting place after being forced to wander halfway around the world.

Homesickness generates the dramatic action of *Wise Blood*. The novel recounts the last leg of Motes's getting home to Tennessee and covers the final months of his wandering and life. Motes's yearning for home and family while absent from them extends his passage across African and Middle Eastern deserts. As he moves from the first to second desert and on from there, Motes drifts further away from the social world to which he has never been firmly connected and further toward marginality. Those who are read in ascetic literature will find themselves on familiar ground when they read O'Connor on the way in which Motes progresses from two foreign deserts to his longed-for home in Tennessee.

Wise Blood does not reproduce the identical perils and cultural atmosphere of those drawn to the deserts of Egypt and Palestine in the fourth century. No modern novel can deal with unbelief in our more dangerous times by duplicating the motives and tensions arising from an era of faith. Nor can the simplicity of the primitive desert mothers and fathers be reproduced. The late twentieth century is too wary of believers and dogma to credit mere updated, pious versions of the simple faith that guided Anthony and his followers in the desert. Thanks to chemical and nuclear holocausts and ubiquitous land mines, even a good desert is hard to find right now. Nevertheless, O'Connor does see our age as right for hermits. She is clearly on the side of those who feel spiritually at odds with the time and need to find a way to freedom from their attachment to a world nose-diving into catastrophe. In their moral position, those on hidden personal searches do not stand alone in space or in history, for their lives are a response to a radical human desire for wholeness. With allowances made for the contemporary experiences of her shrapnel-scarred solitary, O'Connor rediscovers the timeless pattern of solitude and warfare that was vividly limned by the primitive desert-dwellers of late antiquity.

At this point in the first chapter devoted to O'Connor's fiction, when we are on the verge of tracing Hazel Motes's spiritual passage, I think it useful to block out the overarching design of the classical desert quest. Then, with the contour of the search before us, we will be positioned to appreciate certain views or theories that have helped elucidate desert spirituality to others over the centuries. These preliminary considerations will serve as a way into *Wise Blood* and as the groundwork on which to build subsequent readings of the desert poetics molding O'Connor's short stories. Above all, it helps to have in mind a rough outline of the desert struggle as it bears on *Wise Blood.*

Flight establishes the pattern. The ancient monastics in their search for God began their venture by disowning society. To attain their goal of divine union, the renouncers took up life in the wilderness on the fringe of the social world. There, in a deserted place, they battled against inner and outer forces of evil to repress any self-will that got in the way of approaching God. By subduing their private will, the solitaries grew in knowledge of the transcendent good that reforms the mind and heart into the likeness of the higher will that they strive to obey. For the ancient hermits, this will is the mind of Christ. For the self-battering Motes in *Wise Blood,* the hunt for home also requires that he set himself apart from the social world; and his separation also, as shown, brings him to several deserts, the two that the army sent him to and the adjoining wilderness of his nihilistic convictions. In these empty places, Motes grapples with his will. First he indulges his personal desire; then he fights to stamp it out. In both stages, self-will is Motes's fiercest demon; and almost to the end, that dark power rules him as he becomes the darkness of the void that he has evangelized to others. When near death, as he battles his demons, the light of discipline illuminates the way to his goal.

As soon as the flight to the desert began in late antiquity, the solitaries and their admirers began to look around for principles to explain the experiment. Theorists were as ready then as now to propose systems and paradigms to make understandable the first hermits' austere approach to God. Two prevailing philosophical concepts in the Greco-Roman world were at hand for the earliest commentators. One was the Stoic idea of the progress of the moral life. Stoicism was useful to account for the ethic and psychology of discipline that defined Christian renunciation. The other notion was from the rich Platonic inheritance of the time. Platonist language lent itself to the idea of contemplating God by pure mind. Moreover, Platonist mysticism harmonized with Christian doctrine to put forth with enduring cogency the ascetic search to find God as the journey or quest.

These two ancient philosophies, with certain important qualifications, underscore several features of Motes's asceticism. There is something Stoical about Motes's being unmoved by joy or grief. He certainly achieves an austere indifference to pleasure or pain. He remains unflinching under bad fortune and suffers calmly. In his unconcern for suffering, Motes's resemblance to the ancient Stoic ends. Impulsiveness rather than philosophical ideal determines his actions. Zeno would be hard put, for example, to find in Motes's detachment the rationality out of which wise

Stoics followed virtue by their own inner lights. As for Plato, the exponent of the world of Ideas to which the soul aspires, his teachings bear less resemblance to Motes, who denies soul and spirit. Motes in his way is occupied in the practice of dying, as Plato says true philosophers always are; but systematic thinker Motes is not. We can see Motes's movement as a journey of the soul, but we would have to aggrandize his unknowing fits and starts and refurbish his tin lizzie Essex to call his rambling a search for the Platonic realm of immutable essences. In the end, these ideas from late antiquity hover in the distant background out of which desert asceticism arose. Besides, O'Connor's talent is not one that yields philosophical allegory; but in so far as Stoicism and Platonism shaped ancient asceticism, it is useful to consider to what degree they enter O'Connor's treatment of the experience.

O'Connor's sensibility is scripturally based, and one biblical application of Platonist thought has opened the way for centuries of reflection on the desert experience. Origen (d. 254) enriched the understanding of the spiritual journey through his commentaries on the Bible. Origen interpreted the Exodus as the pilgrim's journey of the soul. Each soul for him retraces the Israelites' passage through the desert/wilderness to the promised land of God, the Canaan of knowledge and faith. Origen's moral allegory, which is couched in Platonist language of contemplation, was and remains theologically illuminating as a model for the lives of the desert elders who made efforts to live by the Bible. The Exodus was for the hermits a conscious guide for their search. The momentous account of deportation, trial, and confession under divine oversight also provides a suggestive parallel for the anagogical method that O'Connor employs in her art. She repeatedly sends her wanderers shouting their cries for help on a journey from bondage to deliverance through the desert/wilderness. Hazel Motes numbers among those following the footsteps of the Israelites through the Sinai of conversion.

Modern readers can use help in tracking Motes's ascetic exodus, and the patristic writer who offers the best guidance is John Cassian (c. 365–435). Unlike most early theorists, Cassian wrote from inside the actual experience of ascetic life and addressed his observations to those unfamiliar with the hermits. Born in what is now Romania, Cassian as a young man lived in a monastery in Bethlehem and traveled throughout the East, where he learned about the desert firsthand from the great teachers of Egyptian spirituality. Inspired by the desert masters, Cassian then traveled to Marseilles, France, to found a monastery based on the eremitic life of the East that he admired. The lessons he learned were incorporated into his *Conferences*, which brought desert life to Western Europe.

Cassian's *Conferences* is a work by a monk for monks. The single collection includes twenty-four imagined discussions (by fifteen renowned Eastern abbas) of how to come to know God. Even though written for the instruction of monks and nuns in southern France, these conversations and interviews ("conferences") speak far beyond their original time and audience. They are to this day invaluable directives for spiritual life in the cloister and for those seeking a spiritual life in a secular world.

Cassian's appeal lies in the artistry with which he vivifies the life of the spirit. Earthiness distinguishes his presentation of the way to holiness. In his commentaries on the hermits, Cassian develops characters, puts them in dramatic situations, has an eye for concrete particulars, and comes to asceticism through basic psychology. His intellectual rigor does not make him shy away from the excitement, tenderness, and love experienced among the hermits. Although there is no evidence in Arthur Kinney's *Flannery O'Connor's Library: Resources of Being* that O'Connor read extensively in Cassian's writing, her knowledge of church history and patristic writing and of Alban Butler's *The Lives of the Fathers, Martyrs, and Other Principal Saints*, which she knew well (Kinney 52–53), would have put her in touch with Cassian's place in the tradition. He is that important. For the purposes of this book, we should be aware that Cassian's kinship to O'Connor is a matter of affinity rather than of direct influence. That deep resemblance becomes more striking as O'Connor in her later fiction goes into kindlier zones of ascetic life such as friendship, mourning, compunction, and tears.

The *Conferences* endures because of Cassian's warmth, his respect for human weakness, and his unvarnished view of inner life. Happily, the loftiness of the desert ideal did not keep Cassian from taking a down-to-earth course in introducing the Egyptian elders to Western monks. The upshot is a pragmatism that effectively translated the wisdom of the fourth-century desert into a response to the new context of Cassian's fifth-century milieu. By standing in deference before the revered past and his needy present, Cassian explained the desire for God that bridged both eras. He tapped the wellspring of the spirit. Cassian's ability to perceive similar spiritual urgency in different times and places often extended beyond the cloister. Cassian takes account of persons who could be more fervent outside the monastery than those within the walls in shedding their sins to make their way to God. This far-reaching embrace of desert spirituality is especially helpful in examining O'Connor's relation to the tradition. O'Connor goes even further in exploring the desire for transcendence. She uncovers in many nonbelievers a spiritual probity that avowed

Christians lack. With Cassian, and from a comparable appreciation for the varieties of ascetic experience, O'Connor recognizes that all those looking for the kingdom of God beyond the kingdom of humankind are desert searchers at heart.

The heart is where all the theoretical axioms and exegetical precedents come together; and in the human heart, Cassian discerns the fundamental renunciatory movement toward God. *Conference* one cites the biblical story of Mary and Martha as the example of the soul's growth in knowledge of God. The story concerns choosing what matters most or, as O'Connor would say, about many wills vying in one person. Martha works hard at numerous tasks in extending hospitality to Jesus, while her sister Mary sits listening at Jesus' feet. When Martha asks Jesus to summon Mary to help with the chores, Jesus responds by turning the tables on Martha's worthy request: "Martha, Martha, you are full of worry and are upset over many things where actually it should be over a few or even one thing. Mary has chosen the good part and it will not be taken away from her" (*Conferences* I, 8 [43]). This quotation from Luke 10:41–42 illustrates that the part Mary has chosen is to listen to the word of God. Her absorbing interest becomes the basis for Cassian's exegesis of the passage, in which he outlines three stages of ascetic effort: the attention to "many things," the attention to "a few," and the attention to "one thing"—namely, God. Cassian's reading of Jesus' response does not devalue Martha's labor but rather places the fretting surrounding physical labor in perspective. Service of the body, for Cassian, while altogether virtuous, lasts only as long as the person is present, whereas zeal for the divine word can never end. Mindfulness of God "will not be taken away." The third stage culminates in the soul's union with God, and it comes about through an ascesis and stripping down of inner focus.

Wise Blood traces a similar triadic pattern. Motes's attention sharpens from many worries, to a few, and finally to the one concern that counts. This distillation is his ascetic act of mind. A multitude of thoughts and distractions fall away until Motes is restricted to the poverty of a single thought. O'Connor dramatizes this inner ascesis through Motes's gradual narrowing of the objects of his attack from many enemies, to a few, and, at last, to the one. The one opponent that counts for Motes is the blasphemous demon within himself. With his body guiding his will, and his will honing his soul, Motes gains the one thing that endures: the truth he contemplates is that his will has played him false. Sixteen centuries after the hermits expressed the conviction that our wills are our demons, Hazel Motes proves them right.

The aim of desert life is stillness (*hesychia*), and that is Motes's goal. Enveloped in a haze of disquiet, Motes also casts about for rest. Whatever else the stricken nations may seek amid the war's spoils, he wants peace. He, one of the walking wounded, has had his fill of guns and government and people and Jesus. For a man longing solely for detachment from the warring world, however, Motes still carries many worries. We can readily sense the depth of Motes's turmoil. Everything he says and does and everyone he meets create distress. Each step of his flight from social engagement is an ordeal. The first sentence of the novel reveals that the battlefield he thought he left behind has moved inside him. *Wise Blood* begins with Motes on the train riding south: "Hazel Motes sat at a forward angle on the green plush train seat, looking one minute at the window as if he might want to jump out of it, and the next down the aisle at the other end of the car" (*CW* 3). Opposing forces precariously bind him. His body wants healing and draws him to rest; and yet his will drives him forward to fight, press on, and dominate whatever lies before him. The first glimpse we have of Motes is of his body enslaved by his private will, deluding him to think that he can make reality an extension of his personal desire. He has made up his mind, for instance, that the black porter from Chicago is not from Chicago but is instead the son of Cash Parrum of Eastrod, Tennessee. The passengers, too, are swept up into the nagging conflicts of his will. When they resist their assigned roles in Motes's psychodrama of Jesus and sin, they become his enemies.

The desert-dwellers understood the private will in its inclination to defy God's will and to dominate others as demonic; as Poemen states: "For our own wills become the demons, and it is these which attack us in order that we may fulfill them" (*Sayings*, Poemen 67 [176]). The truth of Poemen's insight comes to the reader immediately that night as Motes tries to sleep in the upper berth in the sleeping car of the train. Motes's family history returns with ghoulish vividness as he lies like one of those medieval monks in a coffin, contemplating death. We see the spooky adversary Motes is fighting to overcome in the form of his grandfather, a frightening circuit preacher who used Motes as a boy to point up the extreme example of human evil for which Jesus died a gruesome death. Before he was twelve years old, Motes was publicly shamed, emotionally scourged, as that "mean sinful unthinking boy," who was and always would be directly responsible for the crucifixion of Jesus. Transferred into his grandson's mind, Jesus, the slaughtered victim, becomes the pursuer of souls that he died to save; and the young Motes stands as living prey of this bleeding, skulking Jesus. "Jesus would have him in the end!" (*CW* 11), shouts the ghastly old preacher through years of memory. The old man succeeded in searing his ambush theology into Motes's mind, where Jesus takes on the force of the assailant, the liar, the enemy—in short, the demonic.

Whatever harm the grandfather caused, he instilled in his grandson "a strong confidence in his power to resist evil" (*CW* 11). In effect, he made Motes a desert fighter before he took up arms in the desert during the war. Motes has been combat ready since adolescence. Back on native shores after being discharged, he wages war against the enemies of truth, his truth, the truth he wills to be right. In America, adversaries abound, and Motes can detect their dishonesty with the exactness of a radar wave detecting a target miles away. There are those who vaporize belief in Christ, those who capitalize on it, and those for whom belief does not matter. All are spectral materializations from the past, when his grandfather accused Motes of causing Jesus' horrible death. To the warrior of integrity, all are hypocrites deserving denunciation. Motes stands over and against contemporary pretenders to belief as Jesus stood ready to cleanse the temples of defilers (Matthew 21:12–17).

The conflict in which O'Connor has Motes engaged is the most scrambled of holy wars. On one side is the force of untruth led by an army of one, Motes; he is a nihilist by conviction. On the other side are all the other characters. They declare themselves Christian but are pagans in practice. These are money changers in the house of God and modern Pharisees who cover themselves with a mask of justice and dogma to dispense with an interior life and do away with acknowledging themselves as sinners. O'Connor describes such persons in a letter of 23 December 1959 to her friend Cecil Dawkins. While referring specifically to members of her own church, the observation applies to other Christians as well. She writes that there are many "unimaginative and half dead Catholics who would be startled to know the nature of what they defend by formula" (*HB* 366). In *Wise Blood*, O'Connor commissions Motes to take on these many Christians and unnerve them with bolts from the "spiritual reality" to which they are blind, thus indicating how that unseen actuality "affects us in the flesh" (*HB* 365).

Miss Wally Bee Hitchcock is the first to be attacked and reminded of what lies behind her stance of Christian virtue. She sits prim and proper opposite Motes on the train, judgmentally prattling on about various persons with the confidence of one who has satisfied her moral obligations to life. Out of the blue, Motes twice charges the woman: "'I reckon you think you been redeemed'" (*CW* 6). He strikes again in the dining car, where he is seated with a group of women who are "dressed like parrots" and act like shrikes. He feels their condescending cruelty and does not let them get away with it: "'If you've been redeemed,' he said, 'I wouldn't want to be'" (*CW* 7). Motes confronts these "respectable" travelers with the hard truth of sin and penance, assailing their smugness that passes for goodness and superiority. In his mind, only those who have paid their debt to the Cross can act as they do about their worth. Seeing through their sham virtue, he dissociates himself from whatever god has guaranteed the salvation these women believe is their due. Motes the nihilist takes Christianity more seriously than do the Christians in *Wise Blood*, and his blunt honesty exposes their secret rottenness.

For all of its integrity, however, Motes's campaign can only increase his tribulation. O'Connor admires his zeal in piercing the deceit before him, but she shows him judging the modern Pharisees pharisaically. Motes, like his opponents, puts up his private will as absolute. This is idol worship, which invites the demons of pride to embroil Motes more deeply in the trap they set for him. The numerous antagonisms in which Motes suffers show that in the spiritual struggle pride is his weakest weapon. *Wise Blood* prepares the reader for a simple truth that guided the hermits in their grappling with evil: "Do not trust in your own righteousness" (*Sayings*, Anthony the Great 6 [2]). Confidence in one's virtue leaves no room for aid from others or God's help. The scene in the dining car comically bears out the desert elders' understanding of how pride weakens one before malice. When Motes retaliates against the women baiting him and says that he would not believe in Jesus "'even if He existed,'" his self-congratulating effrontery begets a more swollen disdain from the woman with a venomous voice, who chirps: "'Who said you had to?'" Motes's blasphemy is no match for the casual profaning of the sacred that pervades society. Backed up by years of culturally approved faithlessness, the woman's offhand insult of the divine stuns Motes: "He drew back" (*CW* 7).

Such a defeat, along with the humiliation before his grandfather and the soldiers' mockery at the bordello, would have a positive side for the ancient solitaries. The enemy offers knowledge to the spiritual fighter: "A man knows nothing about the powers that are outside him; but if they enter into him, he must fight them and drive them out" (*Sayings*, Poemen 199 [194]). By revisiting the many agents of dread and terror (his grandfather, father, and mother) and by meeting the exponents of nihilism (the military powers of World War II, his own government, the army, his fellow soldiers, and the travelers on the train), Motes meets the evils stirring in his soul that he must learn to conquer. The next phase of his ascetic education requires that he be a solitary in society, allowing his concerns to winnow from the many to a few.

That schooling takes place in the city of Taulkinham. The moral atmosphere of Taulkinham combines the fright of nightmare with the actual menace of daily life. "As in a terrifying dream," Frederick Asals writes, "characters assume strange and distorted shapes, appearing and disappearing in defiance of waking probability; the familiar landscape of the modern city turns foreign and forbidding; and objects and gestures shimmer with symbolic resonance" (48–49). Asals's chimerical verisimilitude redescribes how the desert appeared to the ancient solitary when attacked by demons. "For when they come," Anthony warns, the demons' "actions correspond to the condition in which they find us; they pattern their phantoms after our thoughts" (Athanasius 42 [63]). Depending on the victim's vulnerability, the demons work their will by imitating "women, beasts, reptiles, and huge bodies and thousands of soldiers" (Athanasius 23 [48]). If one phantasm fails to overcome the solitary, the demons fabricate another. There is no end to demonic wiles because there is no cessation in their scheming against God's plan and because there is no limit to the weaknesses in their human victim. But as each guise represents the solitary's own thought, the demonic figure offers the possibility of self-awareness. Among the swarm of demons, O'Connor condenses the few that Motes needs to drive out of himself.

The desert of Taulkinham, first of all, brings Motes to confront estrangement. Nobody really belongs in this city. Like Motes, the people are drifters and waifs from a disaster who somehow end up in the town. For Sabbath Hawks, daughter of the false blind preacher, the place is a dead end. After being abandoned by her father—and after Motes tries to get her out of his bed and life—Sabbath twice pleads despairingly: "'I ain't got any place to go'" (CW 95). Taulkinham is also the end of the line for the runaway Enoch Emery, who finds the city insupportable: "'I ain't never been to such a unfriendly place before'" (CW 25). Having endured rejection and abuse all his eighteen years, Enoch speaks from considerable familiarity with the harrowing conditions of Taulkinham. And there is no escaping his ostracism. He sees an actor in a Gonga costume shaking hands to draw a crowd to a movie. The anticipation of human contact thrills Enoch: "No gorilla in existence, whether in the jungles of Africa or California, or in New York City in the finest apartment in the world, was happier at that moment than this one, whose god had finally rewarded it" (CW 112).His hope for a mere handshake, however, is dashed, because he frightens people off. The brute god of rejection drives its subjects into deeper isolation. Deliverance for Enoch comes in the form of sitting by himself on a rock, gazing "over the valley" at the city skyline below (*CW* 112). The dark pit that Enoch blankly contemplates is the yawning abyss of Taulkinham that is waiting to swallow up Motes.

Once Motes arrives in the city, he rushes into the black hole of modern life. Just as the first demon to attack Anthony was the demon of fornication, so Motes's first trial is sexual. Both Anthony and Motes are in their early twenties, the age when the softness of sexual pleasure has powerful sway over the body. Anthony conquered the seductive devil through humility. On his own, the young ascetic would have succumbed to the sexual power of the demon, and so he relied on God to help him resist the demon. By incorporating the control of sexual desire into his ascetic search for holiness, Anthony resolved his erotic confusion. Motes also tries to bring sexuality into his search, which is to prove that there is no sin; and the result is carnal unruliness. With Motes, who puts all his trust in his will, sexuality takes a schizophrenic turn. Sexual activity essentially occurs in his head. His mind has so much power over his erotic inclination that he seems sexless at twenty-two. This dissociation from his body plays itself out by manipulating women. When losing his virginity with Mrs. Watts, Motes uses her body "not for the sake of the pleasure in her" but "to prove that he didn't believe in sin" (*CW* 62). All he really demonstrates is that his will does not so much control his body as it forsakes his body to *anhedonia*, the inability to experience pleasure. Try as he may to turn flesh into mental verification, Motes only manages to intensify his turmoil.

The other urban adversaries appear in the animal shapes in which Anthony saw demons centuries ago. During his second night in town, Motes encounters "a tall cadaverous man with a black suit and a black hat" and dark glasses over scars that make him like "a grinning mandrill" (*CW* 20). Next to this baboonish creature is a young female in black. The grisly pair are Asa Hawks, a religious spoofer, and his daughter Lily Sabbath Hawks, who hands out pamphlets entitled *Jesus Calls You*. Completing the zoological bugbear is a young man "who looks like a friendly hound dog with light mange" (*CW* 23). The chummy canine is Enoch Emery. These are the embodiments of hypocrisy and mindlessness that Motes must learn about, and their dehumanized physical appearance issues the moral warning.

Hawks's face demands closer scrutiny. His cheeks are hideously streaked with injuries from his bungled lime stunt that was to imitate Paul's blindness as proof of faith and that he used for cash reward. His lesions accord with the "Deep scars of thunder" that God entrenches on the face of Milton's Lucifer as the archangel turned archfiend is hurled from

Paradise (*Paradise Lost* I, 601). The ugly woundings bespeak the same conscious pride and shameless daring in the latter-day deceiver as they did in the first creature, the benighted messenger of light, who sought to put his individual will before the will of God. O'Connor's delineation of Asa Hawks is an early example of her lifelong dedication to giving the devil his due. There is no mistaking Hawks's show of evangelical perfection for various psychological tendencies. The macerations of a greedy religious poseur playing to a crowd make equally obvious the self-destruction that results from such violent assertion of one's personal will. Hawks's mortification of his body is about his will; and in displaying his will by scourging his body, the evangelist brings vanity to a new level of flamboyant hauteur. And yet, Hawks's histrionic abuse of his body speaks with almost no force to a jaded populace. Their nihilism, rather, finds confirmation in his debasing his body for money. Hawks's creases and furrows exemplify a prideful, discredited ascesis that goes with false prophecy, an art form all its own in the thriving Jesus industry of Taulkinham.

It bears observing that neither Hawks's pretense nor greed initially rankles Motes. These corruptions of Christianity slide from his attention, which is entirely focused on his being in the right. The angularity of Motes's vision indicates the deluding power of his demons. The ability to "recognize something to be true and from God or false and from the devil," Cassian explains, requires humility (*Conferences* II, 9 [67]); but Motes sees only what his prideful demon lets into his vision. Repentance, which is Hawks's message, is blocked out because it is a summons to sinful persons, and Motes must resist such a call if he is to cling to his conviction that there is no such thing as sin. Repentance implies personal culpability; and this admission of responsibility looks to interior change (*metanoia*). Conversion, Motes learned from his grandfather, means he must suffer to share in the merit of the Cross. Motes, however, believes that sin has not entered him; therefore, he owes nothing to Jesus. In inimitable Motesian fashion, the man of integrity conducts the good fight for truth for wrong-headed reasons. By attacking the messenger (Hawks with his call to repent), Motes can deny the message. And so, as Hawks preaches the Church of Christ, Motes in prideful reaction founds his Church Without Christ, in which "'the blind don't see and the lame don't walk and what's dead stays that way'" (*CW* 59). This altogether logical and antimystical proclamation is the gospel according to Motes's will, whose power eventually unmasks the false Hawks, who then vanishes like a dispelled desert mirage.

True to the desert elders' predictions, another adversary appears to replace the defeated demon. The improvised team of Onnie Jay Holy and

Solace Layfield, flag-waving promoters of the sunset and friendship, materializes with their gospel of Soulease. Motes knows all too well that the soul's search for God is anything but tranquil. This new violation of truth as Motes sees it enrages him. Ensnared by the rectitude of his own fury, the soldier who fought fascists in the faraway desert now imitates them at home. In the name of his private truth and out of the demand that another person must conform to his abstract notion of the world, Motes exterminates Solace Layfield. On a lonesome road on the outskirts of town, a deserted spot favored by demons to incite O'Connor's characters to act as executioners, Motes strips Layfield of his masquerade and slays him with his Essex, the temple and war chariot of his truth. Later we will see how Motes's savage ascesis of Layfield comes back to him with equal devastation; but at this juncture, we see Motes falling into the satanic trap set by his claim to virtue. His irreproachable life develops a tightly involuted self-love and intractable spiritual pride. Secure in himself, Motes easily turns this confidence into severity toward others. The result is death.

The cold-blooded murder of Layfield completes Motes's projection of his inner furies onto others. Shrouded by night under moss-laden trees, the last of Motes's few local enemies lies shattered at his feet. The haunted warrior of truth thinks that he has finally conquered his enemy. Although he is ready to move on, he cannot just yet. Looking up from the puddle of blood gushing out of Layfield's head, the victim's grimace and voice buttonhole Motes. Motes squats down next to Layfield. Before Motes are the cruelties he received over the years and that he thought he had put to rest, as well as those cruelties he committed on others and denies. Motes, however, is too firmly under the power of his wrathful and prideful demons to feel anything but coolly justified by his moral cleansing of a man who "'ain't true'" (*CW* 114).

Motes's callous blindness has its counterpart in the narrator's brisk, matter-of-fact presentation of his killing of Solace Layfield. Bloodshed in the Tennessee woods slips quickly into the passing round of daily American life without exciting alarm. And yet certain excisions of the narrator are conspicuous and, therefore, morally telling. There are no witnesses to the slaughter, and the account pays no attention whatsoever to the crime's legal consequences. This abridgment allows O'Connor to embed her ascetic passion into the story. Instead of bringing the action to the anticipated outer social inferences, O'Connor's spiritual poetics channels the reader to the inner world of moral discernment and judgment underlying the killing. The interior view is the desert perspective, which, guided by humble compassion, always takes the victim's standpoint. By looking at Layfield's death from within his suffering, we can see what Motes misses, and we can open our hearts to what he cannot yet feel. It is in this inner world that O'Connor locates her hope for each person to change the direction in which he or she looks for happiness and for the whole world to alter the nihilistic course taken through the "dark night of the soul" (*HB* 100). With careful restraint, O'Connor shows how desert ascesis, even when hurriedly packed into Layfield's dying moments, undoes the demonic power ruling the world.

To see the world as Solace Layfield does from the hard ground of death is to stare at the demons of hatred and anger unleashed from Motes's soul with all the fury he learned in war and from his grandfather. Layfield is physically defenseless in utter loneliness. There is no way out for him. The hour of darkness, dread, and death is on Layfield. In Layfield's appointed crisis, O'Connor replicates a predicament Cassian describes in his tenth conference as a "night the devils surround me with their horrors." To be horror-struck is to be poor in spirit as well as alone in battle. As Cassian states: "And so if I am to deserve liberation from this bleakness of spirit from which my groans and sighs have been unable to save me I shall be obliged to cry out 'Come to my help, O God; Lord, hurry to my rescue'" (*Conferences* X, 10 [135]). The recognition of the poverty of spirit avails the solitary to the blessing of the first of all the beatitudes. In the blackest moment of wrath in *Wise Blood*, O'Connor, like Cassian, dovetails a glimmer of resistance to the fiends' attack. That opposition arises from Layfield's naked, bashed body in a mere sigh for escape. In the final solitude on the last desert of death, Layfield confesses his sins of troubling his mother and father and of stealing. Motes's efficient brutality requires that O'Connor abbreviate Layfield's petition to God. Scorned and revictimized by Motes for repenting and ordered to shut up, Layfield wheezes out three words: "'Jesus hep me'" (*CW* 115).

Prayer does not get more concise than Layfield's three words, and O'Connor cannot get any closer to the essence of desert spirituality. "'Jesus hep me'" seals Layfield's liturgy of repentance. He is a guilty man who has given himself over to correction, not to the unjust blow of Motes's car but to the chastisement of God. In at least one respect, Motes judges Layfield correctly. He calls Layfield a liar because he preaches the Holy Church of Christ Without Christ even though he, Layfield, believes in Jesus. Layfield does believe in Jesus, and his belief costs him everything. Stripped of the mask of unbelief, which earned him $15.35, Layfield becomes a solitary despite himself and, like Jesus in whom he believes, becomes a scapegoat to a pharisaic executioner by virtue of Motes's attack in that deserted spot. Without guidance from a wise elder, with only

the harrowing recognition of his total helplessness after Motes's scourging, Layfield the fake prophet turns out to be a person of true prayer and
authentic ascesis. His blood-garbled plea, "'Jesus hep me,'" which further
contracts into "'Jesus,'" reverberates with echoes from the ancient desert.
Cassian could not forget nearly identical words that he heard when he
was with the hermits, and he passed them on to Western monks to remember when "the devils surround" one "with their horrors." Cassian
records the prayer for rescue and protection with anxious regularity:
"'Come to my help, O God; Lord, hurry to my rescue'" (*Conferences* X,
10 [135]). Should the desert-dweller's struggle grow fierce and should the
need become dire, then "'Lord, help!'" suffices, says Abba Macarius. The
Lord "knows very well what we need and he shews us his mercy" (*Sayings*, Macarius the Great 19 [131]).

Cornered by evil spirits, quivering with a terror that drags away any
hope, Solace Layfield wins the grace of humility through contrition. His
simple prayer throws off the yoke of pride. His terrified groan, uttered in
his last gasps, calls on his protector to rescue him. Nothing more is said;
and O'Connor makes its plain that nothing more is needed. "'Jesus hep
me'" is the sturdiest defense the desert fathers and mothers had against
the onslaught of evil. Their wise blood taught them that meekness overcomes anger. By means of hard self-renunciation, Layfield comes to the
same hard faith in the power of human meekness (2 Corinthians 8–9).
Whatever the indignity, the pain, or the gloom of thought, Layfield's three
last words keep him from despairing of redemption because they proclaim
the One he calls on and the One who sees his great struggle.

Solace Layfield's death marks the end of Hazel Motes's social war in
Taulkinham. Having beaten down the last of the enemies of his Church
Without Christ, the circuit crusader of truth retreats for a night's rest in
his Essex. The Essex, bought in a used car lot "between two deserted
warehouses" (*CW* 37) and fit for desert travel, is the ark and armament
of Motes's fate. The vessel also serves as his cell for reflection. After killing Layfield, Motes spends a sleepless night in the car "thinking" (*CW*
116) about a new life, the upshot of which is a decision to preach in a new
city. As he speeds along the highway in his rolling sanctuary, a sense of
massive emptiness overtakes him. The road slips beneath him, pulling
the Tennessee landscape back into the boundless foreign desert halfway
around the globe where he was shelled. "He had known all along that
there was no more country," and soon he will understand that "there was
not another city" (*CW* 117). The entire world for Motes is the desert, a

vast Sahara of his own making that yawns wide to ease his moving deeper into its propitiatory mystery.

Motes's willfulness made the world a desert; and now willfulness ushers Motes into the deepest desert of his wrathful furies. As Motes took the law into his own hands in killing Layfield, the law now takes Motes into its custody. The battle of Taulkinham is won and lost by self-willed anger. Once again, O'Connor sets the scene in the outlands. Five miles away from town, a patrolman stops Motes because he does not like his face. The cop follows the pretense of checking Motes's driver's license; then, taking pleasure from meanness, the officer of the law pushes the Essex over the embankment. The ark of Motes's covenant lies thirty feet below in shambles. Motes in shock sits on the edge of the embankment, staring at the car that he believes is his salvation and that is now disintegrated before his eyes. What the wreckage reveals to Motes is devastating: he created the Church Without Christ as a mere edifice to separate himself from pain and suffering. The buzzard hunched on the roof of a one-room shack nearby seems to be waiting for the last picking of Motes's belief to be dumped in its valley of dry bones. The cop, taking the demon's delight in destroying illusions, puts his hands on Motes's shoulder for the conqueror's claiming touch before driving off. Motes is left behind in the bleakness of spirit into which he drove Solace Layfield. No human enemies remain for Motes to demonize. He must shoulder the burden of his terrors. He must follow Layfield's way of ascesis directed not outward toward others but turned inward against his own personal demons.

Motes's last campaign is fought on the battleground of his own being. O'Connor brings him to the desert within so that he discovers the barrens of his nihilism. In this terrain, he must undo the delusion that his private will can save him. The only resource he has left is his shrapnel-filled body from his desert campaign in Africa. Having failed to fight his way to truth by using his body as an instrument of his will, Motes now attempts to reverse that control so that his diminished body, whose eyes have seen his Church Without Christ razed, can reinstruct his will. His fragile body, the badge of his struggling humanness, must achieve the goal that his Essex failed to reach. For this to happen, Motes must remake his body into a finely calibrated vehicle that can negotiate the long return of his person, body and soul together, to the end.

In remaking his body, Motes pays special attention to his extremities of feet and eyes. His feet support his body and soul to keep him upright; his eyes are the source of light and understanding. The process of anatomical realignment begins with a five-mile walk back to town in the slow, deliberate passage of three hours. The measured pace is the stride of self-scrutiny. It is the moral infantryman's strategic retreat. A lowly foot soldier in the desert during World War II, he remains an infantryman in the Armageddon of his will. Motes repents by going back over his actions to replace self-deceptions with clear-sightedness. This correction involves a turn away from the visible to the invisible world. To make this turn permanent, Motes sacrifices his eyes to his new obedience. On reaching Mrs. Flood's boardinghouse, he blinds himself with quicklime. His purpose is to gut the organs of sight that played him false by mistaking the surface of things for all of reality, for thinking that Hawks's show of evangelic perfection meant belief. It is as if the quicklime can burn through Motes's eye sockets to scorch open a pathway into the invisible reality that the optic nerve alone cannot perceive.

In Cassian's third conference, Abba Paphnutius speaks of the ascetic's drawing away from the visible world until the attention is mainly on the invisible and future world. "Our passion is for the unseen," Paphnutius says (*Conferences* III, 6 [85]). Motes has learned that reality takes multiple forms. There is the reality of war, fragments of exploded shells troubling his body, and of the Essex; but there is another kind as well, a different reality that constitutes the essence of his ascetic search and of O'Connor's eremitic art. Here the modulation of the unseen inner world is reality. During his final months, covered in the last chapter of *Wise Blood*, Motes's eyeless gaze fixes once and for all in the direction of that distant reality. His one passion at the end is for the unseen, the one task that will not be taken away from him.

Motes's passion for the unseen places him in relation to the absolute, the One. This new bond with the supreme integrates the shards of his life and erases the boundaries of his world. The limitless expanse depicts the desert of his spirit, which impinges on eternity. Motes is so immersed in this deserted cosmos that he seems removed from the experience of time. A question that Mrs. Flood asks Motes in the morning might be answered in the afternoon or not answered. When she encourages Motes to return to preaching, he becomes irritated. Going back into public life would take him away from the infinite stretch in which he has been advancing. "'I don't have time'" (*CW* 125), he says, walking off the porch into the enticing dark enormity that has opened before him. The comment may seem to express contempt for time; but when considered from Motes's ascetic aim, it does not devalue time. Rather, by setting the present moment over against timelessness, Motes gives time its true depth in eternity. Time stands still in Motes's spiritual Palestine, as it did for the desert-dwellers in late antiquity.

Not the clock but Motes's body marks his progress through the desert darkness that is his final domain. The drastic changes in his physical condition during his final months of mortification indicate with terrifying exactness the determined course of his ardor for the unseen. He lines the bottom of his shoes with gravel, broken glass, and bits of stone. Half of each day is devoted to walking: in the morning around his room, after breakfast until midday outdoors, always following the strict route of four or five blocks circling the rooming house. One day while lying in bed with influenza, Motes hears the swirling of winter wind making "a sound like sharp knives" (*CW* 128); and he climbs out of his sickbed to embrace the cutting wind that will intensify the hewing of his body. The pain of this grinding walk goes beyond physical penance to satisfy Motes's need to subdue his will, a will that to the very end tries to seduce him into comfort and away from the joy of obedience. But he does not stray from the newly found path through the invisible world. The ascesis of his body keeps his will in line with the absolute.

The most unnerving of his restraints is the practice of wrapping three strands of barbed wire around his chest, which, we should remember, is already punctured by fragments of artillery shells from warfare in his other desert. There is no getting around the violence of this girdle of punishment. Motes's metal hairshirt confronts the reader in an extreme way with the controversy over O'Connor's images of the human body that surrounds her entire fiction. The cartoonish figures and mangled anatomical parts strewn over her stories and novels have led one commentator to assign O'Connor's writing to "the literature of disgust" and to accuse her of regarding "the body itself as repulsive" (Hendin 28–29). This response, which runs through O'Connor criticism, is certainly in keeping with Mrs. Flood's initial recoiling from Motes's excoriated chest; but then, Mrs. Flood is in the novel to reflect the reaction of our age—not that of O'Connor.

Far from confirming either a repulsion of the body or a noetic detachment from the body, as other critics have argued, the poetics of desert ascesis in *Wise Blood* invites a different understanding of Motes's bodily mortifications. O'Connor condenses in her hero's wracked flesh and bones the century's history of war, emotional violence, willfulness, and godlessness. These are the satanic outbreaks of our time; Motes's scars embody their effects. O'Connor felt compelled in a letter (9 July 1960) to remind "A," who apparently thought that Motes was too naïve to support the large meaning surrounding him, that her hero, "even though a primitive, is full of the poison of the modern world" (*HB* 403). That contagious evil is the source of control that society exercises over and inscribes in Motes's body. But also circulating in the moral atmosphere of *Wise Blood,* as has been shown, is the current of renunciation, which flows as an antidote to the history of sin and violence. Within the dynamics of Motes's fervor, O'Connor follows the movement of Motes as he struggles to rid himself of the toxins defiling him. He disciplines his body to correct his will. It is in Motes's surrender of his resistant will that O'Connor sees a way to reclaim the body from society's domination. Ascesis can cleanse the body of the killing agents generated by a nihilistic and avaricious culture.

Like the early desert anchorites, and unlike modern Manicheans, Motes intuits a continuity between his body and soul. If groping through the timeless dark teaches Motes anything, it is that his physical life and his spiritual life are insolubly united. Before the destruction of his sham Church Without Christ, Motes's will dominates. After seeing the deceptions of his will in the wreckage of his Essex, Motes allows his body to teach its wisdom to the soul. In the end, Motes thinks of himself not as a monk, a believer, a preacher, nor in any category of identity. Rather, he is a person who is paying for the rare freedom to repent his transgressions and to mortify his newly imagined body. This new body, cleansed of sin's stain, might gain a future glory for his body. Motes tames and lacerates his body in the belief that he can bring it to a fresh, uncorrupted state. Motes's word for this pristine condition is "'clean'" (*CW* 127). This inner stainlessness corresponds to the "purity" that Abba Paul says Adam enjoyed "in Paradise before he transgressed the commandment" (*Sayings,* Paul 1 [204]). Motes's speaking of "'no bottom'" in his sightless eyes is his attempt to evoke the unfathomable reality or paradise into which his purged body will be assimilated. "'If there is no bottom in your eyes,'" he explains to Mrs. Flood, "'they hold more'" (*CW* 126). The added dimension of "more" is the realm of transfiguration. Far greater than the realm of pure spirit, the transfigured world for the Christian is that state in which the physical body is glorified through the grace-bestowing event of Jesus' resurrection.

Motes's ascetic effort brings his body to the threshold of this transfigured world. After the policemen return his corpse to Mrs. Flood and, at her request, put the dead man on her bed, she notices that her tenant's "face was stern and tranquil." Severity is to be expected in Motes, but bodily serenity is surprising, even improbable, because this quietude overcomes his gruesome scars and emaciation to make him a new man. The effect of Motes's salutary inner change is tangible. His peace mesmerizes Mrs. Flood, who "had never observed his face more composed." Such equanimity can only lie deeper and reach higher than any other human trait or aspiration. His comfort speaks to her comfort. Mrs. Flood grabs Motes's "hand and held it to her heart" (*CW* 131). This is the only time in *Wise Blood* when two characters touch without intending to control or harm the other person. At this moment, the woman who knows that the world is an unfriendly and empty place seeks help from the man who has lived as an exile in the world. One of the fruits of Motes's solitude is the comfort his life gives a woman who lives as an outlander in the society Motes rejects.

This rare moment of union between two isolated characters links several features of desert spirituality that profoundly affect the relations between human persons and their bond with God. The tenderness in Mrs. Flood signals a penetration into her heart that goes deep enough to alter her way of regarding Motes and his practice. In the poetics of solitude, the heart is the source of all human and spiritual vitality. The hermits refer to the piercing of the heart felt by Mrs. Flood as *catanyxis*, a stark inner upheaval that O'Connor will bring to fuller meaning as her fiction develops. With Motes, the heart is not suddenly stirred but finally brought to rest. For him to enter the depths of the heart marks the freeing from its idols and its being stripped of its layers of pride and illusion. With his will sapped of opposition, he can rest in God. It is his ease of heart that arouses Mrs. Flood and dramatizes the aim of desert ascesis. *Hesychia* is the term for the heart resting in God. This is the repose that settles in Motes's body and flows into Mrs. Flood. In death, he becomes a teacher, a reluctant teacher for our resistant times.

The conversion of Hazel Motes from cruel nihilist to unperturbed hesychast embodies O'Connor's radical wisdom for those seeking to dispel the poison of the modern world. She proposes a detachment from a decadent society, a withdrawal not with proud contempt but from a need to be true to oneself. For Motes to find his true self, he must cast off the rule of fabricated social and political compulsions. Because he, like the culture, is so fully captivated by the power of self-will, only a stronger power outside himself can force a clean break from the world. The destruction of his Essex catalyzes his letting go of the past and society. As he humbly walks back to Taulkinham, Motes steps outside the American life that was promoting power and violence and an artificial self rooted in ego. Motes luckily sees that he cannot fit in. He does not want the usual life anymore, and society no longer wants him. For Motes to lead the ordinary life means denying the vast hidden world that holds more than his eyes hold. If there is repressed desire in O'Connor's questers, it is a passionate attachment to God without their being aware of the affinity. They both wish and oppose their own desires, but their yearning wins out. "Haze is saved by virtue of having wise blood," O'Connor remarks to John Hawkes; "it's too wise for him ultimately to deny Christ" (*HB* 350). Renunciation offers Motes a way to affirm his wise blood.

Motes's pathway to his innate wisdom is costly. O'Connor has her Taulkinham hermit detach himself from social relations and his ego to a degree that is altogether dreadful. He dares to risk being lost in the dark void. Against the modern cult of personality, O'Connor has Motes incur the danger of anonymity that covers his lostness in God. The part of him that mentors his will to slough off the ego is, as we saw, his scarred body. His wise blood demands that he give that up, too. Motes's body initiates and fulfills his ascetic calling. His complete self-giving expresses, for O'Connor, nothing less than integrity. The desert mothers and fathers understood this total yielding to God's will as singleness of heart. Their more common phrase for this dedication is *purity of heart.*

Although the phrase "purity of heart" may put Motes's strange life into historical and spiritual perspective, it also places a high tone on a life that is essentially as squalid as it is marvelous, as brutal as it is quiet. Whatever truths the desert tradition opens up in the larger implications of *Wise Blood,* Hazel Motes must yield to mystery. Renunciation transcends any political ideology and religious dogma in which it is practiced. O'Connor as hermit novelist is postdogmatic in portraying Motes in the way some writers are postmodern. For certain people of belief or unbelief, the frank confrontation of their mortal condition simply makes asceticism an urgent necessity. Suddenly, wealth, pleasure, and power fail, and self-will proves false; and the loss of inner vitality puts one to the test. These are the persons commanding O'Connor's scrutiny.

O'Connor brings Hazel Motes, her first and most far-ranging quester, to an exacting interrogation from the most stripped position. Motes has neither a tried rule nor a sage guide to show him the way through his trials. Rather, he succeeds as a spiritual solitary because he is ignorant enough of ascesis not to be awed by it nor to label it. He is lonely, and he lives out his loneliness. He is attacked by demons, and he fights back. The world has no place for him, and he faces out the consequences of dispossession in a barbed-wire moral enclosure. The desert and darkness alone, and Motes's ventures into them, provide the grounds on which his heart must settle its opposing desires. But holiness, O'Connor reassures us, lies in unsuspected places. The stories coming up bring us to more of those untracked territories.

3 Sporting with Demons

> Examine yourself, then, my brother, and see if you have
> not been the sport of the demons, for you have lacked
> perception in this matter.
> —Macarius the Great, *The Sayings of the Desert Fathers*

> Vigilance, self-knowledge and discernment; these are the
> guides of the soul.
> —Poemen, *The Sayings of the Desert Fathers*

IN THE PREVIOUS CHAPTER on *Wise Blood*, we saw that
renunciation guides Hazel Motes to integrity. By facing out his unbelief
through bodily mortification, O'Connor's nihilist saint finds a consoling wholeness in solitude that is denied him in the broken modern world.
The insights that Motes gains in solitary warfare clearly take firm hold
of O'Connor's moral imagination, for as we turn to *A Good Man Is Hard
to Find and Other Stories* (1955), her first book of short fiction, we see
the tantalizing desert of the East that Motes carried back in his spirit
after World War II merge with O'Connor's South. Here in ten "stories
about original sin" (*HB* 74), as O'Connor with an elder's heuristic moralism calls the collection, the desert life of solitude and trial provides
the ideal against which O'Connor judges the heart-wounding dissensions
of American life.

Such a comprehensive use of ancient spirituality to throw modern life
into relief may seem improbable, because we tend to think of the desert
mothers and fathers as women and men of a different stamp from ourselves, persons of a remote age bred in a rarer atmosphere, searchers some-

how tougher and larger than we and therefore summoned to a greater destiny. But O'Connor brings us to another view of their—and our—calling. In doing so, she shows how deeply she plumbs the modern condition and how greatly she cares about our fate. Our age, O'Connor believes, can avail itself of the dignity and wisdom of the past. Despite the political and cultural differences between twentieth-century American democracy and the late Roman Empire, the intrinsic predicament of the desert-dwellers and their motives to struggle against the poverty and vastness of inner solitude remain as they have always been. The commands heard and answered in O'Connor's South reverberate with mandates received and obeyed in the ancient East. It turns out in *A Good Man Is Hard to Find* that O'Connor's plain country people are expected to face the same sufferings and confess God and die before God as did the primitive hermits. Those who are not heroic are the ones O'Connor chooses to share the lot of God's legendary warriors in the battle against evil. Given the faithlessness of the modern age, the demons' perpetual trickery, and the desert's sheer hardship, the odds are against the footsore and weary southerners O'Connor mobilizes into combat. Her stories do not falsify this inequality. In the deserts of this volume, triumph over evil is as hard to find as it is difficult to recognize a good man or woman in a gulch or farm off Georgia's dirt roads. If you find one, you will find the other. Survival entails, as will be shown, the habits of humility, self-scrutiny, and prayer. These virtues develop from a rigorous discipline that is difficult to practice in a world that rewards egotism, betrayal, and power.

All the protagonists of *A Good Man Is Hard to Find*, like Hazel Motes in *Wise Blood*, are unwitting solitaries; they are forced out of their social relations and into aloneness. Like Motes, these solitaries *malgré eux* set their private wills against that of God. Never one to minimize the tempting power of evil, O'Connor frequently shows her besieged solitaries succumbing to the gratification of their personal desire. *A Good Man Is Hard to Find* is as sternly realistic about spiritual struggle as are the desert *Sayings* and *Lives*, which frankly depict the fall of some ascetics who seek God. Fully five of the ten stories in O'Connor's first volume end with the heart of the protagonist vanquished by the demonic temptation to love her or his own desire above the good of another character or above the will of God. This subjection into satanic thrall marks "The Life You Save May Be Your Own," "A Stroke of Good Fortune," "A Circle in the Fire," "Good Country People," and "A Late Encounter with the Enemy." There are hints in these stories of a victory of heart offered and narrowly missed, but the decisive incident in each battle shows the demons in ascendancy.

These five stories are O'Connor's sober reminders of the long demonic shadow cast over "our fractured culture" (*MM* 140) in this "unbelieving world" (*HB* 382). Against this horizon of darkness rising, O'Connor sets five accounts with glimmers of light: "A Good Man Is Hard to Find," "The River," "A Temple of the Holy Ghost," "The Artificial Nigger," and "The Displaced Person." These stories tell of characters who fight their attachment to their own will and rise to the occasion of the desert ordeal. These protagonists respond to the call of the desert by fighting the good fight. Through a process of inner emigration, to reword the reflective journey that Seamus Heaney as "inner émigré" celebrates in his poem "Exposure" (453), O'Connor's searchers survive the era's evil without being corrupted by it. Before one can appreciate how the solitary advances the cause of good, however, it would do well initially to take up the five stories in which the cause of evil wins out. The first order of business for the desert elders and O'Connor is "to be certain that the Devil gets identified as the Devil" (*HB* 360). That is the task of this chapter.

At base, the desert presents the challenge of survival. For O'Connor, the desert is what it is for Moses and the Israelites in the Exodus: "the great and terrible wilderness, an arid waste with poisonous snakes and scorpions" (Deuteronomy 8:15) that taxes human strength to the uttermost. Simply to endure desert hardship is a victory of sorts. For the Christian desert-dwellers, the struggle also entailed fighting the moral forces that swirled around the long stretches of their inner loneliness. Patristic lore gives many accounts of this conflict. No sooner does Anthony the Great take up isolated life amid the desert's harshness than the devil bombards the young man with reminders of the comfortable family life he left behind, tempting him to give up his solitude. When this temptation fails, the devil tries to seduce the youth, who at twenty-two would be erotically susceptible to thoughts of "the softness of pleasure" (Athanasius 5 [34]). But Anthony can see through the trickery to recognize his enemy's true intention of turning him away from God. Anthony's weapon in resisting his demons is his power to see evil for what it is. As the devil traffics in deception, the solitary fights back with discernment.

For the desert ascetics, then, the power to cut through deception is an armament requiring repeated use to be serviceable. Abba Poemen explains the honing of such discretion in a typically down-to-earth analogy: "A man can spend his whole time carrying an axe without succeeding in cutting down the tree; while another, with experience of tree-felling brings the tree down with a few blows" (*Sayings*, Poemen 52 [174]). Training makes for proficiency. So too with moral skills. One must keep exercising the faculty of detecting and dispelling evil as the forester must stay at perfecting his technique to knock down the tree. Such elementary knowledge determines the spiritual quester's success in the desert. Without practice in making a clearing of truth, the solitary can get lost in a thicket of demonic shams. The virtue of cutting through deception was so important to John Cassian that he elevated discretion to the status of maternal protector: "For discernment is the mother, the guardian, and the guide of all the virtues" (*Conferences* II, 4 [64].

There is another maternal prototype who is eager to hand the searcher along the way. She is pride, the mother of all vices. Pride disables her victim by getting in the way of the solitary's ability to distinguish between the truth presented by God and the falsity promoted by the devil. "The Life You Save May Be Your Own" dramatizes how stupid presumption restrains and supplants discernment. In this cautionary tale of betrayal, pride leads the mother of Lucynell Crater into falling prey to the illusion of her own cunning, and this mother's defeat results in the added suffering of her daughter's abandonment by the trickster that the mother trusted. So fully does vain overconfidence dupe the mother that she trusts the emissary of Satan as if he were actually the bearer of light. The offshoots of the prideful demon in "The Life You Save May Be Your Own" are the blinding of oneself and treachery for another—in this case, the innocent daughter.

These forces meet in the desert, of which there are as many such places in *A Good Man Is Hard to Find* as there are characters. Mrs. Lucynell Crater's desert is a "desolate spot" (*CW* 172) out in the country that has been wasting away since her husband died fifteen years earlier. The garden house needs a roof; front and back steps are broken; the fence requires mending; a hog pen has to be built; and the old Ford has not run all those fifteen years. Mrs. Crater's body also tells the story of her desert life. The demands of the tumbledown place have burdened the old Crater woman to the degree that she has now dwindled down to "about the size of a cedar fence post" (*CW* 172). Most of her physical substance seems to have been used up in her head, where years of adversity have hardened into shrewdness, a cunning required to protect her in advance of many fears. Mrs. Crater enjoys an intrepid confidence in what she deems to be her ability to judge people. Her ingenuity meets its test one evening when a stranger named Tom T. Shiftlet appears on the horizon. As he encroaches with the darkness, the self-assured owner of the dried-up farm slides to the edge of her porch. The drifter's mere silhouette reveals all to her; and her impression is all wrong, dangerously so: "Although the old woman lived in this desolate spot with her only daughter and she had never seen Mr. Shiftlet before, she could tell, even from a distance, that he was a tramp and no one to be afraid of" (*CW* 172). The vagrant's shabby clothes and injured body—he is missing one arm—bespeak his low status and harmlessness, and such insignificance affirms her power as foxy landowner. These illusions are just what the spirit of evil seeks to create and will appeal to. He disguises himself as a "'poor disabled friendless drifting man'" (*CW* 179) so that no one need fear him. The demonic trap is set through delusion.

There is nothing like presumed superiority to invite catastrophe from the leveling forces swarming O'Connor's desert. Actually, the battle in the desolate spot of "The Life You Save May Be Your Own" is over before it begins. Vanity has lured Mrs. Crater from her porch chair to the cavern of blindness. She cannot see the enemy. But O'Connor's reader can. Tom T. Shiftlet, with his "long black slick hair" smoothed down behind his pointed ears that neatly balance his sharp features "over a jutting steel-trap jaw" (*CW* 172), has come to devour the spoils of the old woman's self-defeat. The desert teachers repeatedly warn that the enemies of the soul appear in disguised forms of the victim's own disordered passions and weaknesses. Mrs. Crater looks down on Shiftlet, who in turn disregards her in favor of the sun setting on the mountain peak of his egotism. Her caginess and old age are matched by the young man's old, ancient knowledge, expressed in "a look of composed dissatisfaction as if he understood life thoroughly" (*CW* 172). Cunning meets shiftiness, and pride prevents the victim's recognition of the semblance.

Besides pride, the demon of covetousness tempts Mrs. Crater. She clings to her ramshackle possessions as weapons of personal dignity against the impoverishing desolation around her. If pride distorts Mrs. Crater's vision of others, then greed readjusts her visual acuity to pick up what in another person she can take for her own use. What the old woman wants in the strange man is his body, however impaired, for the work she can get out of it. The drifter's toolbox seems to invite a claim on his physical industry. But his case of tools is another smoke screen, just as his offer to the woman of a piece of chewing gum is a fake rural potlatch. On arrival, Shiftlet, with a mere "pale sharp glance," swipes "everything in the yard" (*CW* 173) along with the old rusty Ford in the shed before he puts his one good hand on anything. Mrs. Crater rises to greet the man with one combat-ready fist on her hip. Wordlessly, she spars with the intruder, attempting to capture him, but her gambits are futile. Her enemy lies within, in her blinding pride and greed.

Shiftlet has the advantage of knowing desolate places and their effects on people all too well. In fact, the wizened visitant embodies the desert. Besides withering his body, the desert's thin dry air has invaded and taken over his inner being. This interior aridity (*acedia*), which corresponds to the physical dryness of desert, was well-known to the hermits. Acedia was the besetting evil that took the form of an emotional flatness, leading to a general distaste for life. An attack of acedia brought about a despondency that—as Amma Theodora, a celebrated desert mother, warns—"weighs down your soul," making one fainthearted and open to evil thoughts (*Sayings*, Theodora 3 [83]). The condition experienced by the ascetic in solitude does not readily lend itself to the language we now use to describe inner states. Modern clinical terms lack the very theological dimension, the component of sin in despairing of life, that the mothers and fathers experienced and fought when attacked by acedia. "There is no worse passion," Abba Poemen says (*Sayings*, Poemen 149 [188]). The gravity that the hermits felt in this most harmful passion suggests that, for those seeking fuller life in the desert, the inability to experience joy in their practice violated the will of God that called them to ascesis in the first place. Acedia is a sin and a state of sinfulness. Indeed, before there were seven deadly sins, there were eight for Evagrius; acedia was thus the eighth deadly sin in his *Praktikos* (6 [16–17]) before being absorbed into sloth.

O'Connor portrays Shiftlet the despiser of life as the personification of acedia. Life for this roaming predator is running down like a clock marking progressive deterioration: "'Nothing is like it used to be, lady,' he said. 'The world is almost rotten'" (*CW* 173). His project as enemy of life is to help bring the world to total decay. And there have been many opportunities in desolate places for Shiftlet to work his inimical will. As he tells it, he has performed all kinds of work all around the globe. Not one to miss the chance to share in the organized slaughter of his time, Shiftlet "fought and bled" for his country and "visited every foreign land" (*CW* 175). He certainly is a favored traveler, one with the speed and ubiquity of his wily species. One can imagine Shiftlet as trawling the centuries, snaring whatever or whomever he can on and off the beaten path. Along the way, he apparently paid a call on and was fascinated by the ascetic practice of a medieval monastery, because when he justifies to Mrs. Crater his proposal to sleep in her old Ford, he cites as precedent that "'the monks of old slept in their coffins!'" (*CW* 176). His vast experience has taught him a great deal about human nature, and he uses his knowledge to gratify his will. He has achieved a timeless cynicism for a man of twenty-eight. At Iago's age, and serving the Italian soldier's master, misbegotten Shiftlet possesses a future that Shakespeare does not allow his handsome, satanic forebear.

Like Iago, Shiftlet can coil his way into the mind of his victim to manipulate it. As an aspect of Mrs. Crater's own dark will, this opportunist does not have to hear the woman's sweet talk about her nearly thirty-year-old deaf and mute daughter, Lucynell Crater, for him to detect the old mother's scheme to get a husband for the daughter and a handyman for her place. "Mr. Shiftlet already knew what was on her mind" (*CW* 177) and works his way into Mrs. Crater's trust to strike a deal. He will marry Lucynell for the Ford, which will speedily get him back on his nomadic stalking. Their pact momentarily appeases Shiftlet's craving to take advantage of people. Cruelty amuses Shiftlet. Each small success in forcing his will on Mrs. Crater brings out an expression, always quick because it is surreptitious, of his true nature. On hearing Mrs. Crater's consent to pay for the paint to spruce up the Ford, "Mr. Shiftlet's smile stretched like a weary snake waking up by a fire" (*CW* 179). The warmth provided by the newly painted car, however, has no staying power against his cold, insatiable avarice. Pleasure sinks into Mr. Shiftlet's dejection like a drop of water in a parched desert. Such is the absorbing barrenness of acedia, the sterility of which pervades "The Life You Save May Be Your Own."

The only sign of life in this desolate spot is the innocence of young Lucynell Crater. The narrator, who apparently knows the desert and savors its unforeseen efflorescence, finds in Lucynell a hint of sprouting life amid desiccation: "Every now and then her placid expression was changed by a sly isolated little thought like a shoot of green in the desert" (*CW* 180). The youth behind the counter at the forlorn eating place, The Hot Spot, where Shiftlet abandons Lucynell, discerns something fresh in Lucynell's presence. "'She looks like an angel of Gawd'" (*CW* 181), he murmurs, gently touching her "golden hair" (*CW* 182) to confirm his recognition. Lucynell is a messenger. The counterboy notices what the holy Anthony discerns when he prays to overcome acedia. When afflicted by listlessness, Anthony asks: "How can I be saved?" The answer comes in the figure of a man like himself working and praying: "It was an angel of the Lord sent to correct and reassure him. He heard the angel saying to him, 'Do this and you will be saved'" (*Sayings*, Anthony the Great 1 [2]). Anthony's angel works and prays his way out of dejection. O'Connor's herald cannot say, Do this. Instead, she delivers her message in silence: Be this and you will be saved. In a conniving universe where schemers babble, Lucynell's silence is noble and expresses her directive of simplicity and humility. Lucynell shows the way out of moroseness and greed.

But Shiftlet can no more discern the truth in Lucynell's silence than Mrs. Crater can see Shiftlet for the monster he is. As the story concludes, the demon who defeats both his opponents turns out to batter himself deeper into despondency. One way or another, Lucynell will return to the safety of her native desolate spot, and Mrs. Crater will manage without the car that did not work anyway and her $17.50. But Tom T. Shiftlet experiences the pain of his own tricks. He suffers from the delusions of his self-will. An anonymous ancient solitary reminds us how the desert can easily assail those who, as Shiftlet does, presume to know life thoroughly and consequently miss the reality before them. "Many have injured their bodies without discernment and have gone away from us having achieved nothing," says the elder, because they have not learned "that which God seeks: charity and humility" (qtd. in Burton-Christie 237). Without humility, Shiftlet has recourse only to himself, and more and more of himself means that he deals less and less with reality and not at all with God.

O'Connor's study of the demonic goes still further to warn us of its destructiveness. She shows the inner workings of deception, pride, and acedia by putting them on a level congenial to Shiftlet's material desire— his car. The Ford he covets is a booby prize. It offers no delight in life but is an alien joy, another fix that does not work. At the wheel of the machine, Shiftlet momentarily forgets "his morning bitterness," and then, only a hundred miles into his escape, the fixer "became depressed in spite of the car" (*CW* 181). It is not the betrayal of Lucynell that drags him down; guilt requires a moral sensitivity that Shiftlet lacks. After he gets rid of her, he is "more depressed than ever as he drove on by himself" (*CW* 182). Again, the hitchhiker that Shiftlet picks up to ease his gloom darkens it more by cursing Shiftlet's sentimental lies and jumping out of the car. Always adept at parrying the shock of truth and rationalizing his latest deceit, Shiftlet blames the universe for his inner darkness. Alone with the self he serves, "Mr. Shiftlet felt that the rottenness of the world was about to engulf him" (*CW* 183). His last words are fittingly hypocritical: "'Oh Lord!' he prayed. 'Break forth and wash the slime from this earth!'" (*CW* 183). The demon's prayer is hatred disguised as faith, the condescension of the proud man who loves his own illusion and self-sufficiency. Shiftlet's self-deception points up the desert insight of "The Life You Save May Be Your Own": a lapse of discernment can lead to a despondent sinfulness. As he barrels down the highway to Mobile, Shiftlet's pride keeps him impervious to the renewing waters crashing down on the Ford. The seemingly unbeatable opponent suffers a defeat he cannot comprehend. Deception has immured him in lies. In the end, the world becomes invisible to Shiftlet. Inside the car, a storm of deceit and self-sorrow compounds the outer downpour blanketing the windshield.

The defamer of life cannot see where he is going, for he has been thunderstruck and is crying out as if trapped in his own anxiety.

No roving enemy suddenly appears to attack Ruby Hill in "A Stroke of Good Fortune." Rather, the enemy has been lurking within Ruby for some time. Although married and living in a city, Ruby is alone and lonely. The wilderness in which she finds herself is her body. Whereas the young Lucynell Crater's inert body and blank mind are a desert out of which innocent green thoughts sprout, Ruby Hill's body is a fertile confusion that bursts forth with anxieties and thoughts of death. Ruby is conspicuously pregnant and denies the undeniable. For all her eagerness to join the mainstream of suburban life, Ruby in her fearful solitude stands to profit from the experience of ancient solitaries with whom she would feel no link. The radical dissociation of her mind from her body creates in Ruby the need for the remedial lesson of the desert that body and spirit are one. Desert ascesis assumes that body can instruct the soul, and that is what happens to Ruby. Ruby's disordered emotions—her demons—taunt her until their calumnies force her to accept her pregnant body.

Ruby's desire to forsake her body does not arise in a vacuum. The urge to discard her body reflects Ruby's family history as reinforced by cultural pressures. Ruby's mother was pregnant eight times, and with each child she "got deader" until she looked "like a puckered-up old yellow apple" (*CW* 186). Her mother's screams in giving birth to her last child, Rufus, still pierce Ruby's consciousness. Pregnancy and childbirth terrify Ruby, who feels that ignorance trapped her mother and two sisters, each of whom already has had four children in four years. Pregnancy to Ruby means being subject to physical assaults that rob her of her femaleness, youth, and freedom. Pregnancy is pain, and Ruby wants to avoid pain by controlling her body. Young looking for thirty-four (though she does touch up gray hair), Ruby wants to stay that way. And she has her eye on a duplex bungalow out in Meadowcrest Heights, where she and her husband Bill Hill can enjoy all the good things promised to the perpetually young in American suburbia. A baby would interfere with her plans. Ruby's body, swollen with unwanted, unacknowledged, and unbearably different life, sums up past terrors that she projects onto her future.

The story takes up Ruby's passage through her desert of disordered feelings as she ascends the dark stairway up four flights—128 steps agonizingly counted—to her city apartment. The steps map a tributary of the highway of delusion and despondency that Tom T. Shiftlet follows. Whether frenetic (as is Shiftlet's getaway) or lumbering (as is Ruby's climb), their shared course of acedia leads inescapably to the infirmity of body and soul that the great mother Theodora advises other desert-dwellers to resist.

Acedia, Amma Theodora warns, "also attacks your body through sickness, debility, weakening of the knees, and all the members. It dissipates the strength of the soul and body, so that one believes one is ill and no longer able to pray" (*Sayings*, Theodora 3 [83]). The equivalent of prayer for Ruby is her hope for the good life, which pregnancy threatens to rob from her. Acedia blackens her spirit as the steps get "darker and steeper" (*CW* 190). The stairwell takes on the atmosphere of a solitary's cell besieged by demonic phantasms "transformed into all shapes" (Athanasius 25 [50]). Each flight of darkening stairs mocks Ruby's attempted flight from her body by confronting her with the emotions she is denying. First it is the toy pistol of six-year-old Hartley Gilfleet that torments Ruby with thoughts of maternal stupidity. Then the spooky second-floor tenant Mr. Jerger, seventy-two, a goatish creature with "little raisin eyes and a string beard" (*CW* 188), grates and startles Ruby with the odor of decay that she associates with pregnancy; his presence emits the lecherous stench one gets from under a buzzard's wing that maddens her with the shriveling, degenerative effects of aging that she fears. Finally, Laverne Watts, "an especial friend" (*CW* 190) as experienced through Ruby's acedia, torments Ruby with the coup de grâce of truth: "'MOTHER! MOTHER!'" (*CW* 193).

Try as Ruby does to "stop this gory thinking" (*CW* 188) about being pregnant and therefore turning into a monster, she cannot by sheer volition remake her body by denying her pregnancy. Every attempt to satisfy her personal will runs up against reality and dejects her even more. Ruby slams Laverne's door, looks down on her swollen body, takes a few steps, and crumbles into a feeble cry: "'Noooo'" (*CW* 195). Delusion, the demon's stock in trade, seals Ruby's eyes: "She gasped and shut her eyes" (*CW* 195). Amma Theodora's warning about acedia accounts for what happens to Ruby as her "'Noooo'" seeps inward to hobble her defenses even more against her demons. With self-blinding desperation, she moans: "'It couldn't be any baby'" (*CW* 195). When Ruby does open her eyes, after little Hartley gallops up the stairs shooting two toy pistols, she gazes "down into the dark hole"; and in the final pant of an illusion destroyed, Ruby's "hollow voice" utters "'Baby'" (*CW* 196). The blow to Ruby's delusion is the most fortunate stroke of all; but her private will, still in the grip of acedia, pitches her into darker denial as she tries to separate her body from the rolling sensation and to think of the fetus as "if it were not in her stomach" (*CW* 196).

Ruby's struggle comes to the reader with cartoonish exaggeration. The mode may suit the ridiculous lengths to which Ruby goes in denying her pregnancy; but slapstick does not satisfy O'Connor, who found

"A Stroke of Good Fortune" too farcical to sustain the serious moral implications of Ruby's "rejection of life at its source" (*HB* 85). In falling short of O'Connor's high artistic standard, the story nevertheless instructs us about the permanent spiritual interests in her evolving art. Even when not up to technical speed, O'Connor cannot help but present her protagonist as the solitary at war with her demons. This is her essential drama. Nor can O'Connor at lower pitches of creativity avoid making the human body the battleground on which the war for independence and dignity is conducted. Ruby Hill does not rise to the occasion of O'Connor's own accepting self-humor in seeing herself early on in her physical condition as "a large stiff anthropoid ape" hobbling around with Aristotle and Saint Thomas on her mind (*HB* 104), but Ruby's deadly denial over dragging her body up the stairs draws from the unaffected humor typical of desert stories that invite laughter over the preposterousness of the private will trying to push nature and God around. Such an attempt for the elders and O'Connor is the folly of Lucifer.

Folly is part of desert solitude. How could foolishness not show its droll aspects in a world of demons and mirages? Folly accompanies aloneness as vanity goes with a mirror. The inner danger takes the form of egoism and madness, which hover over the desert dweller, ready to seize the person who loses touch with actuality. Demons are native to the sandy stretches of the human mind and are cast loose to snare the solitaries in their illusion. Although the devils are invariably subject to O'Connor's humor because she trusts the power of God to hand them their final defeat, her stories stress demonic craftiness because she knows how easily humans are taken. And so diabolic spoils litter every story in *A Good Man Is Hard to Find* and appear in full comic display in the festive aftermaths of "A Circle in the Fire" and "Good Country People."

"A Circle in the Fire" and "Good Country People" recount the arrival on a secluded farm of a stranger or group of strangers. Though intrusive, the unexpected visitors seem manageable to the owners of the places they visit. The owners' attitudes are based on property rights, and such pride is the illusion that undoes them. The proprietors are females who are keenly aware of their prerogatives. The strangers, all male, are intelligent and uninhibited—both socially and sexually. They feign a certain compliance to goad the owners' female sense of power. The women take the bait and end up as vicious sport for the intruders. Several cultural deceptions dispose the women to defeat. These southern females believe that feminine verbal decorum will overcome brute male physical assault. With this social deceit comes its sexual counterpart, which holds that female eroticism can be refined into mental superiority over unscrupulous male sexual aggression. Male cunning, however, evaporates female intelligence and sexuality into paralytic rage and shame.

The evil forces in "A Circle in the Fire" and "Good Country People" derive their power from their female victims' prideful attachment. The women cling to their property in the belief that it can confer security. The protagonist in "A Circle in the Fire" defines her worth by her land; the heroine of "Good Country People" gains her status through her mind. Besides blocking self-awareness, such attachments for O'Connor are especially dangerous because they get in the way of knowing God and, if maintained, can take the place of God. That idolatrous substitution of land or mind for God is the ultimate risk for the protagonists in these two stories. Abba Isidore of Pelusia puts us on guard against the socially approved instinct to raise our esteem by accumulating material or intellectual property. The urge can consume and inevitably plays into the devil's hand: "The desire for possessions is dangerous and terrible, knowing no satiety; it drives the soul which it controls to the heights of evil. . . . For once it has become master it cannot be overcome" (*Sayings*, Isidore of Pelusia 6 [99]). The patristic warning is direful but no more bleak than are the eventualities in "A Circle in the Fire" and "Good Country People."

"A Circle in the Fire" tells of Mrs. Cope's obsession with her farm. She slavishly worships it as a deity, the source of her identity and permanence. The land, however, resists the trust she deposits into it and, more ominously, presages the ruin that Abba Isidore of Pelusia predicts will come from such attachment. The earth obeys only the laws of creation. At this moment, the land is bone-dry to the point of being a serious risk for fire. Mrs. Cope believes it to be her paradise; but it is her desert, parched, resistant, and a toil. The first glimpse we have of Mrs. Cope shows her on her knees bent in service to her dirt god. She is squatting on the ground, fighting the noxious plants that threaten to destroy the order of her sacred acres: "She worked at the weeds and nut grass as if they were an evil sent directly by the devil to destroy the place" (*CW* 232). Mrs. Cope is at war against the wrong enemy. Herbage is not a demonic vendetta. The enemy is her self-will that interprets the innocence of nature and people as defiance of her will. When Mrs. Cope looks up from her compulsive devotion, she spies another menace, which appears in the form of Culver, the black worker, who is driving the tractor the long way through the gate that opens into the field: "Her Negroes were as destructive and impersonal as the nut grass" (*CW* 233). Still on her knees, always prostrate before the land, and waving her trowel-scepter of authority, Mrs. Cope wastes more time, energy, and good will than Culver uses gas by reprimanding him. But Mrs. Cope must get her way. In the far-off Georgia desert where money rules, employees must obey. The exchange typifies the illusion of superior status that the demon of possessiveness gives Mrs. Cope as recompense for the bondage in which her demon holds her.

If economic control over others masks Mrs. Cope's inner subservience, then the desert's overmastering power can be her blessing, for the counterweight to attachment is renunciation. Since Mrs. Cope is unlikely to loosen her own grip on people and things, she must have her claims forcibly ripped from her tight fist. That happens in her next battle. The enemy is a troop of three boys from Atlanta: Garfield Smith, W. T. Harper, and Powell, the single-name commander. Though young, they are a match for Mrs. Cope, because they embody her self-will in more aggressive form. They want to spend time in the country riding horses and riding their will before school begins. Driven by their hell-bent will, they invade Mrs. Cope's fortress. The boys march up with white, penetrating stares. Their eyes have the steel-pointedness shared by O'Connor's demons that pierces into their victims' secret places, hidden to the victims but known to their demons. On arriving, Powell's eyes make Mrs. Cope feel pinched by "a pair of tongs" (CW 236). The boys descend to the occasion of her controlling politeness that deliberately misconstrues their unwelcome raid as a "'real sweet'" (CW 236) visit. Feigned cordiality cannot mask her fear of strangers, of fire in the dry woods, and for the vulnerability of her twelve-year-old daughter, Sally Virginia. Most of all, Mrs. Cope is afraid to see the boys for the danger they are. The deeper her fear, the greater the power of the invaders. A mere stare from Powell fixes Mrs. Cope in silent intimidation. The more she relies on prim manners, the more she empowers the willful boys. Because Mrs. Cope's decorum is false and manipulative, the strangers need only to be their ruthless selves to demolish her. The lady is a coward, and the boys know it. Later, Garfield Smith, the big boy, surely threatens Mrs. Cope's propriety by taking off his shirt to display his sweaty chest and the cut on his arm that came from riding horses in the woods.

Sally Virginia has more sense than her mother. Common sense is clear sight and courage. The girl would physically attack the brazen thugs and chase them from the place. Her mother, of course, will not countenance such unladylike conduct. Instead of acknowledging her fear and getting help to fight the hoods, Mrs. Cope abets her enemies with pleas. It is only a matter of time before Mrs. Cope is reduced to assert her false kindness in a way that belies her airs of ownership. "'Haven't I been nice to you boys?'" (*CW* 246), she begs, trying to stop them from vandalizing her mailbox. She is nice to the devils; but politeness actually feeds her pride, which her enemies recognize as covering anger. Mrs. Cope's declaration of ownership, the last assertion of the vain mind, drives the young devils beyond the distant woods for a farewell rendezvous with spiteful malice. Sally Virginia witnesses their caper when she crashes through the woods. In mock assault with toy pistols, she champions herself as a fighter in the war against the rampant evil. The spectacle she witnesses is a demonic sabbath. First the girl sees the boys completely naked, washing themselves in the cow trough. Orgiastic abandon rules. They feel that the place is an unclaimed wilderness that is theirs for the taking, and they take it. "'It's ours'" (*CW* 249), asserts W. T. Harper, the smallest and most aroused of the three, giving unrestrained expression to Mrs. Cope's own avarice. Jubilantly, Powell leads a race of naked bodies, dashing twice around the field and staking out their spoils. Their white, glaring eyes communicate the next move, and Powell leads the dancing warriors in setting the place on fire. The insatiable desire to possess, as Abba Isidore of Pelusia warns, "drives the soul which it controls to the heights of evil" (*Sayings*, Isidore of Pelusia 6 [99]). That gluttonous greed consumes the bacchants, the place, and the owner. The last sentence of the story lifts their unbridled war cries, through Sally Virginia's distant perception, into "wild high shrieks of joy as if the prophets were dancing in the fiery furnace, in the circle the angel had cleared for them" (*CW* 251).

The merrymaking that concludes the story is unnerving. The boys' fiery guffaws burn down illusions along with dry woods. Unrepentant and with brilliant ferocity, the boys gloat over the destruction and pain they cause. Their demons win out. Their lurid laughter exposes the folly of Mrs. Cope, who believes that she, unaided and without fighting back, can cope with evil. The woman's investment of herself in the land goes to the heart of desert instruction about attachment. The hermits saw possessiveness and evil as challenges to inner growth. One story illustrates the extremes to which the solitaries went in responding to both threats. When Abba Anastasius learned that a brother stole a parchment containing the Old and New Testaments, Anastasius not only refrained from asking the brother about the book for fear of making the brother lie; Anastasius also would not accept the parchment back when the thief returned it (Merton, *Wisdom* 17 [30–31]). What is given cannot be stolen. Anastasius spared the thief further guilt and freed himself from concern over losing a sacred object. The elder dealt with loss through charity. Interior growth depends on discerning the possibility for charity, which leads to change and freedom. This desert lesson permeates O'Connor's writing. Her letter to "A" of 11 August 1956 offers one of her many reflections on the need to be transformed by losses. This especially memorable saying from the hermit novelist arises in a rare, deeply moving comment on her father's need for people: "We are all rather blessed in our deprivations if we let ourselves be, I suppose" (*HB* 169). Such letting go of the heart is a lot to ask of Mrs. Cope, but then O'Connor's desert teaching does not speak to timidity, although it is for everyone.

If Mrs. Cope would let herself be gladdened by her losses at the end of "A Circle in the Fire," she would experience a relief from the anxiety over weeds, nut grass, and ownership that almost crushes her with the monotony of their threat. She prays on windy nights that "'there won't be any fires'" (*CW* 233), but she cannot keep these forces at bay—and never really has to. Her orisons and frenetic activity are mere holding actions against unplaced terror. The fire is a warning of the all-consuming effect of any attachment to property and status. Mrs. Cope's dry place has been trying to instill in her an awareness of her vulnerability and solitude in the desert. From the beginning of the story, a glaring white sky tries to break through "a solid gray blue wall" (*CW* 232), marking the tree line of her property that doubles for the border of her identity. Later, the evening sun "seemed to be trying to set everything in sight on fire" (*CW* 241), not just to ignite the beauty of the place but also to conspire with the afternoon sky to cut through Mrs. Cope's blindness and kindle in her an awareness of her demons. It takes the fiendish boys to stoke the fire that can break through the wall of her ignorance. Finally, we do not know if it does. The conclusion leaves us knowing only that it can and that Mrs. Cope can gain from letting her attachment and faith in herself go up in the flames. The fire threatens the security she has built, and the circle cleared in the fire by the divine messenger reveals the freedom that follows detachment. The misery on Mrs. Cope's face at the end of the story expresses both the great effort of surrender that she must make to endure the blessing and the care that she will be freed of if she does let go with her heart and submit to the ascesis blazing in the fire before her eyes.

As painful as it is to separate oneself from the security conferred by physical property, it is still more agonizing to become indifferent to the distinction bestowed by intellectual property. The human mind, it seems, will give up anything before yielding its cherished idea of itself. "Good Country People" looks deeper into this most fortified zone of human attachment by putting a microscope to the inner workings of the will that are hidden from the heroine herself. Hulga (formerly Joy) Hopewell, the heroine of "Good Country People," has decided that her mind is the only possible dwelling place for her. She chose as a child to retreat into her head. At ten, a gunshot during a hunting accident resulted in the loss of one of her legs. Along with the limb, the bullet took the girl's sense of female wholeness. To feel a completeness that she believed would be unavailable in her body, Hulga spent the next twenty-two years forsaking her body in favor of developing her mind. She uses her mind to get back her body and turns ideas into attacks on her physical being for its imagined betrayal. Thus, the name Hulga replaces Joy.

Hulga's animosity toward her body brings her to develop a perverse asceticism. She uses her body not to transcend and open herself up to the world but to barricade herself against the deprivations that her shame and culture project onto her physical loss. Her "bloated" (*CW* 268), deliberately clumsy bulk serves as an instrument of her defiant will. She trusts in her will to gain dignity in a humiliating society, truth in an ignorant world, and footing amid treacherous sands of alienation. Hulga's will guides her all the way through the educational system to get a Ph.D. in philosophy. Now thirty-two and approaching an early death because of a weak heart, Hulga has been forced to return to the family farm, where she lives under a proper and solicitous, if controlling, mother. Cut off from kindred intellectual spirits, Doctor Hopewell is displaced against her will. Life for her in "these red hills" among "good country people" (*CW* 268) is a withering death in the wasteland. Hulga Hopewell is an outcast living in a desert; and she is at war, not against her besetting demons but against her body and life. Anger is the trajectory of her desert life. Wrath seals her alienation and sustains the momentum of her willful battle against her circumstances. She makes it insultingly clear that were it not for her heart, she would be faraway from the farm and in the groves of academe, lecturing to people who could understand her. Dislocation generates a "constant outrage" (*CW* 264). With her mother, whose indefatigable sunniness grates Hulga's sullenness, Hulga presents a "glum" face spouting "ugly" (*CW* 265) remarks. Her spleen explodes when the magpie Mrs. Freeman, the wife of Mrs. Hopewell's worker, uses the name Hulga instead of Joy. On such an occasion, Hulga "would scowl and redden" (*CW* 266) because the privacy of Hulga's willful rebuke through the name *Hulga* against the world is thrown back on her as a public mock. Hulga's twenty-two years of intellectual effort nurture resentment and result in a temperamental lopsidedness that is far more pronounced than the hobble made by her artificial leg.

Graduate school may have put the finishing touches on Hulga's refashioning of her intellectual self, but course work, examinations, and a dissertation do not fully account for the steady inner darkening of her spirit. Nor does pride, of which Hulga has a full measure, alone explain the puffed up contempt with which she treats her body and meets every situation. As all relationships derive from a relationship with oneself, so Hulga's disdain originates and comes back to self-hatred. Loathing begins with the revulsion of her body after the gunshot. Although medical science repaired Hulga's leg, Mrs. Hopewell's sense of shame over what she believes is the loss of her daughter's femininity never allows the injury to heal fully. The trauma moves inward into the girl's psyche, building into a grudge that hardens into cold rage. Rage is a seductive demon that gives Hulga a fleeting, illusory comfort. Isolation intensifies the destructive power of her indignation and brings about an affective mutilation that corresponds to the cutting off of her leg in the accident. The demon of rage entices the crippled Hulga into feeling protected from further hurt by allowing her to spurn the offending world in advance, but this defense demands that Hulga serve her demon with idolatrous devotion. In obeying her demon, she makes wrath the source of her being. The nihilism that she picks up at university enhances her veneration of anger by putting her scholarly work and the world on a level of disgust congenial to her galled disposition. In sum, Hulga's wrathful demon is the true antagonist in "Good Country People." Hatred is a self-wounding passion that brings her renewed suffering and eventually leaves her body as carrion for the devouring egoism of her adversary, who will appear as her suitor.

Loneliness is thwarting enough to well-being; but Hulga's anger, tempered in bitterness, severs her from the new growth that is available if solitude is honestly faced out. Hulga, however, chooses to exacerbate the exile forced on her. Taking walks around the farm confirms her dislike of dogs, cats, birds, and flowers. The sky, trees, and lakes no more register their vitality on Hulga than the light of day can break through Mrs. Cope's maddening obsession with weeds and dirt. With determination smacking of self-punishment, Hulga retreats into the cell of her mind where, warmed by anger, she can feel self-contained and secure, breathing the unventilated, toxemic air of nihilism, which maims her mind as the gunshot injured her leg. In the imagined freedom of her mental hermitage, above the frightful incompleteness and captivity of her body, Hulga becomes the complete twentieth-century person. She is the sage par excellence who sees "'*through* to nothing'" (*CW* 280), as she brags to her seducer, Manley Pointer, up in the hayloft. No belief, no creature, and certainly no creator command the respect of so wise a person. The usefulness of experience in her economy lies in its capacity to destroy illusion. The more one knows, the less there is to value. Practice makes perfect; "'I don't have illusions'" (*CW* 280), states Hulga dogmatically, laying claim to the grandest illusion of them all. Her rejection of trust in morality or design in the world gives Doctor Hopewell a sense of belonging to the evolved, intellectual world that is elsewhere. This locale of the mind's negation exists far beyond her mother's incarcerating red hills. It lies in the deep desert of our age, where the wrathful demon rules. More than a psychological release, wrath has been institutionalized and no longer seen as evil but exalted as the righteous power, driving what Hannah Arendt calls "a doomsday machine" (74). Although not a direct agent of military violence, Hulga's passion implicates her in the age's wrath. In making ire the ground of her intellectual integrity, she shares in the belief that anger is a sign of strength and a vehicle of truth. Frightening when multiplied en masse, as it has been this century, anger in Hulga is also funny and delights the reader in the teeth of larger meanings. And it is those wider consequences (gas chambers and racism, for example) that O'Connor repeatedly invokes to make us understand, as Hulga does not, that anger is chilling and destructive.

For a healing view of anger, Hulga might look back further than her admired Malebranche to the women and men of the fourth-century desert, who thrived in the solitude that incenses Hulga and who fought the demon that she cultivates. In the ancient desert, where love of God and neighbor is the task of the day and the work of the soul, anger posed a great danger to the search for holiness. The human was human; and in the solitaries' encounters with themselves, their expectations, the abrasions with other solitaries during their weekly assemblies, and the intrusions by visitors, old grudges and new hostilities inevitably flared up. To the hermits, however, resentments indicated failure to love, weaknesses to be overcome, and threats to the peace they sought. Above all, the elders were realistic. They knew that anger comes with one's humanness and that only unrelenting determination can control and eventually overcome its power: "I have spent fourteen years in Scetis asking God night and day to grant me the victory over anger," says Abba Ammonas (*Sayings*, Ammonas 3 [26]). Subduing anger was more important than working miracles: "A man who is angry, even if he were to raise the dead, is not acceptable to God" (*Sayings*, Agathon 19 [23]). The hermits consecrated themselves to God by struggling against anger. Abba Pityrion explained the total ascetic understanding of evil and its conquest through anger: "If anyone wants to drive out the demons, he must first subdue the passions; for he will banish the demon of the passion which he has mastered. For example, the devil accompanies anger; so if you control your anger, the devil of anger will be banished" (*Sayings*, Pityrion 1 [200]). Conversely, by giving in to anger, one invites the devil by doing evil's bidding.

The isolated Hopewell farm, where anger answers the unavoidable hurts of daily life, seems to draw danger to the place. Enter Manley Pointer, the itinerant Bible salesman of nineteen with an erotic attachment to detachable female prosthetic parts. Pointer finds a welcome in the peevish Hopewell women. Although Mrs. Hopewell has no interest in the Bible and finds the salesman tiresome, she pridefully refuses to be rude and send him away so that she and Hulga can have dinner. When Pointer explains that he has a heart condition, Mrs. Hopewell's weepy association with Hulga's coronary problem brings her to invite him to dinner. Her hospitality, however, is not friendly. Being gracious with Pointer is her way of attacking Hulga, who "looked at nice young men as if she could smell their stupidity" (*CW* 268). The unexpected arrival of a tall, sycophantic male allows Mrs. Hopewell to confront her daughter's misandry by showing the girl a thing or two about agreeable conduct with a gentleman caller. Once these women begin to play out their animosities by sporting with this wily opponent, the fun inevitably turns ruinous. Mrs. Hopewell's anger with Hulga gets Pointer a seat at the dinner table, and Hulga's hatred of men brings him back the next morning for a frolic in the hayloft. Mother and daughter use Pointer, who is pleased to be used because he makes a specialty of exploiting female delusions of superiority. The rules of the game favor him. Hulga, the vampish philosopher, holds Pointer so low that he is barely worth seducing; but he is male, and he is on hand. Moreover, Doctor Hopewell, deprived of a university classroom, at long last has a student on whom she can work her pedagogical will in the form of sexual instruction. The sexual sport is all worked out in her mind. Whatever remorse the simpleton will feel because of his Christian mores after being lured into sin, as he will naively call their tutorial, the enlightened woman will convert the credulous student into an understanding of the world's nullity.

Hulga's nose for male stupidity answers her libido's need to gratify itself on male oafishness. Given her taste in men, most readers understandably come away from "Good Country People" with the judgment of Hulga as a dumb blonde with a Ph.D. whose dreamy sexuality ends up pathetic before Pointer's refined fetishism. Most readers also chuckle over the picture of Hulga's abstract nihilism being demolished by Pointer's living belief in nothing. In their erotic bent, however, Hulga and Manley are made for each other, just as Mrs. Hopewell with her matchmaking revenge had hoped, although her eyebrows would rise if she saw how right she was. Hulga's erotic desire is as demonic as Pointer's. For both, the sexual game is about contempt and mutilation. Philosopher and Bible salesman both take a human part for the whole person. She dismantles him down to a mental object that she can manipulate; he takes apart her wooden leg to fondle and steal as a trophy for future titillation. The intellectual removes the body; the rake dispenses with the spirit. They are two sides of the Manichean sensibility manifested in sexual arousal. Anger links both extremes. Misandry generates Hulga's plan to bring them together; and misogyny is the patent source of Pointer's bringing the meeting to completion by acting out his desire to dismantle the female body.

Abba Pityrion's warning that anger draws evil to itself proves to be gravely and hilariously true about reclusive life in Georgia's red hills. Wherever anger thrives, the devil easily conquers. In this lovers' war for human parts in the barn, the victory goes to Manley Pointer. He gets the wooden leg and the pleasure of piercing the illusions of the woman who has no illusions. In exposing the virtual nihilist to actual nihilism, the diabolical lover shows Hulga what life in the desert is all about. The demon, a sharp prober of souls, strips Hulga of her eyeglasses, artificial leg, and dignity. The loss of these imitative devices and of her spurious esteem opens Hulga's spirit to genuinely deep emotions. If her autonomy is an illusion, her suffering is real. At the end, Hulga's face is "almost purple" (*CW* 283) with an enraged helplessness that surely endangers her weak heart. Exiled on a farm, the lonesome scholar feels the added pain of abandonment. Hulga's pride and anger—the weapons she draws from the culture's ordnance—prove to be feeble defenses against her adversary's attack. Compared with the loss of her leg for the second time, the grand themes on which Hulga's formal education usually touches are trivial. Her last four words are a desperate screech: "'Give me my leg!'" (*CW* 283). That futile imperative best expresses the impotence of Hulga's personal will. When Pointer locks up the leg in his valise, taunts her, and gleefully disappears, the articulate doctor, who is usually not lost for words, is reduced to tearful silence. The heroine is the butt of her own joke. Hulga mocks the world, but the devil mocks her misguided philosophy, a system of truths that fails to instruct the philosopher. Her defeat dramatizes some of the perils of solitude. The solitude in which Hulga has lived produces a spiritual mutilation that is much more deforming than the severing of her leg. Given her inner distortion, it follows that her spiritual amputation results in a rise in anxiety, since it encourages in her an artificial attitude toward life.

"Good Country People" does not end with Hulga's offended dignity. Her drubbing is certainly humiliating; and yet Manley Pointer accomplishes in Hulga a cruel ascesis that she does not elect for herself but can profit from. O'Connor brings her heroine to this inner poverty in a deserted spot to suggest that anger and pride contain the basis of their own negation. The lesson to be learned is that demons are not to be played with but cast out. Pointer is the spiritual amputee that Hulga will become if she persists in her negative pride. Hulga can at least cry; and her tears open the way of change, for she is left on the verge of self-scrutiny. There is in the action only a pointing toward a possible new direction. The ending stops short of showing Hulga's conversion because O'Connor aims—through Hulga's defeat—to warn of the demonic power generated by a lapse in discernment. To show the universal importance of that teaching, O'Connor carefully sets the final scene at some distance from the heroine's venerable ideas and rhetoric. The two short final paragraphs shift quickly to Mrs. Hopewell and Mrs. Freeman digging onions as they watch "'that nice dull young man'" cross the meadow toward the highway. The spiteful humor that settled on Hulga's belated recognition of evil broadens into a wary chuckle over the patronizing dismissal of the "'simple'" (*CW* 283) Bible salesman by the knowing, superior farm women. Manley Pointer has left two other female victims in the wake of his invasion, and they do not have the benefit of knowing that they have been taken. They continue to sport with their illusory demons.

The loss of vigilance, self-knowledge, and discernment also brings about spiritual disaster in "A Late Encounter with the Enemy." The fierce August sun that can burn Georgia dry is the agent for the wrathful demon's victory over George Poker Sash, who has led a long, embittered life. Sash's automatic response to persons, places, and situations is "'God damm it.'" It is the codger's mantra. There is no curbing his anger because it has persisted long enough to harden into indignation about life. He feels injured constantly. When his granddaughter Sally Poker Sash dresses Sash in his coveted Confederate uniform for her August graduation ceremony, the old man mutters: "'God damm every goddam thing to hell'" (*CW* 258). As resentment and malediction consume him, so the throbs of curses carry him to death. His story is not a moving one in that his transgressions are largely on his own inner life, from which there emerges little self-awareness. Nevertheless, his fate sends out a caution about solitude lived without self-scrutiny. Isolation and warfare, when rooted in anger, lead to debility and hallucination.

Sash's identity is invented by Hollywood for a premiere in Atlanta of a movie about the old South. Probably only a foot soldier during the Civil War, he gets a new rank and name, General Tennessee Flintrock Sash of the Confederate States of America, to go with the movie's romantic fraudulence. Sash and his granddaughter accept the masquerade as fitting their confected notions of themselves, and they delight in being trotted out in public ceremonies to display antebellum glory before chauvinistic audiences. The story uncovers the inner harm caused by the modern cult of personality and captures the sadness behind quaint costuming that has been taken as absolute fact. In living by pretense, the dotard loses dignity, behaves dishonestly, and ends up a spiritual coward. Sash is that rare old man in O'Connor's fiction who does not command her reverence. He is the antimodel of the wise old *geron* that O'Connor will come on later in her desert exploration.

Like all abstractions, Sash's storybook notion of himself is unchanging and therefore not subject to the death that alters all human identity. This would-be general feels himself to be high enough in rank to exercise command over mortality: "Living had got to be such a habit with him that he couldn't conceive of any other condition" (*CW* 252). What began as a silly promotional stunt grew by virtue of Sash's narcissism into megalomania. The illusion of glory may seem innocent, even charming, but O'Connor shows Sash's self-involvement to be grievous in its folly. The old man is a prisoner of his own fake selfhood. To be trapped in oneself is to be in hell and cut off from any need of transcendence. Sash's will, a most fierce demon, sustains his world. People exist for him insofar as they define his centrality. Sash has no use for history "because he never expected to meet it again" (*CW* 253). Instead of a birthday, he has a celebration when the Capital City Museum exhibits him along with memorabilia in a musty room that lends his wizened body a crumbling authenticity. Memory and history shape conscience; lacking both, Sash is an ego in a general's costume.

As a crucible for grandiosity, there is nothing like the desert. Its forces can break through ossified defenses against dread and mortality so that the desert-dweller either is strengthened by humble acceptance or is driven deeper into deranged fantasies to ward off the desert's unsparing truths. Sash's desert is his head, which is as untenanted as any sandy stretch that Hazel Motes was stuck in during the war. Instead of confronting the emptiness, Sash creates a mental Disneyland of the way things used to be (and never were) in the South. Hostile and ornery, he resents all company, including his own. The dictates of his personal will sprawl his mental waste to the exclusion of anyone else. The last stand of this toy general on the graduation stage is taken in the desperation of solitude. The trials of longevity in solitude were known to the ancient hermits. The subject goes back to the Greek encomium celebrating the ideal and wisdom of age and was the basis for Athanasius's fourth-century *Life of Anthony*, which remains the ancient model of hagiography. The battles lost and won in old age engage O'Connor's imagination; and as an exercise in farcical contrast, we might compare the profile of Sash to the classical model of the *sophos,* the wise man among the elders. Sash lives to be 104, just one year shy of Abba Anthony's 105 years. Longevity in the desert is not the only similarity that the tin general bears to the legendary warrior hermit. Both men bring their entire history to their death; how they die reveals how they lived. The final condition of their bodies expresses the outcome of the battle against their inner demons, which keep up their onslaught to the bitter end. Anthony fought his demons even on his deathbed, where he lay with a "bright" face, cheerful to be "going the way of the fathers." He met death without any illusion that the enemy would retreat to make his struggle easier in the final hours. Instead, with a commanding voice, the clear-seeing father warned his disciples that "the treacherous demons" remain "savage" even when "weakened in strength" by the solitary's lifelong struggle (Athanasius 91–92 [96–98]). Anthony shared none of King Lear's fond wish to "unburthen'd crawl toward death" (Shakespeare, *King Lear,* I.i.41). It was warfare to the end for the holy man, and his body gave proof of his wisdom, as Lear's protracted suffering exposed the folly of his trying to live out his final days free of strife and responsibility.

Athanasius makes a special point of adding that, after 105 years of ascetic combat, Anthony's body "remained free of injury." His sight stayed "undimmed and sound"; he died with a complete set of teeth. Warfare and fasting nourished, not depleted, Anthony's physique: "He also retained health in his feet and hands" (Athanasius 91–93 [96–98]). The image of the saint's body is noteworthy. Whatever the theological implications, Anthony's physical wholeness is an outcome of his spiritual state. In any era, such physical sturdiness at 105 is astonishing; but in the ancient world, whose population lived under constant fear of starvation, Anthony's body was nothing short of miraculous testimony to the plenitude available in the austerity of the desert way of life. Nothing was lost over many years of renunciation, which began when Anthony was about twenty and was maintained until his death. Anthony's intact constitution demonstrated that ascesis and love remade his physical body in preparation for the incorruptible state of its resurrection. The Antonian case for desert spirituality was and remains compelling: with prayer and humility, Anthony waged war against the evil in himself, and his entire body harmoniously incarnated its equilibrium with his purity of soul. Battling demons vitalized Anthony's body, just as his body—with reciprocal power—instructed his soul through discipline. Anthony's practice centered on the fundamental directive shaping the desert search of "dying daily" (Athanasius 91 [97]), a charge which Abba Evagrius puts plainly when he says: "Remember the day of your death" (*Sayings*, Evagrius 1 [63]). Besides making one mindful of eternal judgment, an awareness of death cultivates an attitude of dealing with anything recognized as dangerous in the course of a day. "A man who keeps death before his eyes will at all times overcome his cowardice" (Merton, *Wisdom* 139 [76]).

Keeping death before one's eyes is important in all of O'Connor's stories. In "A Late Encounter with the Enemy," we see the spiritual harm of not doing so. Sash expends all his energy avoiding his death and cultivates bitter cowardice. Death has come before Sash's eyes in the Civil War and in the deaths of his wife and son, and death is working its way through his wasting body; but after a century of reminders, he still "had no more notion of dying than a cat" (*CW* 257). Unaware of his end, this slumberous old tom purrs to the attention showered on his general's uniform that implies a symbolic world where all the battles are won and life goes on endlessly. Despite his ignorance, death does come as a reality to Sash. The great foe arrives in the academic procession that marches from the stage into his head. Concealed within the black-robed graduates crossing the platform to receive their scrolls from the college president, the enemy ambushes Sash with a round of musket fire. Sash cannot see over the crepuscular mass, nor can he dodge the bullets, which at last force his eyes "wide open" (*CW* 261) to something beyond himself. Although O'Connor does not reveal what Sash sees, she does inscribe in his body the consequences of closing his mind to death and his habitual refusal to confront the demons of egotism and anger. His body is the veritable shambles of vanity. Wrath has consumed him, leaving him "as frail as a dried spider" (*CW* 258), an insect trapped in the demonic web spun over many years by entangling animosities. As Sash does not allow the daily dying of his body to teach his soul about the perishability of things, so his demons reduce his material substance, foppishly draped in the symbolic garb of power, to the puniness that it really is. In his defeat, Sash's corpse issues two allied warnings from the desert. The attack of death weighs down his soul through acedia, and his cursing fury betrays his deepening anxiety about life. Whereas a frank and ceaseless encounter with death finally freed Anthony from care, Sash's negligence pushes his soul into deeper anxiety.

Keeping death before one and combating demons are challenges beset with perils arising from the great inborn power of the enemy as well from the limitations inherent in the human condition. Evagrius comments on this inner battle with a healthy modesty: "The spirit that is engaged in the war against the passions does not see clearly the basic meaning of the war for it is something like a man fighting in the darkness of night" (83 [37]). To see what is at stake in the battle and to get through the persistent dangers, the soul needs "vigilance, self-knowledge and discernment" (*Sayings,* Poemen 35 [172]), habits of spiritual warfare that are themselves difficult to sustain. O'Connor appreciates the imperfect vision with which her solitaries must negotiate their demonic darkness, but she makes no concessions to their refusal to be vigilant and to look within themselves to root out their faults. Rather, knowing that dignity is something one gives, O'Connor pays her affectionate respect by upholding the high standards to which her protagonists must rise but from which they have fallen short.

The bodies of the desert-dwellers discussed in this chapter are freighted with care at the end, and their burdened bodies sum up O'Connor's judgment: Sash's corpse slunk in his wheelchair; Tom T. Shiftlet's upraised arm, cursing the world's rottenness; haggard Ruby Hill, clutching the banister and the dissociating fantasy that she is not pregnant; Mrs. Cope's berserk screaming over the fire; and Hulga Hopewell floored without her leg. The outcome for each is an inexorable move into spiritual disaster, for they put their faith in themselves, where their diabolical illusions, undetected and therefore unchallenged, triumph. What the poetics of their solitude captures so graphically is the distance and separation of all these souls that O'Connor has put on the page for our reflection. But there is more to consider in *A Good Man Is Hard to Find.* The next five stories tell of solitaries in whom a frank admission of helplessness lets in a higher guidance that shows the way to safety.

4 Entering a Strange Country

> Now the Lord said to Abraham, "Go from your country
> and your kindred and your father's house to the land
> that I will show you."
> —Genesis 12:1

> The good man comes from God and returns to Him.
> —Thomas Merton, *Thoughts in Solitude*

A Good Man Is Hard to Find also tells of those who combat
against rather than sport with the demons besieging them. Their struggles come to us in the remaining five stories of O'Connor's 1955 collection. Like those in the preceding chapter who suffer defeat in solitude,
the protagonists in the second group of stories are called to the desert,
where they are attacked by demons; but unlike the searchers in the previous stories, these solitaries are receptive to a wisdom beyond themselves and discover the aid required to tackle their demons and therefore
get through their trials with integrity. Their survival makes clear the
source of divine sponsorship and rescue in the war against evil.

Once again, a patristic writer provides guidance into O'Connor's
presentation of her modern desert lives. The ways in which people were
initially summoned from a relatively secure life to the certain peril of the
desert caught the attention of John Cassian, the fifth-century interpreter of the first hermits whose *Conferences* was so helpful in clarifying
Hazel Motes's search for renewal. Cassian saw firsthand in Egypt and
Palestine that different sources inspired people to enter the secrets of the
desert. He distinguished among three kinds of desert calls: "The first is

from God, the second comes by way of man, and the third arises from necessity" (*Conferences* III, 4 [83]). Each call urges people to abandon human company to establish a total relationship with God. Cassian's distinctions about the origins of the flight to the desert explain the various makings of desert solitaries in *A Good Man Is Hard to Find*. The five stories discussed in this chapter dramatize the three kinds of desert calls (from God, humankind, and necessity) that Cassian observed in the ancient East. To begin with, God calls the young protagonists in "The River" and "The Temple of the Holy Ghost." Then, "A Good Man Is Hard to Find" and "The Artificial Nigger" locate the call in human persons. Finally, Cassian's third call to desert life, the command arising from necessity, which impinges to some degree on all of O'Connor's stories of solitude, takes on culminating importance in "The Displaced Person."

For all the varieties of calls and the depth of O'Connor's interest in the spiritual life, the focus in *A Good Man Is Hard to Find* is not on the few professed religious characters (a preacher, several nuns, and an old priest) who appear in the stories. The most prominent of these figures is the priest, who is an active minister seeking souls for God and not a cloistered devout alone seeking God. O'Connor seems intent on exploring the ascetic call in ordinary people and ignoring those who are conscious of being solitary ascetics or who take a vow to give up the world in favor of consecrating themselves to the contemplative life. One of the strict observances of the desert tradition in institutional form, that of the Cistercians, was familiar to O'Connor. She knew and visited the Trappists at the Cistercian monastery of the Holy Spirit in Conyers, Georgia, outside Atlanta, and she was interested in other monastic orders; but she did not write about monks. And with good reason. The social and ecclesiastical message of organized monasticism—uniformity, regimented social station, and reverential decorum—would constrain O'Connor's imagination and bind her ecumenical faith. Besides, the original flight to the desert was a movement of laypersons who were unfulfilled in the cozy church of their time.

Like the primitive solitaries, O'Connor is after something deeper than vows, legislated rules, and liturgical satisfactions. She goes to the deepest law in each person's being, and the law for O'Connor is the need for God, who is life itself. Monks are women and men who structure the day by this need according to historical rule. *A Good Man Is Hard to Find* erases that traditional understanding of monastic life. The stories discussed in this chapter uncover the *monachos* (solitary) that lies hidden in the center of everyone's nature. Her southerners emerge as alone and poor and surrounded by as much silence and peril as were their ancient predecessors. Through them, O'Connor can show that perhaps there is no greater glory than to be reduced to insignificance by the unjust and stupid temporal powers tyrannizing the modern world so that God may triumph over evil through human insignificance. Together, her plain country people portray the paradoxical truth proclaimed by Paul and fleshed out through O'Connor's spiritual poetics: God's "power is made perfect in weakness" (2 Corinthians 12:9).

Weakness takes an especially poignant form in the children of O'Connor's fiction. In her narratives, girls and boys are equally wounded. Some survive the initial trauma to meet the hard destiny laid out for them in later years; others, most memorably O'Connor's three young males, are summarily and totally destroyed. In their time on earth, their awareness of the world, and their ability to protect themselves, these boys are O'Connor's most vulnerable figures. There is the dim-witted Bishop Rayber in *The Violent Bear It Away* (1960), who is murdered at age seven; there is the mentally slow Norton Sheppard, ten, in "The Lame Shall Enter First" (1962), who kills himself. In "The River" (1953), their predecessor in rejection is spunky Harry Ashfield, four or five, who drowns himself. Harry, the youngest, is the first of O'Connor's innocent and solitary children to exhibit God's supremacy at its best in human weakness.

As with all children, Harry's story is a family story. Although Harry lives with the couple who are physically responsible for his birth and welfare, his parents do not emotionally live with him. They inhabit a solipsistic temple elsewhere that is dedicated to their god of pleasure. For them, Harry is a nuisance who gets in the way of the parties that the Ashfields are either giving or recovering from. The leftovers of parental selfishness define Harry's desert and how he feels about himself. He thinks of himself as merely another particle in the powdery remains of the Ashfields' negligent self-indulgence. Bewildered, ill at ease, and a missing child with an address, Harry is the lost son looking for his father and mother. In his search, Harry negotiates a waste as dusty as any desert inhabited by the desert elders, and he is as alone as they were. Moreover, Harry's goal in solitude is no less spiritually urgent than theirs; he seeks the source of meaningful life.

Evagrius's description of the spirit's battling evil as a dim-sighted fight in darkness, an image with which the previous chapter concluded, renders Harry's predicament. Harry first appears limping through "the dark living room" (*CW* 154), which is strewn with the leavings from the endless night-before of his parents. At 6:00 A.M. on this particular cold Sunday, Mrs. Connin, the latest of many sitters, has arrived to get Harry off his parents' hands. The gloom, thick with the carcinogenic cigarette butts that name the family, condenses the toxic ways in which the Ashfields lead their lives and devalue their boy. Harry is hungry; he is exhausted and turned out of the house sleepy. He has runny eyes and a nose that the Ashfields do not wipe dry. Mother and father say that they love their child; and given the heathen, immature culture in which they express their love, they can be confident that they are loving. And yet, that night, after a weary, lonely day, Harry goes to bed without a hug, a kiss, or a comfort. Instead, his mother, feeling guilty and needing reassurance from Harry, pulls him up and down by the shirt he has worn all day and must sleep in and brushes "her lips against his forehead" (*CW* 168). Junk food and junk feelings bespeak the inadvertent moral oppression enveloping Harry. Understandably, Harry feels that he does not count. That sense of paltriness pervades Harry's interior desert.

Where parents are children—as are the Ashfields—their children must parent themselves, for children's basic inner needs cannot be grasped or answered by the parents. O'Connor points up the spiritual chasm by having the narrator call Harry "the little boy" (*CW* 155) to remind us of his neediness, whereas Harry's father calls his son "'old man'" (*CW* 166) to hasten the child's independence. The paternal endearment is accurate. In Harry's need to be taken seriously, the four- or five-year-old is more mature than his parents. Harry hears no call from the pulpit, as Anthony did, since church is not part of the Ashfields' social faith. But the call to flee nevertheless comes to Harry. Before he hears the words, he feels the need to count—which is the need for God without using the word *God.* The living and active word of God (Hebrews 4:2) discerns the urgency of Harry's heart and summons him toward God. From one sun-up to the next, Harry lives out his desire to count. By intuition and in solitude, the young searcher silently pursues the life of the spirit with a zeal that transports him from the known to the unknown.

Harry's true father is Abba Anthony. They are related through the deepest lineage as sons of Abraham. In Genesis 12:1, God called to Abraham: "Go from your country and your kindred and your father's house to the land that I will show you." With the Lord's command to Abraham, the momentous story of the desert and scriptural revelation begins. God's call sounds a clean break with the pagan past in Israel's history. Under God's auspices, Israel will migrate to a place of God's choice, where Abraham and his descendants will receive God's blessings. In cutting loose from home in wordless trust in God's call, Abraham exemplifies the person of faith. The ground of that faith is the desert. John Cassian adds a fifth-century spiritual interpretation of the call to Abraham by applying Israel's sacred history to the individual's interior journey. For Cassian, the three parts of God's instructions to Abraham express ascetic goals. In leaving one's native place, one gives up wealth from the earth and the world; departure from family severs one from the past way of life, character, and faults that cling from birth; and, finally, leaving the father's home separates the spiritual searcher "from all worldly memory arising before our eyes" (*Conferences* III, 6 [85]) to contemplate the future. Obedience to these three renunciations leads to fulfillment in the land of God's promise.

As with Abraham, the scriptural exemplar, so with Anthony, the Christian model, and so too with Harry Ashfield, the bereft child of our time. In "The River," God calls and promises, and the young searcher responds. God's perfecting power in this story accords with the condition of a boy who has never heard of Jesus and wanders without emotional moorings. There are, as in the *Sayings* and the *Lives,* messengers to help Harry along the way. First, Mrs. Connin materializes out of the cold dark. She sees the negligence and utters, "'You pervide'" (*CW* 155), which, as a prayer, points toward the origin of the message she will impart. Mothering Harry, the sitter cleans his nose, feeds him, and holds him in her lap. Harry, child of emotionally empty parents and therefore accustomed to not being heard, communicates principally through his hands. Hesitant and lonely, the "little boy put a slight pressure on her [Mrs. Connin's] hand" (*CW* 156). Later, Mrs. Connin holds Harry's hand as her entire family walks to the river to hear the Reverend Bevel Summers, a healer, into whose hands Mrs. Connin delivers her young charge.

Summers speaks directly to Harry's inner search by pointing to the water that will bring life to his desert. Arms and head lifted, the evangelist shouts to all—both to those who know and those who expect otherwise—that life is suffering and that Jesus shows the way to make sense of suffering: "'It's a River full of pain itself, pain itself, moving toward the Kingdom of Christ, to be washed away, slow, you people, slow as this here old red water river round my feet'" (*CW* 162). This message of healing puts into words the feelings Harry experiences. He is awash in the detritus of rejection and lives the truth of pain. When Summers asks Harry if he wants to be baptized in the river of suffering, the child utters, "'Yes'" (*CW* 165), the one decisive word. In confirmation of Harry's *yes,* the healer's hand tightens his grip on the child, swings him upside down, plunges his head in the water, and says the baptismal words. The turning over of Harry's body reverses his topsy-turvy inner world. Now he counts. The word *yes* stirs a deep countermovement in his will, a young, pliant will that carries him riverward as well. Like Abraham, Harry turns his back on the past to take up his river life and thinks: "I won't go back to the apartment then, I'll go under the river" (*CW* 165). Getting to the river is Harry's new battle to be fought against old enemies. First there is the child's abiding loneliness; then his parents thwart his need to be taken seriously; finally, Mr. Paradise, the cynic, tries to stop and divert Harry. These adversaries do not disappear after Harry is baptized. Rather, Harry's desire for a secure home in the river gives him the courage to overmaster them.

O'Connor makes a point of celebrating the baptismal day that fortifies Harry to meet his opponents. The bright sun brings Harry to warm life. His body springs with anticipation. As Mrs. Connin, her children, and Harry walk along a long, red-clay road, Harry begins "to make wild leaps and pull forward on her [Mrs. Connin's] hand as if he wanted to dash off and snatch the sun which was rolling away ahead of them now" (*CW* 160–61). The child's hand and feet, not words or ideas, manifest his hope. For the right words to describe Harry's superaliveness, we can listen to the taciturn Abba Isaac describe how God's call comes through physical vitality: "I feel that my spirit has once more found a sense of direction, that my thinking has grown purposeful, that because of a visit of the Holy Spirit my heart is unspeakably glad and my mind ecstatic" (*Conferences* X, 10 [135]). The Spirit of God suffuses Harry's "dreamy and serene" (*CW* 160) mind with a goal that prefigures the tranquillity in store for him. The term for the calm that fulfills the desert searcher's desire is *hesychia*; but to attain this peace, Harry must first pass through the dreadful unknown. The further Harry drifts from his city home and into a bewildering terrain, the more deeply he takes in the tangible call to divine life. After Mrs. Connin's entourage leaves the dirt road, they cross a field and then enter a wood. This transition, a recurring movement into deeper obscurity that appears throughout O'Connor's fiction, startles Harry, for the woods are a new, revelatory experience for the urban child. Cautiously, he makes his way through the wilderness, "looking from side to side as if he were entering a strange country" (*CW* 161).

The strange country that Harry approaches is the boundless, primeval forest through which all of O'Connor's solitaries—young and old, ambulatory and prostrate, eager and reluctant—must pass. It is the deep lair of beasts and perils, enemies lurking within and without the person who enters the uncharted territory. The woody "shadows" of this locale (*CW* 161) encompass Dante's dark wood (*una selva oscura*), the scriptural ways of darkness (Proverbs 2:13–14), the wilderness, and the desert. O'Connor's "strange country," which lies adjacent to her true country of

God, is dark with ignorance and sin, the forces blinding the sojourner to the stealthy adversaries determined to impede any spiritual progress. O'Connor, a fine landscape artist, consistently embeds her spiritual poetics into the topography. The site Harry traverses as he draws near the river reflects O'Connor's special anagogical detailing. She makes Harry's strange autumnal country a mixture of mellow beauty and incipient danger to show the hard and magnificent ground of being on which even a young wayfarer must find the meaning of life. A carpet of "purple weeds" paves the way to the woods, where the earth is covered with "thick pine needles." The bridle path twists down a slippery hill through "crackling red leaves" and takes Harry alongside "two frozen green-gold eyes enclosed in the darkness of a tree hole" (*CW* 161). The perplexed child leaves the spooky stare and other menaces behind as the path opens out to the red river that the healer calls "'the rich red river of Jesus' Blood'" (*CW* 162).

The signs of Harry's rushed, inner maturation are unmistakable: O'Connor's child of four or five must suffer the passion that all must suffer—and more because his infinite longing is so freshly formed. O'Connor compensates Harry for his youthful inexperience by endowing him with two weapons that the ancient hermits spent a lifetime developing. After his baptism, the child forges a singleness of purpose that the hermits understood as purity of heart: Harry will give up everything for the one thing that cannot be taken from him. Also, his humility makes room for the only power—God's attention—that can comfort his restless heart. These virtues, purity of heart and humility, are the two most powerful inner shields that any solitary can have against the enemy. The final action of "The River" shows Harry traveling the road of innocence to death and rest fortified by a humble, unalloyed need for divine reality.

Other children of God may need warning of the terrible speed of God's mercy, but Harry does not. He hastens toward it. He wakens the second morning, Monday, amid the constant dark despondency that has sunk his life so low. Shriveled vegetables, brown oranges, and a fishy something in a paper bag exude the stale, heathen distaste for life that has made Harry feel so alone. His parents' overindulgence pollutes the air, which he inhales as a judgment against him. The nagging sense of being expendable seizes Harry sharply, and he cannot get rid of the disgust and anger in his heart by tearing up his picture books, rubbing ashes into the rug, or kicking the sofa. But this morning his old dejection is short-lived. "'The pagans are gloomy,'" the holy man named Apollo used to say, but those "'who are going to inherit the kingdom of heaven must not be despondent about their salvation.'" With Saint Paul, Abba Apollo urges the solitary "'to rejoice always'" (*Lives*, Apollo 53 [78]). Hope in the form of remembering the river quickly changes Harry's mood.

The day before, when Harry was reaching out for help, his hand expressed his desire; on Monday, with Harry knowing the way to count as a person, his feet mark his spiritual progress. His damp shoes connect him to the river. The water calls him out of half-sleep and darkness to recover light and life. He takes a car token from his mother's handbag, gives his slumberous, hungover parents a parting glance, and goes from his father's house. Harry takes nothing for his journey. Wordlessly and still dressed in the soiled clothes of the previous day that, it should not be forgotten, are his baptismal garb, Harry retraces the route that Mrs. Connin took to the healing. But now Harry ventures alone. That he is also alone in a landscape charged with the overtones of the desert and wilderness is striking. Harry gets dusty, he sweats, and he passes over purple weeds. The crossing is Harry's exodus. To heighten the child's passage through the desert from bondage to deliverance, O'Connor's recasts the image of Jesus from *Wise Blood* as a ragged figure moving from tree to tree in Hazel Motes's mind to add hints of the Gospels' Passion to Harry's final journey. At the end of "The River," Harry follows the same current of Jesus' surrender to a higher will as he wanders "from tree to tree" (*CW* 170) until the steep trail brings him down to the river. On reaching the water, Harry's inner yearning outruns his half-formed sensibility, and he jumps into the rich red river to get home, to rebaptize himself.

Baptism for Harry is not a one-time ritual ablution but a permanent living out of his desire to belong. The healer taught Harry that through the red water, Harry claims membership in the kingdom of Christ, and the degree to which the boy takes this lesson to heart is simple and appalling: he drowns himself. Literalness and emotional need are one. His body receives the instruction that mentors his will. There is a clue to this shocking interaction in O'Connor's response to the baptism of her correspondent "A" as an adult. After informing "A" about the three kinds of baptism in Christian theology—"water, blood, and desire"—O'Connor goes on to add her personal amazement about those who on their own find the need for the fundamental sacrament, one that O'Connor was given before the age of reason (and thus which she might never have chosen for herself): "All voluntary baptisms are a miracle to me and stop my mouth as if I had just seen Lazarus walk out of the tomb" (*HB* 130–31). The wonder in "The River" is the reader's seeing Harry walk into the tomb and float on his watery bier to sacral regeneration. To stop our mouth even longer, O'Connor finds a way to combine all three forms of baptism in her child solitary. Water covers Harry; the blood of sacrifice witnesses his need; and his desire to count impels him home to God. Harry's cleansing and sanctification compose a fully enfleshed incorporation, at once liturgical and individual, into the mysterious sovereignty that the healer had promised.

Harry attains new life through ascesis. The sudden mortification of his young body redirects his inquisitive soul and compliant will to the red river. His newly focused will fights against whatever impedes his advance—the water included. The last denizen of the shadowland Harry is leaving is Mr. Paradise, the misshapen old cynic who one reader astutely notes is "an ugly amulet" deflecting any sentimental reading of Harry's drowning (Di Renzo 131). O'Connor's placing of this human eyesore at the end of the story further indicates the inner strength Harry has gained. Mr. Paradise sums up in a single presence the unsightliness behind the hedonistic field of ashes. At the end, Mr. Paradise sets out with a peppermint stick to bring Harry back, but nothing can deter Harry. When recognized as a delusion, Abba Anthony teaches, the pleasure offered by the tempting spirit dissipates into repugnance (Athanasius 42 [63]). Finally seen by the boy from beneath the water as a porcine ghost, Mr. Paradise "like some ancient water monster" (*CW* 171) stares down the river for the prey set free from the allurement.

Harry is on his way, escorted by the desert call from God. To escape, after unsuccessfully fighting the water, Harry takes a determined plunge. With a single "low cry of pain," he sinks, getting caught in the current. As the desert elders understood the struggle in solitude, the outcome depends on God's help. That aid at the end of "The River" brings us back to O'Connor's association with Lazarus's rebirth. Lazarus in Hebrew means "God has helped," which is a way of saying that the divine coexists with disaster. As Harry dives into the red-yellow water, the "long gentle hand" of the flow pulls him forward. "All his fury and his fear" (*CW* 171) leave Harry; for, as Abba Anthony says, "all things are in the hand of the Lord" (Athanasius 42 [63]). The cradling hand is ready with God's affirmation to wipe away his runny nose and eyes. The snug grasp only hints at the benevolence now within the boy's reach as he plunges deep into Jesus' misery and redeeming destiny. The young hesychast rests in serenity.

The other desert call from God rouses a girl of twelve, the heroine of "A Temple of the Holy Ghost." The girl shares Harry's sense of not fitting into the world and his need to count. Neither family nor community offers a suitable explanation of who she is. The girl feels that a true understanding of herself lies beyond the prevailing culture. This desire to know herself in depth launches the heroine on a lonely quest that leads to a strange disappearance into the hidden ground of love, the desert to which God calls her. Her search becomes acute during the weekend visit of two second cousins from the convent school, Mount St. Scholastica. Their strange and inimical way of speaking about sexuality and the hermaphrodite they saw at a fair brings out the heroine's loneliness, an incompleteness, she believes, that is apparent for all to see in her metal braces and fat cheeks. The child is young enough to admit her lonesomeness but not old enough to create a social surface she could present to the world to hide her difference. She is, in her own knowing words, "out of it" (*CW* 197) and "a born liar" (*CW* 204). Pride also sets the girl apart, for she is "deliberately ugly to almost everybody" (*CW* 204).

The trait that most distinguishes this child, however, is the unseen attribute of spiritual ambition. She wants to be a holy person. Sanctity, she believes, will unify her disconnected parts. Being a saint is "the occupation that included everything you could know; and yet she knew she would never be a saint" (*CW* 204) because she lies, sasses her mother, and is lazy. And so she will have to settle for martyrdom because it is quick and would leave her no time to sin. Her knowledge of martyrdom comes from the secure, Hollywood banalities of an MGM rendering of the persecution of Christians in the Roman Empire. In the Colosseum of her mind, a gold light shines on the girl as lions charge her, only to fall at her feet in conversion to God; then, failing to burn her hallowed body, the Romans behead her so that she can enter paradise triumphantly attended by her lion friends. Martyrdom confers the importance that society and her peers deny the girl. As in *The Life of Anthony* and with other holy persons, the child's rapport with animals—especially with lions, the kings of beasts—authenticates her privileged relation to the divine (Elliott 144–59). She who is prohibited from going at night with her cousins to the fair to see the hermaphrodite takes the sideshow performer's place as the central attraction and in nothing less spectacular than the Roman stadium.

The child's display of beatific nostalgia humorously evokes a parallel between O'Connor's treatment of religious desire in "A Temple of the Holy Ghost" and the situation that gave rise to desert asceticism in the first place. Several historical facts explain O'Connor's smile over the girl's fantasy of heroic torture for faith. Constantine's conversion to Christianity and edict in 312 A.D., which ended the Great Persecution, established a relative comfort for the church. That ease in turn stirred yearnings that went beyond conformity in those seeking God. With venerable martyrdom no longer possible as Christianity became the official state religion,

Christians sought new ways of living out their belief. Assimilation of Christianity into Roman imperial society prepared the way for ascetic renunciation in late antiquity. Seizing the impulse, Abba Anthony pointed to the desert as the new way—extending the oldest way—to God. His example was a leaven to the society provided by a small, dedicated group within Christianity itself. Their flight to the desert was in part a protest against a society in which Christianity was becoming too cozy and had veered from Jesus' call to sacrifice.

It would be going too far to argue that through "A Temple of the Holy Ghost," O'Connor reproaches a despotic imperial state for thwarting the child's search for integrity. But it would be entirely in keeping with O'Connor's sensibility to say that the story levels charges against a Christianity, modern or ancient, that has been complacent, smug, sentimental, and antithetical to Logos. In fact, her fiction frequently depicts a decadent Christianity that has become a civic religion or a genteel association sanctioning oppression (Bacon 134–36). Fashionable Christianity of late antiquity and the modern equivalent both create the need for fresh ways of living out Jesus' proclamation. In the fourth century, Anthony revolutionized religious life by returning to the desert of the Gospels, and O'Connor in this century points toward another reformation by taking her characters back to the ways of Anthony. If it is late in the Christian day for martyrdom, it is the right moment for a return to the simple, practical life of the desert mothers and fathers as a means to witness faith.

This renunciatory teaching reaches the girl in "The Temple of the Holy Ghost" in two stages. It first comes through an acceptance of her alienation and then with an identification with the two-sexed performer. Above all, the girl wants to escape the dullness of the people around her, who inhabit a porcelain world that offends the heroine's seriousness. Joanne and Susan, the convent cousins, are gigglers who trivialize the idea that God might dwell in each person. It would be particularly unthinkable to them that God inheres in the hermaphrodite. In their Manichean minds, one must look a certain cute, conventional way to be human. Moreover, the notion of being a temple of the divine Spirit deprives Joanne and Susan of their sexuality. The heroine, not yet tainted by the modern anxiety leading to contempt for the flesh, welcomes the possibility of the Spirit dwelling in her as receiving "a present" (*CW* 199). But she looks in vain to adults for any confirmation of such sacramental intuition. Her mother merely promotes benevolent manners, and the Sisters of Mercy—with their lectures on temptation (reminiscent of the popular social guidance films of the 1940s)—are not much better.

The girl's feelings of being cut off from society forge a link in her mind with the hermaphrodite and the religious past. Ritual images of public scapegoating explain to the girl the pain of her lonesomeness, the hurt caused when people do not respect the quality of difference and do not see their own capacity for evil. In the child's fantasy, the performer, who has been turned into a forbidden object of curiosity, speaks to the necessity of seeing otherness in ourselves: "'I'm going to show you this and if you laugh, God may strike you the same way'" (*CW* 206). The marked person of two sexes confronts an audience that does not hesitate to defend its threatened prejudices by stigmatizing exceptions to its arbitrary rules, and he/she summons the crowd to respect those it would victimize: "'I'm showing you because I got to make the best of it. I expect you to act like ladies and gentlemen'" (*CW* 206). In the harsh conformist culture dominating the O'Connor world, the hermaphrodite holds the moral authority by calling for the self-scrutiny that sees the malice in displacing difference and evil onto others.

This shadowed sideshow figure, though never seen, activates the child's mind. The night that she hears of her/him, the girl lies awake trying to fathom how a person can be both woman and man. Too sleepy to figure out the riddle of two sexes in one person, she instead rescripts the sideshow performance by linking Sister Perpetua's comment about the temple of the Holy Spirit with the performer's declaration: "'God done this to me and I praise Him.'" The self-accepting and divine-praising words in the child's invented version of the spectacle also create a wiser audience that lifts its approving voice with "'Amen. Amen.'" All the voices unite in the unattributed affirmation, "'I am a temple of the Holy Ghost'" (*CW* 207), which surely speaks for the girl's inner desire. Without solving the physiological enigma of how two genders become one, the child's reverie touches on the mystery of two natures, divine and human, in one.

O'Connor does not leave the question of how the human body can receive the divine up in the air as a child's intuition or a symbolic hint. All theological matters for O'Connor must come to light in the body itself; and that is what happens as the story ends. The next afternoon, when the child and her mother leave the convent after returning the cousins, a big nun rushes to embrace the child goodbye. The affectionate clasp mashes the child's soft face into the hard crucifix that hangs from the nun's belt. Just as God strikes the hermaphrodite's body with a physical burden, the Cross imprints the hermaphrodite's disturbing wisdom into the child's flesh. The cruciform cut is the wound of love bearing the lesson of the desert: suffering entails warfare against evil. Anthony's call came from the pulpit; Harry Ashfield's call comes from the river; the child's call comes from the Cross. God directly calls each to enter the strange country of renunciatory warfare against the evil within. The child's path ahead is taken up in solitude, in the loneliness she now experiences, and through self-investigation, a struggle she is already waging.

Desert spirituality is never a matter of pieties but of seeing through illusions; and the child has made a good beginning, for she sees herself with the peeled eyeball of the ascetic. She admits to being "a born liar and slothful." Her rigor is mature enough to know that the enemy's grip is consuming: "She was eaten up also with the sin of Pride, the worst one" (*CW* 204). Her habit of berating others instructs the child to control of her tongue. And there is more to her awareness than a seeking of verbal politeness; the child is on to the hermits' powerful recognition of the harm that words can cause. "No passion is worse than an uncontrolled tongue," says Abba Agathon, "because it is the mother of all the passions" (*Sayings*, Agathon 1 [20]). With the child, her intemperate tongue feeds her devouring pride, giving vent to the illusion of superiority, as when she maligns Baptists. Combating her pride would lead to humility. "Hep me not to talk like I do," she prayerfully reflects during the convent liturgy. This simple desert entreaty brings about in her a hesychia of "quiet and then empty" (*CW* 208) mindfulness. Such a sustained scrutinizing of her weakness, not heroic martyrdom in the great arena, will guide her in solitary pursuit of holiness. She must learn with the hermaphrodite that she too is broken, incomplete, and disparaged and that something is right in the hermaphrodite body and in her that society and the demons have made wrong.

The child's call is summed up in the eucharistic vision that concludes the story. Child and mother are riding home from the convent in their car. The child looks out to a sun setting on the dark wood that greets the solitary's entering the strange country through the red-clay path, an image that runs throughout O'Connor's fiction: "The sun was a huge red ball like an elevated Host drenched in blood and when it sank out of sight, it left a line in the sky like a red clay road hanging over the trees" (*CW* 209). The figure of an oozing, consecrated wafer draws on late-medieval eucharistic worship. In this devotional setting, as Caroline Walker Bynum's study of nourishment and the religious life of medieval women explains, "the host becomes flesh to announce its violation; the bleeding is an accusation" (63). The charge warns of sin's harm to the mystical body and further calls for restoration. That call was answered by the self-donation of Jesus, whose communal sacrifice unites all humanity in his streaming blood. Bynum continues: "Exactly because the host became so insistently Christ's body—whose firm outlines had been violated by Roman (or Jewish) spears and nails—it remained a powerful corporate symbol, a symbol of humankind, of Christendom, and of the church" (61–62). O'Connor goes a step further to turn the symbol into the actual blood-stained streak in the child's vision that maps the interior path to the holiness she seeks. The inner course of repentance ends in the place of the Cross, which is permanently the strange country of the desert.

———————

The grandmother in "A Good Man Is Hard to Find" is an unlikely person to encounter a hermaphrodite. Hers is a family world upheld by the traditional Atlanta ways of nice people against the fast-changing, corrupt social and moral forces that threaten her understanding of what is right and her due. And yet for all of the grandmother's staunch protections against the outer world, she meets a two-sided person who is much more unusual than the two-sexed performer. More remarkably still, the staid old lady heeds the performer's call to sympathize with the way in which this odd, truly freakish, and fatal stranger is struck by God. She, the prim lady securely placed in society, bears the burden of disfigurement and of being an outcast.

These by now familiar amazements in the O'Connor world come about in "A Good Man Is Hard to Find" through another ascetic experience in the desert life of O'Connor's warring solitaries. Although she acts like a matron who is perfectly situated in her social context, the grandmother really has lived a lonely and combative life for many years. Her awareness, however, quickly catches up with her condition, for she advances to the ground of her essential battle at breakneck speed. It takes no more than the morning and early afternoon hours of a single day for her to reach the empty place where she gains the insights embedded in her solitude. It all happens during a family car trip south from their Atlanta home. What is meant to be a vacation with freedom from care turns into a transformative interval of tribulation. As a way into the importance of the old lady's adventure, it is necessary to look at the condition of her body at the beginning and end of her journey. She has the body of a woman who for years takes pride in caring for her physical appearance, and her trim, firm-set posture conveys determination in having her way. The story begins with the grandmother standing "with one hand on her thin hip" as she badgers her son Bailey to change his plans to visit Florida and drive instead to see relatives in east Tennessee. She brandishes the newspaper report of The Misfit who has escaped from the federal penitentiary to make her point. Her precise directives fit her body language of con-

trol: "'Now look here, Bailey,' she said, 'see here, read this'" (*CW* 137).
At the end of the story, she meets The Misfit and ends up on the ground,
half-sitting "with her legs crossed under her like a child's" (*CW* 152) in a
pool of her own blood.

The enemy rends her body. The solid contour of the old lady's carefully groomed body disintegrates. Her flesh gushes blood. Her deformed,
bleeding corpse re-presents the eucharistic wafer oozing blood that we
just observed in the girl's vision that concluded "A Temple of the Holy
Ghost." As with the oozing host, the grandmother's streaming body declares its violation and calls for reparation; but there is an additional note
present at the end of "A Good Man Is Hard to Find." The old lady lives
out the blood sacrifice recalled in the Eucharist and, through self-denial,
becomes the one who calls directly to her slayer, The Misfit, to atone.
The grandmother, a most improbable exemplar of ascetic self-denial,
sends an inspiration into the heart of her killer, in whom there stirs a
longing for God. The source of the old lady's change can also be seen in
her bodily collapse. Her stance at the beginning, with one hand on her
hip, is the posture of self-will. The story's first two sentences state her
personal desires. She "didn't want to go to Florida." Instead, she "wanted to visit connections in east Tennessee" (*CW* 137). Where she wants
to go should determine the direction. Just as she stands while the family
sits, so the rights of the grandmother remain over and above the agreed-
upon wishes of her son, her daughter-in-law, and three grandchildren. The
three-day outing is about her. Naturally, she is the first person to get in
the car. When she is ready, it is time to go. Her wishes drive the excursion. Her iron will announces the departure, regulates the conversation,
gets the family lost, and speeds them into extinction. Along the way, her
will acts as tour guide, cautioning about police and pointing out scenic
details. A small but by no means insignificant indication of her controlling will is the presence of Pitty Sing, the cat, which the old lady hides
in a black valise to take along against her son's wishes. The grandmother does care about the cat, but she also cherishes her need to manipulate.
In the end, it is the cat, the instrument of her devious will, that dooms
the family.

All the events in the story go back to the grandmother's self-will; and,
as the desert teachers made clear, the will takes individuals right to their
demons. These demons are most gratified when they misguide, and that
is what the grandmother's disordered passions do. The route on which
her imperious will takes the family bears the distinct features of O'Connor's landscape of inadvertent withdrawal and trial. The family drifts
away from the settled world into "the outskirts of the city" (*CW* 138).

There is a stop at Red Sammy's The Tower for lunch, after which they accelerate deeper into strange territory. Outside Toombsboro, the grandmother schemes to get her son to make a detour to see an old plantation. This swerving off their course takes them down a lonely dirt road treacherously parched into pink dust. Besides being dry and skittish, the road has "sudden washes" making for "dangerous embankments" and "a red depression" running through "dust-coated trees." The place is scorched and forlorn. "The road looked as if no one had traveled on it in months" (*CW* 144). Suddenly, the grandmother remembers that she has mistaken the place where she saw the plantation. Blinded by her will, jolted by embarrassment, she upsets the valise hiding Pitty Sing, which jumps on Bailey. He loses control of the car, which turns over; and they all land in a gulch. The family is stranded in a bewildering void. The uninhabitable place is the desert. The demons that have been driving the grandmother have succeeded in getting their prey into the desolate place where disordered impulses readily unleash their forces. The disaster about to break loose is marked by the "tall and dark and deep" woods (*CW* 145) surrounding the ditch in which the family members, like so many O'Connor sojourners, lie in various aspects of defenseless exposure.

The forsaken gloom takes human form as The Misfit, with two accomplices, steps out of a black, hearse-like car. The escaped criminal brings many satanic forces into play (Evans 3–7). Above all, he epitomizes the evils of self-will that the grandmother has been exercising in smaller domestic ways and that have brought her to meet up with her double, The Misfit. The Misfit's thoughts and actions constitute nothing less than demonic tyranny. To enter The Misfit's mind is to be ensnared within a fierce web of willfulness. He will not stay within the walls of the federal penitentiary. He will take the clothes, the car, and the lives of people as and when he wants to take them. He insists that he "'ain't a good man'" (*CW* 148) and takes pride in the distinction conferred by his evil choices. He tells Bobby Lee and Hiram, his henchmen, when to take the family members to the woods to be shot, thereby putting assailants and victims under his willpower. The Misfit, like his parent Lucifer, explicitly puts his will above the will of God when he insists that he should have been around for Jesus' crucifixion so that, as he says in the droning first-person singulars of self-sorrow, "'if I had of been there I would of known and I wouldn't be like I am now'" (*CW* 152). What he is like is Satan. And he will personally kill the grandmother by firing three precise shots into her chest. The will of The Misfit is so massive that its satisfactions outstrip the pleasures available in earthly creation: "'Nobody had nothing I wanted'" (*CW* 150), he explains to the old lady when she asks if he was sent to jail for stealing. Theft would imply his recognizing ownership by others, and a will of The Misfit's grandiosity assumes that the world is his for the taking.

Taking human lives is the culminating act of his demonic mastery. The Misfit deals in death; he is a spree killer. As the opportunity of a car or clothing arises, he kills to get it. This is one nasty misfit. The latest six corpses that he leaves behind are testimony that The Misfit lives in a cell of his own making and continually fortifies the jail he is trying to escape. In describing prison, he effectively depicts his inner state: "'Turn to the right, it was a wall. . . . Turn to the left, it was a wall. Look up it was a ceiling, look down it was a floor'" (*CW* 150). What his private will chooses is its own imprisonment. Guilt and captivity are the gods his will serves. The demon of acedia acts as gatekeeper. Although he complains about being trapped, he loves enslavement. With each murder, this escaped convict freely wills his own pain and punishment and convicts himself anew. The Misfit's self-will gradually brings death to his soul. He sums up the consequences of this inner extinguishment in his bitter outburst to one of his cohorts, who says that killing people is "'fun.'" "'Shut up, Bobby Lee,' The Misfit said. 'It's no real pleasure in life'" (*CW* 153). The killer's inability to find delight in the world results from his desires being out of line with the rights of others and the will of God. Such maladjustment of his will, not his being a social outcast, gives the gravest meaning to his name, The Misfit.

The Misfit's cursing life as dismal concludes "A Good Man Is Hard to Find," but his denunciation and self-loathing are not the final words of the story. The more we understand about The Misfit, the more we can appreciate the grandmother's refusal to meet his wrath with her own wrath as she dies. His parting utterance emerges from a dialogue between The Misfit's acedia and the silence of the grandmother's twisted, bullet-riddled body. As she lies flattened in the gulch, he hovers over her like an incubus incapable of leaving its victim. Killing her is not enough; he needs to drain the last drop of her attention as well. As he complains about having to live without delight, the grandmother dies with her face beaming a smile upward at the cloudless sky. The agony of having to witness her family systematically killed before she herself meets her inevitable end turns everything about this old lady into clear light and freedom. She enjoys much more satisfaction in availing herself to her killer than she ever received from pushing people around or being smartly dressed.

To understand how the bungling grandmother attains this joyous state, we need to double back to the place on the highway where she makes Bailey reroute the car onto the dirt road to visit an old plantation that she misremembers. The detour marks the turning point in the grand-mother's life. From this moment on, a twofold action evolves. One details the outward drama of the multiple murders. The other traces the inward ascesis in the grandmother. Both are fast and furious. The unseen development brings to final form the poetics of solitude shaping the entire story. The grandmother's interior movement begins with her awareness of her error. Suddenly, she realizes that she saw the plantation in Tennessee, not Georgia, where they are driving. Not being in the right and being aware of her fault destabilize the old lady. A new sense of herself opens up. Once she loses her geographical and moral bearings, the once perfectly assured woman experiences a series of additional losses. Her inner demons have a field day. Her self-confidence slips away. Distraught, she feels deprived of control over the trip and the family's actions. Because she is too weak to take responsibility for the accident, the old lady must rely on self-protecting maneuvers. To get sympathy from The Misfit, she lies about the car overturning twice when it overturned only once. Caught in dishonesty, she relinquishes her poise when it is most needed; and she gives up whatever moral ground she might have stood on. Then she tries candor by blurting out her recognition of The Misfit. In being forthright, she infuriates Bailey and forces The Misfit's trigger-happy hand. The foundations of the grandmother's world are shaken. Her disordered passions reduce her and the family to utter vulnerability. She has no ploys left, and The Misfit must get rid of the family.

The way in which The Misfit kills the family is designed to instill fear as he destroys. He employs the rawest means of coercion, a common and for this century the signal demonic method of political brutality, terrorism. But O'Connor, specialist in violence that she is, has a response to terrorism just as she faces down war, death camps, racism, and suicide. O'Connor gives new meaning to The Misfit's reign of terror not by turning the scourge back against him—as some readers might hope and as a sensational writer would settle matters—but by using the terrorist's brutality in favor of his personally chosen victim, the grandmother. The precedent for O'Connor's treatment is in the Gospel Passion narratives of Jesus' self-surrender that The Misfit himself speaks of. The Misfit's appalling slaughter acts on the old lady as an ascesis, excruciating and unwanted. One by one, her family is taken away from the old woman to the dark thicket. Removed from her sight, the violence cuts deeper into her soul. She must consciously witness the murder of those she loves. There are outer signs of what is going on in the grandmother's soul. Her hat comes off; her social standing vanishes summarily. Her voice goes. She thirsts. But these are mere hints of what she endures. As she hears the shot that kills her son, the old woman cries out for him in a drained voice; but he is torn away from her, and the wound of love shatters her heart.

The stripping away of the grandmother's personal attributes and of the human bonds by which she has defined herself over a lifetime leaves the old lady painfully reduced and alone. She is alone two or three times over. Physically, she is without aid or comfort in a fatal encounter. Psychologically, she is bereft of the things that are important to her feelings of security and well-being. And she knows a deeper deprivation and loneliness, not so much a loneliness for people as a metaphysical emptiness and a sense of being in a void, a sickening void, a place where no one can follow her, which O'Connor depicts in the harsh contours of the gulch surrounding the grandmother. Given the old lady's usual success in getting her own way and her peevish reactions to even slight opposition, one might expect the grandmother to respond to impending death with devious cowardice or self-sorrow; and one would not be surprised if the injustice of it all made her strike out in rage at the man who has coolly wiped out her family. But she is neither caught up with herself nor angry. Something entirely out of keeping with her usual behavior occurs in the pit. At a time when a sense of the nothingness of herself and of life must seize her, the woman who has been babied by her family abruptly matures. She calls out in a parched voice to The Misfit with the brightness of discovering her own flesh and blood: "'Why you're one of my babies. You're one of my own children!'" (*CW* 152). Her life and her death are with her killer. She looks at the stranger's face and finds herself. She looks into her killer's heart and hears a summons to her duty. His torment is hers; his ultimate fate weighs on her. Solitude teaches the old lady solidarity and is the spiritual basis for the tough "new realism" (136) that Thomas Hill Schaub sees in the story as O'Connor's response to the ineffective liberalism and political ennui of the postwar years (130–33). To solemnize her call, the grandmother reaches out and touches The Misfit. He responds by shooting her. For him, life is only tolerable when kept at arm's length; but for the grandmother, life and death become meaningful when she answers the call for compassion that draws her closer to all that she has wished for in life.

It is now evident that, although the grandmother got the car to take the wrong turn in the wrong state for the wrong reason, the new direction at the intersection of the deserted road rights the grandmother's faults. It is her iron will that causes the pileup, and it is her self-will that is bent and demolished by the demonic attacks in the gulch. In the act of forcing his will on the grandmother, The Misfit unknowingly imposes on her the task that the masters of solitude recommend as ways to strengthen the solitary's spirit in adversity. "To throw yourself before God, not to measure your progress, to leave behind all self-will," says Abba Poemen, "these are the instruments for the work of the soul" (*Sayings*, Poemen 36 [172]). These are the very means of change in the grandmother. She would not choose to throw herself before God; but when fate hurls her there, she leaves her self-will behind. No longer is her chief concern to dominate or be found properly dressed or be right—still less to survive. The will she now obeys is the will of God, which comes to her in a bleak, hostile environment through the needs of another person. In this case, the person is her executioner, which makes her consent to put her interests aside all the more amazing. She seeks the good of The Misfit by trying to assuage his torment so that he can be saved. She urges him to "'Pray, pray'" (*CW* 149). As we can see, and the killer can feel, there is already at work the prayer of her body offered in The Misfit's behalf lying at his feet. The grandmother has given herself up totally to God's will.

In abandoning her self-will, the grandmother illustrates the goal of desert life by living out one of its basic tenets. Abba Anthony states the means and the aim when he urges: "Renounce this life, so that you may be alive to God" (*Sayings*, Anthony the Great 33 [8]). Awareness of the divine presence is a useful way of understanding the nature of grace in O'Connor's characters; and in her fiction, as in the Gospel world and the late-antique desert, this gift of experiencing the divine invariably makes life more burdensome. With the grandmother, intimacy with God brings annihilation. In the battle against The Misfit's external will, she loses; but in the battle of the deep will, she triumphs. Her banality, her incomprehension, does not matter; her deep will is given completely to the call of charity, and that is enough.

Without The Misfit, whose suffering penetrates the grandmother's depths, she could not claim victory. In terrorizing her, The Misfit frees the old lady from herself, from the demonic deceptions about her virtue that have prevented her from being a good woman. He forces her to hit bottom. She has nowhere to go or anyone to push around or turn to. Moreover, there is no indication that she could or should escape this helplessness by returning to the social distractions that she made so much of or by returning to her self-will that got the family into this predicament in the first place. Quite the contrary, she sees that there is no escape from the desert except in God, who—in this dreadful way, more dreadful than ever expected—comes to the old lady. Her conscious effort to give The Misfit a place in her heart is also more astounding and noble than ever expected. Only O'Connor and a desert mother or father could have imagined the fruit of such obedience. "O obedience, mother of all virtues!" exclaims Abba Rufus, "O obedience, discloser of the kingdom!" (*Sayings*, Rufus 2 [211]). Obedience mothers the grandmother into revealing the kingdom.

O'Connor has consistently held that her sojourners must learn to be alone and that they must go (and be forced to do so) to the desert to learn the importance and duties of the interior life. For the grandmother, it takes getting lost on the red, dusty road to set her on the path to awareness. Then dread introduces the confused, lonely old woman to solitude. Solitude in the face of death, in solidarity with another, and in the company of God's love introduces her to freedom. Her freedom in the red-dirt desert introduces the reader to O'Connor's lesson of prayer of the body in silence. Freedom is the lesson to be drawn. O'Connor's way of bringing her heroine to this liberty is to make obedience and love really learned in the moment when obedience becomes impossible and the heart might turn to stone and does not. In the end, we should see much more in the grandmother than a terrorized victim; for she participates in God's call in so far as she extends herself to The Misfit in simplicity and humility. God is content with her good will.

The call in "The Artificial Nigger" brings the antidote of ascesis close to other social evils of our time. Deemed by O'Connor as "my favorite and probably the best thing I'll ever write" (*HB* 209), the story concerns racism, which she called "the tragedy of the South" (*HB* 101). The very title, "The Artificial Nigger," offends many readers, as does O'Connor's casual use of "nigger" in her letters. The debate over O'Connor's presentation of racism gathers heat from her well-known refusal to meet James Baldwin in 1959 because it "would cause the greatest trouble and disturbance and disunion" in Georgia (*HB* 329). But there is a competing impulse in O'Connor. As her faith and social loyalties intertwine with her literary exploration, the subliminal drama of desert renunciation forces a radical conversion in "The Artificial Nigger" that bends the white hero's private will to conform to God's will for justice and equality. The times cried out for correction of abuses. "The Artificial Nigger" appeared in the Spring 1955 issue of the *Kenyon Review*. Eisenhower was the president. Conservatism was the ruling tone of life; liberal democracy was on the defensive. As death and destruction had been causes for celebration during the war, the subsequent momentum of mindless chauvinism made humiliation and personal vendetta occasions for national festivity. The arrogance and vulgar disregard for truth in the name of patriotism epitomized by Joseph McCarthy's chairing of the Committee on Un-

American Activities did not self-destruct until spring 1954. Nevertheless, the social change that accompanies every war was in the wind. America was, in fact, on the cusp of civil rights reform. The 1954 Supreme Court ruled in *Brown v. Board of Education* that separate was not equal and that schools must desegregate.

O'Connor's story enshrines this particular historical juncture: a moral atmosphere of smugness and unchallenged racism that nonetheless presages the urgent upheaval of the civil rights movement of the decades to come. "The Artificial Nigger" quietly brings us to this moment. Whereas the social activist would argue for change through the public anguish caused by bigotry, O'Connor the desert writer makes her case against racism through the turmoil in the characters' inner lives that causes discrimination. Ideology is deeply embedded in the action and comes to us as a felt reality, an attitude toward life rather than a set of political propositions—an interplay of signs, metaphors, and tropes that Clifford Geertz shows to be part of a cultural system (193–229). Viewed through this lens, O'Connor uses ideology to give her political drama spiritual vitality.

The story centers on the intergenerational rivalry between two white males: Nelson, age ten; and his grandfather, Mr. Head, age sixty. Child and grandfather have only each other; they are solitaries creating a male world of two set apart in the Georgia backwoods one and one-half hours by foot from a railroad junction lying some distance from Atlanta. Necessity unites them; isolation and competitiveness sustain them; feisty independence and social dislocation suit them. And they mean to keep things that way. They live in poverty but do not consider themselves poor, and their seclusion is a critique of society without their being conscious of protest. Their homespun Georgia relationship unfolds along ancient lines. O'Connor engrafts onto their connection through blood the spiritual bond linking moral teacher and disciple. Mr. Head's eyes hold the look of wisdom that aligns him with "the great guides of men." This country sage might be none less than "Vergil summoned in the middle of the night to go to Dante, or better, Raphael, awakened by a blast of God's light to fly to the side of Tobias" (*CW* 210). By virtue of Mr. Head's doubly exalted status, Nelson lives under two rigorous disciplines. Medieval Tuscan patriotism and ancient piety superimpose great moral authority on the power Mr. Head holds over the child as father-protector and mother-comforter. The cumulative effect of these obediential forces recreates the primitive desert relationship between spiritual father (abba) and disciple. Like the ancient desert abba, Mr. Head assumes the task of being father to the son that he begets in God.

Because Mr. Head is O'Connor's first developed example of the abba, this is a good place to provide a few words about the elder's place in the desert adventure that this study has been exploring. To put it most plainly, the abbas or ammas preserved the desert way of life in their personal experience. They were not theologians, tutors, counselors, therapists, or even spiritual directors (as currently understood). The ancient fathers and mothers were simple, unlettered, prayerful persons of few words. They spoke in response to this remembered phrase: "Speak a word, Father." What was collected composes the *Sayings*. The various sayings were spare and practical. Their point was not to enlighten or to make the disciple feel good but to nurture the younger person in the life of Jesus. As with Jesus, the elders engendered new life most successfully by living out the words they spoke. Their lives were their words enfleshed. The *Sayings* preserves what the elders said; the *Lives* presents their achievements. Neither fidelity to a rule nor prescribed roles established their place. The sign of their success was humility. The elders' distinct charism was manifested indirectly, shyly, in the psychological effect on the aspiring solitary or curious visitor. The abbas and ammas had little; yet one of their hallmarks was their sumptuous generosity in responding to the authentic spiritual needs of others.

Abba Isaiah speaks for the entire desert experience when he advises those wanting to make a good beginning to put "themselves under the direction of the holy Fathers" (*Sayings*, Isaiah 2 [69]). The elders' authority was a function of holiness, and what conferred holiness came from taking on "all the commandments of God" (*Sayings*, Psenthaisius 1 [245]). At a time when harsh Roman law regulated a highly stratified society, the desert-dwellers were professedly egalitarian, even anarchistic. Holy persons became the laws of God alive and therefore were challenges to imperial claims of supremacy. As the elder lived in submission to divine will, so the searching disciple heeded the abba's example. By exemplifying the commandments, the abba or amma became, to repeat the splendid phrase previously applied to the grandmother, the "discloser of the kingdom" (*Sayings*, Rufus 2 [211]), which sums up O'Connor's adaptation of the elder. The infinite complexity of the human personality meant that the elders brought the kingdom into view through unpredictable means. Beneath the historical glow of perfection, the abbas were altogether human; and since the human will be human, even the elders' flaws can reveal the way to God to the postulant. Such a defect appears in a saying by a monk who lived in Scetis. The abba tells of a certain curmudgeonly old hermit who had a virtuous disciple. For an unstated reason, the elder drove the young man outdoors. When the abba opened the door, he saw the young brother still sitting there, and the abba repented, saying: "O Father, the humility of your patience has overcome my narrowmindedness. Come inside and from now on you are the old man and the father, and I am the younger and the disciple" (*Sayings*, An Abba of Rome 2 [210]).

"The Artificial Nigger" presents a modern analogue of the late-antique story of reversed discipleship. In so doing, O'Connor squarely places the moral lesson on a level of anguish appropriate to our bigoted time. She darkens the elder's limited mind into Mr. Head's unquestioned racism and sharpens abbatical rejection into paternal betrayal. Because the innocent obedience of the ancient disciple is beyond O'Connor's stern view of youthful nature, she replaces unflagging patience with determined pride and fear of abandonment in her young figure. The insularity of the ancient relationship thus remains. So too does O'Connor preserve the self-scrutiny that brings about obedience. As in the saying, repentance levels difference in age and moral training. O'Connor's grandfather becomes "like an ancient child" and her boy seems "like a miniature old man" (*CW* 230). Then touching the deepest matrix of desert asceticism, that of atoning for Adam's sin, "The Artificial Nigger" ends with an evocation of Eden. The old man accepts his faults along with the boy's forgiveness. The acknowledgment discloses the kingdom as gerontic child and fledgling elder stand ready "to enter Paradise" (*CW* 231).

The action begins in a homestead too remote even to have a name, moves through "a black strange place" (*CW* 228) called Atlanta, and returns to the backwoods. The movement updates a geographical conflict that was at the heart of the desert flight. In patristic times, the desert stood in opposition to settled land or the city. The counterposition was both spatial and moral (Chitty 1–5). The *Sayings* and the *Lives* convey a strong dissatisfaction with the inhabited land; yet the early hermits did not regard the city as evil but rather embraced the desert as a more conducive locale from which to seek God. Popular reflection over time, however, polarized the regions. The desert was exalted, its harshness spiritualized, so that it stood for the pure and holy fortress against the world. The city, epitomizing worldly desire, was devalued into the evil district. Although this later romantic dichotomy shades the urban topography in O'Connor's fiction, her desert/wilderness preserves its ancient ambivalence. It is the territory that witnesses satanic victory and defeat. Whenever her characters force their personal will on people and nature, the deserted place becomes the ground of hair-raising brutality. Whenever her characters renounce the selfish claims of the private will, the lonely spot offers the possibility of atonement and intimacy with God.

In O'Connor's scheme, the city is a desert of confusion that drives her protagonists back to the hermitage. This view of the city is rooted in O'Connor's personal experience, most notably her loneliness in New York and during her later medical visits and hospital confinements in Atlanta. O'Connor had no stomach for New York; and southern cities were no more palatable. "The only time I enjoy Atlanta," she wrote to "A" on 17 November 1956, "is when I'm leaving it" (*CW* 1006). The country whites in "The Artificial Nigger" encounter the worst forces behind O'Connor's associations. In one day in one southern capital, Mr. Head and Nelson put up with the vicious circling of Dante's hell, intensified by the trials of Israel's wilderness, all brought to felt life through the demonic attacks sustained in the fourth-century desert. Battered and diminished, the pair also feels O'Connor's sense of release. On leaving Atlanta, they rejoice. Joy, however, was not in their plans. Grandfather and child expect little pleasure and merely hope to avoid pain in Atlanta. At most, the city could gratify Mr. Head's ego and teach Nelson not to boast about being born in Atlanta. In the struggle of self-asserting youth against tough old age, Atlanta is a phantom locale founded on the will's tenacious desire to prove itself right. As their battle intensifies, the cityscape waxes into a demonic projection of both protagonists' pride. By displacing their rivalry on to Atlanta, they turn the city into a desert—indeed, a second and third desert—for the two must travel from the desert that is their refuge and home to the stranger and deeper desert of Atlanta that is their dark inner reality.

At heart, Mr. Head and Nelson love each other, but their terror of Atlanta masks their bond. Mr. Head tries to overcome his natural fear of the city by relying on his "will and strong character" (*CW* 210). Nelson, in his pride, wants to best his grandfather any way he can, even by rising to cook breakfast before Mr. Head awakens at 3:30 A.M. It is a small advantage but threatening enough to Mr. Head that he fights back with one of his fiercest demons. Just in case the child thinks that he can retain the upper hand during the trip, Mr. Head puts Nelson down by singling out Atlanta's most distasteful feature to ignorant whites: "'It'll be full of niggers'" (*CW* 212). Racism is the old man's demonic weapon in disciplining Nelson, who has never seen a black person. Twelve years earlier, Mr. Head and other benighted whites had run blacks out of their county. "Nigger" is now a curse in search of a reality to confirm its menace. By reiterating the malediction, Mr. Head spins "webs of significance," as Clifford Geertz defines cultural habits of mind (5), that the old southerner misconceives as the network created by God.

Mr. Head not only demonizes blacks; he also brings the boy and the entire journey under the influence of his demons. From the beginning, the story's atmosphere comes to the reader charged with the self-doubt stalking Mr. Head. The most ordinary things loom with threats to his status. The two arrive at 5:30 A.M. for the 5:45 train and are fearful that it will not find them worth picking up. The ghost train arrives out of the woods and into Mr. Head's head, where the old man reels in all the people and places encountered on the trip. The conductor approaches with "the face of an ancient bloated bulldog" that combines the monstrous Minos that guards the entrance to Dante's hell (canto 5) with the gruesome Cerberus that blocks Dante's progress (canto 6). Sneaking up from behind, the conductor "growled, 'Tickets.'" Under the sway of the old man's demons, phantoms ride this train to Atlanta. A "pale ghost-like face scowling" from the window looks back at Nelson (*CW* 214). Across the aisle, a bleary man with "heavy purple circles under his eyes" has just the right grimace to be pulled into Mr. Head's psychodrama as an eerie conspirator to degrade Nelson. Speaking through the boy to the dim passenger, the punishing demon in Mr. Head says of his grandson: "'Ignorant as the day he was born, but I mean for him to get his fill once and for all'" (*CW* 215).

The chance to expose Nelson's naïveté arises as "a huge coffee-colored man" (*CW* 215) escorts two black women through the segregated coach on their way to the dining car. "'What was that?'" Mr. Head quizzes Nelson, who replies with a moral freshness that vanishes in a flash: "'A man.'" Glee fills Mr. Head. With one stroke, the master—an old, slight, 110-pound redneck—can show up his pupil and alleviate his sense of puniness by putting down the imposing, heavyset black man who confidently bears his worldliness. "'That was a nigger,'" proclaims Mr. Head with pathetic oracularity. Crestfallen, Nelson resorts to unavailing visual exactitude to defend himself. "'You said they were black,' he said in an angry voice" (*CW* 216); but self-affirmation and parental acceptance lie not in empirical neutrality but in the child's adaptation to public prejudice. Nelson's newly confirmed racism finds quick release in visual violence.

The human inclination to put oneself first is a diabolical trap. The desert solitaries knew the peril and fought it vigorously. The *Sayings* is filled with warnings about pride, because pride not only replaces God with the self but also undoes the closest human ties: "And of what use is love where there is pride?" asks Abba Elias (*Sayings*, Elias 3 [71]). Centuries later, O'Connor answers by showing how Mr. Head's need to lift himself on the suffering of blacks imperils his longstanding love for Nelson. Once Mr. Head's prideful demon confers the delusion of superior social knowledge over Nelson, the old man cannot resist the temptation to lord his status over the child through the social solidarity created by racist perceptions and conduct. The old man is dangerous, if laughable. "'That's his first nigger'" (*CW* 216), Mr. Head pipes to the shadow across the aisle, as if the expert hunter has brought the tyro to catch his initiatory quarry. Deviousness, too, is a satanic gambit. Mr. Head's presumed alliance with the white stranger blinds Mr. Head to his personal guilt of corrupting a ten-year-old boy and stigmatizing all black people.

Demon arouses demon, and moral sight suffers the consequences. Nelson's initial blindness to color swiftly becomes blindness to evil. He finds in his grandfather's appeal to white male superiority a balm that moderates his aloneness. From now on, the lost backwoods child has a place in the larger social world that provides a black scapegoat to support his standing. The child's inner need summarily finds a corresponding psychological mechanism to answer it. Nelson displaces blame—his, his grandfather's, and society's—by believing that "the Negro had deliberately walked down the aisle in order to make a fool of him and he hated him with a fierce raw fresh hate" (*CW* 216). The boy's prideful demon awakens his wrathful demon. At age ten, Nelson has learned that he can prove his worth in his grandfather's world by despising black people. But the will to harm, as the desert solitaries knew by confronting their sinfulness, is futile. As Abba Poemen says, "wickedness"—actual or perceived—"does not do away with wickedness" (*Sayings*, Poemen 177 [191]). Rather, vengeful anger draws evil, weakening the ability to perceive clearly by enveloping the person in a vulnerability that John Cassian calls "the blindness of sin and the blackness of passion" (*Conferences* II, 2 [62]). Whereas modern culture celebrates anger as power, desert spirituality sees anger as weakness, a flaw to overcome. Anger alienates one from others and from God. For Abba Evagrius, anger was the "most fierce passion," operating with a corrosive intensity that can bring about emotional and bodily exhaustion and even generate hallucinations (11 [18]).

The startling chimera and the debilities that Evagrius warns against are the conditions that overtake the protagonists of "The Artificial Nigger." By the time Mr. Head uses the black passengers to humiliate Nelson, the demon of anger has been welcomed into his company as a guardian devil. The demon's directives build gradually with a few slurs to bolster Mr. Head's social ignorance. When a black waiter stops Mr. Head from inspecting the dining car, the old man snipes that people are kept out because the roaches would overrun the passengers. The angry demon is sly. Other travelers may laugh at Mr. Head's gaucherie; but Nelson, newly enfranchised in the old man's racist system of perceptions, takes "keen pride" in Mr. Head's foolish insult. The barrage of intimidating new circumstances leaves Nelson little choice. Mr. Head's denigrating wit is all that the child has to assuage his terror of being "entirely alone in the world if he were ever lost from his grandfather." But they are already lost. Anger stirs Nelson's fear of abandonment. Having strayed from their love for each other, they will soon lose their bearings with each other in Atlanta. Sinister sounds and sights (Evagrius's hallucinatory signals) flicker. The black conductor "snarled" (*CW* 218) the first of two Atlanta stops. Then, around the terminal, the confusion of silver tracks under an eerie rose-gray sky marks a forbidding entrance. Atlanta emerges from the grim artistic domain O'Connor discovered as her own. On reading her own fiction, she found that her "subject in fiction is the action of grace in territory held largely by the devil" (*MM* 118). As the cartographer of Satan's bailiwick in "The Artificial Nigger," O'Connor is precise and poetic, current and anagogical. Behind modern Atlanta, deepening it at every point, O'Connor layers Hawthorne's haunted forest, Dante's inferno, Augustine's Carthage, and the biblical wilderness.

The geography summing up these locales is the lonely expanse inhabited by the desert questers. With their forebears, Mr. Head and Nelson enter the underworld of their inner demons. Here they will come, like Abba Poemen, to recognize about themselves: "I am thrown into the place where Satan is thrown" (*Sayings*, Poemen 171 [190]). Dislocation puts Mr. Head and Nelson in the grip of the adversary who "accompanies anger" (*Sayings*, Pityrion 1 [200]). The demon mocks Mr. Head with self-misgiving and taunts Nelson with possessive desires, yearnings immediately dashed as he stands mesmerized in front of every store window. Before the material array that betokens urban prestige, Nelson, with futile claim to all that he cannot have, blurts: "'I was born here!'" Mr. Head takes the bait. He brings the child to a sewer entrance and pushes the child's head into the drain. The angry man momentarily controls his fear of losing his way by detailing the deep, rat-infested, "endless pitchblack tunnels" that suck people down into the nether parts of the world. Mr. Head's reinvented hell is the spiritual darkness being dug by his and Nelson's private wills. Each assertion of their wills plunges them deeper in pain. "'This is where I come from!'" crows defiant Nelson. Mr. Head stiffens and utters his ritual jeer: "'You'll get your fill'" (*CW* 220). Their guardian devil obliges them both by sending them to the left (*sinistra*) in Dante's own sinister direction so that they get progressively lost. Their aimless wandering now entails a swerving from common sense as well as from love.

The large black population of Atlanta provides easy targets at which the two embattled country whites can discharge their self-blinding sorties. Nelson, a quick learner, can render the otherwise incomprehensible social context of a poor black neighborhood meaningful by repeating the code words: "'Niggers live in these houses'" (*CW* 221). The child's motive is merely to gain his grandfather's approval, but the phatic language of group solidarity deepens Nelson's racism. Black city-dwellers whirl around O'Connor's wanderers with the force of assaulting moral distortions born of their ire toward each other and their fear of the city. Through their dread, O'Connor gives us the mindscape of ambush. The neighborhood jumps with skulking dissuasions: "Black eyes in black faces were watching them from every direction" (*CW* 221). Through a ten-year-old's spiritual turmoil, O'Connor shows what ideology first feels like and how it develops. The child's racist demon proves emotionally and socially useful when Nelson feels most lost and angry in that he can disguise self-doubt through kinship with his grandfather's world.

The very newness of Nelson's racism, however, leaves room for honest feeling. There is a place in Nelson's heart that remains unafraid, open to others; and O'Connor indicates the child's moral freshness by having his fear of blacks cohere with an attraction to them. The first lure comes from a large black woman wearing a pink dress over her shapely body. She leans in a doorway barefooted. Her hair sprouts "straight out from her head" (*CW* 222), radiating Medusa's enamoring power. She combines fearsomeness with beauty, sexuality with extinction, and hauteur with engulfment. She astounds Nelson, who feels a new excitement in her sparkling black flesh that gets him helplessly lost in her sinews and fluids as he suckles at this terrifying, mammary presence: "His eyes traveled up from her great knees to her forehead and then made a triangular path from the glistening sweat on her neck down and across her tremendous bosom and over her bare arm back to where her fingers lay hidden in her hair. . . . He felt as if he were reeling down through a pitchblack tunnel" (*CW* 223). Nelson takes a free fall into a transfixing sexual mystery that leads to spiritual revelation.

The child encounters the beautiful black woman because he and Mr. Head are lost. She then not only directs Nelson to the train station; she redirects the boy through his swoon to a strange depot in himself. In an unpublished manuscript, O'Connor linked the black American in southern writing to "our darker selves, our shadow side" (qtd. in Asals 86); and that underworld is the inner zone to which the woman dispatches the countrymen. Frederick Asals gets to the heart of Nelson's encountering black people when he says that the white child meets his "dark unacknowledged self" (Asals 87). Grappling with one's inner darkness goes to the core of eremitic pursuit. Racism is one historic evil, O'Connor argues, that American culture might overcome by heeding the desert teachers' calls to self-scrutiny. Solitude forces the habit of looking inward and relying on love and God for survival rather than on prejudice for enfranchisement. Beneath the shadowed self that fabricates lies of its superiority, Thomas Merton saw the true self that tries to break free of spiritual and political shackles to find God; and in Merton's anguished writings about racial and military evil in American life, he suggests that desert life could cast off those dark forces and bring us to "our inalienable spiritual liberty and use it to build, on earth, the Kingdom of God" (*Wisdom,* "Introduction" 24).

O'Connor's goal is precisely to give her characters a desire to enter, through social justice, a liberating relationship with God. Her theology is not a stiff tradition but a vibrant reality, one that resonates in our daily habits. "The Artificial Nigger" thrusts her rural solitaries into the alien desert that exposes man and child to the angry pride that dissembles itself through racism. Put another way, by experiencing the racist agony created by the false self, Mr. Head and Nelson are forced to find the interior place that will not be lied to, the heart's true center lying just beyond the horizon of the cruel desert. Although a sudden external encounter can force a confrontation with one's dark self, to be sustained, as the hermits learned, raw exposure to harsh truth demands persistent renunciation of the private will. "The Artificial Nigger" delivers the heroes to this exacting discipline. As with all those whom O'Connor favors with a new spiritual awareness, Nelson has no idea what hits him upon facing the black woman. Tender age, orphancy, and erotic awakening have something to do with the child's receptivity but cannot fully account for his arousal. Only an interior power could explain Nelson's being dumbstruck by the woman; and in the O'Connor world, we see effects long before we have even a glimpse of their cause. The narrator describes Nelson as "burning with shame" (*CW* 223), a special fire O'Connor uses, most strikingly at the end of *The Violent Bear It Away,* to indicate a consuming change effected by self-judgment. Neither of Nelson's two fears—ridicule from black children or physical terror of black men—materializes. Rather, the child's own "sneering ghost" (*CW* 223), first seen in the train window, nabs him. The dark woman has somehow sounded the dark of his heart. The narrator does not tell us what Nelson touches in himself but, with a simple hand clasp, shows that the willful boy who was bent on flouting independence tacitly admits his insufficiency. In a rare gesture of dependency, quietly foreboding, Nelson takes his grandfather's hand to follow the commanding woman's directions to the streetcar.

Although the pilgrims reach the streetcar, they do not board it. The

bane of urban pandemonium prevents Mr. Head from yielding what little control he feels to the ominous "long yellow rattling trolley" (*CW* 223)
coiling toward them. Instead, the countryman follows his own will,
which is the road map to disaster. His decision eventually gets them lost
again. Until the decisive moment of recognizing the dangers of his will,
Mr. Head holds the upper hand, an imaginary position from which he
cannot resist berating Nelson for "'grinning like a chim-pan-zee while a
nigger woman'" tells him where to go (*CW* 224). The burning rebukes
and counterrebukes, along with the heat of the pavement, wear Nelson
down. Both of their bodies, in fact, show signs of grappling with their fiery,
demonic passions as they wander. They weaken, and their bodies become
instruments of instruction for their proud souls as Atlanta resembles less
the modern city and more the ancient desert. The sweltering heat, the
long trek, the energy dissipated in vain quarrels to gain power, all exact
a somatic fatigue that can penetrate down into the resistant crannies of
the unbending will to chasten it. Forgetfulness contributes to their unintended ascesis. Having left their packed lunch on the train, Mr. Head
and Nelson inadvertently turn their sojourn through parching Atlanta
into a fast that will discipline their appetites.

The sharpest confrontation with evil in the stifling urban desert
comes when the prideful demon, as Abba Evagrius warned, concocts in
Mr. Head's mind a mirage of Nelson as newly impudent after dozing.
Silently, the old man distances himself from this imagined affront and
walks twenty feet down an alley where, from a garbage can, he keeps an
eye on Nelson. The malevolent spirits of the desert stir. First they invade
the child's fitful nodding as "vague noises and black forms" swell up
"from some dark part of him into the light" (*CW* 225), and then they seize
Mr. Head. Haunted by fear of missing the 6:00 P.M. train, though it is only
2:00 P.M., Mr. Head kicks the garbage can to awaken Nelson. In a flash,
obscure noises and dim forms seem to reify Nelson's daymare, and the
possessed child dashes wildly down the street and knocks down an elderly
white woman.

We are still in a halcyon time of American life when such adolescent
behavior would evoke guilt. Enraged, a crowd of white women gather "to
see justice done," shouting and plucking at Nelson's shoulder. Caught
between responsibility for the accident and fear of city police, Mr. Head
creeps toward the mayhem, where the women might "dive" on Nelson
and "tear him to pieces" (*CW* 226). These white furies stun Mr. Head.
Their demand for retribution articulates the unacknowledged, punishing
self in the old man, the part that is hell-bent on breaking Nelson's obsti-
nacy once and for all. When the injured woman shouts for the police,

Nelson, seeing Mr. Head, runs and clings to him for protection; but the demon of fear has a tighter grip on the old man's heart, and he denies knowing the child: "'This is not my boy,' he said. 'I never seen him before'" (*CW* 226). Dread born of pride, as Abba Elias foretold, can and here does destroy love. Presented with the chance to show his paternal loyalty, Mr. Head instead succumbs to the screaming demons binding his heart and refuses to acknowledge his own grandson.

The trap set by the prideful demon for Mr. Head was well known to and fought by the primitive hermits. When entangled in pride, Abba Anthony pleads: "What can get through from such snares?" A voice says to him: "Humility" (*Sayings*, Anthony the Great 7 [2]). The wisdom of the Egyptian desert seeps through the centuries to touch "The Artificial Nigger," where O'Connor vivifies in the bodies of Mr. Head and Nelson the word given to Anthony. Before Mr. Head's denial, both walked in the stiff-necked confidence set by their own will; but after the betrayal, they lumber, subdued by a greater will into bent figures of sagging meekness. The instant Mr. Head disowns Nelson, the child unlocks his tight hold on the old man's hips. The release affects Mr. Head as a loss of his own anatomical parts: "He felt Nelson's fingers fall out of his flesh." The whole body of their ten-year kinship is dismembered. The women can see in Mr. Head the face of evil and recoil from him in horror of his disclaiming his obvious flesh and blood. His behavior is so painfully dishonest that the crowd simply has to turn away. Reviled, unworthy, and exposed, Mr. Head enters "a hollow tunnel that had once been the street" (*CW* 226). When Nelson's fingers fall from the old man, they seem to take with them the backbone that Mr. Head failed to show. Now Mr. Head's shoulders sag; his neck hangs so far forward that it is invisible from behind. His glance backward catches Nelson's two small eyes, which spear the stricken man's back "like pitchfork prongs" (*CW* 227).

Nelson's stare of rejection feels like the devil's punishing instrument because it pays back Mr. Head for his previous vocal and visual stabs at black people. Retribution is painful yet purgative. The old man's demons pierce his muscles with a humiliation that cuts into his soul and resurfaces on his face, now scarred into "all hollows and bare ridges" (*CW* 227). The discipline of mortification, however, cuts deeper. He thirsts and offers water to Nelson, whose refusal sinks the forlorn man "into a black strange place" (*CW* 228). For several hours of the fading day, each moment freighted with feelings of abandonment, grandfather and grandson wander in trials of despair in Satan's own dark, where the wily enemy unfolds his charges in his crepe wings. The sun drops; the strangers enter a suburb of white mansions. Going from heat to cold externalizes the heroes' shift from familial warmth to frozen detachment. They experience the desert extremes of burning day and icy night: "Here everything was entirely deserted" (*CW* 228). Eyes lowered, not knowing where they are, Mr. Head and Nelson, under the spur of necessity, move into a sharper ascetic condition. A *kenosis*, or self-emptying, sets in (against their will, of course). They are helpless to close the distance between each other and to break the chains of prideful autonomy. But the sheer force of abandonment tears away the illusion that, on their own, Mr. Head and Nelson can find their way out of isolation and back to each other. When the old man feels Nelson's rejection, "he lost all hope" (*CW* 228).

It is not the rephrasing of Dante's inscription over hell's entrance, however, that expresses the predicament. The defining metaphor comes right out of John Cassian's *Conferences*, the seminal fourth-century interpretation of the Egyptian hermits. For Cassian, for Merton, and for O'Connor, humanity's drifting along by prejudice and cultural indoctrination leads to disaster. Cassian writes of "the wandering mind" seeking "a haven of peace after long shipwreck" in social oppression (*Conferences* X, 8 [131]). O'Connor knows the desperation and comes upon the same image. Mr. Head frantically waves to a passerby, calling, "'I'm lost!'" like "someone shipwrecked on a desert island." This rare nautical figure in the writing of the landlocked O'Connor bespeaks her fourth-century sensibility grappling with twentieth-century disasters. Only the stranded person can feel the need for rescue, and Mr. Head knows he is on the rocks. "'Oh Gawd I'm lost!'" he exclaims to a bald-headed stranger (*CW* 228). The monastics adrift in the trackless sands lived out the anxiety of needing guidance and found a simple solution. Frank acknowledgment of helplessness was a good start. It was the ground of the only prayer the hermits felt was essential. Nothing systematic or elaborate was required for prayer. Honest need and trust in God were enough because prayer (like ideology) was inseparable from everything one feels and says. "There is no need at all to make long discourses," says Abba Macarius; one needs only to say: "'Lord, help!'" (*Sayings*, Macarius 19 [131]). In Mr. Head's own time and from his inner, forsaken place swells up the great simple prayer of the desert. Drifting toward despair, Mr. Head repeats: "'Oh hep me Gawd I'm lost!'" (*CW* 228).

One of the many desert stories about finding the way bears on the ending of "The Artificial Nigger." In *Histories of the Monks of Upper Egypt*, Paphnutius tells of Isaac, who, roaming the dangerous desert, encounters Abba Aaron. Elderly Aaron is standing alone with a rope tied to a stone hanging from his neck, but the surprise for Isaac is not the millstone, which would astound a modern person. Abba Aaron asks the bewildered Isaac: "'Where are you going, my son, in this place?'" Isaac answers: "'Forgive me, my father, for I am lost.'" Aaron explains to the lost Isaac: "'Come, sit down, my son. Indeed, you are not lost; rather, you have found the good path'" (91 [117]). What captures Isaac unexpectedly is the elder's total welcome. The weary drifter finds the person who will give him rest.

The Egyptian story stresses two aspects of desert spirituality: the discovery of a master with whom the searcher can live in obedience and the power of admitting dependency to lead the lost person to a spiritual home. "The Artificial Nigger" recasts with finer precision both motifs of spiritual pursuit through the contemporary racial politics that expose the defects in Mr. Head's guidance. On the way to the train station, Mr. Head sees on a low brick fence the plaster figurine of a black servant eating watermelon. It is a lawn ornament meant to be cute in a rich neighborhood, pretending that slavery never happened. Through the decorative denial of historical anguish, O'Connor emphasizes the invisible millstone of racial subjugation that weighs down the South as conspicuously as the millstone of past sins hangs from Abba Aaron's neck—and she does so to the same redemptive end. The lawn ornament displays its defilement and calls for reparation. The statue has a chipped eye and sits bent over, about to topple from the crumbling putty in the wall. The burden on the black figure is, of course, the more than three-hundred years of being the despised other, the scapegoat. Like Isaac, Mr. Head and Nelson find the guide they did not expect. With more than usual pathos, Mr. Head breathes: "'An artificial nigger!'" (*CW* 229). The term "artificial" underscores O'Connor's political argument about racial ideology. The fake grotesquery of the watermelon-eating figure epitomizes Mr. Head's viewpoint and his cartoonish way of expressing it. The "artificial nigger" on the manicured lawn further points up the moral fakery in the racial ideology that sustains white solidarity and displaces class tensions. But the racist symbols are being challenged by O'Connor and history; the crumbling statue accordingly captures George Wallace's South at the moment of its own half-conscious awareness of change.

Mr. Head's exclamation—"'An artificial nigger!'"—is a jejune remark made to break the ice; and it works because grandfather and grandson want to reunite. That desire disposes them to the lessons depicted in the cheap, racist figurine. Its brokenness embodies both the ageless misery brought about by individuals who fail to see their inner capacity for evil and a culture that legitimizes the ensuing moral derangements. By mirroring the tilted posture of Mr. Head and Nelson, the effigy of suffering warns that assailants get back what they send out. Their collective physical abjectness, however, points the way out of bigotry. The statue bears the humility that calls Mr. Head and Nelson to atone and, more joyously, to be themselves bearers of humility. If pride brings the rural solitaries to the deep desert in themselves, then lowliness rescues them from its snares. Nelson's misery makes him eager to find a way back to his grandfather's protection; and so the boy, accepting the clumsy, breathy slur as an indirect apology, repeats: "'An artificial nigger!'" (*CW* 229). He then forgives Mr. Head for denying him. Like racism, compunction has a ripple effect. The ancient story of reversed discipleship expands to two would-be moral experts and their cultural legislators. The statue is the teacher that turns the tables. The child's forgiveness teaches the old man how to bear his treachery. In forgiving, the boy learns anew how to love. Man, child, and black statue become one. In that union, the "artificial" African American has a healing effect on those who maltreat black people. This lawn image of oppression emblematizes the victory of humility—the highest moral ground even in political struggles—in which the proud, white protagonists feel "an action of mercy" (*CW* 230) dissolving their differences. Mercy acts as a fiery ascesis. Old man and boy are burned free of personal and cultural supports so that they may be dependent on God.

Divine mercy brings the Atlanta trip to an end with the unpredictable whirl of a mighty desert wind—not fast enough for the homesick journeyers but too sweepingly for many readers. Like Catullus, the ancient Roman poet preparing to return home after a painful absence, Mr. Head and Nelson are afflicted with happy feet (*laeti pedes*). They summarily catch the 6:00 P.M. train, reach the tree-marked junction, and step into a moonlit garden that feels like a sacred space holding the deepest spiritual welcome. Found culpable of betrayal and racism by his own conscience, the old man goes from the junction garden to the Garden where he identifies with Adam's sin and stands "appalled" at "his true depravity" (*CW* 231). Solitude in the desert teaches Mr. Head things about himself that he would rather not know. Having learned about his hidden evil, he is open to contrition. With O'Connor's quiet touch of theological feminism, she gives her bereft old man the great female gift of divine mother-love, mercy, used here in the Hebrew meaning of *rahamim*, a mother's unconditional attachment to her helpless children (Psalm 103:13). The climactic sentence proceeds: "He saw that no sin was too monstrous for him to claim as his own, and since God loved in proportion as He forgave, he felt ready at that instant to enter Paradise" (*CW* 231).

The voice here is not Mr. Head's; it is that of the narrator rendering the hero's recognition that the only limit to God's mercy is the hardness of the human heart. The elevated language is at odds with the rhetorical capacity of the plainspoken hick, and this dissonance has sparked a debate over how the narrator's exhilaration fulfills the dramatic action. Many readers find the ending to be a lyrical ventriloquism that distorts the issues raised by the events themselves in favor of O'Connor's homiletic enthusiasm. Some complain that sexual tensions are brushed aside; many are irritated by the narrator's shift from the political to the eschatological resolution of racism. Finally, readers have even questioned the authenticity of Mr. Head's religious experience. Marshall Bruce Gentry has charted the lines of the dispute for us and has proposed that both Mr. Head and Nelson, by virtue of their religious ideals, will go beyond the narrator's disengagement from the world to have their insights retested (*Religion* 85–87); and the racist language of Nelson's last words suggests that Gentry is right.

The controversy will not go away. Indeed, it goes with reading Flannery O'Connor, whether one's convictions are humanistic or postmodern. In "The Artificial Nigger" and all her fictions, O'Connor approaches sexual desire and political relations only to turn her back on those insistent urgencies in favor of the spiritual implications they raise. O'Connor either could not or would not pursue the sexual and political dimension of her stories to the satisfaction of contemporary readers, whose predilections for material resonances are simply not O'Connor's. Ideology comes to us through the characters' habits of living. This mediation of politics through spiritual life defines O'Connor's strength and her poetics of solitude. Her habit of art is to sweep the human body and social relations up into the vastness of salvation history, into the Paradise that Mr. Head feels ready to enter.

Readers familiar with patristic writings will have no problem with this absorption of erotic and racial emotions into the hope of regaining Paradise. Far from being at odds with the Atlanta journey, Mr. Head's transition from the railroad junction to the Garden of Adam's sin and then to the redeemed Eden is in perfect keeping with the story of desert search. O'Connor's ending revives for the modern age the motive recorded in the ancient *Sayings* and *Lives*. The sharpest conflict of the desert solitary was not so much a battle with sexuality or political rights as it was with disciplining the will. The earliest desert-dwellers saw their asceticism as a way to recover the innocence of Adam and Eve and then to earn the glory purchased by the new Adam. An elder known for his power over snakes pointed to the original intimacy that Adam knew with God as the source of his power: "If someone has obtained purity, everything is in submission to him, as it was to Adam, when he was in Paradise before he transgressed the commandment" (*Sayings*, Paul 1 [204]). The belief in late antiquity was that the first sin was an act of voracious greed rather than one of sex, and so the ascetic's fasting and renunciations were to undo in part the fatal sin of our first parents.

O'Connor remands Mr. Head to wander "into a black strange place" where "everything was entirely deserted" (*CW* 228) and to undergo the ascetic experience that she sees as a corrective to the racism and pride contributing to the violence of our time. The daylong struggle—in the physical desert of Atlanta and in the inner waste of anguish—rekindles something of Abba Paul's power over snakes; for as Mr. Head and Nelson compose themselves at the junction, the Atlanta train "disappeared like a frightened serpent into the woods" (*CW* 231). O'Connor leaves the wayfarers ready to go back home. Renewal of their love for each other and their covenant with God, so painfully breached in the city, is presented, just as in Scripture, in terms of a return to the desert, their backwoods hermitage.

"The Artificial Nigger" ends with a palimpsest. Within the representation of 1950s racism, O'Connor inscribes a timeless spiritual tableau. The chastened protagonists stand poised inside a living refuge, a place of the empowering Spirit, where every thought, every emotion, becomes a humble offering that can completely topple the bigotry supporting the plaster figure of the black American, which is already pitched forward toward collapse. By bringing the still unfamiliar voice of the fourth-century solitaries into twentieth-century fiction, O'Connor dramatizes a way to strike blows against our political demons. In an echoic voice, drawn from the intimate desert of her own personality, O'Connor has forged a worthy artistic vessel for the modern era's painful social history. After the shaking of their moral foundations in Atlanta, Mr. Head and Nelson can no longer live merely as social dissenters in the backwoods but must struggle as affirmers of the Spirit forging a deeper connection with God.

"The Displaced Person," published in 1954, illustrates most directly O'Connor's proposing desert ascesis to counteract the political evils besetting the modern world. The story concerns the aftermath of World War II, which was the watershed that redirected the flow of American life from its local tributaries to international rapids. The change was especially difficult for the South. Moored as the region had been to a past securing its stratified social order, southern consciousness resisted the preponderant currents from the larger world. But the tides were too powerful for its ardent defenses. In a 1987 essay, Leonard Olschner outlines the court battles and global conflicts that reach all the way into middle Georgia to play out their fatal effects in "The Displaced Person." Olschner cites the enactment of civil rights legislation, the northern migration of blacks, the shift in the southern white population, higher prices for farm products, a corresponding increase in land prices, and the Displaced Persons Act of 1948, which opened the United States to 400,000 refugees over four years. Olschner contends that these influences and longstanding provincial fears, especially the anxiety over the influx of strangers and the concern that Catholic Rome might take over the country, contribute to the "eruptive violence" (72) marking "The Displaced Person."

Jon Lance Bacon uses this historical background to deepen our grasp of the politics of O'Connor's art in "The Displaced Person." Bacon sees cold war animosities breaking in on O'Connor's "pastoral setting" to threaten the South's confidence in the tried and true "American way" (87). Unlike the South at large, of which she is a loyal daughter, O'Connor as artist goes against the grain of her compatriots' trust in the status quo. In face of these challenges, O'Connor was, in the language of the left that Bacon applies to a writer seemingly of the right, "an advocate of cultural resistance" (139) against the cold warriors and xenophobes who held sway in America. O'Connor, Bacon concludes, saw the need for reform and was open to foreigners and new ideas.

I wish to add certain details from religious history to these cultural insights to suggest that O'Connor's adaptation of the desert tradition furnished a spiritual position that supported her critique of the social and political consensus. To be sure, the planet was a killing field. From the German invasion of Poland on 1 September 1939 to the Japanese signing of an unconditional surrender on the battleship *Missouri* on 2 September 1945, over fifty million people were slaughtered. The earth was also awash in waves of castaways. Millions more were deported from their homes to serve as slave laborers or had fled from persecution and were, in the bland official language of the hour, "displaced persons." The modern technology of death, with its bombs and concentration camps, erased the boundary between bizarre fantasy and a sober grasp of statistics.

The hot war left a contradictory legacy as well. Out of murderous destruction came a resurgence of Christian asceticism. The response was summed up in the person of Thomas Merton. When Merton reflected in his autobiography *The Seven Storey Mountain* (1948) on coming of age during the mid-century, he perceived the darkness of the era in his personal predicament. He had become "the complete twentieth-century man." For Merton, a person such as he, who had assimilated the culture of egotism and savage aggression, was one who lived "on the doorsill of the Apocalypse, a man with veins full of poison, living in death." Citizenship in "my own disgusting century" meant alienation from God (*Storey* 85). To recover the connection with God that Merton saw as the fundamental bond of each person, he severed his social relations in December 1941 to became a Trappist monk in the Kentucky hills. He elected poverty, silence, solitude, and penance. It was a drastic reaction to an extreme crisis in human affairs. In its severity, Merton's stunning action spoke directly to the inner needs of the age. He changed the way many people lived. So strong was Merton's example that the renunciatory adventure quickened into something of a postwar romance, inviting other disquieted persons into the tantalizing immensity of eremitical solitude. Thousands followed Merton into the cloister; many more took up the ascetic spirit in their workaday lives. Another sign of America's coming of spiritual age was the arrival of the Carthusians, who established a Charterhouse in Whitingham, Vermont, in 1951, and later moved to a larger setting in Arlington, Vermont. The Charterhouse has historically been known as a "desert" where the monks live as hermits far removed from contact with the social world. The Carthusian way of life, founded in the eleventh century in France, is the closest in vitality, integrity, and rigor to the fourth-century practice in Egypt.

Now as in antiquity, asceticism expresses more than social distance. The logic of ascetic life, as we have seen, is the total opposite of the logic of the world. That contrast holds emotional appeal and political possibility to those who flee to the monastery and adjacent desert places of the mind. Obedience to the will of God could subvert the monopolies of power and violence. Whereas modern politics and culture are training grounds for hatred and death, solitude is a school "in which we learn from God how to be happy" (*Storey* 372). Such happiness consists of participation in God's selfless love and freedom. The desert teachers pioneered a way to that liberty. They withdrew from the world of despotic Rome to live among sandy wastes to find their true selves that could draw close to God. The means of gaining divine intimacy was through rigorous self-scrutiny. The pitfalls along with the victories experienced in this inner combat yielded insights that have been for centuries a rich source of spiritual renewal. To participate in this radical experiment, each age must discover and reinvent the solitary experience to negotiate the physical or psychological desert in which it finds itself. Merton strongly believed that "ours," the era of the wasteland, "is certainly a time for solitaries and for hermits" (*Wisdom*, "Introduction" 23) and that we should follow the solitaries of late antiquity. Their fearless striking out into the unknown landed them on the frontiers of their bodies and personalities;

there, through hardship and physical discipline, solitaries waged war against Satan. Merton enlisted us in that desert campaign. In so doing, he hoped that, trial by trial, surrendered will by surrendered will, modern solitaries could check the narcissism of our time that compels us to dominate and destroy others.

Flannery O'Connor judged the age as Merton did. "If you live today," O'Connor wrote on 28 August 1955, "you breathe in nihilism" (*HB* 97). Time and again she protested against "the Manichean spirit of the times" that "infected" (*MM* 33) our minds and devalued physical creation, and she despised the avarice that saw only personal profit in it. The toxic atmosphere of this "terrible world" created the "modern consciousness . . . Jung describes as unhistorical, solitary, and guilty" (*HB* 90). The violence pervading O'Connor's fiction registers her denunciation of the way we live now. Her writing and Merton's are resounding manifestos of religious dissent against the prevailing cult of brutality and materialism. At a time when America was saluting its global power in winning a morally just war, O'Connor turned her back on national triumphalism to follow the hermits' path to freedom through solitude. "The Displaced Person" takes up that ancient route by synthesizing the three desert calls observed by John Cassian in his *Conferences*. The preceding discussions showed how O'Connor reconfigured the calls from God and by way of another person. Cassian also describes the call from necessity; and "The Displaced Person" incorporates this directive (along with the other two) into its story of totalitarian evil unfolding on the home front with backbiting, racism, slow stares, and even a farming tractor that are every bit as lethal as the guns and tanks on European battlefields.

Whatever their nationality, Polish or American, whatever their race, black or white, and whether believer or nonbeliever, all the characters in "The Displaced Person" are summoned after the war to a struggling dairy farm in the Georgia countryside. The remote tract of land has touches of distinctive beauty, especially the elegant radiance of the peacock that struts along the red, rolling ground; but the farm is decaying. The seed of ruin has been planted by human inhabitants and lies deep in the soil. The deterioration can be seen over time in the diminishing presence of peafowl, once numbering thirty, then twenty, and, by the end of the story, down to a mere single peacock. O'Connor in a letter used the word "evil" (*HB* 118) to describe the powers working their wiles on the land and the people. On this sparsely settled stretch, the inhabitants' duty is to encounter the demonic forces set on destruction. The place, in sum, is the desert, beautiful and terrible as deserts everywhere are. The characters' struggle is the vocation of the desert.

The desert contest at root involves discernment and survival. These two skills are reciprocal because staying alive in the alien barrens depends on recognizing the powers intending harm. These habits are as hard to develop in the modern wasteland as they were in the late-antique desert. Then as now, the natural human bent is toward slothful indifference and self-interest in ignoring evil. In addition, there is in the air a national contentment over defeating the foreign enemies in the war and on their own ground. As a result, the stalwart Americans in "The Displaced Person" are slow or reluctant to admit the presence of evil on their native soil. Some are even willfully blind to evil—except, of course, to that of others. Having militarily conquered fascism, Americans can further separate themselves from evil. Evil is in Europe. Atrocities come no closer to home than do the frames of newsreels depicting tangled human body parts piled high. As Mr. Head in "The Artificial Nigger" blames blacks and Atlanta for his bigotry, his country cousins in "The Displaced Person" put responsibility for their greed and hatred not only on "'those shiftless niggers'" but also on the victims in a strange locale "'back over yonder where everything is still like they been used to'" (*CW* 290). "Yonder" pinpoints those wicked, unreformed, transatlantic nations and "their wars and butcherings," as though American guns and bombs left no carnage. Europe darkens in the local imagination until it becomes "the devil's experiment station" (*CW* 296).

Satan also has a testing ground in Georgia. His project at this substation is very shrewd in that it builds on postwar xenophobia. He gets people on the Georgia farm to feel about virtue and innocence as they ought to feel about evil and complicity. A sure sign that the demonic operation thrives is the pervasive denial of the devil's presence at the place. The owner, Mrs. McIntyre, and her workers have cultivated a keen sense of tumult in the outer political world but have little awareness of the shifting winds buffeting their society and especially their inner world. Victory in war makes these isolated farm people certain about who and where the enemy is, and they can readily identify virtue. In their world, a good person is easy to find; one simply looks in the mirror. Such egotistical confidence marks their moral subjugation, for the art of Satan's warfare is to give these provincials the illusion of virtuousness. Satan, in fine, traps O'Connor's good country people in self-love.

The snare of righteousness was keenly felt by the desert mothers and fathers, and they searched out ways to avoid the temptation. Their struggle centered on self-examination, the very habit O'Connor's farm people lack. Mrs. McIntyre and her workers are quick to spot who is loafing and who is dishonest. Fretting over the faults in others comforts them. The

ancient hermits, on the other hand, drew no such contentment from judging others. In fact, they were strong enough to leave their neighbors and
their neighbors' actions to God's mercy. The transgressions of others
alarmed the desert solitaries less than did their own personal laxity. Those
watching to see faults in others, it was taught, lose their capacity to see
their own shortcomings. There is the story of "a man who beats his servant because of a fault he has committed." In recounting the injustice,
the elder avoids the easy moralism of indicting the assailant in favor of
calling on the listener to take responsibility on oneself: "To bear your own
faults and not to pay attention to anyone else wondering whether they
are good or bad" (*Sayings*, Moses 7 [142]). Rigorous inner attention spared
one from the illusion of virtue, the devil's most seductive gambit. The
elders at every turn encouraged one another to scrutinize themselves.
This need fills the *Sayings* and *Lives*. The counsel frequently arises in
the exhortation: "Go, watch yourself" (*Sayings*, Ammoes 4 [31]). The
failure to examine inner desires causes far-reaching inner devastations
that can do great harm to others. In "The Displaced Person," the refusal
to look within causes the savage murder of an innocent foreigner.

"The Displaced Person" begins with a warning about inattention by
focusing on Mrs. Shortley. She, the wife of the white farmhand, sums up
the claustrophobic workings of self-delusion. The woman's final weeks
on the farm/desert record the life of a lonely, nomadic woman tormented by her demons. Although Mrs. Shortley has a husband and three children, she feels entirely alone in the world. Her shiftless husband,
Chancey, provides no economic security; her son is off preparing to found
a church; her two daughters are destined to remain dependent on her. All
this witlessness forces Mrs. Shortley to act as though she is strong and
self-sufficient; but deep down, she is a weary solitary with "an immense
weight to carry around" (*CW* 301). The millstone is not only her inept
family but also her fear of not having a place in the world. That anxiety
begets aggression. The first paragraph shows Mrs. Shortley ready to defend her recently gained stronghold on the McIntyre farm against the
newly arrived displaced persons from Europe. Her body is massive in girth
to support her burden and to protect her threatened turf and beleaguered
ego. As Mrs. Shortley, with protruding stomach and "grand self-confidence" (*CW* 285), mounts the hill toward her lookout prominence, she
manages to assume a place even in front of the peacock.

Gorged on fear and ignorance, Big Belly, as one black worker calls
Mrs. Shortley takes potshots at all who enter her range. Although she
laments the destruction caused by two world wars—into which, she says,
America was dragooned by corrupt foreign powers—Mrs. Shortley has

been spoiling for a fight all her life. The opportunity flares up when the Guizac family arrives from a refugee camp. The Guizacs are among the twelve million Poles dispersed when Russia took over their country during the cold war landgrab. In a way, one can understand part of Mrs. Shortley's fear because the Polish family's destitution starkly puts before her the insignificance that she most dreads. She sees not the family's vulnerability with its call to love; instead, she views their very presence as competition demanding destruction. To allay her anxiety, the demons of fear drive Mrs. Shortley to stigmatize the foreigners as "rats with typhoid fleas" that carry "all those murderous ways over the water with them directly to this place" (*CW* 287). Ousted from their homeland, the Guizacs are now deprived of their humanness. Understood as sources of pestilence, the intruders become to the frightened Mrs. Shortley satanic agents of an unreformed religion determined "to cause disputes, to uproot niggers, to plant the Whore of Babylon in the midst of the righteous!" (*CW* 301). The mastermind behind this fantasy cabal is the long-legged, insectile, old Catholic priest Father Flynn, who gathers peacock and turkey feathers when he visits to divert attention from the loot that Mrs. Shortley thinks he really intends to pick up on the place. On the fringe of this righteous community that Flynn, who is the devil's operative to Mrs. Shortley, aims to overturn are two black workers, Astor and Sulk. Although they see themselves as "'too low'" (*CW* 297) for anyone to bother with, these "'shiftless niggers,'" as Mrs. Shortley calls them, are suitable as foot soldiers in her jihad. She warns the black workers that "'ten million billion'" (*CW* 290) more aliens are preparing to turn out both blacks and whites from house and home. Mrs. Shortley's attacks on the innocent Guizacs are a printout of the prevailing cultural assumptions, all rooted in ignorance and developed by tightly involuted self-love, a shadow play of misled apocalypticism.

These gloomy theatrics are a mere curtain-raiser to the spectacular pyrotechnics looming up from the lower frequencies of Mrs. Shortley's disordered personality. Trapped in the desert of pride, the woman resents the economy and drive of Mr. Guizac, the refugee hired by Mrs. McIntyre. Mrs. Shortley sees in the man's reviving of the barely productive farm not industrious vitality but an attack on her survival. This fear of displacement is the passion that can overcome Mrs. Shortley; and Satan, as Abba Matoes says, "supplies nourishment to the passion which he sees the soul is slipping towards" (*Sayings*, Matoes 4 [143]). Everything feeds Big Belly's gluttonous imagination of displacement. When the peacock, a most unlikely contender for Mrs. Shortley's position, unfurls his tail, the bedeviled woman's "unseeing eyes" transform the king of birds' rings of green and gold and salmon-colored swirls into "an inner vision" swarming with billions of displaced people "pushing their way into new places over here" (*CW* 290–91). The hallucinations caused by one's demons, as Abba Evagrius warned, have seized Mrs. Shortley. On the heels of pride follow the demons of anger and sadness; and, "last of all," Evagrius says, "there comes in its train the greatest of maladies—derangement of mind, associated with wild ravings and hallucinations of whole multitudes of demons in the sky" (14 [20]). Thus, Mrs. Shortley's furies attack her.

Mrs. Shortley's ears are phantasmagorical—as is her inner vision. Words become events. Father Flynn's "rattling talk" with Mrs. McIntyre opens up into revelations of conspiracy to evict her and her family. Again, the rhythms and sounds of spoken Polish suddenly acquire the disclosive power of the refugees' seditious purpose. Mrs. Shortley has her own demonic hermeneutic of the spoken word. Words are living presences situating Mrs. Shortley in the midst of the historical battle between good and evil: "She saw the Polish words, dirty and all-knowing and unreformed, flinging mud on the clean English words until everything was equally dirty." The immense power of this war of words threatens to engulf Mrs. Shortley into the murderous horrors she saw in newsreels of European concentration camps. Here she is on the brink of self-generated extinction: "God save me! she cried silently, from the stinking power of Satan!" (*CW* 300). Her anguish is real, and the enemy is accurately named; but the source of that putrescence is misconstrued.

No ancient solitary felt the devil's attack more severely than does Mrs. Shortley. In their trials, the desert elders looked for help in Scripture, which, Burton-Christie explains, "provided guidance, understanding, and wisdom as well as strength and protection in the midst of this struggle" (193). The besieged Mrs. Shortley also turns to the Bible. Although her need is the same as that of the elders, her disposition undermines her effort to find aid. She does not want to receive the sacred word but to use it; she seeks not help from Scripture but confirmation of her power. Her instinct for vehemence in the face of cataclysm brings her to pay special attention to the prophets and the Apocalypse. She searches for ways that she—as one of the chosen strong—can guard against the invading destroyers. The desert mothers and fathers had a more humble, realistic sense of themselves as weak before the devil and sought in the sacred texts the strength that they lacked. Since Mrs. Shortley has already replaced God with herself as the liberator of blacks and whites, there is nothing she can receive from Scripture to mollify her anger; but there is much that she can select to justify her rage. To obey the biblical command to expose the wicked, she pushes the demonic fantasy of her prophetic calling by turning self-pity into the moral indictment of the priest and the strangers he brought over from Poland.

Mrs. Shortley's demons, trials, and scriptural obsession coalesce when she overhears that Mrs. McIntyre will fire Mr. Shortley; as a result of this, her family will be evicted from the place that has been their home for two years. In response, a panoply of biblical figures implodes in her imagination. Ezekiel's fiery wheels spin off human body parts from John of Patmos's shattering vision of the End. Prophetic voices reverberate out of legendary wildernesses. The cartoonish imbroglio captures Mrs. Shortley's wrestling with her demons. O'Connor is not so simplistic (nor were her desert teachers) as to equate demons merely with personifications of disturbing ideas and desires. The devil, for O'Connor, infiltrates our subtlest psychological engagements. Peter Brown's astute explanation in modern terms of the late-antique mind helps us understand O'Connor's presentation of the demonic in Mrs. Shortley. The demonic, to reiterate Brown's insight, "was sensed as an extension of the self. A relationship with the demons involved something more intimate than an attack from outside: to 'be tried by demons' meant passing through a stage in the growth of awareness of the lower frontiers of the personality. The demonic stood not merely for all that was hostile *to* man; the demons summed up all that was anomalous and incomplete *in* man" (*Making* 90). The inward bursting of Mrs. Shortley's self-imagined displacement and revelations sends her and her family on a trip. Rocking chairs, beds, mattresses, boxes, a cat, and people all get stuffed into a car topped with chicken crates. Before 4:00 A.M. in a drizzling rain, the clumsy "overfreighted leaking ark" (*CW* 304) sets sail to actual displacement—she to death and the others to the next leg of their exilic wandering.

The Shortleys' obscure journey follows a mysterious course known to the desert mothers and fathers. About the Shortleys and all who by necessity embark toward a strange country, Amma Syncletica says: "We sail on in darkness. The psalmist calls our life a sea and the sea is either full of rocks, or very rough, or else it is calm." How we negotiate the passage determines the outcome. Setting course by the "sun of justice" saves the sojourner in "tempest and darkness," whereas negligence sends one to the bottom (*Sayings*, Syncletica 25 [235]). Watchfulness and fair judgment, however, are not the magnetic poles of Mrs. Shortley's compass: "She had never given much thought to the devil for she felt that religion was essentially for those people who didn't have the brains to avoid evil without it" (*CW* 294). Brains she has. In the solitude of fear, she uses her mind to ruminate bitterness and foment discord with the new neighbors. She lives and dies by her wits. The result of her crafty acumen is that she goes out of her head. With deluded suspicion instead of common sense as the true north of her intelligence, her overloaded mind erupts. As the sun rises on the road not far from the McIntyre place, Mrs. Shortley suffers a stroke and dies convulsed in the chaos of her demons. In middle age, she dies a violent death, one portentously linked to her inner life.

The devil may succeed in pushing to extreme the fantasy that drives Mrs. Shortley's self-banishment, but all is not lost. Her struggle "to avoid evil" recommends Mrs. Shortley to O'Connor. In O'Connor's fiction of the desert, the anguish of the solitary counts; and that suffering can count on help. Abba Moses says that "if the soul gives itself all this hardship, God will have mercy on it" (*Sayings*, Moses 5 [142]). Trust in God's loyalty undergirds desert life: "He knows very well what we need and he shews us his mercy" (*Sayings*, Macarius 19 [131]). The haggard and lonely Mrs. Shortley needs to be rescued from final defeat. Help comes in the form of separation and ascesis. At the moment of death, she feels "displaced in the world from all that belonged to her." Her greatest attachments are not material—she is, in fact, poor—but are the dark cares and tensions that she clings to as a miser clings to money. Mrs. Shortley's deepest attachments are to thoughts of greed, anger, sloth, and pride. These are the anxieties that drive her to fight the wrong enemy in the right war. In the moment of being freed from her misdirected animosities, Mrs. Shortley enjoys "a great experience" that is dreadful and gentle, routing and enfranchising. She seems "to contemplate for the first time the tremendous frontiers of her true country" (*CW* 305). Delivered to the ramparts of freedom, the snoop becomes the woman of prayer. Amma Shortley survives despite herself. The exile makes it home.

Mrs. Shortley's roiling death brings the action to a high point (at which nearly all of O'Connor's stories usually end); but "The Displaced Person" goes beyond the paradigm. Instead of ending in a sudden death, this story traces a parabola with an ensuing downward curve. After Mrs. Shortley's stroke, there comes the murder of Mr. Guizac, which leaves an eerie quiet that then enshrouds the bodily disintegration of Mrs. McIntyre, which marks the entire farm's going to ruin. This montage of death brings the story to a repose that is very much at odds with the grim historical context out of which the conflicts arise. One expects something more destabilizing from the account of a Polish family's exodus that has its roots in Nazi carnage and ends in murder on an American farm. Rather than stunning us, O'Connor repositions the reader as a desert adventurer entering into the final desert of Mrs. McIntyre's slow dying.

Seen through this protracted focus on expatriation and loss, "The

Displaced Person" provides an exemplary vehicle for the desert teachers' primary teaching about life—namely, death. "Remember the day of your death," says Abba Evagrius. "See then what the death of your body will be . . . so as to be able to live always in the peace you have in view without weakening" (*Sayings*, Evagrius 1 [63]). A certain peacefulness, a balance forged in courage, comes from keeping death before one. Mortality for the desert-dwellers was by no means a morbid preoccupation. Mindfulness of death meant remembering the last judgment, which was for them a vivid reality that set everything true. Since they lived in the joy of hope, the end infused both compassion and endurance in the solitary. Losses that might have stirred excessive fear actually emboldened those who looked squarely at death, because they saw the vanity of the world and the limits of their human resources conquered in the kingdom of God. Death served as a reminder that earthly attachments captivate and dissolve, whereas freedom lies in God's power. The entire emotional tone of the primitive solitaries' struggles with evil and affliction acquired a gentleness that stood out against the rough desert and their severe renunciation. Rather than take on the harshness of their circumstances, the hermits developed an acute sensitivity to pain, to deprivation, to sorrow, and to others. So keen was their disposition that their sympathy could penetrate the heart to the point of causing tears. Patristic records testify that the hermits dared to enter the most vulnerable zones of feeling. Here in the dust of displacement were women and men who were not afraid of tenderness. Tenderness was something one gave to another as a gift in its most affecting form: the gift of *penthos*, the offering of godly tears.

In an undemanding way, "The Displaced Person" calls for such tenderness in that the action laments the modern neglect of this ancient habit of tears. O'Connor expresses the loss through the coldly calculated murder of Mr. Guizac. The Polish émigré's death is a ritual lynching that results from a temperament untouched by the pain and death it inflicts. The character responsible for the slaying of Mr. Guizac is Mr. Shortley. He is stupid and lazy in everything except bloodshed, for which he exhibits an innately efficient genius. His aptitude for killing was honed in a close call with death in war, proving that death can harden the heart as well as cut it to tears. By Mr. Shortley's account, he has experienced more than his share of death; and by his actions, the reader knows that he has gained no wisdom from his encounter with human mortality. Instead of allowing the threat of extinction to penetrate his emotions, Mr. Shortley wears death over his heart as a badge of courage. His logic has all the duplicity implied in his serpentine shadow that glides halfway into the sunlight, cunningly ready to strike in whatever direction serves his interest. On two occasions, he reminds Mrs. McIntyre that he faced death in the form of a German hand grenade that almost killed him in World War I. With ease, he brings this past war experience around to the target at hand. His mortal enemy was a small man with eyeglasses resembling the pair Mr. Guizac wears. Mr. Shortley presents himself as a living Purple Heart ready to cash in on the special considerations coming to a wounded veteran after risking "'my life and limb'" for his country. Self-excusing and vain as it is, Mr. Shortley's language is worth summoning up, for it reveals how the demonic voice replicates the seductive jingoism that passes for virtue in a culture that allows military violence to stand for courage: "'Gone over there and fought and bled and died and come back on over here and find out who's got my job—just exactly who I been fighting'" (*CW* 323). And there is no cutting through his desperate, interminable *and*s as they coordinate shibboleth and sentimentality, German and Pole, First World War and Second World War, assailant and victim, himself and deserving sufferer. *And* he recently endured the death of his wife, *and* he figures "'that Pole killed her'" (*CW* 318) and not the stroke.

Life may have put death before Mr. Shortley, but his self-love blinds him to any implication of human perishability except the desired death of Mr. Guizac that would satisfy Mr. Shortley's revenge. The consequence of his blindness is self-pity and, as the desert-dwellers warned, cowardice. The two-bit egotism and lack of discernment making up Mr. Shortley's character are common in O'Connor's fiction. What is rare in her writing until the last collection of stories is the prominence of tears. There are a few drops from Mrs. Flood's self-grief in *Wise Blood*, but these are not from true compunction. To distinguish between the syrupy weeping that manipulates by putting oneself first and the tears that pierce the heart by drawing one into the concerns of another, O'Connor presents Mr. Shortley as one of her few early characters to cry. Her portrait is devastating. When he reflects on his dead wife, his eyes squeeze out wetness to use her death to promote himself. Mr. Shortley's ooze is an egocentric film over his eyes. Not surprisingly, when death at Mr. Shortley's hand comes before him in the body of Mr. Guizac under the tractor, Mr. Shortley averts his gaze to seek the consolation of his personal will, which is his moral center. Mr. Shortley's refusal to keep death before his eyes lets the most savage prompting of his self-will rule him. To regain the dairy job, he schemes to kill Mr. Guizac, the conscientious foreigner who actually loses his life and limb in struggling for his family's survival. Mr. Shortley's angry demon distorts everything. He confounds what he thinks he deserves with what he is. He is a slave to evil passions. His demons

so control him that malice seeps from his will into his facial musculature. When he returns to the farm after his wife's death, "the hollows in
his long bitten blistered face were deeper than they had been a month ago"
(*CW* 318). The fiendish lines of satanic intent sharpen still more over the
weeks during which Mrs. McIntyre fails to fulfill her promise to fire Mr.
Guizac. Soon, Mr. Shortley's murderous resolve hews his entire body into
a death-dealing instrument, part slashing, part venomous, and entirely
darkened. He is malice made visible. Mrs. McIntyre sees at the end of the
barn "a long beak-nosed shadow glide like a snake halfway up the sunlit
open door and stop" (*CW* 323). Warming up to bloodthirsty satisfaction,
Mr. Shortley slinks to his master's command, branded as his silhouette
is with the image and likeness of the lord of death.

If encountering evil and death does not positively affect Mr. Shortley, the death he visits on Mr. Guizac does transform Mrs. McIntyre.
Although Mrs. McIntyre holds the deed to the land, she, like everyone
else in the story, is brought to a place that is not her own to face out the
consequences of her most intimate attachments. In her case, through
forced renunciation of property, the landlady gains an abiding awareness
of God. By turn of fate and cast of disposition, Mrs. McIntyre is a solitary. She leads a lonely life eking out a living on the margins of society.
Her dwelling place is fifty acres of resistant land. She came to the farm
as an outsider to work as secretary to the owner, who is simply known
as the Judge, a wizened, snuff-dipping old man with the "peculiar odor . . .
of sweaty fondled bills." The scent appeals to his much younger secretary, who instinctively follows the smell to its source. They marry after
three months. Actually, she does not know what she is looking for, and
she gets it. The aura of wealth was all that the Judge had. He left her a
bankrupt estate of a mortgaged house and land stripped of marketable
timber. This legacy is her desert, harsh and inhospitable, and "she had
survived" (*CW* 309) its impoverishment.

The history of Mrs. McIntyre is very much the story of desert struggle and survival. Her life is perpetual warfare. The enemies change their
form, name, race, and tactics but sustain the object of their aggression:
Mrs McIntyre. Enemies swarm her desert. The land resists her effort; the
cows demand more care than she can afford. And there is an endless band
of drifters passing through who take what they need to survive, pull up
stakes, and leave. These trials enforce an identity between land and land-
holder, and Mrs. McIntyre sees herself as an arid waste and has a dehy-
drated voice edged with the desert's lashing harshness. "'Sorry people.
Poor white trash and niggers,'" Mrs. McIntyre complains to Mrs. Shortley, who is herself among the fleeting takers: "'They've drained me dry'"

(*CW* 293). The men in her life gradually made marriage an extension of desert hardship by exacerbating her aloneness. Her second husband's craziness saps her; her third husband drinks himself useless and leaves her nothing but a name, McIntyre, the final erasure of whomever she originally was (which the reader never knows). For twenty years, she has been battling depletion. Solitude and warfare, the essential motives of desert life, are in the air that she breathes and the body she develops. Combat becomes second nature to her to the degree that she cannot accept victory over economic adversity when it finally happens in the form of Mr. Guizac's skill. Instead, accustomed to abuse and emotional destitution, she turns the rescuing foreigner into her foe.

Mrs. McIntyre's turning against Mr. Guizac is more than her shooting herself in the foot. At the heart of her self-destructive rejection lies the American South of myth and fable. Long before the Pole arrives, the demon of racist hatred has caught Mrs. McIntyre in a cultural web so entangling her assumptions that it does not feel like the trap it is. Mrs. McIntyre might have discerned the snare; but, thanks to the solidarity born of social animus, prejudiced hostilities provide social participation in lieu of personal conscience. The racist demon for centuries has succeeded in disguising bigotry as virtue and patriotism, thereby making openheartedness, especially to foreigners, seem evil. For O'Connor, the moral distortions in the political world are isomorphic with the devastations in the inner world out of which they arise. We see the link when Mrs. McIntyre learns that Mr. Guizac is arranging for Sulk, the black worker, to marry Mr. Guizac's cousin of sixteen, who has been in a European internment camp for the last three years. The news overwhelms Mrs. McIntyre. There are many ways for her to express an objection to the plan, but she responds entirely from the feeble position of personal anxiety conditioned by a cultural dread over miscegenation. As a result, she loses emotional control and caves in to self-pity, which erupts in anger. Her demons take control of her heart.

The defining feature of Mrs. McIntyre's distress is the way in which she manifests the desert ideal of penthos, or compunction in reverse. She is open enough to discern the Polish woman's plight, but the pain felt is for Mrs. McIntyre, not for the young woman detained in a refugee camp. Self-pity goes deep enough to pierce Mrs. McIntyre's heart, and its rapid palpitations make her cover her chest with a hand to hold her heart in place. These inner tremors cause her "to cry quietly, wiping her eyes every now and then with the hem of her smock." Tears bring relief but not the hesychia of resting in the duty to love. Her peace comes from insulated self-remorse and protective withdrawal. She retreats to the back hall into "a closet-like space that was dark and quiet as a chapel" (*CW* 312). Clois-tered amid the Judge's old bankbooks and the tabernacle of a safe, the solitary contemplates her years of being done in by those who owe her deference. The calm that settles on her is the lull attending the croco-dile tears presented to her coddled self-will that invariably feels cheat-ed. Her behavior poses a simple question: How is it that a woman who has married three times for economic security to feckless men cannot sympathize with the interned young woman's willingness to marry for basic freedom?

From hard experience, the desert-dwellers cautioned those who strug-gle to survive adversity—such as Mrs. McIntyre—against allowing self-indulgence to seize one's will. Mrs. McIntyre evidences the harmful ef-fects the ancient solitaries warned about. All of her resources are spent in enforcing the compliance of others to her will. As she prepares to de-mand that Mr. Guizac stop the marriage, Mrs. McIntyre's natural smile constricts, and her eyebrows come together in an ominous web of lines that are "fierce as a spider's leg." Armed with counterfeit sympathy and blunt racism, she confronts Mr. Guizac as if he were a monster who must be stopped from forcing "'this poor innocent child'" on "'a half-witted thieving black stinking nigger!'" (*CW* 313). But it is not Mr. Guizac who gets caught in the net of fury. He shrugs off her preemptive charges, swal-lows his grievances, and returns to work. Rather, it is Mrs. McIntyre, needing to control the lives of people working on "'my place,'" who gets caught in the twisted resentments webbing her face. Bound to her mur-derous demons, Mrs. McIntyre folds her arms in a vindictive display of power and stares at Mr. Guizac "as if she were watching him through a gunsight" (*CW* 315).

Death is the ultimate expression of the private will's control over another person; and Mrs. McIntyre, like the age in which she lives, has murder in her heart. While a world unravels outside in war's aftermath, life on a disintegrating farm unravels inside the owner. The good Mrs. McIntyre harbors the same demonic monster that drove Mr. Guizac from his homeland, but her righteousness and ideological distortions blind her to the demon driving her self-will. She, too, is at war. Besides stirring "some interior violence" (*CW* 315), Mrs. McIntyre's private desires spin a web of hostilities. Any defiance of her wishes stiffens her scheme. Mr. Guizac's indifference to her complaints provides an excuse to exploit him. Before expelling him, she is determined to get as much work out of him as she can. As a result of her appropriating Mr. Guizac's humanness, the Georgia farm participates in the persecution that produced forced-labor camps and death camps during and after the war from which Mr. Guizac fled. And at the moment of his slaying, the red hills of Georgia and the barbed-wire compounds of Europe become one.

Mrs. McIntyre soon gets caught in her own trap. The body of Mr. Guizac, with his backbone broken by the tractor carefully released by Mr. Shortley, puts murder starkly before Mrs. McIntyre and presents Mr. Guizac's execution as a consequence of her inner will. In life, Mr. Guizac "was not very real to her" (*CW* 310); but in death, the man sacrificed to prejudice, vengeance, and greed vividly confronts Mrs. McIntyre with the alienation and mortality that she has endured for decades. She tries to avert her eyes from Mr. Guizac's bloody body and to run "somewhere." She either faints or blacks out. An impulse in her conscience pulls Mrs. McIntyre, shocked and disoriented, back to the murder scene, which now composes a pietà of a family grieving over the slain husband and father. The sight transports Mrs. McIntyre to "some foreign country" (*CW* 326) where she, the stranger, must bear witness to the truth of her worse passions. Her moral banishment is to the deeper desert in herself. In that alien place of the heart, Mrs. McIntyre is no longer a stranger to her capacity for evil.

At the end of "The Displaced Person," Mrs. McIntyre follows Mrs. Shortley to discover her true country of humility, where God wants us to go and offer sacrifice (Merton, *Wisdom* 138 [53]). Sacrifice for Mrs. McIntyre comes through a loss of material and psychological possessions as well as through bodily diminishment. After the murder, the hired help, like so many malevolent spirits, promptly vanish from the scene; then an auctioneer sells the cows at a loss; and Mrs. McIntyre is left at sixty, alone on the deserted farm. Her body undergoes a similar wasting through a neurological degeneration that manifests her earlier loss of nerve to resist her demonic promptings to use and banish Mr. Guizac. The disease leaves Mrs. McIntyre bedridden, almost blind, voiceless, and forgotten by nearly everyone. A shrouding solitude effectively surrounds her. It is a terrible, a very humbling thing, to have all this silence and security represented by the land turned against her, accusing her of failing to value and protect the foreigner who saved her and the farm in which she placed her security. The systematic enervation of Mrs. McIntyre's body dramatizes how her demons, if not subdued, can conquer her by taking her strengths into themselves.

Even in grave physical debility, however, there remains the opportunity to prevail over the ever-present demons. O'Connor shows Mrs. McIntyre's last struggle—with its possible victory—by presenting her terminal illness as an ascesis, a self-emptying that she certainly has not chosen for herself and yet by force of physical necessity cannot ward off.

Ascesis involves all the surrender that Mrs. McIntyre's willfulness has resisted, and it entails breaking down the barriers her defensive pride has erected. To raze these walls, O'Connor grants the paralyzed Mrs. McIntyre the attentive guidance of Father Flynn, who makes weekly visits to the fallow farm. O'Connor's priest bears no resemblance to the smooth, crooning, postwar model as presented by Hollywood in *Going My Way, The Bells of St. Mary's,* or *Boys' Town;* nor would he fit next to Fulton J. Sheen, trimmed in monsignorial red and competing on television with Milton Berle's comedy hour. O'Connor's cleric is from a drier moral climate. Father Flynn serves as an abba to the woman solitary confined to her cell on the final desert. The terminally ill Mrs. McIntyre, who had her heart set on crops and money, could not have a better guide to profit her soul. At eighty, the plain-speaking priest has cultivated a heart that discerns undercurrents of the inner world. In Mrs. McIntyre, he sees the "'tender heart'" (*CW* 322) that readers and her workers are likely to overlook and that she herself has yet to tap. During Abba Flynn's weekly liturgies of friendship, he "would come in and sit by the side of her bed and explain the doctrines of the Church" (*CW* 327). Flynn fathers the dying woman in the life of Jesus. That is the aim and regular training of the solitary: to be as Jesus was. Nurturance is Flynn's nature. As he earlier slipped the host into the mouth of Mr. Guizac's broken body and supplies manna for the ailing Mrs. McIntyre, Flynn also carries breadcrumbs for the surviving peacock.

The sustenance Flynn brings each week to Mrs. McIntyre provides for the great adventure that is opening before them. Their itinerary, like Jesus' great journey toward Jerusalem, is not in essence spatial but spiritual. Flynn has recognized all along in Mrs. McIntyre a need for more than life was giving her; he sees in her yearning a desire for God. Like the spare sayings of his desert ancestors, Abba Flynn's words go toward bringing the woman who seeks God, or the woman who is not sure what she seeks, nearer to God. As soon as necessity calls the stricken woman, the summons constitutes her as a new person. Deprived of her material securities and bodily resources, Mrs. McIntyre can only live by faith. For O'Connor, trust in God is all that is needed to move close to God, and physical diminishment can assist in the spirit's progress. O'Connor, like the ancient hermits, believes that through ascesis "the soul prospers in the measure in which the body is weakened" (*Sayings,* Daniel 4 [52]). In the desert of "The Displaced Person," the struggle is ceaseless. Father Flynn is on hand with prayers, and "prayer is warfare to the last breath" (*Sayings,* Agathon 9 [22]).

Although Mrs. McIntyre's body has nowhere to go physically, she is launched on a momentous exodus across the wastes of her body to the boundary of her personality—and on to the absolute. Flynn is the right guide for the journey to God. Himself a foreigner who still speaks with a brogue, he is a man for others in whom prayer becomes action. He is a clear-eyed man of tranquil feelings who carries himself in the aloof dignity associated with that archetype of humble strength, the desert abba. Nothing perturbs Flynn's "long bland face" (*CW* 315); he remains serene before every adversity, even the slaughter of Mr. Guizac. Such calm has the power to transform vexation. Over the previous months of meeting with Mrs. McIntyre to discuss the arrival and subsequent performance of Mr. Guizac, Abba Flynn patiently takes in her irritable selfishness and returns good will and judicious advice to her. She does not always heed what he says, but wisdom allows the old man to see what is good in and for Mrs. McIntyre. As she lays dying, Flynn directs his attention to freeing Mrs. McIntyre of anxiety and care. He receives her helplessness and makes of it the hope of rest. In turn, the silent woman learns the living desert art of holy dying, which imbues the narrative with incompleteness and expectancy. "The Displaced Person" concludes with an image of the unfinished soul poised for new growth, as Mrs. McIntyre's path gets lost in obscurity; and this, without dramatic effect, is absorbed like water in desert sand.

At the point of death, Abba Theophilus said to Abba Arsenius: "You are blessed, Abba Arsenius, because you have always had this hour in mind" (*Sayings*, Theophilus the Archbishop 5 [82]). Mrs. McIntyre in her last days is blessed because at her side is the prayerful old man who has kept death before him and brings this courage as a living accompaniment to her own slow encounter with death. Remembering death with his trust in the promise of the fullness of life enables Flynn "to live always in the peace [he has] in view without weakening" (*Sayings*, Evagrius 1 [63]). This peace born of eremitic solitude is the remedy O'Connor holds up for the catastrophic cruelty of modern social history. The grim evocations of the Holocaust, prison camps, and massive deportations—along with the stark, American-style murder—in "The Displaced Person" resolve themselves not in the violence that usually concludes O'Connor's stories but in the consoling recollection of Father Flynn's serenity. The killing of Mr. Guizac is malevolently planned, furtively carried out, and cold as the ice on which his body lies crushed; but countervailing this evil scheme is the design of the ending, which emerges smooth, beautifully layered, warmly intimate, and open. O'Connor brings all the other nine stories of *A Good Man Is Hard to Find* to this final understated poetics of solitary repose, preferring in the face of modern brutality, as did the ancient hermits during the savage Roman Empire, nobility to hand-wringing.

5 The Prophet and the Word in the Desert

> Go, lie down; and if he calls you, you shall say,
> "Speak, Lord, for your servant is listening."
> —1 Samuel 3:9

> Do not be always wanting everything to turn out as you
> think it should, but rather as God pleases, then you will
> be undisturbed and thankful in your prayer.
> —Nilus, *The Sayings of the Desert Fathers*

FROM 1938 TO the summer of 1952, visitors to the back-woods of Tennessee would have seen a man devoting the last fourteen of his eighty-four years to raising his grandnephew from infancy to adolescence. Getting to the site would take some doing. To reach it, one turns at the junction of Highway 56 onto a dirt road running ten miles. The route then becomes a twisting, lovely passage. The wide, unpaved road goes through thick growths of trees before narrowing into a rutted wagon path that crosses a field rising to a crest. The view is healing to the eye. Through a forked birch at this promontory, the visitor can see one-quarter mile down to a clearing with an unpainted, two-story shack settled between two chimneys. The homesite is Powderhead. Its inhabitants are Mason Tarwater, the great-uncle, and Francis Marion Tarwater, his grandnephew. These backcountry figures, comprising a male world of two, are the heroes of O'Connor's *The Violent Bear It Away* (1960).

It would do well to pause at the journey's end to see how these woodsmen live and to look closely at the locale in which they make their day. Patient, discerning eyes will find much to take in. Here is a snapshot of master and disciple epitomizing an ancient way of life that defines the ascetic sensibility shaping all the stories that O'Connor tells. The old man and the young boy are offspring of a family bloodline that George Rayber, the third male relative, describes as "flowing from some ancient source, some desert prophet or pole-sitter" (*CW* 402). For the Christian, that genealogy finds its fullest expression in fourth-century Egypt, in the life of a solitary, young peasant-landowner named Anthony. One day, he heard these words of Jesus read in church: "If you wish to be perfect, go, sell your possessions, and give the money to the poor. . . . then come, follow me" (Matthew 19:21). Jesus' charge spoke directly to Anthony; he sold all his property and went to live with an old man who had devoted his life to solitary prayer. In time, Anthony withdrew from the feet of his teacher into the desert, where his struggle to follow Jesus transformed the lonely waste into a paradise. Alone, the hermit developed a practice of fighting demons and controlling his body to find peace with God. If Anthony sought anonymity, he found fame. His daily discipline appeared to others as spectacular physical and spiritual feats that attracted widespread attention and many recruits. The man's fame multiplied through Athanasius's influential celebration entitled *The Life of Anthony*, which appeared about ten years after the renowned Egyptian's death in 356 A.D. *The Life of Anthony* combines in this one man the prestige of the pagan wise man and the honor of the Christian holy man with the biblical "man of God." The man of desert solitude became a spiritual exemplar for all ages.

George Rayber cites the models of the unbridled Hebrew prophet and Simeon Stylites, the legendary mid-fifth-century Syrian saint who stood atop a sixty-foot pillar in the desert, to explain the religious call besetting his family as an "affliction" (*CW* 402). For Rayber, a man of reason, living out God's word before others is an invitation "he knew to be madness;" for him, prophecy and chosen alienation from society are "irrational and abnormal" (*CW* 401) demands that he personally fights against through ridicule and even attempted murder. In scorning the desert call, Rayber is not alone. For some, Simeon's standing on a pillar was an extravagant instance of the morbid phenomenon of asceticism. Others, however, found the solitary figure seeking freedom up in the open air a holy man to be admired and emulated (*Lives of Simeon Stylites* 15–23). For Simeon's followers, his pillar (where he spent twenty-eight years) was not a place of punishment but an altar. From his lofty perch, the renouncer moved heavenward by means of taking into himself the suffering and cruelty of the world around him. More than an icon, Simeon's body gave witness in flesh—not metaphor—to sickness, hunger, and pain. Rayber is aware of the harsh extravagance of ascetic life but not of its contradiction. The schoolteacher's one-sided judgment is instructive about desert spirituality and its expression in *The Violent Bear It Away*. Whereas Rayber remarks the physical outrage of Simeon on the pillar, he misses how in withdrawing for spiritual reasons the saint changed people's lives—not only through miracles but also in simple acts of kindness and justice. By devoting oneself to God, as will be shown, the hermit is called to serve all in need.

O'Connor's heroes in *The Violent Bear It Away* are modern variations drawn from the ancient profiles of desert life. Elder (abba) and younger Tarwater, described most simply, are solitaries. As noted earlier, the Greek word for solitary is *monachos*, which yields our word *monk*, a forbidding word for O'Connor's good country people and an alien status in every culture. Deliberately separated from society, they are hermits, which comes from *eremos*, meaning desert. In Hebrew and Christian reflection, desert and wilderness are interchangeable conditions in sacred history; and at different times in *The Violent Bear It Away*, Powderhead resembles both desert and wilderness. *Monk, hermit, desert,* and *wilderness* are charged words in the spiritual vocabulary. To appreciate life in Powderhead, one would need to intensify matters by paying even more attention than in the previous chapters to the loaded term *ascesis*, which in *The Violent Bear It Away* involves a training and practice whose essence seeks to imbibe the spirit of Scripture. That vital principle embraces the prophetic call of the Hebrew prophets and the renewed embodiment of that vocation in the life of Jesus. This continuum has its basis in spiritual discipline; the practice commended in Powderhead is that of the desert. O'Connor's recluses are authentic ascetics. They lead a disciplined life of prayer, study, and subsistence farming as rigorous as the regimens maintained in many organized cloisters or charterhouses. Asceticism is a universal phenomenon, and not necessarily religious or even salutary (as becomes clear when one turns to the life of George Rayber). Christian ascetics embrace the rigors of bodily and spiritual training in solitary starkness to draw close to God. The Hebrew prophets and Jesus, who were themselves models for the desert mothers and fathers, guide Mason Tarwater and reign in Powderhead. As in biblical time and during late antiquity, the search in Tennessee involves not speculative knowledge but the religious experience from which ascetic practice is born. The fruits of this experience are fulfilled in the nitty-gritty of daily life.

The ruling culture beyond the secluded Tarwater world has little sympathy for old Mason's ways in the woods. Mason need not concern

himself with the hostility, however, for controversy has always surrounded the ascetic life. In Edward Gibbon's famous analysis, Christianity's
alteration of the ferocious Roman temper and civic structure led Gibbon
to a stern attack on the indolence of those ascetics who disturbed the
accepted way of Christian life by retreating to the nearby Egyptian and
Syrian deserts. The Reformation, of course, saw this solitary kind of
monasticism as disparaging the body and regarded its denials as unscrip-
tural. The latter charge holds partial truth because Jesus was not a solitary, except on crucial occasions, but a man of public involvement. Such
reservations about ascetic solitude would not bring Mason Tarwater out
of the woods. Mason, O'Connor's prophet for our time, is not at all inclined to give up his antisocial life in favor of public acceptance. Far from
being persuasive, advice from the heathen culture that Mason abjures
only reassures him of the value of flight. Indeed, the old man celebrates
his status as stranger in an estranging world. He is incomprehensibility
in human form. Besides his enigmatic ways, there is his unfathomable
goal of intimacy with God through service as a prophet; and that relation is an extreme Christian mystery holding truths beyond Mason's own
understanding. He does know that to reach God he must pull away from
society, and his place on the edge of the settled land marks a more daring displacement than geographical remoteness. Mason's fearless striking out into the unknown of divine union lands him on the limits of his
body, spirit, and personality. There, beyond society and self, old Tarwater seeks to recover the connection with God that O'Connor believes is
the fundamental bond for each person.

This chapter explores the primary impulses and cultural significance
of asceticism and the trials of solitude in *The Violent Bear It Away*. The
discussion first sketches the historical context giving rise and meaning
to religious withdrawal in the novel and then takes up the biblical and
patristic sources generating the novel's ascetic action. That action involves Tarwater's combating his demons and traces his flight and return
home. As O'Connor concludes the hero's weeklong struggle with a rite
honoring his self-donation, so this chapter ends by showing how, through
the poetics of solitude, the novel O'Connor called "a very minor hymn
to the Eucharist" (*HB* 387) comes together like a liturgical song.

O'Connor precisely brackets the climactic events of *The Violent Bear It
Away* within one week and sets its essential antecedent action between
1938 and 1952, a period corresponding to the formative years of the modern world that she judged "terrible" (*HB* 90). Briefly to historicize the

novel is to glimpse a world where the engagements register both the terrors driving a person to find refuge from society and the political urgencies calling to the solitary for help. During the fourteen years that Mason lives as a solitary—fighting his inner demons and dedicating himself to raising his grandnephew to be a prophet—the powerful nations committed themselves to turning the planet into a charnel house. In November 1938, the year Francis Marion Tarwater was born, Kristallnacht inaugurated through mob violence the systematic oppression of German Jews; then there was the wearing of the yellow stars, followed by deportations and finally the camps. The moral distance between Hitler's Germany and O'Connor's Powderhead is telling. The people who are hated in the mighty European power are honored in the primitive Tennessee woods. In Powderhead, Israel's prophets hold the healing answer to the terrible wounds evidenced in the ravages of World War II. Through their keen awareness of evil and misery, these ancient bearers of God's word articulate the ways through which to overcome oppression and break spiritual chains. Israel's prophets are heroes of the word; but, even more through their exemplary alienation from the sinful life, they are heroes of being. *The Violent Bear It Away* reaches all the way back to Moses, Ezekiel, Elijah, John the Baptist, and Jesus to show how asceticism and prophecy join forces to combat the demons spreading their crepe wings over the modern world.

The vaunted scientific progress of the twentieth century spawned a technology of death. Ovens, crematories, gas chambers, and artillery wiped out over fifty million people during World War II with business-like productivity that occasioned patriotic celebration. On the Christian Feast of the Transfiguration, 6 August 1945, the United States displayed its expertise by employing atomic fission on humans, thereby changing the shape of fear while altering the earth's future. Disintegration continued after peace treaties were signed. Millions more were exiled and became "displaced persons" (an impassive epithet that O'Connor recharged, as seen earlier, with theological power). Then there was the Korean War (1950–53), which raged while Mason was teaching Tarwater the history of the world from Adam's eviction from Eden to "the Day of Judgment" (*CW* 331). Even within the shielding Tennessee pines, there persisted the anguish of racism and the prophet's own violence and iron self-will in disobedience to the command of God, whom he vows to honor.

These were some of the social forces darkening the period in which the Tarwater chronicle unfolds. Acutely alive to the moral climate in which she lived, O'Connor summed up the state of things with more than usual precision: "Right now," O'Connor wrote on 6 September 1955, "the whole world seems to be going through a dark night of the soul" (*HB* 100). Whereas the clinician Walker Percy diagnosed the institutionalizing of death as the thanatos syndrome, and the cultural observer Don DeLillo later saw the proliferating technologies swell into a cult of death, the ascetic O'Connor defined the malady as an inner extinguishment. For the hermit novelist, the vortex of political and psychological turmoil is the inborn center of the person, of the spirit. Terror, impotence, and egotism seep into the inner world to distort the characters' perception of themselves and creation. Divided within, they are uprooted from their native ground and alienated from God.

During these bloodthirsty years, O'Connor witnessed humanity's stark capacity to destroy its own species and habitat, and she described that willful malice in the warring human relations of her narratives. The "dark night" that O'Connor observed not only eclipsed decency but disabled the soul's discernment of evil, blurring the line between mad fantasy and sane recognition of evil. But the ruins of society are, for O'Connor, as the shards of the Roman Empire were for the desert fathers and mothers, stuff for the kingdom. The ancient hermits believed, Thomas Merton explains, that they could "pull the whole world to safety after them" (*Wisdom*, "Introduction" 23). In her own seclusion, O'Connor developed a similar concern for her age. The effect of her eremitic withdrawal was different than Merton's political militancy but equally vast. In advance of and alongside Vatican II (1962–65), she conducted a one-woman aggiornamento that brought her readers and church into vital confrontation with the modern world, which in a sense became her hermitage.

O'Connor's good country people would be shocked to learn that they had any connection with a primitive way of life centered on self-denial. Ascetic life belongs to the unreformed past that these advanced people of gumption, whose guidance comes from their own private will, have outgrown. The pangs of flesh, however, make known the infirmities of desire as O'Connor's characters stare into a drainage ditch, a pool of vomitus, puddles of blood, a raped body, and sweeping tides of darkness. Willful they are, but renouncers they become, amazed and blessed by having their cherished personal wishes violated and brought into alignment with God. They all end up where there is no company, where nobody can follow. Long before illness sent O'Connor to this forlorn place, a desert father reassured humankind that "humility is the land where God wants us to go and offer sacrifice" (Merton, *Wisdom* 83 [53]). This strange land of surrender is Powderhead.

The Violent Bear It Away sets out to draw more firmly that vanishing boundary between a world hostile to life and a sphere of true human order fostering dignity and holiness. Powderhead marks off that border. Its red hills contain a deep withinness. Here is an "empty place" "where there's nothing" (*CW* 352), a "'lonesome place'" (*CW* 357) that has the force of a character. The woods are a wilderness with the desert's stark isolation that drives its inhabitants to their spiritual roots. Daily life is a struggle to maintain footing on the hard ground of being. The truths of Powderhead are known to old Mason, for they run deep in his nature and teaching. With death in sight—and mindful that his young charge might turn to George Rayber, who disavowed his prophetic call—Mason admonishes young Tarwater: "'And when I'm gone, you'll be better off in these woods by yourself with just as much light as the sun wants to let in than you'll be in the city with him [Rayber]'" (*CW* 344). The red soil, fed by the sun, reveals the plan and promise of God as taking all time to complete.

Mason sees himself as a child of the promise—the prophet and heir obliged to train Tarwater as his successor to speak God's word before others. Before confronting society's apostasy, Tarwater must admit to and fight against evil in himself: his demons. Mason's training is rigorous because the battle for Tarwater will be daunting. This hidden warfare demands a life of self-denial and discipline (ascesis) to resist the enemy. Mason is a seasoned veteran of this unseen war against inner evil, and he knows that the struggle is excruciating and fought with meager human resources against superior opponents. To begin with, there is always the human inclination to take the easy way by following one's own will rather than the hard commandment of God. And so, over the years, Mason wanders into the remotest parts of the woods to thrash out his willfulness with the Lord. Alone, he endures blistering assaults that culminate in a consuming interior fire, leaping in a wildcat's fury, to claw away any resistance to God. There are other powerful demons in Mason to rend. His faults include wanton violence, a misguided apocalypticism, and a share in Rayber's following a different moral course than he had hoped for. Even the teacher needs correction. The battle is a ferocious taming of Mason's tigerish will, and the agony continues until he "couldn't stand the Lord one instant longer" (*CW* 358); and then he got drunk. The wounds Mason suffers in wrestling with God are acute. Exhaustion plunges Mason deeply into his heart so as to know its waywardness, its capacity for evil, and its self-deception. He grasps these modulations from within the shattered condition he shares with all humankind. Such depth of passion consists of participation in God's love and freedom and is made known by the wooden cross that Mason wants over his grave.

To recognize the extent of Mason's sinfulness and the intensity of his inner warfare is to marvel at the outcome of his struggle. Mason achieved the almost impossible task of being a holy man in evil times. He stood guard over sacred texts in the face of public reproach. His is a life well lived. Those around him could feel the old man's profundity of spirit. "'He was deep in this life,'" Buford Munson eulogizes at the beginning of the novel, "'he was deep in Jesus' misery'" (*CW* 360). With Jesus, Mason fights against Satan. By opening himself to the full range of experience to endure the painful fight against his personal evil, Mason holds all of humanity in the healing presence of Jesus' passion and obedience to God's will. The outcome of his solitary warfare and the goal of his teaching are one and the same: freedom. "'I saved you to be free, your own self!'" (*CW* 339) Mason reminds Tarwater. Being one's true self, as Mason's immersion in Jesus' misery exemplifies, frees one to love, to see Jesus in the suffering of others, and fearlessly to proclaim God's word before others to liberate them from the captivity of sin. As Mason goes deeper into Jesus' life, he translates over time the Gospel into the many various circumstances of life. In this sacramental way, Tarwater, his disciple, comprehends the search for God through living principles in everyday activities.

The route to this recognition for young Tarwater runs across his pubertal body, through the wilderness of his tormenting choices, and into the solitude of his cracked heart. The front line of Tarwater's decisive battle is his will, just as it was for the ancient solitaries. For O'Connor, freedom of the human will involves, as seen in *Wise Blood*, "many wills conflicting in one man" (*CW* 1265). O'Connor's emphasis on the will in its multiplicity reiterates a crucial desert issue. In their quest for holiness, the ancient ascetics were preoccupied with contending desires, and it was precisely the private will that blocked their search. Only by taming the personal will can one move toward God (*Sayings*, Poemen 54 [174]). Out of the struggle to overcome the impediments of the self-will, the desert-dwellers perceived a connection between human passions and the devil, and that patristic understanding of demons inhabiting our disordered emotions opens a direct way into O'Connor's controversial reintroduction of Satan into the postmodern, postsuperstitious world of *The Violent Bear It Away*.

A better position from which to understand the demonology in *The Violent Bear It Away* can be achieved if one pauses briefly to consider the view of evil forces held by the desert mothers and fathers. With the rest of the ancient world, the hermits believed in supernatural beings, both helpful (angels, or messengers) and harmful (satans, or adversaries). The ammas and abbas persistently probed from various directions the operation of these powerful beings. Dorotheos of Gaza, in his *Discourses*, puts his inquiry with the prosaic brilliance characteristic of the desert-dwellers. He asks his brothers: "Why is the devil called not only 'enemy,' but also 'adversary'?" Dorotheos's answer goes to the heart of the inextinguishable spiritual energy of the satanic: "He is called 'enemy' because he is a hater of men, one who hates what is good, a traitor; an 'adversary,' because he always puts obstacles in the way of good" (2 [95]). Such clear-eyed perceptions provided the groundwork on which the solitaries built their knowledge of their opponents. Demons (from the Greek *daimones*), the hermits came to realize, were deceitful agents waging war against the true God and Jesus. Demons had a power over humans, who must vie, in Saint Paul's words, "against the cosmic powers of this present darkness, against the spiritual forces of evil in the heavenly places" (Ephesians 6:12). The desert solitaries mortified their wills and bodies to develop the self-mastery needed to combat the hosts of wickedness assaulting them. That same ascetic control is the discipline that young Tarwater must cultivate to overcome the identical evil agents attacking him. Satan targets the boy precisely because he is raised to serve God.

Indeed, the demons swarming both the modern and the ancient worlds hold a special animosity for anyone with spiritual longings. The moment Anthony takes up the life of prayer, the devil hurls thoughts of sexual pleasure before him to turn Anthony's attention from God. Whether defeated or successful, the devil never lets up. No sooner does Anthony recover from horrible whippings by a demonic multitude than the throng of "beasts and reptiles" attacks him (Athanasius 9 [38]). Never far away and always dusting the human mind with dissuasions, the evil spirits rush to check any inclination toward God. The demons' intention is to ingratiate their presence into human consciousness by any means. The demons attacking the desert ascetics reassert their malice in *The Violent Bear It Away*. With updated garb and southern vernacular (easy maneuvers for spirits), the demons pursue their fixed goals against Tarwater: they hate him and put obstacles before any good that his great-uncle had taught him to seek. Insinuation is a mere preliminary to the domination they seek over him. It is a measure of how intimately desert spirituality runs in O'Connor's sensibility that she intuitively dramatizes Tarwater's trial as being caught in the swift downward tide of the satanic "thought-flow" charted by the ancient solitaries.

The metaphor of thought-flow comes from the Greek *logismos*, an important word in patristic texts that means thought or idea. In ascetic-monastic usage, logismos most frequently occurs in the plural, *logismoi*, and is invariably allied to *demons* to mean evil or passionate thoughts. "Evil thoughts," says Poemen, "are suggested by the demons" (*Sayings*, Poemen 21 [170]). The word *logismoi* recurs in *The Life of Anthony* and in Origen (Bacht 956–58). Evagrius, a learned Greek among unlettered Egyptian hermits, intending to teach the cunning of demons, in the *Praktikos* enumerates eight logismoi (the seven deadly sins plus *acedia*) through which the evil spirits harmfully influence humans. As demons are the source of evil, the logismoi describe for Evagrius the means and effects of stirring up the human senses (6–14 [16–20]).

The logismos usually begins by appealing to the human mind through physical gratification and then imbues the mind as an idea that tempts the person to commit evil. If the person yields to the thought, the temptation gathers a propulsive momentum of its own, and the demon penetrates from the conscious mind into the heart. The heart's obscure passages are the estuary of the demonic flow. Here the evil stream swirls and thickens to occlude the heart so that its responsiveness to others and its yearning for God are stopped. When this blockage occurs, Peter Brown writes in *The Body and Society*, the person becomes lost "to the powers of numbness that still lurked in the hidden reaches of the universe" (167). The logismoi register their invasion of the heart in eerie ways. The fantasies and obsessions commonly associated with demonic possession take hold. More sinister than these histrionic displays is the unseen deadening inertia of the spirit at the very center of emotional life. The heart loses its fluidity of freedom in favor of becoming a bound accomplice to the demon burrowed into the heart, twisting its rightful attention from God into self-interest. At this final stage, the evil flow, by clogging the heart, seizes the person's will, and the victim's will becomes the demon's.

The attempt of the evil logismoi to control Tarwater makes up the essential drama of *The Violent Bear It Away*, and Abba Poemen's description of the demonic flow anticipates the young hero's psychological struggle and early defeats at the hands of the devil. The boy's initial and repeated submission to sin, O'Connor emphasizes, has to do with the conquests of his private will, and she stresses that Tarwater's will becomes the demon whose savage commands he fulfills. Because the final goal of conquering the victim's heart is always the same, the devil wastes no time in getting started. The demon begins by instigating Tarwater's disobedience of Mason's burial orders. Then, for several days, the demon incites rebellion against the boy's prophetic vocation. To that end, the demonic flow steadily pours self-interest into Tarwater's heart until it dams up the boy's capacity to feel anything other than proud independence. At this point, the demon gets Tarwater to drown in cold blood the very child that Mason ordered Tarwater to save by baptizing him. O'Connor's dramatic pattern not only replicates the movement of diabolical machinations in desert literature; she intensifies Tarwater's spiritual trial with his demons by placing him in two deserts: the external wilderness of Powderhead and the inner barrenness of desolation. What makes this interior desert so painful for Tarwater is that, unlike the elders and Mason, the boy does not seek it. In fact, he flees from hardship, restraint, and solitude; but the discipline of his two unsought deserts is crucial to his moral calling.

To grasp the full importance of Tarwater's grappling with evil in two deserts, one must add a biblical perspective of the young hero's spiritual pursuit to that of the ancient hermits' psychology of evil. O'Connor compares the ascetic training of her two protagonists in Powderhead to the experience of Elijah and Elisha (*CW* 356); and in so doing, O'Connor draws on the link in Christian reflection between the Old Testament prophets and the desert fathers and mothers. In their humility before the Bible, the desert elders believed that Elijah and the prophets invented the desert life and that they, the fourth-century followers of their forebears' word, lived out the Scriptures. As the hermits reflected on sacred history, desert solitude was in their consciousness the basic experience of prophetic life. Desert trials bring Elijah to feel the unfailing care of the Lord, who attends Elijah's "journey to the wilderness" with food and drink all the way to Horeb (1 Kings 19:15). There on the mountain where Moses saw God, God reveals himself to Elijah (1 Kings 19:1–10). The desert that imposes hardship is for Moses and Elijah the ground of contact with God. Elijah, above all, exemplifies the paradoxes uniting the prophetic vocation, desert spirituality, and O'Connor's religious sensibility. As Elijah comforted the distressed, he also made the comfortable into the uncomfortable. Gentleness and denunciation were indicative of Elijah's deep trust and reliance on the only God; and this is the very singleness of heart that the desert solitaries sought and that O'Connor's solitaries, against their will, must learn. To show the making of a new prophet for our time, *The Violent Bear It Away* incorporates the wisdom of fourth-century elders with the scriptural precedent on which prophecy rests.

―――――――――

The very first scene of *The Violent Bear It Away* links the prophetic vocation with the desert call. The old prophet Mason Tarwater has just died, and his death marks Tarwater's entrance into this interlocking ascetic adventure. Mason leaves young Tarwater with two momentous obligations, each requiring the boy to act as an agent of bringing new life through death: first he must bury the old prophet; then he must baptize Bishop, his cousin, Rayber's son. Both ministries are onerous. Digging a grave in sand and solid brick for "two hundred pounds of dead mountain"

(*CW* 343) taxes the teenager's physical strength, and baptizing little Bishop goes against the young hero's personal desire to follow his own plan for his life. This conflict immerses the future prophet in a trial of wills. Such warring of multiple wills in one person is the first and unceasing struggle of the desert and the essential drama of *The Violent Bear It Away*. The interior battle against self-will is the first phase of the young boy's spiritual training. Combat begins in mourning, which is a solitude not shared with his uncle-protector or any other person.

The summons to solitude is to prepare Tarwater for the important work in his future. As solitude initiates the novice into the trials of the desert, the situation simultaneously incites the ancient adversary into aggressively taking up his opposition to anyone called to carry out the plan of his sempiternal opponent, God. When the boy is alone, the devil makes his move; and the logismos stirs. Always cozy near death's shiver, the demon flutters from within Mason's bodily death rattle across the breakfast table to Tarwater. The communication is subtle yet tangible. The satanic brushing is just light enough to be tolerated but so unfamiliar as to make Tarwater experience a "sullen embarrassment as if he were in the presence of a new personality" (*CW* 336). The bereft boy does come into contact with a force that he had never before felt so intimately. The spookiness registers a revealing sensation. The arrival of this alien psyche causes a physical discomfort that warns of the numbness and morose pain to come from the subsequent demonic provocations.

The emphasis on the physical nature of Tarwater's encounter derives from O'Connor's belief that moral knowledge comes "through the senses" (*MM* 67), which accords with the patristic concept of the logismos as penetrating the body. The first part of this instruction takes the form of an insensibility that the devil deliberately instills in his victim and that Tarwater welcomes as an excuse for not digging Mason's grave. Deceit occasions Tarwater's schooling. The devil pretends to offer comfort and aid but actually aims to control the boy so that he will reduce Mason's corpse to ashes rather than burying it. The demon first nestles inside Tarwater's head as a "loud and strange and disagreeable" voice (*CW* 337) promising the orphaned boy companionship. Among the devil's toadies buzzing about, three cohorts spearhead the attack on the boy's body. The nasty voice, by disparaging the dead, speaks to the boy's inclination to defy Mason's orders. Demon rum joins the fray to inebriate the boy. Drunkenness is Tarwater's mourning, his version of wearing black. Although Tarwater embraces the stupor as pleasing to his will, O'Connor shows the slothful pleasure to be the result of a disgusting infiltration. The stump liquor he has been drinking feels like a "burning arm" that "slid down Tarwater's throat as if the devil were already reaching inside him to finger his soul" (*CW* 358).

The demonic invasion of Tarwater's body captures perfectly the patristic-monastic understanding of logismos. John Cassian, the fifth-century interpreter of eremitic spirituality, maps out the flow and the malice generating it: "A train of thoughts comes into being from the devil when these undermine us with the attractiveness of sin and when the devil gets to us with his hidden snares, when with the subtlest of skills he deceitfully presents evil as good and on our behalf transforms himself into an angel of light" (*Conferences* I, 19 [53]). Sure enough, O'Connor's stranger comes as a sly, appealing messenger. With Tarwater, the devil presents himself as an avuncular surrogate who will undertake responsibility for the bereaved nephew's education and spiritual welfare. This self-appointed sponsor then waxes like a wise counselor purporting to reveal truths about the boy's choices in the outside world that Mason kept hidden from his charge. One bit of inside information that the devil offers his petted friend concerns the visitant himself: "No no no, the stranger said, there ain't no such thing as a devil" (*CW* 354). Disappearance is the illusion behind all demonic illusions. Vanishing tightens Satan's control on his victim. It turns Tarwater into the dummy for the demon's ventriloquism and, more ominously, into Satan's proxy in his war against God. The battle is no longer against evil: "It's Jesus or *you*" (*CW* 354).

Tarwater chooses himself. He torches Powderhead under the soused belief that he is cremating Mason and flees to his uncle, George Rayber, in the city. The next leg of Tarwater's spiritual wandering begins with the hope of finding a refuge for his pride, perhaps in the form of praise from Rayber for defying Mason. Like Elijah, the ancient desert-dwellers, and Saint Francis of Assisi, Tarwater takes nothing material for his journey. Unlike his predecessors, however, the Tennessee boy in his poverty relies not on God but on himself. The result is the greater poverty of egotism, a magnet for the demonic preceptors of adolescence ready to coddle him with delusions of adequacy. As the boy roams through a series of deserts and adjacent wildernesses of his mind, demons materialize, serving as the wind beneath Tarwater's wings of escape. These velocities assume various guises but share the common ruse of befriending Tarwater for what is least admirable in him.

The logismoi carry Tarwater into the mainstream of American life. Moving in the urban currents, he can live and breathe a culture that exalts the private will over everything else. The selfishness, optimism, materialism, and humanism of Tarwater's tempters form the negative image of the dark night that O'Connor saw enshrouding our age. T. Fawcett Meeks, a salesman of copper parts, drives the boy in darkness to the city and promotes its vices. "'And now,'" he gloats, "'you're coming to town to run to doom with the rest of us, huh?'" (*CW* 381). Meeks's rules for prestige in "the big world" (*CW* 364) are familiar. Time is money; people are money; love makes money; money is god. Wealth in the *Sayings* and *Lives* of the desert is frequently linked to sadness and aggression, and Meeks exemplifies the connection. As possessions are the sources of Meeks's gratification, so they generate his violence and define his sexual gratification. Everyone this grim huckster encounters becomes the object of emotional assault as he breaks down their humanness into sales figures.

The desert ascetics, who struggled with material attachments, came to an understanding of clinging to things that exposes the demon in Meeks and the suffering he brings on himself. A vignette from the *Sayings* also warns of the psychological harm to the person who values goods over people and effectively disregards support from God. The story even has a comic touch that O'Connor would savor. The saying tells of an old man who helped some thieves when they were stealing. "When they had taken away what was inside his cell, Abba Euprepius saw that they had left his stick and he was sorry. So he took it and ran after them to give it to them" (*Sayings*, Euprepius 2 [62]). For those seeking God, like the old abba, mercy outweighs justice because robbery is a test of the ascetic's reliance on God for sustenance. From that dependency emerges another truth in this saying, one that lies at the heart of O'Connor's treatment of poverty and her psychology of renunciation: As sadness marks possession, joy is the patrimony of those who become poor for God. Such profound faith frees one from care. From this detachment and inner freedom flows compassion toward others. Meeks, the flagrant antithesis of this freedom from care, rushes around the South in the anxiety of spirit that the ascetics and Mason struggled to avoid. The salesman's bitterness manifests the demonic effect that avarice wreaks on his soul. Attachment to material gain enslaves Meeks to the point at which he has cut off feeling for others. "'And that's the way it ought to be in this world,'" he brags, "'nobody owing nobody nothing'" (*CW* 362). During Meeks's protracted self-aggrandizing, Tarwater is too attached to his own willful disobedience of Mason to be engaged with the demonic salesman. If Tarwater's attachment to his personal will is at this moment a protection against Meeks's indoctrination, Tarwater's will is also the warning of the spiritual disaster awaiting the truant boy.

The danger of serving one's private desires is idolatry of one's self. Ascetic spirituality sees self-will as the impulse that replaces God with the self as the source of life and meaning; and for that reason the will, for the hermits, presents the greatest danger in solitary life. For the desert teachers, self-will is hell; and hell is what Tarwater experiences in the city as anger and pride impel him deeper into his personal desires and further from God. There is no mistaking the boy's infernal descent into himself. Upon entering the city, the atmosphere imposes resistance, emits peril, and inflicts reprimand. Terror clutches at Tarwater the instant he bangs on Rayber's door. The place dares to defy his bidding, seeming "immune to his fury." Tarwater feels "a trap" (*CW* 385). The ambush is laid by Tarwater's own disordered passions. The logismoi swell his head and distort his perceptions. People, places, events, and God come into his view as challenges to or validations of his will. Hallucinations and bodily depletions, the punishing effects that the desert ascetics felt from unchecked pride, punctuate the urban phase of Tarwater's spiritual vagrancy—a phase his uncle George Rayber accurately calls "five days of madness" (*CW* 455). Tarwater's excursion in the city reveals the interior deformities of solitude that leave him a prisoner of his egotism. The worst of these torments comes from Tarwater's closing himself in the hell of the heart that resolutely refuses to love and is sealed by the iron walls of the will to defy Mason's orders and assert his autonomy from God.

During Tarwater's stay with Rayber, every experience dilates to the boy's inner disorder. The three characters Tarwater encounters torment him merely by their presence. Lucette Carmody unnerves Tarwater by her apostolic zeal, which reminds him of Mason and the call to prophecy. The crippled girl evangelist lives by the singleness of heart and vision that recognizes the material world, the human person Jesus, and his rising from the dead as outpourings of the Logos. "'Jesus is the Word of God and Jesus is love'" (*CW* 412), Lucette cries out at her revival service. She shouts: "'Are you deaf to the Lord's Word?'" (*CW* 415). Later, Tarwater says in a convulsive murmur to Rayber that he came to the service "'only . . . to spit on it'" (*CW* 416); but at the prayer meeting, the narrator goes beneath Tarwater's vocal contempt to show that Lucette has struck dread in his heart by reminding him of things he thought he sent up in smoke in Powderhead. When he goes to bed that night, "the boy's white face" is "drained but expectant" (*CW* 416), exhausted by the logismos and provoked by Lucette's reminder that God's Word, the Logos, becomes flesh to speak to him through the direct and visible presence in the person of Jesus.

For Lucette, each person's response to the demands of love expresses an attitude toward Jesus, the enfleshed Logos, that defines one's relation to God. O'Connor gauges her characters' relations to God through their responses to little Bishop. Bishop is joy and love—qualities of the Logos—love unguarded and a capacity for pleasure bound only by the reaction of others to his spiritual freshness. The two most important persons around Bishop impose on the child's joy constraints out of their own fear and severity. Because the child has Down's syndrome, his father rejects him as an ugly burden created by a brutish deity. Because Mason orders Tarwater to baptize Bishop, Tarwater scorns the boy as a menace to Tarwater's freedom. Simply for being himself, Bishop becomes the declared enemy in Tarwater's battle to defeat Mason and reject his prophetic vocation. At the park where Bishop is delightfully splashing in the water fountain, we see the painful effects of these demonic misrepresentations of the child's innocence. To prevent the possibility that Tarwater might spitefully christen Bishop, Rayber yanks his son from the water. Bishop, cruelly snatched and wounded, howls and then settles into "crying quietly" with "his face red and hideously distorted" (*CW* 422) by the fiends who have dragged the innocent boy into the hellish dark of their sinister wills. Thanks to the competing logismoi, pain unites Rayber and Tarwater where love could not; for as Bishop sobs, father and cousin remain unmoved by anguish and deaf to the Logos.

Tarwater's five delusional days culminate in the disaster that the desert solitaries saw as the goal of the baiting demons: "A time is coming when men will go mad," says the knowing Anthony, "and when they see someone who is not mad, they will attack him saying, 'You are mad, you are not like us'" (*Sayings*, Anthony the Great 25 [6]). The demonic logismoi, now tunneled into Tarwater's heart, single out the person, Bishop, who is not like us: "It's only one dimwit you have to drown" (*CW* 462). The crazed attack comes the day after the park excursion, as night sets in at the Cherokee Lodge, where Rayber takes Tarwater and Bishop for an overnight outing. Tarwater lowers Bishop into the boat, takes him to the opposite bank of the lake, and drowns him. The murder is the sheerest butchery.

There is another demonic horror at work in the scene. Rayber observes the killing from his room in the lodge, and he feels nothing as Tarwater drowns Bishop. Writing from an intimate grasp of desert spirituality, O'Connor shows what the inner person becomes when the logismos saturates one's being and possesses one's heart. During his son's horrible slaying, Rayber "remained absolutely still, wooden, expressionless, as the machine [his hearing aid] picked up the sounds of some fierce sustained struggle in the distance" (*CW* 456). Rayber can no longer hear the sound or word at any pitch; he is deaf, as Lucette says, to the Lord's word. The distant din is Bishop's death roar; the cry of suffering is the voice of God. The excruciating bellow blares out one last time, "rising out of its own momentum as if it were escaping finally, after centuries of waiting, into silence" (*CW* 456).

The background of silence marks the enormous changes in the inner world of all three characters. For Rayber, this silence is the chill demonic aftershock of deafness to the Logos. Trained in Mason's stern self-control, Rayber over the years uses his "rigid ascetic discipline" (*CW* 402) to keep God from controlling him. The silence surrounding Rayber at Bishop's slaughter indicates that he is spiritually dead while physically alive. The silence waiting to embrace Bishop is a different stillness; this quiet opens to fuller life. Bishop's silence, which inheres in his physical condition and is broken only by crying, embodies the desert ideals of silence as the source of humility and tenderness. The child lives alone and in the poverty of total dependence on God for his dignity. Without making a choice, Bishop is the humble prayer alive that the desert mothers and fathers valued in silence. Humility made the inarticulate child proof against Rayber and freed him from the self-absorption that separates the human person from God. God never leaves the child; God is present at the sparkling fountain and God is with Bishop at the blackened lake. In the dark water, the rescuing flow of the divine spirit softens the child's death. Baptized by his killer, Bishop is buried in mystery, enshrouded in silence. In Bishop, the Logos reveals itself and acts.

The significance of silence in Tarwater's case is far more complex and central than in the case of the other two characters. It involves a dialectic with speech that rises from some of the subtlest insights that the ancient hermits gained in solitude. Silence attends the young killer's crossing into the deepest zones of the still desert world of warring tribulation, the inner combat that profoundly expresses the faith that O'Connor's art brings to life. For the desert elders, silence entails more than not speaking. It encompasses a positive receptivity to language at the inmost center, the heart of personal integration of human faculties. Silence is a habit of being; it links the inner life with action, which is to say that silence is a prerequisite for linguistic integrity. "Teach your mouth to say what is in your heart," says Abba Poemen (*Sayings*, Poemen 164 [189]). Again, Abba Moses reminds us: "If a man's deeds are not in harmony with his prayer, he labors in vain" (*Sayings*, Moses 4 [141]). For the ascetic and prophetic life to have the truthfulness it seeks, words must be tested by experience. "When words and life correspond to one another they are together the whole of philosophy" (*Sayings*, Isidore of Pelusia 1 [98]); and then silence reaches fruition. It is a smooth transition from the *Sayings* of the ancient hermits to the sayings of the modern hermit novelist.

"Conviction without experience makes for harshness" (*HB* 97), says Amma Flannery. Silence can bring about the union of experience with expression that signals prophetic integrity and desert holiness. Holiness in words is, of course, O'Connor's true subject. In working out the training of her prophet-elect, she brings Tarwater back to the silent source of his integrity and spiritual vitality. His future work depends on this return, because silence nourishes and supports the message he must deliver in its full revelatory force. Silence will teach his heart to guard that which his tongue teaches (*Sayings,* Poemen 188 [193]).

Part 3 (chapters 10–12) of *The Violent Bear It Away* concentrates on Tarwater's tongue to enact the drama of silence, in which he confronts his torturing consciousness. In this inner war, the powers of good and evil, life affirming and life denying, Logos and logismos, pull in opposite directions to get the boy to speak or be silent according to their aims. Never talkative to begin with, Tarwater wants to be stone silent after leaving the lake to hold back admitting that he uttered the christening words in the act of drowning Bishop. Tarwater's silence is more than an attempt to suppress the guilt caused by his murdering Bishop. Tarwater has been taught by Mason that the tongue expresses the depths of the heart and that words effect and reveal invisible powers. Tarwater fears that hidden world. Words in the prophetic and patristic economy bear a unique relation to the sanctifying sacrament of rebirth through the death of sin, the baptism Tarwater was ordered to perform on Bishop and unknowingly accomplished. O'Connor's treatment of Bishop's drowning carries the special understanding that the early Christians found in the Word becoming flesh to give life. They developed an extensive theology of the Logos that described (with magnificence in Origen) the mystical communion of the Logos with the baptized. And so the baptizing words blazoned forth by the Logos itself, uttered over and against Tarwater's demonic will at the lake, consummate Bishop's life in death, the death of sin accomplished by the enfleshed Word.

Although Tarwater tries to rationalize his voicing the baptismal words while drowning Bishop as "'an accident'" that "'don't mean nothing'" (*CW* 458), the words plague him because the they were pulled from his tongue against his will and do mean something to him. The most powerful force, the Logos itself, has claims on Tarwater's tongue and lips. He feels yet another tug at his tongue from the slumberous trucker who picks him up and wants nothing but meaningless words from him. Like the other demons assaulting Tarwater, this operator with a serpentine nose tries to reduce his victim to a machine, a device sputtering gibberish. When Tarwater opens his mouth to speak words, "none came" out of it (*CW* 457). Tarwater is tongue-tied, gripped by secret forces—Logos and logismos—fighting for his voice, the instrument of the prophet's mind and heart. As the Word overcomes all words, a silence affixes other silences. A mute vision of the murder scene burns its unexpungeable details into Tarwater's memory as he rides the truck "in silence." In Tarwater's mute recollection, Bishop's "light silent eyes" stare pleadingly at Tarwater, who is yielding to the "violet-colored" eyes of the devil (*CW* 461) who is engineering his human cargo to the "silent" lake bank (*CW* 462). The sudden cry of the baptismal words shatters the dream and hurls Tarwater out of the silent rig and into the soundless dark. Back on the road, he plans to return to Powderhead, where he can be silent about the murder and can be his own man spared from "the torture of prophecy" (*CW* 465) and live by his own will. The very silence that he seeks to deny his sinful disobedience, however, will teach him "the blessings of obedience" (*Early Fathers*, Dorotheus 3 [153]). In silence and solitude, Tarwater's will begins to bend away from himself and toward others and God.

As with the desert searchers, Tarwater, who is now wandering in the wilderness of sin and loneliness, receives through his body the lesson for his soul. Throughout the novel, his body registers particular needs that his proud mind and egotistical will deny; on his return to Powderhead, these bleak and insistent physical urgencies begin to sink in. He hungers. He thirsts. He sees Bishop in a black child. He smells the demon near him. He hears the stinging denunciations of the unmistakably angelic woman who nabs him for shaming the dead and scorning "'the Resurrection and the Life'" (*CW* 468). This messenger of truth leaves the boy speechless except for an unstated obscenity that his controlling logismos spits out. Need and anxiety drain Tarwater's musculature of its pubertal sap to the degree that "his skin seemed to have shrunk on the frame of his bones from dryness" (*CW* 468). Ascesis has taken hold of his body, which bears the desert's aridity; and an unsparing mortification ensues. Along the highway, his demonic friend rematerializes in a fancy car. Dressed to kill, the devil drugs Tarwater with liquor and rapes him in the "silent" woods (*CW* 471). An hour later, not a coherent word but a "loud dry cry" (*CW* 472) tears from the boy's mouth. Having gotten the use he wants of Tarwater for the moment, the demon discards him.

O'Connor's presentation of rape draws less on the modern understanding of rape as a political crime (with its attendant sympathy for the victim) and more on the timeless spiritual effects of this notorious weapon of degradation. The hour-long rape in the silent woods off the dirt road, the site where O'Connor's devils feel most free to indulge their malice and will, brings out into the open the extent to which the logismos spiritually penetrates the boy. Rape consummates Tarwater's self-plunder-ing, which has taken the form of his assenting concourse with the logis-mos of his will. Under his demonic partner's brute sexual force, Tarwa-ter experiences the loss of control that his fierce will imposed on Bishop and the loss of freedom brought about by his demons. Those who fill themselves on personal desire, says Gregory of Nyssa, in *The Life of Moses*, become "empty and a vacant container" under Satan's tyranni-cal power (61 [68]). Gregory explains the hollowing of O'Connor's young killer in preparation for prophecy. As the satisfactions of Tarwater's pri-vate will take their toll, Tarwater's violated and desiccated body begins to bear the primal themes of the desert.

The desert fathers and mothers had a cure for the loss of control Tarwater experiences in rape and with language. "If you cannot contain yourself," says Abba Matoes, "flee into solitude" (*Sayings*, Matoes 13 [145]). Solitude enforces a positive self-emptying (*kenosis*) that brings the hero to the "beginning" (*HB* 359) of his vocation and the novel to a close. The drama ends with the renegade back in Powderhead. In the last chap-ter, Tarwater does not say one word. Buford Munson speaks four brief sentences to inform the prodigal boy that he, Buford, buried Mason while Tarwater was drunk; and Buford's truthful words demolish Tarwater's residual self-confidence and shut him up for good. Also, the velvet voice of the logismos sighs its final importunings; but the fresh ache from be-ing raped teaches the boy that loneliness is preferable to his attacker's conjugal alliance. Tarwater, for the first time, discerns his demon as his "adversary" and torches the nearby tree to get rid of the wraith. This "roaring blaze" (*CW* 475) declares the boy's war on evil.

Declaration of war, however, requires weaponry to fight the adver-sary. In the unseen combat of the spirit, humility alone overcomes the devil (*Sayings*, Anthony the Great 2 [2]; Theodora 6 [84]). The efficacy of demonic power depends on the human victim's prideful assumption of adequacy in meeting the demon. Humility, by contrast, defeats the oth-erwise indomitable enemy by acknowledging weakness so that the Al-mighty can intervene. Thinking the same thoughts as the desert elders, and feeling as they do, O'Connor intuitively reimagines so closely a vi-gnette in *The Lives of the Desert Fathers* that the fourth-century Egyp-tian text serves to introduce and elucidate Tarwater's final action. John of Lycopolis tells of a young man who had sinned gravely and repented mightily. "At God's bidding this youth was struck by compunction for his many sins. He made straight for the cemetery, where he bitterly la-mented his former life, throwing himself down on his face and not dar-ing to make a sound, or to pronounce the name of God." The youth renounced his life with groans "from the depths of his heart" (*Lives*, John of Lycopolis 37 [57–58]).

Like the young man in the ancient *Lives*, O'Connor's youth, also not daring to make a sound, mourns his sins at a burial place. Death is the final experience of the human body and the first lesson of inner growth for ascetics. "A man who keeps death before his eyes," says an elder, "will at all times overcome his cowardice" (Merton, *Wisdom* 138 [76]). By keeping "death in mind," Tarwater will "not forget the eternal judgement" (*Sayings*, Evagrius 4 [64]), as the hermits and Mason before him did not. Evagrius's saying expresses the wisdom issuing from the encounter with death that concludes so many of O'Connor's narratives. In every instance, O'Connor's protagonist finds meaning and joy in grief. Tarwater's facing death is the founding experience of his relationship with God. As the desert blossoms with divine promise (Hosea 2:14–15), so the wild field around Powderhead yields a vision of Mason among the multitude miraculously being fed the loaves and fishes at an eternal meal.

In both Mark 8:1 and Matthew 15:33, the feeding occurs in the desert. The slope on which the crowd sits in the novel links the revelation of God to Tarwater with the divine disclosure on Mount Sinai to Moses. As God was with the Israelites at every step in the wilderness (Exodus 15:26), so the Logos has been an abiding presence with Tarwater on his stumbling desert passage. When the banquet dream seizes Tarwater at the end, he sees that his journey stands at and under the charismatic authority of Mason, whose ascetic solitude informs his instruction. Central to that teaching is Mason's belief that the world was made for the dead—which the novel's ending dramatically corroborates. In this confirmation, a dynamic need imbues the old man's envisioned body. His bulk is leaning forward on the ground, looking up with hunger to the single basket of the messianic banquet. What Mason yearns for is satisfied by the very nourishment that leaves his desire unsatisfied, in the way that Dante in the *Paradiso* moves and grows deeper in love through the yearning that carries him to love itself. Stunned by the revelation, Tarwater remains in Powderhead from dusk to midnight to take in the ambient gift of the great feast before his eyes. Understanding again comes through his body, especially his mouth. Tarwater's hunger is "so great" (*CW* 478) that he takes on his dead uncle's ache for food as his own.

Tarwater's struggle presses beyond his privileged gaze of the festive meal. The lesson in his exodus through the desert is a venture of integrating into practical life the stern training and wisdom he received right there in Powderhead. O'Connor marks this concurrence through the respiratory act essential to life and meditation. Tarwater's breath (in Latin, *spiritus*) goes "out to meet" (*CW* 478) the fire that he knows tested Daniel and transported Moses. This fire is the purifying element in the divine word that Tarwater expects to hear. Like the youth in the *Lives*, the boy throws himself on the ground to receive the word. His gesture of love insolubly binds asceticism with prophecy as he physically lays down his life for others (John 15:13; *Sayings*, Poemen 116 [184]). In the scorched face and prostrate body of the living nephew, we see honor for his great-uncle and the other dead.

Tarwater's low point of self-abnegation prepares for the high point of the novel. Tarwater rises from the ground, sees the ruinous fire he started, and stoops to smear his forehead with dirt from the grave. He who loved the excellence of his self-will now confesses his persistent destructive will as the inner enemy that he must fight. His admission of personal sin is a first effect of grace in Tarwater, and the dirt above his brow forms the seal of the experiences preceding it. It is not Mason's body but Tarwater's ego that lies in ashes. The boy learns what the desert solitaries taught and what modern preceptors deny: his own being is the subject and source of his pains. Whipped, bereft, raped, scorned, and broken of self-will, the boy makes room for God in his soul, a sacred space that expands through self-scrutiny. Exposure to his sinfulness and hunger for the bread in the baskets teach Tarwater that salvation lies in the bread of life and in loving others. For all its introspection, the solitary life is a life for others. "Our life and our death is with our neighbour," says Anthony (*Sayings*, Anthony the Great 9 [3]).

Readers who find this eschatological evocation too exuberant have only to glance at patristic writings to see how naturally the course of Tarwater's renunciation sweeps him up into the hope of regaining paradise. The desert mothers and fathers saw their practice in solitude as a way to recover the innocence of Adam and Eve and then to earn the glory purchased by the new Adam (Burton-Christie 231–33). The ending of *The Violent Bear It Away* revives for late twentieth-century readers the motive pervading the ancient *Sayings* and *Lives*. The desert ascesis of dying to oneself aims for a rebirth of love of others in God. The hard Tennessee earth on which Tarwater prostrates himself is the severe training ground of that inclusive love. The war ahead of him will be fought by drawing from the austere practice of love and humility developed in the grace-filled backwoods.

It is precisely O'Connor's understanding of ascetic life as the basis for a universal communion that brings her to say in a letter to T. R. Spivey of

9 April 1960 that *The Violent Bear It Away* "is a very minor hymn to the Eucharist" (*HB* 387). The reference to the Eucharist may strike some readers as a devotional aside that can be passed over in favor of looking into more conspicuous issues raised by the novel. Others may find O'Connor's crossing from art to worship to be abrupt and baffling. But those who are attuned to the spiritual currents in O'Connor's fiction are in a position to appreciate her linking artistic practice with sacramental action. To follow this transformation is to approach anew the heart of O'Connor's poetics of solitude. Seeing how *The Violent Bear It Away* becomes a song of praise to God is the goal of the final portion of this chapter.

First, a word is in order about the word Eucharist. In the original Greek sense, Eucharist means to give thanks for "goodly gifts." By extension, the word has also come to be associated with the Last Supper (Luke 12:19–20), during which Jesus gave his body and blood to be taken in the form of bread and wine. Jesus' offering at the table anticipated his supreme gifts of suffering and dying. As the sacrifice is for all, all are invited to the table to share in the meal. Each subsequent liturgical celebration of this oblation, then, brings the past sacrifice alive in the present. The eucharistic action accomplishes a new sacrifice of the single historical sacrifice, for which the recipient gives thanks. Gratitude, like Jesus' original self-donation, has a collective and communal dimension. As the gift freely given is for all, so the grateful response for the divine offering is universal.

The public aspect of solitude and ascesis has been part of Tarwater's destiny from the beginning. If his self-consecration at the end is only for himself, it would lead to spiritual pride or a merely symbolic moment that O'Connor would dismiss, effectively condemning it, as she did when Mary McCarthy condescendingly allowed that the Eucharist was "a pretty good" symbol (*HB* 125). A disincarnate faith offends O'Connor. But to express her belief, O'Connor sacramentalizes Tarwater's graveside genuflection by making it the pivot of a twofold liturgical action that has been quietly built into the entire novel. Up to the ending, the events emphasize the writings of the prophets as amplifying God's call to Tarwater to be spokesman of the divine word. In Protestant and Catholic worship, this movement would constitute the Liturgy of the Word. Tarwater's submission to the prophetic call, however, enacts a shift. In a nonverbal way, he acknowledges that he is unworthy to receive the Lord; but if the Lord only says the word, he, the broken sinner, will be healed and prepared for God. The transition is from the Liturgy of the Word to the Liturgy of the Bread (or Eucharist), from preparation to reception.

There is also a theological transition in this movement. Surrender previously moved Tarwater's conflict toward reconciliation with God—that is, the Father. Now the turn is toward Jesus, the divine word enfleshed, and toward communion with the Son. Far from being symbolic, the liturgy that ensues is disturbingly incarnational. Jesus enters Tarwater's blood. God not only says the word but does the word once again. The words of command silently rise from the dirt into the boy's veins. He is a word of His. "GO WARN THE CHILDREN OF GOD OF THE TERRIBLE SPEED OF MERCY" (*CW* 478). A trio of embracing prepositional phrases, each introduced with the *of* of God's belonging, unites through forgiveness Tarwater and all the people of God as members in the body of Jesus.

Although the movement from word to Eucharist follows the order of worship that O'Connor experienced in her church, her artistic rendering is more radical in its intense corporeality and theological poignancy than the rite she knew. O'Connor takes the words that might appear symbolic and puts them back on the track to living things themselves. Words become organisms, seeds breaking into Tarwater's blood to make flesh, seeds for new life. In the parable of the sower, Jesus says that the "seed is the word of God" (Luke 8:11). In *The Violent Bear It Away*, Jesus' words are made flesh. What appears to be an object, the seed, hides a story with an unfolding future. The redeeming death that flowed from the incarnation of the Word now abides reincarnated in Tarwater. In the masses that O'Connor attended, the rites celebrating these events, the Liturgy of the Word and the Liturgy of the Bread, were separate; but she joins them into a primordial sacrament.

The combined rite brings Tarwater backward and forward in time. By setting Tarwater's reception of the blood within the dream of the paradisal repast, O'Connor restores the most ancient association of the Liturgy of the Eucharist with Jesus' resurrection. The future arises from that event. The Eucharist is not merely a private exchange between Tarwater and Jesus; for the dream depicts a crowd, and the commanding words speak of the multitude. As Jesus' suffering and dying were for all, so Tarwater's prophetic life must be for all "the children of God" (*CW* 479), for people he does not know. O'Connor wants to get into Tarwater's skin the words that unite all in a seamless identification with the divine. Rooted in the dirt of the backwoods, this union comes about in silence, including the silence in which readers bring the text to life, for the true heart of *The Violent Bear It Away* is not heard but felt. The silence of solitude composes an interior attitude of attentive listening, of interior receptivity to the interior God, who would keep aside all that might interfere with the Spirit's voice.

The "great asceticism," says Amma Syncletica, is "to control one-self in illness and to sing hymns of thanksgiving to God" (*Sayings*, Syncletica 8 [232]). O'Connor did both. She made of her stricken body and her forced withdrawal from the world the condition of her extraordinary art. Gratitude was the bedrock of her response to life, as it was for the elders. "I work from such a basis of poverty," O'Connor wrote, "that everything I do is a miracle to me" (*HB* 127). That "everything" drew sustenance from the Eucharist that O'Connor deemed "the center of existence for me" (*HB* 125). In the marvel that is *The Violent Bear It Away*, she offers, to reiterate her words, "a very minor hymn to the Eucharist" (*HB* 387). Although it may be slight next to the handiwork of creation against which O'Connor measured her effort, *The Violent Bear It Away* has become astonishing and urgent for our spiritually starved age. The book is a song to the Eucharist in its original meaning as the thanks of one who has received great gifts. In gratitude for what O'Connor has received, she in turn passes on the story of prophets, who have been on the endangered species list for some time, who receive the word in the desert of our time. Through the depiction of Tarwater's evil, she raises the question our century must ask: How can someone who has done something so horrible make something of his life? Through her prophet-elect's wrenching spiritual upheaval, accomplished by means of fire and loss, she explores inner zones of thought and feeling that our era needs to face out for its moral survival. This modern yet ancient story of a bloody, renunciative adventure through the arid wastes and across the human body forces us to realize how rarely the warring life of the soul is probed in contemporary literature. At the moment, power more than inner truth preoccupies us. To countervail this bias, O'Connor invites us through Tarwater's inner struggle to recognize the value and insights of solitude and spiritual combat.

O'Connor reminds the age that even the most willful and murderous among us are forever at the mercies of inner eddies of submission, self-denial, and desire for transcendence. The mysterious connection between our body and our soul is not one that many writers even try to consider at great depth, for to contemplate its spiritual textures would be to refute postmodernism's treasured claim, as one of Don DeLillo's characters in *White Noise* tells the hero, that "'you are the sum total of your data'" (141) or that we are products of culture, playthings of chemical processes (as Rayber holds), whose destinies are set by political and evolutionary powers. In open warfare against all this, O'Connor recalls in her hymn to the body the experiment of the desert fathers and mothers to affirm that our bodies are capable of transformation and that we are free to define ourselves and to bend the fixed self-will to align our identity with God.

The Violent Bear It Away is the story of the ancient Egyptian desert set in the American South. The subject matter is shaped by the new meaning derived from modern anguish. To bear her goodly gifts, O'Connor chooses a hero who at fourteen has already participated in the lethal violence of our time. Like many before him in sacred history, the Tennessean will be a holy terror in distributing the news that pulsates in his blood. His ruthless manner and remedy are necessary to cut through the impassivity that the contemporary prophet faces. The good news lies in Tarwater's stern character. He learns with Abba Alonius that "in the world there is only myself and God" (*Sayings*, Alonius 1 [35]); and by reaching the deep knowledge of himself in communion with the absolute, Tarwater embraces all others and all of physical creation.

Flannery O'Connor has become a habit of knowing for the late twentieth century. Her writing is a vade mecum in how to live in desolate times, a handbook for constant use drawn from the words and examples of the primitive monastics she admired. And the hermit novelist of Milledgeville is a match for the great teachers of the ancient desert. As the primitive solitaries are the spirit-bearers of the divine word in obscure and unspectacular practice, O'Connor is the modern writer of daily love and self-donation exercised within the context of ordinary human weakness and brutality. Her letters stand alongside *The Sayings of the Desert Fathers* in their wisdom, and her fiction rivals the remarkable stories in *The Live of the Desert Fathers* in their edification. In personal correspondence, fiction, and lectures, she writes with tremendous freedom; yet her basically joyous and mystical outlook unfolds through an intellectual approach that could be severe. That stringency derives from the probity with which O'Connor faced out the great cost of love in the modern century, an era that she penetrated beneath the exterior surface of appearances to the fundamental secret of inmost life.

From her remote perch in Baldwin County, O'Connor saw an America that no other writer has got right. Now we cannot see it without seeing O'Connor. From our basis of poverty in the desert, we can only be grateful for the miracle of O'Connor's correcting our vision by her perception of divine love revealing that we, greatly loved, are participants in the lasting drama crystallizing around the word uttered and acted in the desert.

6 Acedia *and* Penthos

The demon of *acedia* . . . is the one that causes the most serious trouble of all. . . . He instills in the heart of the monk a hatred for the place, a hatred for his very life.
—Evagrius Ponticus, *Praktikos*

He who wishes to purify his faults purifies them with tears . . . ; for weeping is the way the Scriptures and our Fathers give us, when they say, "Weep!" Truly, there is no other way than this.
—Poemen, *The Sayings of the Desert Fathers*

BY WAY OF INTRODUCING the spiritual poetics that O'Connor develops in *Everything That Rises Must Converge* (1965), I want to reconsider two events in *The Violent Bear It Away.* One scene concerns George Rayber; the other centers on Francis Marion Tarwater. In both situations, the respective character is alone in a secluded spot. Though distant from each other, the two locales are places of death and decision. For Tarwater, the place is the Powderhead gravesite of his great-uncle Mason; for Rayber, it is the Cherokee Lodge murder scene of his son Bishop. Violence, gravity, and tenderness imbue the moral atmosphere of both burial grounds, for they are at once haunted by the devil and hallowed by God. In these separate encounters with the death of a loved relative, divine and satanic powers assert their claims on the young Tarwater and the older Rayber, forcing each in solitude to choose between his private will urged by the devil and the law laid down by God. Rayber succumbs to his demons, feels nothing, and collapses. Tarwater, conversely, in open resistance to his demons throws himself to the ground in repentance for his previous sins.

What is striking about these scenes is that something expected is missing: tears. Even in the O'Connor world, known more for its steely rather than emotive responses, a father's witnessing the slaying of his child cries out for tears; but George Rayber goes numb. The *logismoi*, the satanic thought-flows, which for years have planted thoughts of contempt in Rayber's mind for Bishop because he has Down's syndrome and have even incited his murder, have finally overtaken Rayber's heart to deprive him of the power to feel. At Bishop's murder and elsewhere in O'Connor's fiction, the devil's victory proclaims itself in the drying up of the source of tears. A cold heart leads to dry eyes.

Rayber's desiccation and insentience manifest the condition the ancient hermits called *acedia*. The Latin word *acedia* (in Greek, *akedia*) defies accurate translation into English (accidie). It is a monastic term that the late-fourth-century writer Evagrius called one of the eight basic categories of evil. Acedia is a state of the soul that is invariably linked to solitude, and so it follows that hermits have a deep understanding of the condition. The *Sayings* and *Lives* show indolence, tedium, disgust, despondency, and bitterness as some of the features of acedia. Most simply described, the solitary no longer finds life meaningful. Evagrius, who offers the fullest development of the concept, warns that the demon of acedia "causes the most serious trouble of all" (12 [18]). This demon can take over one's entire being and in particular darken the mind by driving away thoughts of peace and God. It "weighs down" the soul through "faintheartedness" and "also attacks your body through sickness, debility, weakening of the knees, and all the members" (*Sayings*, Theodora 3 [83]). Acedia was not taken lightly by the desert-dwellers; nor can one dismiss the workings of the demon as safely confined to superstitious antiquity. O'Connor saw in the modern world the terrible ravages caused by the demon of acedia and depicted such devastations in her solitaries. For O'Connor, acedia is an extreme affliction of the heart. This sickness sinks the victim into desolation and lifts the servants of Satan with delight. Because Rayber can neither mourn for his sins nor weep for his son, his demons can dwell over his crumbled body with malicious satisfaction.

Satan has nothing to gloat over, however, in the graveyard scene with Tarwater. At the end of *The Violent Bear It Away*, Tarwater too lies on the ground but not from caving in to the forceful logismoi that have been attacking him. Rather, on returning to Powderhead with the ache of sexual assault still in his body, the prodigal boy reacts to his rapist-demon's fresh importunings by sending the demon up in a roaring fire. Then, as Tarwater goes deeper into himself, he acknowledges his evil. Self-scrutiny leads to remorse; remorse elicits repentance; and repentance opens Tarwater to his new life as a prophet. His heart and body quicken. With the fire of forgiveness burning within, Tarwater grasps the suffering of others in need of salvation, others he does not even know. Tarwater's eyes burn with dedication to others and contrition, but they do not weep.

The sorrowful disposition of the soul that seizes Tarwater at the conclusion of *The Violent Bear It Away* concerned the ancient spiritual writers. They sought out whatever sorrow is engendered by repentance and is sensitive to the loss, whether one's own or that of others, of eternal life because of sin. Abba Poemen repeatedly extols this godly sorrow. When a brother asks what to do about his sins, Poemen says: "He who wishes to purify his faults purifies them with tears and he who wishes to acquire virtues, acquires them with tears; for weeping is the way the Scriptures and our Fathers give us, when they say, 'Weep!' Truly, there is no other way than this" (*Sayings*, Poemen 119 [184]). Tears freed the solitaries to show benevolence. Tears were at the center of desert teaching. One day on the way to Egypt, Abba Poemen saw a woman weeping bitterly in a tomb and discerned in her soul a lesson for ascetics: "Even so the monk would always have compunction in himself" (*Sayings*, Poemen 26 [171]). The awareness that especially sensitizes the heart is the reality of the final judgment. For Abba Sisoes, the remembrance of personal faults so heightened the salutary effect of repentance that he made transgression the focus of his day: "I go to sleep in sin and I awaken in sin" (*Sayings*, Sisoes 36 [219]). Such an awareness of the ultimate loss of God through sin leads to compunction.

Compunction is the modern word for the practice the primitive solitaries cultivated to draw close to God through sorrow; the ancient word for this capacity is *penthos*. Penthos originally had no religious meaning. It signified mourning for the dead and sadness over misfortune and also came to suggest a plaint for a dead god. The practice of the desert elders drew on the custom of their prevailing culture; and in doing so, they revealed the transforming power of compunction. As developed by the writers of the Christian East, penthos acquired a constellation of spiritual meanings that linked the awareness of personal sin with mourning for the possible loss of eternal happiness for oneself and all others. Penthos is an expansive, highly charged, and fluid concept that has been a rich source of inner development for spiritual searchers into our own era through such writers as T. S. Eliot, Thomas Merton, Walker Percy, and, of course, O'Connor. However elaborated, penthos remains synonymous with tears. The tears may flow inward; but without tears, there is no penthos. One of the fruits of godly sorrow is the gift of tears.

Penthos takes time to develop and heal the deep wounds caused by sin. Among the benefits, the elders saw penthos as a way to check acedia. "When we meet with the demon of *acedia*," says Evagrius, "then is the time with tears . . . to sow seeds of firm hope in ourselves" (27 [23]). Whereas acedia stiffens the heart and debilitates the soul, penthos softens the heart and strengthens the soul. The remedy, which is by no means easy, demands fasting, vigils, and prayer, the proven and painstaking correctives of disordered emotions. Such a regime fully engages the body, for an abstract and cold repentance is no more capable of bringing about penthos than is a passing outburst of contrition. Moreover, contrite mourning for sin is ceaseless because the risk of losing salvation during life is constant. Perseverance in remorse has the benefit of fortifying the solitary's resolve to follow God's directive. In this way, the gift of tears is bound to firmness of will, for the human will that gives up its personal desires attaches the solitary to the will of God.

Because compunction develops gradually, penthos is not for the young. The distinctive maturity associated with the charisma comes through in O'Connor's subtle treatment of compunction in her children. Her children certainly experience grief; they repent in their own ways; and they can be morally precocious; but there is a limit to their spiritual advancement. They are given to be physically assertive or violent and then peacefully remorseful; and in their sorrow, they experience the grace of contrition without having the time to prove their spiritual mettle. O'Connor's most grown-up youngster, Tarwater, shows how well the author grasps the nuanced desert understanding of godly grief by bringing the boy only to the threshold of tears. Despite Tarwater's wrenching physical punishment and psychological torment, as O'Connor explains in her letter to John Hawkes of 20 November 1959, "I've left him right at the beginning" (*HB* 359). His eyes burn dry, but tears lie in the future of sorrow that O'Connor envisions for her teenage prophet.

The tears implied as part of Tarwater's destiny are realized in *Everything That Rises Must Converge*. Here, in her posthumous collection, O'Connor depicts the triumph of life through nine stories of joyous sorrow. Described scripturally, these stories vivify the second beatitude being lived out in our time: blessed—which is to say, happy—are those who weep (Matthew 5:3). In the patristic order, weeping was the highest expression of joy to be realized in this world, for tears helped the hermits overcome the wounds and losses of life. Basil of Ancyra asks: "How can what was spoiled become unspoiled? How can what has once been violated by desire, corruption and passion become inviolate, when signs of corruption remain in the body and the soul?" (qtd. in Hausherr 21). The answer for the ancient solitaries was in weeping, for those who wept constantly remembered the glory from which they had fallen and how they have been exiled by sin in a place of tears. The violated bodies that lie throughout *Everything That Rises Must Converge* pose the same questions about their restoration; and O'Connor dramatizes the same answer found in numerous desert writings. The final sentence from "Parker's Back" serves to suggest what lies ahead in her last book: "There he was— who called himself Obadiah Elihue—leaning against the tree, crying like a baby" (*CW* 675). The tears flowing from Parker's eyes will hearten him to face out the demons determined to impede his newly found spiritual progress.

Parker is not alone in godly sorrow. Compunction marks the gateway to divine proximity for all the protagonists in *Everything That Rises Must Converge*. Story after story, grief suddenly pours out. Characters who by temperament and rural conditioning stubbornly refuse to show weakness for fear of being mocked or taken advantage of forthwith embrace an inner softness. The reader's astonishment over this moral turn corresponds to the characters' shock in seeing that they had it all wrong about their virtues and fears. The weakness they have been afraid of becomes strength before God; and their new pliancy, with God's aid, gives them courage to resist their demons. Divine help comes none too soon. Immersed in their perilous, misunderstood existence, these loners feel the onslaught of racism, intractable sexism, unbridled violence, sheer madness, and O'Connor's standby, murder. In bringing their warfare against evil to light, O'Connor does not merely recall the Eastern hermits to point up the deficiencies in her southern rustics' responses to evil; rather, with a penthos of her own, O'Connor shows how in the spiritual war tears can help master the evil that cuts off modern nihilists and heathens from the fullness of God's presence.

One additional introductory point needs to be made for us to appreciate the pattern underlying the variety of experiences leading the sojourners to God in O'Connor's last book. As the characters vary in age, remorse, and moral awareness, so they dramatize a range of impediments to and effects of penthos; but whatever the differences, all make headway toward the absolute. Some go further than others; but the form and content of the immersion in sorrow follow the movement that the scattered ancient commentaries on ascetic life collectively set forth. Roughly outlined, the way to compunction begins with a startling shock, or *catanyxis*. Usually originating from the outside, this jolt goes deep into the person's being to plant in the soul a new attitude, emotion, or resolve. The blow acts as an interior lesson to direct the person away from sin and toward God. The experience is so wrenching that the recurring figure for catanyxis in Eastern writing is that of piercing the heart. The solitary "labors night and day in vigils and unceasing prayer," says Abba Hyperychios, so that "by piercing his heart he produces tears" (qtd. in Hausherr 9). Tears manifest the psychological reaction to repentance. With the image of Jesus' outpouring of tears when he entered Jerusalem on Palm Sunday always before them, the desert solitaries saw sorrow as essential to spiritual growth. Only the deepest softening affected by catanyxis, which causes the deepest impact, can get O'Connor's characters to change their ways. The catanyctic blow fits O'Connor's effort to keep a forgetful people from forgetting and to keep their resistant hearts from atrophying.

The sustained attention to penthos and catanyxis in *Everything That Rises Must Converge* brings O'Connor to revise with fine consistency the moral atmosphere in which she is working. Tears create fresh inner climates in these stories. We see the artist of driving rains, the cold drainage ditch, and the bloody, frozen barnyard now writing of warm emotional dependencies produced by grief—erotic whispers, a melting birdstain-icon, a pierced heart, and sobbing entreaties. By following the urgings of these sorrows, the remorseful solitaries in O'Connor's final collection find the magnetic source of consolation with God.

"Everything That Rises Must Converge," the first story in the collection, establishes the themes of dejection and of sin denied and forcibly confronted that inform all the succeeding stories. For some time before the action begins, the spirit of sadness has gripped the hero, Julian. His avoidance of grief is another form of sorrow, one that serves only to darken the mood of the demonic hold on him. Within Julian's gloom, however, there stirs the need for him to plumb the source of pain to be released from his demon's bondage. Spiritually put, an inchoate penthos struggles against a vested acedia. The conflict roiling Julian's inner world affects his negotiations of the outer world—which in 1961, when O'Connor finished the story, is a southern culture shaking with the enmities of race relations. When these social forces collide with Julian's personal antagonisms, his interior world is laid waste, and he finds himself in solitude. The catanyxis or inner burst shatters the hero's resistance to sorrow, and a deep sense of loss moves him to "crying" vocally and spiritually for help. Julian's wail is slow in coming to pass, abrupt in manifestation, and colossal in outcome. At the very end of the story, Julian is swept out of his insensate moroseness into a "tide of darkness" that carries him to the threshold of truthfulness and heightened self-knowledge awaiting him as he enters "the world of guilt and sorrow" (*CW* 500).

Julian clearly is in a bad way and needs to be rescued. He is fearful, hostile, and dishonest about his dependence on his mother. It is possible to consider the chronic foul temper of this son in his early twenties who takes out his self-distrust on the mother who supports him as a symptom of arrested development, for Julian's testiness does come across as a child's constant hitting on a high chair with a spoon (Niland and Evans 53; Hendin 106–7). There is also evidence to support a reading of his spleenful behavior as resulting from sexual repression and his failure to get anywhere with his writing. These frustrations do arise, but they flare up as skirmishes in a greater engagement. O'Connor wants us to see that Julian is grappling with more than juvenile self-absorption and artistic ambition. Julian is up against demons that work to put an end to joy and to feed a bitterness capable of sapping his body's vigor. In portraying Julian's rancor with his mother and his deceit in race relations, O'Connor insists that we go beneath his conduct to consider the spiritual source of his deviousness. Looked at from this perspective, Julian is in the peril brought about by acedia. A clear-eyed view requires that we see him critically, as many readers do (Coles 122; Feeley 103–4); and yet by also defining Julian's character at the depth of his hidden struggle, O'Connor invites a sympathy for him that perhaps only she herself—or a desert mother—could feel.

The demon of acedia reveals its power through the ways in which Julian's grimness blackens every aspect of the story. For one thing, the language used to gauge his gloom makes "Everything That Rises Must Converge" a rich thesaurus of words delineating the effects of acedia. O'Connor goes so far as to use a clinical vocabulary, which is rare in her writing, to show Julian's inner state. "Depressed," "depression," and "more depressed" recur in the first several pages; and each time the term appears, it stresses the anatomical and moral implications of Julian's low spirits. His mother has merely to put on a new hat to sink his emotions: "Everything that gave her pleasure was small and depressed him" (*CW* 485). As they walk to get the bus going downtown to his mother's exercise class, his body becomes "saturated in depression, as if in the midst of his martyrdom he had lost his faith," and he mopes with a "long, hopeless, irritated face" (*CW* 486). When she mentions returning the hat, he becomes "more depressed than ever" (*CW* 487); and, under his demon's control, he viciously lashes out at her for trying to please him.

Julian's intention toward his mother is clear: "There was in him an evil urge to break her spirit" (*CW* 489). Julian's motive to dispirit exemplifies Evagrius's explanation in the *Praktikos* of the aim of the demon of acedia to inculcate a sense "that charity has departed from among the brethren, that there is no one to give encouragement." These deliberate moral injuries follow from the demon's success in imbuing the solitary with "a hatred for his very life itself" (Evagrius 12 [19]). Sure enough, Julian aims to unnerve his mother and succeeds in doing so. The simple act of accompanying his mother to her Wednesday night exercise class at the Y follows the black course of Julian's "'vile humor'" (*CW* 489), as his mother calls it, that leads to her fatal stroke. Their weekly trip to town becomes enshrouded by the "growing darkness" (*CW* 487) of falling night. In darkness, demons flourish. As the forces of acedia and bitterness drive to their goal of death, there seeps through the swelling tide of darkness created by evil the rising flow of remorse. This countercurrent surfaces through sorrow. It is hard to reconcile the emergence of tenderness from the evil forces surrounding Julian's degrading actions, but the interior demonic rapids do emit the flow of penthos that can deliver Julian, in the midst of aching bondage, to the portal of freedom.

O'Connor's intuitive grasp of the desert solitaries' insights into how acedia destroys the human spirit extends to her direct apprehension of the remedy for the affliction. Tears are the enemy of the enemy, and O'Connor brings Julian to arm himself with the softest of weapons against the most adamant adversary. In the desert scheme, asceticism prepares the person for tears, and several versions of austerity mark the life shared by Julian and his mother. Self-denial, of course, is not necessarily religious; and in "Everything That Rises Must Converge," it is decidedly not. The motives for Julian's mother's asceticism are thriftiness and an overweening desire to dominate her son. She scrimps and saves so that he can write and not strain himself selling typewriters. Julian's flight from the world is misanthropic and maladjusted. His renunciation of ambition masks a fear of failure, and his withdrawal excuses the attendant fear of experience. Mother and son together are at least alike in their regressive asceticism. As Julian's mother separates herself from society out of an unacknowledged racism born of nostalgia for the antebellum South, Julian chooses to be alone in a cocoon of bitterness for reasons of neurotic self-protection. Solitude is his protest against his own passivity, his longing to be cared for, especially in the grand old style to which his mother was accustomed and to which he feels entitled.

Strangely enough, their prideful holding back to defend their vulnerability turns out to provide a basis for spiritual growth. In the case of Julian, whose loneliness and potential goodness are the story's subject, it is a matter of seeing how his twenty-odd years are not an idle vacation from ascetic life but an involuntary preparation for it. The impetus for his flight from the world lies in the nineteenth century, when his family was in its heyday. His great-grandfather, a former governor of the state, had 200 slaves working his plantation; and the two family names, Chestny and Godhigh, proclaim genealogical importance. The legacy of this prosperity for Julian is the sadness that usually attends wealth—especially lost wealth. His estate consists of presumed rank and virtue. Within this ancestral decline, social history passes on a form of individual retribution, for it bequeaths Julian the responsibility to live out the poverty and humility that can correct the self-interest and oppression that can come with wealth. Julian's portion of the past is a stripping away of false definitions of himself until, plantation and favor lost, he and his mother, no different from others, are confined to an apartment in a once-fashionable neighborhood now deteriorated into shabbiness, a social desert suitable to their anonymity and decline. These deprivations constitute the frame of ascesis that can dispose Julian to be taught by his heart.

Julian does listen to certain promptings of the spirit, and they come to him through the needs of others. The call arises from the political tensions of the late 1950s and the 1960s, when the civil rights movement was reshaping the South. Also, there smolders within the shards of racism the hatred that erupts in reaction to change. The flunkies of Satan work well in tumult, for their expertise is stoking fear and violence on all sides. To Julian's credit, he sees the evil of racism and tries to correct its injustices. But Julian's words and actions, however well-intentioned, are the gestures of sentimental politics. In sympathizing with the victims, Julian uses black people as weapons to get back at his mother, avenge imagined hurts, and relieve self-dissatisfactions. Julian seeks in ideology the gratification he cannot find either in writing or in social relations. He rebels on principle and anxiously conforms with a prefabricated norm for virtue. The 1960s version of political correctness finds an adherent in Julian.

For O'Connor, racism—as seen in "The Artificial Nigger"—is more than intolerance and suppression sanctioned by a doctrine of the superiority of one race over another. Culture and policy do not get us off the hook in O'Connor's moral scheme; responsibility falls on each person and is inextricably bound to the inner dimensions of our being. We express our spiritual choices through our politics. In short, bigotry for O'Connor manifests inner disorder. The aggression, fear, egotism, and deceit that prejudice evokes are effects of demonic forces. Accordingly, the fight to overcome oppression has two fronts: at the bar and within the soul. Public action to achieve racial equality was not O'Connor's way. Instead of having her characters march in the streets, she has her southerners take the path of self-scrutiny to battle the racist demons attacking their heart and will. The moral force of personal example, O'Connor believes, can unravel power. That was certainly true of Martin Luther King Jr.'s nonviolence and of the desert mothers and fathers' effect on the eastern territories of the mighty Roman Empire, where their quiet ways caused a religious revolution.

Reform sought through inner warfare is as agonizing as is the campaign against guns, attack dogs, and tear gas on the street. In the records of social history, the troops of Satan have far outclassed the police in power; the demons know how to maneuver on both sides to confuse and exacerbate the hostilities. The malefactions of police enforcing unjust laws in the civil rights struggle are obvious; but there can lurk in well-meaning liberal ministrations, as O'Connor shows in "Everything That Rises Must Converge," the emotional violence of Julian's condescension and fake egalitarianism. If facing guns takes stamina, then spiritual activism requires gutty self-investigation. Such discernment comes, the elders repeatedly tell us, only from direct engagement with our demons, a wrestling that Amma Flannery knows and recommends: "A working knowledge of the devil can be very well had from resisting him" (*HB* 92). It is precisely because Julian does not oppose evil in himself that he comes across as ignorant and weak. A lifetime of retirement leads him to his infantile politics of delusion. While espousing racial integration, this fallen patrician wants to be as far away as possible from its concrete fulfillment. The first thought of this socially-minded southern libertarian when he fantasizes about making money is to move "where the nearest neighbors would be three miles away on either side" (*CW* 486). This six-mile hermitage expresses quite a need for separation. Actually, what Julian wants, when calculated, comes to 18,086.4 acres or 28.26 square miles. (The island of Manhattan, by comparison, covers 22.25 square miles.) No ancient hermit needed this much distance, and yet only this expanse will allow Julian to preserve his social consciousness. He who vaunts "radical ideas" and disdains his mother's longing for the ancestral mansion has constructed a reactionary "mental bubble" into which he can retreat "when he could not bear to be a part of what was going on around him" (*CW* 491). Julian has made for himself an ineffective life in seclusion.

Julian's self-protecting motives would not have surprised the ancient hermits. Immersed as they were in their weaknesses, the solitaries understood that some would renounce the world to avoid experiences that would burst the mental bubble of narcissistic self-enclosure. Their working knowledge of Satan taught them how the enemy could use renunciation to his advantage, and they issued a warning about their own life: "There is an asceticism which is determined by the enemy," says Amma Syncletica, "and his disciples practice it" (*Sayings*, Syncletica 15 [233]). This asceticism, as we saw with Rayber in *The Violent Bear It Away*, originates in escape. By turning one's back on experience, one closes off the very openness of the heart that the desert-dwellers saw as the way to holiness. This refusal has the effect of stiffening the private will toward its own, not God's, goals, making asceticism little more than the desperate saving action of the terrified ego. Such a life denounces rather than renounces the world. As a result, what is the desert of God becomes the desert of Satan.

Julian runs the risk of having his mental stockade become the devil's territory. His dependency on and loyalty to his mother frequently expresses itself, as does his sense of social equality, in cruel ways. The emotional distance he keeps from her is malignant. O'Connor brings their relationship and the story to a climax when Julian gratuitously forces his politics on a situation to punish his mother. At this moment, his private will becomes a demonic instrument. Julian's idea of easing racial tensions is to aggravate them. Escorting his mother on the bus provides the occasion. O'Connor knew that a bus in the South in the late 1950s was a potential source of fiery confrontation; and so, six years after Rosa Parks refused to take a back seat in Montgomery, Alabama, in 1955, thereby sparking an explosive, yearlong boycott, O'Connor has her ideologue reformer Julian and his mother take a ride in the rolling tinderbox. The possibilities for violence would not be lost on the devil. Sure enough, personal demons conspire with historical furies to embroil the passengers in animosity.

The demon drawing the riders into conflict is the demon of acedia that has been besetting Julian for years. Evagrius says that acedia "causes the most serious trouble of all" (12 [18]); like a dog, it "snatches away the soul as if it were a fawn" (23 [23]). Acedia is the pit bull in Satan's kennel. The only way to break the viselike jaws of a pit bull is to destroy it, and putting down the beast is what Evagrius urges. Julian, however, sports with the menace. O'Connor trails this cur as it seizes the souls of the bus passengers to trap them in Julian's resentment. The clash begins with idle banter between Julian's mother and another white woman, whose canvas sandals and protruding teeth hint of her biting and baiting in their exchange. They discuss the hot weather and their sons, about whom both mothers are proud: the toothy woman over keeping her son out of the reformatory; Julian's mother over getting her son through college. Julian naturally is too humorless to smile at the banalities of daily life. His resentment invites the demons of paranoia and rancor to ride with him to town, and these passions take the chitchat personally. Threatened, Julian strikes out with his eyes. His "malevolent look" (*CW* 490) has the force to push the bucktoothed woman back against the seat from which she is leaning.

Julian's visual jab brings the submerged tensions of class and race out into the open. As Julian's mother jousts with assertions of pedigree, the sandaled woman parries with pretensions to social adequacy. When a black businessman enters the bus, wrangling about status gets down to the essential southern tension over race. The archdemon anger steps in. The man sits next to the sandaled woman, who demonstrates her solidarity with the reigning satan by promptly rising to take a backseat. Her reward is the "approving look" from Julian's mother, arbiter of all things southern. The alliance is Julian's mother's defense against the black menaces that she believes prowl integrated buses. By demonizing black people, Julian's mother blinds herself to the evil of her duplicitous arrogance. Angered by his mother's fabrications—yet pleased to indulge his own phantoms—Julian "openly declared war on her" (*CW* 492). Julian presumes that the African-American businessman is an ally; but the black man is too absorbed with his newspaper to be goaded into the fray. Missing one target, Julian succeeds in striking the bull's-eye of another. Julian's courting of the black man's favor hits home; and, to Julian's delight, his mother's blood pressure rises.

The family war builds in Julian's head, where the scenes suddenly change as in haunted dreams. Acedia swells his imagination with new demons as Julian visualizes his mother at the mercy of various socially prominent blacks who would destroy her bigotry. Satan's servant summons into being another of his dumb shows. This pageant of dark visitants culminates not with the face that launched a thousand ships but with "a beautiful suspiciously Negroid woman" (*CW* 494) capable of tormenting Julian's mother with the shivers of miscegenation. Ordinarily, the apparition of a comely woman would imply erotic longing in the imagination creating it, as it does with Faust; but the appeal of this fantasy woman lies in "the ultimate horror" (*CW* 494) of shocking Julian's mother.

The moment that a large black woman wearing a hat identical to his mother's boards the bus with her son Carver, Julian has living black people with which to flesh out his demonic musings. The nature of acedia is to reconfigure the world into its ugliness. Through Julian's bitterness, the African-American mother appears "sullen-looking" with a "face . . .

set not only to meet opposition but to seek it out." No detail escapes Julian's morose imagining. The woman's hat, however festive it is for her, is "hideous" (*CW* 495) to Julian. Whatever she does, Julian charges her presence with his own stifled violence: "The woman was rumbling like a volcano about to become active" (*CW* 496). The dormant crater erupts at the bus stop when Julian's mother gives Carver a shiny new penny. This petty gesture speaks to the nickel grievances in others, for whom fury over a coin is as natural as breathing. Carver's mother explodes and uses her pocketbook to knock down Julian's mother. With her blow, all hell breaks loose at a bus stop that is "usually deserted" but "well lighted" (*CW* 493). This is the desert of exposure to which O'Connor brings her characters to meet their demons in the final light of judgment.

With the black mother, the desert uncovers the automatism of habitual acrimony. The penny, or more accurately what the penny signifies, turns her into "a piece of machinery." Fueled by generations of "frustrated rage" (*CW* 498), she blames and strikes the penny-giver, who, though not better off than she is, looms as the dispenser of historical oppression. O'Connor does not condescend to the African-American woman by holding her to a lower standard of conduct than she sets for whites. All are called to resist the urge to harm, a call that accounts for O'Connor's admiring the example of the gentle and tough desert mothers and fathers. Julian's mother experiences another kind of exposure, one left by ascesis. The black woman's blow swirls inward to rip away accumulated layers of useless antebellum dignity. Julian's mother's hair comes undone; her pocketbook and physical stability fall away, leaving her a helpless child crying for her nineteenth-century nurse. Solitude closes in. She feels degraded by the black woman, abandoned by history and society; but most of all, she feels humiliated by Julian. As she dies, she pays him back in kind and attacks him where he is most easily hurt—in his dependency and righteousness. His evil look comes back to him as she rakes Julian's face with the piercing stare of abandonment that combines the breach of filial faith she feels from his betrayal of her with the desolation in which she silently leaves him.

Her death tears away Julian's mask of control. As her pain engulfs Julian, he tastes the cup of her mortification. And rightly so, because his emotional violence has been not only felt but consented to and willed. In this way, he was already committing interior murder. Such a judgment of Julian is stern and yet entirely necessary for readers to see the greater severity awaiting Julian. At the end, he is feeble and at a loss for words. Above all, he is alone. He cannot evade his demons; but there is the possibility of reconciliation. The ancient solitaries point the way: "Go, sit in your cell, and your cell will teach you everything" (*Sayings*, Moses 6 [139]). Julian's enclosure is the silence and grief left by his mother's sudden death. Julian is a promising candidate for this lesson of the desert cell. Since he is given to withdrawal, solitude is a matter of changing the direction of his reclusion. He must turn away from self-justification to self-scrutiny, from judging others to feeling with them; and so arises the convergence John Desmond recognizes as the momentum toward union "through love" ("Lessons" 40). The barrier between Julian and others and to life has been acedia, which has distorted any warm feeling he has into animosity. He says that he hates to see his mother behaving indecorously as she stumbles to death, but what he really hates is having to confront his true emotion, which is that his mother is making him see how much he loves her.

Try as he might, Julian cannot scorn his mother's death to the point of removing its sting. When she dies, a stunning surgical strike of sorrow demolishes his misanthropic hermitism, and the heat of mortality melts his cold impassivity. Julian's change can be heard in his voice, which softens from scolding to beseeching. Describing Julian's final utterances, O'Connor hammers home his remorse by rapidly stressing variants of the word "cry" in the last two paragraphs: "cried," "crying," and "cried" (*CW* 500). The words iterate the narrator's admonishment that the miseries Julian notices in himself be only a more pressing invitation to turn the shouts in his voice into the shedding of tears in his eyes. "'Wait here, wait here!' he cried," as Julian jumps up toward a cluster of light to get help and avert his eyes from the evidence of his emotional cruelty. As his mother's days of waiting for him are over, so Julian's time of patient spiritual learning has begun. His mind bids him to flee, but his feet "moved numbly" (*CW* 500) and keep Julian on the hard ground of desolation, where he can be instructed by grief in the form of a dark tide.

O'Connor leaves Julian on the threshold of repentance: "'Help, help!'" (*CW* 500), he shouts again, his voice now thin with anxiety and unshed tears. Help lies in the ancient answer to Julian's timeless need: "Weep interiorly, for both deliverance from faults and the acquisition of virtues are gained through compunction" (*Sayings*, Poemen 208 [195]). The tears awaiting release in Julian will guide him through the postmortem desert of guilt and sorrow. The dark tide sweeping over Julian is the pull of penthos. Tears will carry him out of acedia by replenishing those emotions that for years have been wasted in sullen escape. Penthos is the founding experience of Julian's life to come.

In the annals of asceticism, the voluntary withdrawal of Thomas in "The Comforts of Home" may never be surpassed for its distortions of the elders' founding principle of self-scrutiny and serving God. Thomas's reclusive practice shows the twisting of truth into a deceit that eventually makes him a deadly agent of the evil he tries to avoid. Put another way, "The Comforts of Home" tells the story of a good servant to a bad master. Thomas tries to lead a good life by retreating from the world into domestic tranquillity. Repose is his fortress. Virtue for him comes not through inner struggle but from maintaining ease in a cozy world. The fruit of his withdrawal, however, is moral sluggishness, which attracts the demons that undermine his impregnable goodness. The more he hides behind the ease of home life, the closer Thomas's demons search him out until they have him under their power. Responding from a state of high dudgeon, Thomas tries to frame his enemy, who appears as a sexy woman of nineteen, only to be ensnared by his demons, who get him to kill his mother and shatter his comforts of home.

Like Julian in "Everything That Rises Must Converge," Thomas lives alone with his mother, who supplies food, clothing, shelter, security, and much-needed affirmation. The fate of both hermit sons is to mourn the death of their generous mother-comforter; but Thomas, thirty-six, must wait longer to receive the gift of godly grief. The additional years entrench Thomas in his solitary habits. The sons' daily routine centers on work, which for both involves language. They use words to relate to the outside world they have shunned. Julian wants to write fiction; Thomas, in keeping with his regressive temperament, writes about the early settlers of his county. The rule of life for the two hermit scribes is according to their will. Having lived longer by his own interests, Thomas exemplifies what Julian would become if the dark tide of sorrow had not come to Julian's rescue. Thomas's story, grimly comic, gets down to the self-loathing that underlies his defensive asceticism.

Thomas is not the only misguided ascetic in O'Connor's fiction; but, historian that he is, Thomas is the only O'Connor anchorite to know and cite the father of all hermits and monks, Anthony the Great (c. 251–356 A.D.). In fact, one researcher found in the O'Connor archives an unfinished draft in which Thomas had studied monasticism and had written "a thesis on Anthony of Egypt" (Burns 79). This detail adds humor to the exposure of Thomas as the great falsifier, for in the final version of "The Comforts of Home," Thomas uses his extensive knowledge of Anthony to justify his own sloth. The passage comes early in the story. As Thomas mulls over his mother's nervy "engagements with the devil," he conjectures that if she could rise to the occasion of his intelligence, "he could have proved to her from early Christian history that no excess of virtue is justified" and "that if Antony of Egypt had stayed at home and attended to his sister, no devils would have plagued him" (*CW* 575). The legendary saint, whose daring exploration of the boundaries of his body and spirit shaped the ideals of asceticism throughout the Christian world, is criticized for the very courage that brought him to greatness. Thomas's self-deception is hard to miss, and readers have caught him in the act of making a "travesty" (Asals 115) of the saint's heroic idea of virtue and of emulating the negative excess he condemns (Gentry, "Hand" 63–64).

From a patristic viewpoint, Thomas's gravest error concerns his idea of the devil. Satan has disappeared for Thomas. With others of our post-superstitious age, he believes that the devil is "only a manner of speaking" (*CW* 575). As a linguistic figment, the devil is a mere residual image from the benighted past, a spurious phantom to be avoided; and intelligence can immunize one to whatever charms the devil might use. Thomas's discounting Satan is far removed from the sensibility of the ancient solitaries. Anthony the Great had a vivid sense of Satan and humankind's involvement with the unseen world. He understood the devil as a vital presence, intensely compelling and determined to gain allies in his war against God. The power of Satan on human persons can range from sinful and foul thoughts to physiological control, all accomplished through endless mutations of gender, species, and tactics. Whereas Thomas would evade demons at all costs, Anthony, knowing his own vulnerability, fought them at any price. With humility and prayer as weapons, Anthony met evil head on. Demons, he learned from direct contact, can instruct the soul by strengthening virtue; and so they did, for through ceaseless warfare Anthony overcame his adversaries.

Athanasius's late fourth-century *The Life of Anthony*, even more than *The Sayings of the Desert Fathers* and *The Lives of the Desert Fathers*, accentuates demonology. The demonic embodies all that Anthony must conquer to become holy. As a person whose loyalty is to God, Anthony is obliged to battle the foes of God. His willingness to fight the devil is synonymous with his sanctity, and so the example of his life teaches other spiritual questers how to disperse evil spirits. His instruction is far from moderate. Having heard Thomas wrench eremitic hagiography into bourgeois narcissism to vindicate himself, one does well to listen to Anthony's own voice in the desert. After being tortured by a multitude of demons, the solitary warrior yells: "'Here I am—Antony!'" Physically battered but spiritually undiminished, he lies beaten on the ground and yet still defies fearsomely ugly spirits: "'I do not run from your blows, for even if you give me more, nothing shall separate me from the love of Christ'" (Athanasius 9 [38]). Goring bulls, raging monsters, and creeping serpents return to give Anthony more pain; and still he does not relent. Believing that any fear in him is "'due to the presence of the enemies'" (Athanasius 37 [59]), he redoubles his guard. His instruments of defense are the matchless powers of cheer and confidence. He scatters the enemy by saying, "'let the soul always rejoice in hope'" (Athanasius 42 [63]). Desire for salvation, accompanied by trust in God's help, fortifies his body and dispels the acedia inspired by Satan in the holy warrior's soul. At the center of Anthony's strength lies an appeal to the fullest possibilities of human life: "'For the joy and the stability of the soul attest to the holiness'" accorded to God's friend (Athanasius 36 [59]). Clearly, Anthony in his own words bears little resemblance to Thomas's flat, grim representation of him and conveys, rather, the exuberance that O'Connor calls "the special superaliveness that holiness is" (*HB* 280).

Thomas is the photonegative twin of Anthony. As Anthony achieves balance and peace by struggling against sin and fear, Thomas relies on anger and deceit, the fruits of acedia, to conquer the threats to his comfort. In effect, Thomas sets demons against demons without realizing that they will inevitably turn on him. As a historian, Thomas might have put his antiquarian interest to good use by considering how Anthony saw the demonic effects brought about by Thomas's impulses: from the evil ones come "terror of the soul, confusion and disorder of thoughts, dejection, enmity toward ascetics, listlessness, grief, memory of relatives, and fear of death" (Athanasius 36 [58]). If one substitutes "other people" for "ascetics" and adds "grandiosity" to the catalogue, it becomes clear just how precisely Antonian psychology explains the effects of acedia, down to the detail of recalled kin, on Thomas.

To see Thomas as the antithesis of Anthony is, paradoxically, to glimpse how his mother's "daredevil charity" (*CW* 573) aspires to the patristic ideal of self-giving. Most readers have to squint in the blinding light of the desert to see this woman's virtues. In variously amusing ways, critics write her off as, for example, a "senile Girl Scout" with "uncanny" instincts (Di Renzo 103). O'Connor, however, sees merit in the woman's undiscerning and dotty habits. "To me," she writes to John Hawkes, "the old lady is the character whose position is right" (*HB* 434). The old lady's incautious stance, commended by O'Connor, recalls certain aspects of desert life. Since Thomas's mother does not have the benefit of misinterpreting Anthony, she can just heed her virtuous promptings; and in her devil-may-care freedom, the woman turns out to be mother in the ancient meaning of desert amma. Thomas's mother is an amma manqué to be sure; but she is an amma nevertheless. The desert mother was, as Thomas's mother is, a simple woman of few words and of direct practical action. The desert mother sought not to enlighten but to nurture a younger person in Jesus' ideal of self-giving. The amma, like the abba, could be foolish and teach through folly, as Mr. Head does in "The Artificial Nigger." The signal feature of the desert mother was how her actions embodied her good words. When the ancient Amma Sarah speaks of repentance, she knows that contrition is not an idea to be analyzed but a way of life, for she spends thirteen years waging war against the demon of fornication, always with humility, prayer, and generosity to others (*Sayings*, Sarah 1 and 5 [229 and 230]).

Thomas's mother does not have to leave town to do her desert work; she wages war against evil on the home front, and her actions bring her words to life. More than any other motive, love defines her conduct. Whatever social forces initially draw her to help people, whatever clichés evince her benevolence, the end of all the woman's desires is ultimately expressed as love. With Thomas, her struggle to love involves devoting her time and energy to his well-being. Her charity also takes the form of instructing Thomas in self-scrutiny, the first lesson of the desert. When he carries on about the return of Sarah Ham, who was jailed for writing bad checks, his mother simply says: "'Thomas, . . . suppose it were you?'" (*CW* 574). Thomas may roar in exasperation over the alluring intrusion by the latest recipient of his mother's boundless charity, but his mother calmly restates her simple call to suspend his judgment of the stranger in favor of looking into himself. The amma in the old lady succeeds in framing her lesson in words of love for Thomas: "'If it were you, how do you think I'd feel if nobody took you in? What if you were a nimpermaniac and not a brilliant smart person and you did what you couldn't help and . . .'" Hearing the identification with Sarah, "Thomas felt a deep unbearable loathing for himself as if he were turning slowly into the girl" (*CW* 575). Sarah's open sexuality strikes terror in Thomas about his own possible loss of erotic control; but would that lust were Thomas's dilemma, for physical desire would at least express a wish to be with another person. Instead, at the bottom of Thomas's self-hatred is an egocentric love that his withdrawal serves by fostering complacency and moral pride.

Thomas's mother's indefatigable effort to incorporate love in her daily life holds the answer to the disgust that Thomas feels for himself. There is nothing glib about his mother's responding in love. Nor is she confident about the results of her struggle. Sarah's thinking of her benefactor as "'an old bag of wind'" (*CW* 582) does not disturb Thomas's mother.

She accepts the insults as lessons in the need to combat the inevitable emotions of defeatism, anger, and judgment of others that check a person's urgings to love. Thomas, of course, is too intelligent to follow such simple impulses. He is sure of his virtue and how to maintain it. Such certainty is one of his domestic comforts. The moral life for him is some fine theory that can be drawn up in advance. Since Satan is to Thomas merely a matter of speaking, Thomas can barricade himself within a "well-regulated house" (*CW* 576) and talk the good talk. This bunker mentality epitomizes Thomas's lifelong resistance to heeding his mother's call issued since his birth, when she named him Thomas, meaning twin, and thereby planted the need for him to recognize his moral twinship with others. To the woman's enduring credit, she does not listen to her son's orders to stop helping people. Instead, she follows her surest instinct for service, an attribute that marks her twinship with the desert mothers. Acting on the Antonian belief that our "life and our death is with our neighbour" (*Sayings*, Anthony the Great 9 [3]), Thomas's mother tries to live out the great desert rule to receive a stranger with hospitality and send the person on the way in peace.

Although Thomas regards his mother's charity and engagements with the devil as excessive, her undertakings are tame next to the ventures of the ancient ammas. Thomas the gynephobe would profit from deepening his fascination with early monasticism by reading in the lives of the early women of the desert. They set the ideal against which he might reconsider his mother's actions and his general disdain for women. Were he to explore Benedicta Ward's *Harlots of the Desert*, Thomas would enter a world of spectacular immoderation. The lives of these women involve extreme sin leading to profound repentance that climaxes in surpassing love. There is Saint Mary of Egypt, for example, who lived as a prostitute for seventeen years in Alexandria, joined a pilgrimage going to Jerusalem and on which she seduced many of the pilgrims, set up business in Jerusalem, and after looking at her life ended up alone in the desert dressed only in her hair (Ward, *Harlots* 27). Mary of Egypt, the liturgical icon of repentance, is not the only amma likely to raise Thomas's eyebrows. To our age and culture, the figure of Pelagia may be more startling and offensive. Pelagia was an actor in Antioch whose great beauty brought lavish attention and wealth. After pleasing many lovers, she sought to please God by discarding "the riches with which Satan ensnared" her and setting her servants free. Pelagia's farewell performance was a ride with scanty attire in Antioch before Christian bishops whose collective interest did not satisfy her; and so she disappeared to a solitary cell on the Mount of Olives in Jerusalem, where, transcending gender difference, she died as a monk. In desert solitude, she sought God's notice, which was the attention she wanted and needed all along (Ward, *Harlots* 72–73). And so go the tales of beautiful and sinful women whose feats in solitude surpassed their prowess on stage or in bed. Their edifying lives recast the scriptural example of Mary Magdalene, who learned about God through a receptivity to the mystery of love.

These holy women could teach Thomas two important lessons: one about sex; the other about the human will. Besides showing Thomas how moderate his mother is in her moral struggle, the lives of the desert harlots, were he to consider them, would school the frigid, dogmatic hermit in a more human view of his repressed erotic longing and of Sarah Ham's sexual candor. The reality and force of erotic desire were vivid in the desert. Because sensual needs were heightened in the desert and had to be faced out daily, it was not the fulcrum of terror that it is for Thomas, who must immediately distance himself from Sarah. No sooner does she get out of the car than Thomas calls her "the little slut" (*CW* 573) to deny his erotic interest in her dress rising above her knees. By demonizing Sarah, he can avoid confronting his inner demons of lust, fear, and hatred. The ancient monastic sources, by contrast, present sexuality as part of the total human experience. Far from ignoring or discrediting physical yearning, the desert ascetics sought to integrate its power into their search for God. In fact, sexual intimacy taught them about divine closeness. The lives of the desert harlots in particular dramatically illustrate the integration of sexuality into their fervent hope for the future. The concern that emerges most vividly in their stories involves conversion. In the harlots' stunning change of heart, we see a way out of the despair the women felt. Their despair, it bears underscoring, was not that of the body, as it is for Thomas, but in the reliance on one's own virtue. Through hard experience, the harlots of the desert came to know better than to trust their own intentions. When they sought God, the women hurled themselves in variously ardent ways before divine mercy, the only help there is.

Reliance on oneself alarmed the desert teachers because it could lead to despair of God's help. That danger becomes evident in Thomas's confidence in his own virtue, which is so fragile that Sarah's mere presence stirs in Thomas an erotic desire that threatens to overwhelm him. His fear of losing control opens the way for the devil to attack, and there is a demon afoot that abets Thomas's pride and male chauvinism. The demon materializes as the ghost of his father. When alive, the old man's severity and contempt for women outraged Thomas; but in death, his father's harshness pleases Thomas because it puts Sarah's intimidation on a level of anger that covers his fear. The dead man's goading comes in a sinister undermining voice that recalls the rattling timbre of the logismos in *The Violent Bear It Away*. In "The Comforts of Home," the ghoulish voice "rasped" assertions of male prerogative in Thomas's head, ordering Thomas to put his "foot down now" to show Sarah "who's boss before she shows" him. Then, the evil thought-flow gains momentum through what probably was the old man's lifelong assault on his "numbskull" (*CW* 582) son's masculinity: "You ain't like me. Not enough to be a man" (*CW* 583). Thomas feels that loss of male strength when he cannot spare his mother from "mourning for the world" (*CW* 587) after Sarah slashes her wrists. Thomas's dejection invites the logismos to enter his brain and from there raid his heart. Like a wasp, the old man takes "up his station in Thomas's mind" (*CW* 585), where he hatches the plan to get rid of Sarah and restore male valor to the home.

Actually, that plot was laid before Sarah arrived on the scene. It was set by the old man back when he bequeathed his son the loaded pistol to go with his scorn for women. Laden with intrigue and contempt, the logismos pushes Thomas around by his sexual anxiety and mocks his laziness: "Idiot! the old man hissed, idiot! The criminal slut stole your gun! See the sheriff! See the sheriff!" The chief law-enforcement officer in this county is named Farebrother. There is no mistaking from whom he takes orders. Farebrother's "sharp creased face" (*CW* 589) wears the badge of membership in O'Connor's fraternal order of demons, and his actions conform to his high standing in the organization. Farebrother is ready with the open arms of deceit and cynicism to ensnare not only Sarah but Thomas as well. He speaks in the voice of flat malice that is heard in the popular films noirs of the time, which feature police who show their toughness through the culture's scoffing at women and less burly males: "'I'll come along about six,' Farebrother said. 'Leave the latch off the door and keep out of my way—yourself and them two women too'" (*CW* 591). If Farebrother's underhanded dealing sounds jaded and abbreviated, it is so because the scheme was invented centuries ago and honed to a quick course of treachery. It is simply a matter of Farebrother's retrofitting Thomas into the old conspiracy against God. With the help of Thomas's father, the dead spiritual brother to Farebrother, the two evil forces take over Thomas's will and voice to make him a collaborator in their attack on innocence.

A few satanic feints complete the web of destruction into which the logismoi have been driving Thomas, his mother, and Sarah Ham. In the end, it is Thomas—not Sarah, as Thomas believes—who is used by the devil to set the trap; and it is his mother who is victimized by Thomas's demonic alliance. First, the old man fires a point-blank barrage of insults to demolish any residual self-respect in Thomas that might resist acting on his evil urges: "Idiot!" "Moron!" "Imbecile!" Knowing his son's sloth, the old man orders Thomas to make "haste" (*CW* 592) and conceal the gun in Sarah's pocketbook. Sloth, which has made Thomas comfortable, finally undoes him. His slight delay allows Sarah to catch him in the act of planting the gun. Exposed and imperiously dishonest, Thomas displaces his personal blame onto creation by damning "not only the girl but the entire order of the universe that made her possible" (*CW* 593). The logismos has succeeded in fathering Thomas into despair, which renders him too self-hating to combat the demonic parent he could not endure. Thomas turns into the old man's foul mouthpiece, proving that the devil is a manner of speaking but also that the manner and the speech are manipulated by a tyrannically real presence. Thomas shouts: "'The dirty criminal slut stole my gun!'" So strong is this satanic "other presence" (*CW* 593) of the father in Thomas's voice that his mother gasps in stunned disbelief in hearing the ghoulish voice of her dead husband.

Under his father's instigation, Thomas pulls the trigger to shoot Sarah when she lunges at him; but he kills instead his mother as she tries to protect Sarah. The corpse, the killer, and the harrier are turned over to Farebrother, the evil twin, for "the Devil's eye view" of the catastrophe, which, O'Connor explains to John Hawkes, "is as the world will see it, not as it is" (*HB* 434). The demonic view casts everything in comforting moral categories. Through the devil's vision, the world all too readily will comprehend the deceit of flesh, here contorting in a breathless Apache dance of shadows with "the killer and the slut" eager to "collapse into each other's arms" (*CW* 594). Cold and trite (as are the explanations in film noir), Farebrother's version merely provides prefabricated overlayings of hastily resolved legal implications. In lieu of genuine feelings before the grisly accident, the demonic sheriff sensationalizes death to gratify the blunted modern sensibility of himself and the old man.

There is more to the ending of "The Comforts of Home" than the cinematic frame of lust and murder provided by the local bailiff. There is also truth behind the charade. In her letter to Hawkes about the conclusion, O'Connor refers to the disaster "as it is" (*HB* 434) with the implication that one person's blind spots can be filled by another's sharp vision. What is missing can be supplied, I believe, by the distant realism of the desert that has evolved in the poetics of the story through Thomas's lonely struggle and his mother's single-handed charity. When the story begins, Thomas excuses his sloth by misinterpreting Anthony the Great; at the end, one might correct the error and adopt the Antonian vision to see Thomas with an honesty that he denied himself. Anthony's desert eye would open a fiercely unsentimental view of sin, death, and obedience, for the Antonian gaze would not spare Thomas from what his eyes have seen. Thomas would see not only what has happened to his mother by his hand but also what she has done for others: her generosity, however foolish, to Sarah Ham; her ultimate act of love in laying down her life for another; and, for the reader, her total example of obedience to the call of charity. For Thomas to recognize his mother's wound of love amounts to O'Connor's way of bringing "Thomas face to face with his own evil" (*HB* 434). Self-scrutiny is what desert solitude demands of Anthony and what Thomas's mother's corpse forces on Thomas. His mother at the end is Thomas's desolation. In her dead body, he must discover the meaning of who he is by genuine awareness of the fatal effects of succumbing to his demons.

The demons besetting Thomas, as we saw, are acedia; its abettor, sloth; and their two offspring, wrath and despair. If identified, these evils can show Thomas the obstacles to the virtuous life he seeks, but he must first find the courage to face them down ruthlessly. That strength has been in Thomas from the beginning in the "sudden burning moisture behind his eyes" (*CW* 573) that he felt when his mother chose to put charity over his comfort and her own interests. His task in solitude will be to get that wetness to flow. At the end of the story, he is overwhelmed. The final shock of killing the mother he loved leaves him a figure of wretched arrogance and shattered denials. And yet, alone in the desert of desolation, Thomas is visited by a mystifying pain. This rare dusting of guilt and sorrow brings him, if not to the verge of tears, then to feel the need of tears, for the curse of understanding one's evil is the blessing of tears. This, the Antonian view, is leagues away from Farebrother's specious dismissal of the killing as a "nasty bit" (*CW* 594) of romantic intrigue or distorted Oedipal longing. The clarity of the desert lays bare the woundings of love that Thomas causes and must endure.

The revelation of these injuries makes "The Comforts of Home" acutely paradoxical. Thomas withdraws to his mother's home as an ideal place, something like a monastery, in which all is ordered in function of the quest for virtue and for the fulfillment of his love for his mother. Such is his expectation; but he carries within him a false notion of its realization. And so things turn out differently. He secludes himself in search of peace, shelter, and the quiet life; but he finds himself struggling with inner forces whose existence he never suspected and, indeed, never believed. His faults are a barrier; his mother is imperfect; the law is different from his; sin mars his relationships; and God appears to thwart his ideas. Against all of this, grace does the great service of stripping away much of Thomas's egoism and childishness. Ascesis establishes Thomas's solidarity of anguish and sinful humanity in penthos, which makes "The Comforts of Home" a moment of the cosmic drama involving principalities and power.

"Greenleaf" enriches O'Connor's exploration of penthos by setting the gift of tears in relation to catanyxis, perhaps the most charged aspect of desert spirituality. "Greenleaf" tells a simple story of backcountry pride and destruction set against the social and economic upheavals following World War II. Mrs. May, the farm owner, finds a stray bull on her land. Furious over the bull's presence and outraged by its owners' indifference, she demands that her dairyman, Mr. Greenleaf, kill the bull, which is owned by his two sons, diligent war veterans whose prosperity signals the social changes Mrs. May finds intolerable. But Mrs. May's orders to kill the bull boomerang, and she is killed by the bull. O'Connor intertwines Mrs. May's display of willful supremacy with the spiritual forces of the desert mothers and fathers that correct the inner demons driving her to ruin. Catanyxis and penthos bring Mrs. May, the protagonist of "Greenleaf," to the awareness of personal evil that she resists. That knowledge, in turn, prepares the heroine for the connection with God that O'Connor sees as the fundamental bond for each person. This intimacy with God comes about through the bull's goring. In a body of fiction known for its unexpected, bloody violence, the impaling stands out as especially jolting and excruciating (Meek 35). Yet the penetration, in its very sudden agony, follows from the primitive asceticism underlying "Greenleaf." To appreciate this story's unnerving action, we need first to consider the prayerful Mrs. Greenleaf, a minor character in the story (as the ancient ascetics were marginal in their fourth-century world). After showing the effect of Mrs. Greenleaf's practice on Mrs. May, the heroine, the discussion concludes by placing their reciprocal relationship within O'Connor's patristic context.

The bull is not the only disturbance on Mrs. May's farm. The animal is a surrogate for anything associated with "Greenleaf," the surname that stands for all that exasperates Mrs. May. The greatest vexation to be found on the place is Mrs. Greenleaf. She is a prayer healer. Her form of prayer brings Mrs. May and the modern reader close to the eremitic experience of catanyxis, or sudden shock that puts a new feeling in the soul, and to a stark recognition of penthos, the tears that flow from the inner shock (Hausherr 7–8). Mrs. Greenleaf's habits are eccentric. She gleans newspaper stories of brutality (women raped), destroyed innocence (children burned), rampant evil (criminals escaped), and catastrophes (train wrecks and plane crashes). Not one to forget that the rich and famous also suffer, Mrs. Greenleaf clips newspaper reports of divorcing movie stars. She takes these stories to the woods, digs a hole to bury the day's fatalities, and prays over them. Her prayer is total. She throws her bulky body on the dirt as a sign of trust that her prayer of flesh and spirit can bring the interred calamities to a favorable end. With raw abandon, this woman tries to love as Jesus loved by hurling herself deep into his misery. It is through Mrs. Greenleaf that the day's tribulations can rest, and it is because of her that the shards consigned to earth are covered by her sheltering body to be made whole.

Mrs. Greenleaf's articulated prayer is as simple and direct as it is startling. "'Jesus, Jesus,'" she groans, and then she buffets the entreaty with repeated shrieks: "'Oh Jesus, stab me in the heart!'" (*CW* 506). These reckless words enact their plea through Mrs. Greenleaf's imposing body. She sways back and forth on her hands and knees until devotion sends her back in the dirt with her heart offered upright for piercing. She then lies supine with "her legs and arms spread out as if she were trying to wrap them around the earth" (*CW* 507). The splayed woman ready for penetration conveys O'Connor's idea of female asceticism. The position combines the posture of mothering with the attitude of compassion, suggesting that Mrs. Greenleaf's body is life-giving because she is pain-embracing. In her clasp of the entire world, she responds to the adversities of her time as did the ancient desert fathers and mothers. Severus of Antioch, concerned about the "strange calamity sent by God to Alexandria," urges his listeners to prostrate themselves to weep and moan. While the indifferent tend to "the amusements of their age," Severus declares, "let us weep over ourselves. . . . Now let us use ardent and constant prayer. . . . But let us pray with tears, bending our knees to earth" (qtd. in Hausherr 57). While Mrs. May tends to cold cream and insurance premiums, tears flow abundantly with Mrs. Greenleaf's prayer.

Without knowing or needing to know the lives and sayings of the desert elders, Mrs. Greenleaf lives out their exhortations for healing in times of crisis. This Georgia woman is a desert mother who is truly maternal. She not only bears two sons and five daughters, but she also presses to her ample bosom all the bereft children of God. On her own, as do all of O'Connor's spiritual searchers, Mrs. Greenleaf catches the essence of desert life and revitalizes the discipline in ways suitable to her own time, place, and disposition. Her rule is very much her own. She hears the cry of suffering in others and, with her voice, brings their pain to God's ears. Here in the Georgia woods, old and deep and linked by agony to the fabled desert, Mrs. Greenleaf brings new life to the directive inspiring Abba Arsenius: "flee, be silent, pray always" (*Sayings*, Arsenius 2 [9]). These words summarize desert spirituality. Flight, silence, and ceaseless prayer do not enforce a specific doctrine, nor does the attainment of the goal require a fixed plan. Primitive desert life was an experimental life—and so too is its modern rediscovery in "Greenleaf." The wisdom of the tradition lies in its radical simplicity and flexible applicability. In truest form, the desert's life-giving power cannot be taught. Desert ascesis touches a nerve, speaks to an unanswered need. Then its impulses are seized, embraced as a way to move toward God.

The "huge" (*CW* 507) Mrs. Greenleaf is not silent. She shares with her age the sense that humanity is separated by a chasm from God. She shouts to transmit that cry of our time across this abyss to God. But flight and prayer are her life, a life of "'prayer healing'" (*CW* 505) that redirects her massive body, simple mind, and capacious heart away from crops, housekeeping, and personal interests to the commands of God. Her prayer healing has the authentic practice of a personal service to God that is offered in charity. Far from being irresponsible, as the haughty Mrs. May declares, Amma Greenleaf, like Abba Anthony, knows that our "life and our death is with our neighbour" (*Sayings*, Anthony the Great 9 [3]). The entire world is Mrs. Greenleaf's neighborhood. Just as the fourth-century followers of Anthony provided the spiritual measure of late Roman society—when Christianity was becoming imperial and too easy, even fashionable—so Mrs. Greenleaf's self-donation calls into question Mrs. May, whose Christianity, hardened by smugness, is losing its requirement of belief (Feeley 96).

Like Anthony the Great, who died after a long life with his robust body intact, Mrs. Greenleaf's girth tells us that prayer and ascesis nourish and sustain rather than deplete the body. But Amma Greenleaf's hugging of all her unknown, wounded "children" does cost. The price of compassion and the source of her inner growth show in her face, which, marked by her tattered offspring, is "a patchwork of dirt and tears" (*CW* 506). The tears attending her prayers are so unceasing that they have reddened and swollen her eyes to the point that sorrow defines Mrs. Greenleaf's entire being. Still, the inner vigor that comes with this weeping is unmistakable. O'Connor checks any sentimental tendency in the modern reader to interpret compunction as morbid or to dismiss tears as signs of female weakness. With more than her usual keen eye, O'Connor describes Mrs. Greenleaf's expression as being "as composed as a bulldog's" (*CW* 506) when she takes on the suffering of the victims. O'Connor provides her faith-doctor with the rudiments of asceticism backed by a dogged commitment. The plucky bulldog, also known for its tender watchfulness with children, aptly suggests the qualities needed to fight against evil. This doubling of gentle calm with power, unflappable poise generating stubborn power, expresses the effects of penthos. Square-jawed, heavily built, and endowed with a strong grip, Mrs. Greenleaf has the courage and self-possession that prove how tears strengthen the body and spirit by softening the heart.

Such bulldog virtues derive from the stab in the heart that Mrs. Greenleaf seeks and sustains. Again, the ancient name for this action is catanyxis. Catanyxis signifies a thrust or sudden sensation of anguish that embeds deep in the soul an attitude, a determination. Scripture offers several examples of this strong impact on the depths of one's being. Psalm 109:16 utters a countercurse to the particularly brutal enemy who showed no kindness to "the poor and needy and the broken-hearted [those stricken in the heart]." The figure of the cut heart recurs as a call of repentance in the celebration of the day of Pentecost in Acts 2. When the house of Israel heard that God made Jesus both Lord and Christ, "they were cut to the heart," and they asked what they should do (Acts 2:37). Even before Mrs. Greenleaf implores to be stabbed in the heart, O'Connor has favored the sharp-pointed blade as the instrument of choice to get the divine word through tough human flesh to teach the soul about God. *Wise Blood* dramatizes the climate and garb of perforation. Icy cold rain and a hairshirt of barbed wire cleave Hazel Motes's body. *The Violent Bear It Away* extends this cutting power to the human voice and eye to make explicit its divine origin. With a dirge-like shriek that echoes Mrs. Greenleaf's wail, Lucette Carmody exclaims: "'Love cuts like the cold wind and the will of God is plain as the winter'" (*CW* 413). Lucette's voice hews with the winter wind, and so do her eyes. After her cry slashes through George Rayber's encrusted defenses, the girl evangelist stares at Rayber, who feels that "a deep shock went through him." He is "certain that the child had looked directly into his heart" (*CW* 413), which is a catanyctic probe. As a spirit-bearing figure, Lucette matures into Mrs. Greenleaf, and the evangelical revival meeting in the grimy building off an urban alley offers an illuminating way into the bizarre prayer healing conducted off a dirt farm road. Together, the scenes show O'Connor's development of catanyxis. As in *The Violent Bear It Away*, O'Connor in "Greenleaf" portrays an agitated evangelist transmitting a shock to a nonbeliever who, in the novel and the short story, is an accidental and reluctant eavesdropper. The shock in the case of Mrs. May lasts longer and goes deeper than it does with Rayber.

Catanyxis in "Greenleaf" comes to Mrs. May in two quaking waves. The first shock is a social jolt. It happened when, fifteen years earlier, the Greenleafs arrived as tenants on the place. The story recounts the past encounter with the vividness it has in Mrs. May's vexed memory. While walking along a wooded path, muttering the latest complaints in her habitual accents of self-sorrow, Mrs. May stumbles upon Mrs. Greenleaf during her loud prayer healing. Had Mrs. May lived in the time of the desert mothers and fathers, when people in mourning and prayer indulged in more boisterous expressions of grief than is often practiced today, she would not have been startled by Mrs. Greenleaf's groaning, sprawled body. But Mrs. May is very much the proper modern woman, and the laws of mourning and faith have changed so that crude shows of belief have been reformed into demure hush. The spectacle of uttering Jesus' name outside of church and writhing in the dirt appalls Mrs. May. "'Jesus,'" she booms to Mrs. Greenleaf, "'would be *ashamed* of you'" (*CW* 507). Over the years, during which Mr. and Mrs. Greenleaf "had hardly aged at all" (*CW* 509), Mrs. Greenleaf's ceaseless prayer healing dilates in Mrs. May's mind as an obscenity, while the healer herself looms up as a monster of vulgar iniquity.

The picture Mrs. May retains of Mrs. Greenleaf is so fierce that it scares her (but no one else). The abjection, the dereliction of this apparently overstrained prayer healer using her body as a shroud over buried reports throws the good Christian Mrs. May into an abyss. Manners alone cannot explain Mrs. May's shock. She could laugh at the scene or ignore it. Nor can temperamental difference account for Mrs. May's aggressive attention to the prayer healer, a fixation so volatile that her son Scofield's mere tease that he might marry a woman like Mrs. Greenleaf sends Mrs. May into a fit. After ranting about the imagined "'trash'" daughter-in-law (*CW* 505) who will ruin all she worked for, Mrs. May launches into a bitter, detailed reenactment of her initial sight of the weird holy roller. To remain in Mrs. May's central nervous system in this nagging way, something of Mrs. Greenleaf's prayer, struggle, renunciation, and aloneness must resonate in Mrs. May. If the reader looks at Mrs. May with the compassionate scrutiny that she denies herself, one can see the qualities in her inner life that she shares with Mrs. Greenleaf. To make this more generous revision, one needs a desert eye, for the ascetic context of "Greenleaf" reveals the saving truth about Mrs. May that is hidden from her until the goring at the end. To begin with, Mrs. May is forced into seclusion. A city woman by birth and instinct (we first see her with curlers and facial cream to remove wrinkles), Mrs. May is cut off from her natural securities when her husband bought the farm, when the price of land was low. After Mr. May's death, she is stuck with the run-down place. The selfishness of her parasitic sons, Scofield and Wesley, further isolates Mrs. May.

Being alone in life and stranded on a hostile expanse creates in the widow the feeling that she must make a go of things by herself. Mrs. May's anxiety over her responsibilities deepens into materialistic clinging (Sexton 39–42). The need to assert control puts the besieged woman in a constant state of warfare that intensifies her loneliness. Solitude and warfare, the very conditions of the desert, are so much her lot that she brags about her vigilant self-reliance and enjoys being embattled. The desert task, writes Helen Waddell in her book that helped to introduce the desert elders to a wide modern audience, is "to do battle with the enemy" (75); and that is Mrs. May's duty. The desert is her true country. She is a desert person because she leads the desert life. For Amma May, the experience is especially trying. As a would-be desert-dweller, she endures its physical and psychological hardships without deriving its inward grace.

Whereas Mrs. Greenleaf struggles to conquer suffering, evil, death, and the loss of salvation, Mrs. May campaigns against the weather, the wrong seeds in the grain drill, government taxes, benefits for war veterans, her sons' failures, her neighbors' successes, her self-esteem, Mrs. Greenleaf's very existence, and the scrub bull—the bull that has the audacity to roam the countryside without regard for Mrs. May's permission, deed, and breeding schedule. At least for fifteen years, and probably all her life, Mrs. May has been on the warpath with a free-floating sense of being a victim in search of assailants to justify her wrath. Mrs. May is the field marshal in the ego war. If Mrs. Greenleaf struggles to save souls, Mrs. May fights to save money, which she believes can redeem her godforsaken plight, to pay homage to pride, which is her source of being, and to keep others under her foot. The means of attack is her will—or, better yet, her wills—for she has countless strong and fixed purposes. To get what she wants, Mrs. May has built a stockpile of demands and prerogatives to overmaster the incessant threats. And there seems to be no end of menaces because she has no sense of gratitude.

There is a hiddenness about the engagements Mrs. Greenleaf and Mrs. May have with the enemy that further differentiates their moral characters. Mrs. Greenleaf retires to the woods to call without distraction on God's help. When stumbled upon by Mrs. May, Mrs. Greenleaf does not conceal her unusual practice. Free of the least bit of embarrassment or cowardice, she brushes aside the intrusion to resume her struggle with determined evangelical fervor. Mrs. May, conversely, is a stealth warrior. Usually she wants to call attention to herself; but when she wants to do harm and shun responsibility, she seeks to escape notice. Property rights and manners camouflage her militant attempt to control the farm and its official mores; and fear makes her victimize others. Her latest sneak attack uses Mr. Greenleaf as a weapon. Mrs. May orders him to kill his sons' footloose bull, a gratuitous bloodshedding that she pretends will protect her cows; but the "exhilaration of carrying her point" (*CW* 520) arises from deeper satisfactions. Shooting the bull is really about power, will power. The animal's destruction will affirm Mrs. May's rule over beast and human. And the sacrifice is about animus. The carcass will relieve her envy of the prosperity enjoyed by its owners, the Greenleaf boys who have made good after the war. By ritualizing her evil passions, Mrs. May creates the smoke screen behind which she can appease the envious demons stirring within her.

Mrs. May comes face-to-face with her demons when she meets forces beyond her will at the end of "Greenleaf." The monstrous collision fits right in with the outlandish demonic assaults described in Athanasius's *Life of Anthony* (9 [38–39]) and lays bare the desert verities shaping Mrs. May's life. This disclosure is anticipated by the similarity of predicament that she shares with her antagonist Mrs. Greenleaf. O'Connor underscores the association by paying attention to each woman's voice, always a good indication of inner life. Neither is silent. Both have high-pitched voices, either because of pressing faith or chronic discontent. Although Mrs. May is stunned by Mrs. Greenleaf's "guttural agonized voice" (*CW* 506), her own "restrained screech" has waxed so "habitual" (*CW* 503) that those within earshot either bait her wickedly, as do Wesley and Scofield, or meet her ceaseless shrills with calm, as do the badgered Mr. Greenleaf and his six perplexed grandchildren. How much easier it is to pass by Mrs. Greenleaf's loud prayers in the woods than it is to avoid Mrs. May's continuous door-slamming, gripes, and orders, which sweep across the farm like a permanent fiery sirocco battering the desert.

Actually, Mrs. May would benefit from pondering those newspaper stories she dismisses as "morbid" (*CW* 505) and from listening to Mrs. Greenleaf's prayers for the victims. Death has been uppermost in widow May's mind since her husband died, leaving her penniless, inexperienced, and exiled. Despite reasonable prosperity, the future still rattles her: "'When I die,'" she says in a "thin voice" to her sons, "'I don't know what's going to become of you'" (*CW* 511). Reminiscing about the future is her way of smuggling in her own anxiety about the present. Insipid self-sorrow leads to preposterous denial: "'I'll die when I get good and ready'" (*CW* 511), she avers, just in case Scofield and Wesley might look forward to lives freed of her peevishness. The blue devils in Mrs. May, however, do express an emotional truth: namely, her fear of death. Were she to keep Mrs. Greenleaf's disasters before her, instead of pretending that death is a function of her will, Mrs. May might learn not "to forget the eternal judgement" (*Sayings*, Evagrius 4 [64]). To find meaning in death is to go beyond terror to courage. This is a basic lesson of the desert solitaries, and this is the lesson of Mrs. Greenleaf's prayers in the Georgia woods.

Mrs. May does come to remember God's judgment. (This would not be an O'Connor story if the heroine were denied the ultimate evaluation of her choices.) God's power comes back to Mrs. May through her resistant will. For O'Connor—as for the desert elders—"our own wills become the demons . . . which attack us in order that we may fulfill them" (*Sayings*, Poemen 67 [176]). These private demands are the powers creating the satanic storm that catches those around Mrs. May in the wind shear of her shifting verbal abuses and commands. As it is her self-will that violates God's law by oppressing others, so it is her will that is bent into compliance at the end. The degree of her resistance to God can be gauged by the violence required to undo her resistance. Violence in "Greenleaf" is swift and appalling. It comes through the bull's horns, one of which "sank" into Mrs. May "until it pierced her heart" (*CW* 523).

Retribution determines judgment. Mrs. May the bully repeatedly stabs people in the back with her verbal and emotional scorn; and now the bull reverses her demons, thereby exposing the impotence of her vaunted will and making a lie of her assertion that she will die when she is good and ready. The bull effectively completes the work of Mrs. Greenleaf, the spiritual tormentor, who is the midwife to liberate Mrs. May from her cold rocky keep. Catanyxis occurs in a flash. Mrs. May has only a moment to see the bull "approaching on the outside of some invisible circle" (*CW* 524). In death, there is hardly a world around her. The desert enters Mrs. May. On the desert of herself into which the bull, against her will, forces her, the proper Mrs. May can cease her petty battle of manners and vicious onslaughts of will. What she has regarded as unbecoming behavior in Mrs. Greenleaf, who prayed to be stabbed in the heart, now fits Mrs. May. Good taste is out of place in the company of death. The bull's head buried in her lap "like a wild tormented lover" (*CW* 523) and embracing Mrs. May with his horns is the essence of extreme bad taste. There is no uncoupling in the story. The bull is shot, but the union is permanent and the faith is radical. Heart-rending is what desert ascesis is all about.

The terrible speed of God's invasion recurs so frequently in Flannery O'Connor's fiction that it ceases to surprise seasoned readers, many of whom understandably dodge the violence through theory or some other kind of abstract explanation. But when grasped in its cruel, bloody particulars, such a tormented impaling by the bull on a beautiful day on a sleepy dairy farm must shock. And it is meant to register a shock seismic in impact and glacial in reverberation. O'Connor is never satisfied merely to craft a dramatically effective comeuppance for the protagonist. The implosion aims for catanyxis in the reader as well, an emotion that cuts deep enough to plant a new attitude or resolution in the unbelieving reader's heart. The art of this hermit novelist is designed to transmit the presence of God to a hard-hearted audience.

The use of the bull horns to deliver the shock squares with an honored tradition of representing the word and spirit of God as a sword. That this creature is a mongrel farm animal accords with O'Connor's special regard for the lame, rejected, and lesser as harbingers of the Almighty. There is, of course, more to the sharp-edged brand. We can appreciate the allusive range of O'Connor's art by noting several examples of the iconography that the story incorporates. The second servant song in Isaiah sings of the prophet's mouth as made "like a sharp sword" (Isaiah 49:2). There is also the mighty two-edged sword emblematizing how God lives and acts in human affairs (Hebrews 4:12); and Ephesians 6:17 speaks of the word of God coming through his servants as "the sword of the Spirit, which is the word of God." The sword gathers special poignancy with Dante, the master poet who stands behind O'Connor's anagogical style. Dante gives dramatic force to the theology of the sword in a way that bears directly on the themes of prayer and healing in "Greenleaf." In the spectacular procession leading to the earthly paradise on the top of Mount Purgatory, a nameless disciple of Hippocrates carries a sword that frightens Dante with the reminder that healing comes from deep wounding (vol. 2, *Purgatorio* 29.136–41).

Deep as the physician's sword cuts, a sharper sword goes even deeper to heal. In the ensuing canto, Beatrice, the spokeswoman for divine wisdom, foretells of the awaiting sword of ultimate justice that inflicts tears; and the eventuality of such weeping strikes terror in Dante (vol. 2, *Purgatorio* 30.55–57). This is an extraordinary shock. Dante's dread is negative in name only, for this terrorism intimidates its subject to liberate the sinful captive. The ice that has restrained Dante's eyes melts, and he cries "with anguish . . . from my breast through my mouth and eyes" (vol. 2, *Purgatorio* 30.98). One has only to look up at the woman who passes judgment on Dante to recognize that this fear issues from love. We sense in Beatrice's speaking from a lofty remove that her love inheres with her stern authority. As she sponsors Dante's journey through the next world, the angel-like lady brings about the tears that draw him to God. In Dante, as in the late-antique desert of the fathers and mothers and in O'Connor's Georgia world, catanyxis leads to penthos, shock to tears, and weeping to the divine.

Finally, one patristic text ties together these various piercings of love. Irenaeus describes the martyrdom of a second-century A.D. woman whose torments surpass Dante's terror and Mrs. May's tribulation and rival in one person the collective agonies over which Mrs. Greenleaf prays. The woman, the slave Blandina, was tortured and left hanged from a stake. After renewed cruelties, she at last died "insensitive to goring by a wild bull, 'rapt in communion with Christ'" (qtd. in Brown, *Body* 73). The meaning of such a violent tableau would have been immediately recognizable to the desert elders, to Dante, and to O'Connor. In all their worlds, stabbing brings oneness with God. Violence bearing away the kingdom is O'Connor's signature moment. In story after story, God vehemently forces his way into the human body. For O'Connor, a person bearing the mighty weight of divine penetration expresses human nature at it zenith. Mrs. May at the end of "Greenleaf" stands for nothing less than this fulfillment.

O'Connor's poetics, which is as exact as is her theology, prepares Mrs. May for her stunning elevation. Just before death, she is most alive. "'Spring is here!' she said gaily" (*CW* 520), as she drives Mr. Greenleaf to meet the bull. When the bull is "racing toward her" with his head lowered for attack, she is most composed. "She remained perfectly still, not in a fright, but in a freezing unbelief" (*CW* 523). Catanyxis makes her most aware. Gored by the bull, she bends "over whispering some last discovery into the animal's ear" (*CW* 524). All along, Mrs. May knew that the world would not come around to meet her demands. The rapier of truth has struck that part of her that will not be lied to, and she is free to speak softly from that inner place. In the end, Mrs. May is a survivor of her fears. The word in desert spirituality to describe her state is *hesychia*, which in Greek means stillness or silence. Hesychia was the aim of the ancient desert-dwellers and remains the goal of the spiritual life. Mrs. May's impaled body sighing her revelation, like that of the gored Blandina, is the holograph of the hesychast resting in God. Receptive now to God, Mrs. May utters what in patristic spirituality is called prayer of the heart, or the experiencing of love and the rejoicing in salvation.

When seen within the story's ascetic context, the raw goring is fundamentally and finally a piercing of love. To be sure, the bull's physical attack is accidental, and O'Connor finds a way to account for the mishap. The bull does not like cars and trucks, and Mrs. May's impatient, sustained honking of the horn attracts the animal. But divine grace is never accidental, for mercy never comes by chance. God's readiness to help those in need comes when the person is open to divine aid; and for O'Connor, divine assistance is the momentum in sacred history bringing humankind back to the Creator. As the bull's "long light horns" (*CW* 512) open up Mrs. May's heart, her heart comes to know the Beloved. No wonder O'Connor calls the jaunty scrub bull the "pleasantest character in this story" (*HB* 132). He romps to a will other than Mrs. May's; and like the expiatory sword that petrifies Dante, the bull's horn is dreadful, beautiful, and holy.

The sundering power of this genial bull brings about the greatest delight in Mrs. May. Held in the mighty animal's "unbreakable grip," she sees that "the entire scene in front of her had changed" and that her "sight has been suddenly restored" through an "unbearable" light (*CW* 523). By this light, Mrs. May shall see the light. Her change in vision expresses a change in her inner world that dazzles with knowing surprise. At a flash of stunning insight, Mrs. May takes the measure of herself and feels how much it contains. Buried beneath her controlling will and anger are things so fine and eternal that the things she most cared for look bare and poor in comparison. The woman who never felt that she belonged out in the sticks and has always dwelled in the desert of the spirit is finally home, no longer a stranger.

In this stronghold of forced submission, Mrs. May is free to be her true self. She is free to cry profusely, as she is inclined to, but the torrents falling from her eyes like a "wall of tears" (*CW* 511) will no longer be for herself. The wound caused by the sleek horns of the bull brings Mrs. May to the source of penthos from which the stream of spiritual waters flows. This auspicious conflux of inner tides comes about by means of the hidden workings of an obscure solitary's unsparing dedication. Through her self-donation, Mrs. Greenleaf, that despised agent from an alien desert cult, not only prays to heal wounds of strangers all around the world, but she also brings down the clemency of God on the Georgia locality in which she lives. In that remote place, Amma Greenleaf helps to bring penthos to life in Amma May's body. Through tears, Mrs. May's trial comes to a merciful end. Flannery O'Connor would have it no other way.

7 *Vision and Vice*

This is the man whose very life is a lie: he is not a simple but a two-faced man; he is one thing on the inside and another on the outside.
—Dorotheos of Gaza, *Discourses and Sayings*

And no wonder, for even Satan disguises himself as an angel of light.
—2 Corinthians 11:14

Be a stranger to the desire for domination, vain-glory, and pride.
—Theodora, *The Sayings of the Desert Fathers*

THREE STORIES IN *Everything That Rises Must Converge* involve characters who see themselves as virtuous in their concern for the welfare of others. By their lights, these upstanding persons are generous in expressing their noble spirit through both emotional and material favors. Such charity is the basis of their dignity and superiority over others. In "A View of the Woods," the patriarch Mark Fortune derives satisfaction from allowing his daughter's family to live on his property in the Georgia hinterland. Mr. Fortune is especially fond of his granddaughter, Mary Fortune Pitts, who receives small daily tokens of his affection and the ultimate gift of being named heir to the entire place. The concern for others in "The Lame Shall Enter First" goes beyond family. Sheppard, an urban recreational director, is a single parent who is not only responsible for his son of ten but in his spare time gives himself over to helping boys at the local reformatory. Sharing his time and energy with juvenile offenders bathes Sheppard in the hue of irreproachable self-contentment. Ruby Turpin, the landowner in "Revelation," has a less activist understanding of her benevolence, but her view of her disposition is not less flattering. Ruby's philosophy is never to spare herself when finding someone in need. Readiness to help others justifies her salvation, about which Ruby is as sure as she is convinced of her magnanimity.

But the human will be human, and virtuous habits are hard to sustain or acquire if one rests in congratulation rather than struggles in examination of fixed attitudes and actions. In fact, the virtue that served the desert teachers as the vigilant corrective for all the other virtues was a healthy skepticism about one's goodness. That "one" practice for Abba Poemen is "for a man to blame himself" (*Sayings*, Poemen 134 [186]). "Self-accusation" about keeping the commandments checks the risk of being what Dorotheos of Gaza calls a "falsifier." For Dorotheos, one can be a liar not only in thought and in word but also "in one's very life." Whether one thinks, speaks, or lives the falsehood, the common motive is the person's "not wanting to acquire the virtue he praises" (9 [161]). If pretext is the conscious or even unconscious intention, then the virtues are a reproach to the falsifier.

The three stories discussed in this chapter submit O'Connor's claimants to goodness to the test by means of demonic attacks on the precise virtues that express their spiritual desire. As in the *Sayings* and *Lives*, only through Satan's exacting challenge can O'Connor's protagonists see what truly drives them. In this contest, their self-will and aspiration come up against the law of unintended consequences, which brings each protagonist to a deserted spot or emotional wilderness. Here, the demons suddenly burst upon these solitaries and sound their hearts to expose the vice beneath their virtue. The shock of recognition demolishes the fabricated vision of themselves. And yet the broken icon offers healing in the form of a new integrity. Now the protagonists can see that to which they are called: not to a neighborliness and virtue according to their own image and likeness but to a shattering sacrifice that plunders whatever is not genuine love.

The story of Mr. Fortune's largesse takes us directly into the territory held by the devil. The bucolic title "A View of the Woods" belies the unspeakable wickedness transpiring under the comely trees gracing the property. The panorama of these Georgia pines is so tied to the inhabitants' self-worth that they torment and kill for the prospect. Whereas murder is common in O'Connor's writing, the configuration of malevolent forces in this story is shocking even for her. There are two killers, and they slay each other. There is also a third evildoer, a psychological killer who is every bit as murderous of the spirit as the two are of each other's bodies. To intensify the horror, O'Connor makes the antagonist a girl of nine and her victim a man of seventy-nine. O'Connor binds them as granddaughter and grandfather. The third member of this triangle is another grown male, the girl's father. The kinship among these three forges an entanglement of unrelieved ugliness. The slaughter concluding this "little morality play," as O'Connor calls her tale (*HB* 186), dramatizes the mortal effects of the wrathful and avaricious demons swarming the place. The tribe making its home on this classical field of spiritual warfare encompasses all eight of the evil spirits cited in Evagrius's *Praktikos*. This time it is the demon of lust that leads the pack, seeking to gratify its taste for disordered sexual pleasure through power over people and nature.

This precinct under the devil's authority is a penal colony occupying 800 hundred acres owned by Mark Fortune. As befits the old man's airs, the narrator customarily uses the alternate title for master when referring to *Mr.* Fortune. Mr. Fortune bolsters his gerontocracy through his prideful demon's desperate attempt to extend itself beyond death by founding a new town. From this newly conceived patch on a clay road fifteen miles off the paved highway, Fortune, Georgia, will rise as a memorial to Mr. Fortune's foresight, an extension, really, of the Pandemonium he now rules. The old man may be "a man of advanced vision" (*CW* 528) in town planning, but he sees people through the timeworn lens of economic control. Two subjects in particular menace his patriarchate: Pitts, his son-in-law, and Mary Fortune, his granddaughter. For ten years, Pitts has been living on the place, trying to make a go of a dairy business to support his wife and seven children. No matter how hard Pitts works, he remains a tenant because Mr. Fortune cuts a hard deal: "What Pitts made went to Pitts but the land belonged to Fortune and he was careful to keep the fact before them" (*CW* 526). The rivalry for the position of dominant male deepens into stalemate with the old man gloating in his humiliation of his younger competitor, who nevertheless retains the upper hand by virtue of his physical might. Mr. Fortune sits at the head of the table; Pitts sits at the side in angry awareness that the arrangement enforces his compromised status. By such tactics, the old man enjoys the delusion of male adequacy so long as the younger man tolerates the position of domestic impotence.

Pitts's demon is too shrewd in the ways of male territorial combat to aim his resentment directly against Mr. Fortune. Younger and stronger, Pitts knows that the best way to deal with a tyrant is to outlive him.

Until that time comes, Pitts gets at his archfoe by beating his daughter Mary. His aim is to make the old man feel the emotional and physical helplessness that lies beneath Mr. Fortune's legal control. The story presents Pitts's savage abuse of his daughter with O'Connor's usual toughness. The reader is made to feel the wounds of futility before raw demonic power. The sacrifice of Mary Fortune is so established and essential to the stability of the household that its violence no longer seems violent to the family and does not incite resistance against Pitts or defense of the innocent girl. The family tolerates a constant crisis of moral incompetence. Whenever Pitts feels Mr. Fortune's control (mealtime for this family whets the appetite for pain), Pitts gets up from the side of the table and takes his daughter to the woods to whip her.

To remark Pitts's attacking his daughter is merely to touch the surface of Pitts's submission to demonic impulses. O'Connor, known to savor the unseemly but to eschew its sexual aspects, succeeds in plumbing Pitts's sadism by means of a demonology that expresses her desert sensibility. A rapid glimpse of the demons' control over Pitts also exposes their political machinations. The obsessed brute follows a liturgy compelled by his lustful and angry demons in obeisance to Priapus, the idol of male procreative power. Its action is simple. "Time and again" Pitts would "abruptly, for no reason, with no explanation, jerk his head at Mary Fortune and say, 'Come with me,' and leave the room, unfastening his belt as he went" (*CW* 529–30). Trained in Satan's domain to submit, Mary Fortune, with a look resembling "cooperation," follows her handler as would an animal on an invisible leash. Pitts drives the girl to a pine tree out of the family's earshot, where he "methodically" belts her around the ankles for about three minutes "as if he were whacking a bush with a sling blade" (*CW* 530). Three minutes would allow for many lashes by means of which the lord of pain can engrave his law into the body of his dependent. The punishment is a demonic method of instruction. It reverses the ascetic aim of controlling the body to bring the will consciously in line with divine law. Instead, Pitts's demons batter Mary Fortune's body to numb her will into bondage.

Pitts knows that fear keeps others buckled under his anger. Through their direct combat with demons, the desert elders recognized that fear gives the devil the upper hand. "Should they [the demons] find us frightened and distressed, immediately they attack like robbers," says Abba Anthony, and so the ascetics must "take courage" and oppose the demons (Athanasius 42 [63]). Mr. Fortune, for instance, observes the beating of the girl from behind a boulder and cannot challenge Pitts's brutality because dread has overtaken him. Trapped in fear, the old man also receives the intended lesson of terror and helplessness from the flogger, and Mr. Fortune's knowledge contains the lesson that the eight other younger victims around the table learn from the attack at the pine tree. Fear feeds on itself by undermining the courage that could check the devil's power. The process begins with a display of Pitts's belt, a proxy for his diminished moral and phallic power, and gains force with Mary Fortune's reciprocal assent. The instruction culminates as the two disappear into the deserted woods, where the assault leaves the everyday world to enter the satanic dark of the girl's fearful self and of those who are left to imagine the pain that Pitts's demons shrewdly forbid them to see.

The clandestine beatings bring the action across the threshold of domestic secrecy into the horror of silence. Instead of raising her voice, O'Connor keeps her language flat. Her desert calm forces the reader to feel the satanic power being internalized unimpeded by victim, observer, or authorial emotion. The forfeiture of authorial response expresses Mary Fortune's loss of her rights and will to paternal cruelty. The girl's degradation simultaneously exposes her tormentor's abasement. Pitts is a slave of power: "'She's mine to whip and I'll whip her every day of the year if it suits me'" (*CW* 531). Though unaware of his indenture, the redneck ox under the guidance of his evil masters is an astute tactician who establishes authority by implementing a harsh, unjust sentence on his daughter's body. The girl and the rest of the family learn to accept an indignity that has always been a sign of Satan's control.

Anguish that seems to have no saving human witness or opponent permeates "A View of the Woods" and shows its damage most fully in Mary Fortune. She lives under two evil regimes—a harsh patriarchy superimposed on a feeble gerontocracy. Whether Mary Fortune is the target of her father's self-hating rage or a prize for her grandfather's egotism, the girl's life as a child and a female is degrading. These men have done what Evagrius saw demons do: they have thrown what is holy, the girl's body, to the dogs of anger ("Introductory Letter" [15]). Mary Fortune's value depends on the inhuman, satanic use of her humanity; and her femaleness lowers the worth of her service and, as she grows up, increases the poignancy of her exploitation. Her very conception is a form of extortion. Pitts and his wife arrived at the place ten years earlier with six children. Knowing that Mr. Fortune resents their presence, the couple soon announce that Mr. Fortune's daughter is pregnant, and they will name the baby Mark Fortune. This newborn will be donated to the despotic idol as a human offering by dutiful subjects. The bribe backfires. The old man spurns the linking of his name to that of Pitts. To increase the disappointment, the child turns out to be a girl, and a female is low coinage in this realm. By genetic chance, however, the girl resembles Mr. Fortune. Vanity wrests some kindness from the narcissist's heart, and the girl receives the name Mary after Mr. Fortune's mother, who died bearing him. Now Mary Fortune Pitts is the namesake manqué for Mark Fortune, but she gradually becomes his soul mate by dint of their emotional ties. Out of this closeness, the girl develops an aggressive self-will to match the light-blue eyes, the florid complexion, and the wide forehead that she shares with her grandfather.

Their age difference and equivalent dispositions make for a confused familial relationship, because the old man's eugenic myth imposes a rigid constraint over the child that he pretends to love. He sets the rules and roles for conduct. As with all satanic power relations, deceits sustain the charade. Mr. Fortune on occasion plays a "suitor trying to reinstate himself" (*CW* 537) after the two quarrel; he can wax solicitous in asking "'sister'" (*CW* 541) what bothers her; and, with his Cadillac, he serves her as a complaisant chauffeur. His adoration accords with Mary Fortune's being his heir. That position not only isolates the girl from her family; it also makes her a weapon in Mr. Fortune's unceasing belligerence. Mr. Fortune serves Mary Fortune so that she will serve him as a posthumous revenge against her family. With the egotist's talent to reminisce about life after death, Mr. Fortune savors the prospect of Mary Fortune's making them all "jump" (*CW* 527) to her orders. The old man's affection for his granddaughter is another bribe, and she knows it. That knowledge is Mary Fortune's power over Mr. Fortune, and her legacy will be her power over Pitts. Being born female may expose Mary Fortune to the demons driving two male parents, but it does not finally determine her relation to power. The demons in both men teach the girl that human emotions serve personal interests; and where love is tied to self-will, its power to free and heal is turned into a force of captivity and pain.

In sum, the opponents in "A View of the Woods" are old and irksome, middle-aged and irksome, young and irksome. Their convergence in the woods unleashes an explosion of unprecedented demonic energy. A consideration of the first and last scenes will show how these evil forces make daily life a living hell only to turn in on themselves to dismantle the demonic structure they have erected. To appreciate O'Connor's crafting of these scenes, one needs to augment this study's usual way of observing human conflicts "with the anagogical way of seeing" (*HB* 180) that O'Connor uses. That way of seeing several realities in one image comes from O'Connor's sympathy for Dante, the seer whose massive insight into the realm ruled by Satan taught him how demonic forces intertwine with human psychology.

"A View of the Woods" begins with the making of hell out of the earth's plain loveliness. Voracious avarice and gluttonous anger are at work here. To guarantee that the Pittses feel the pain of displacement, Mr. Fortune sells off twenty-five-acre lots to various developers. The scheme now underway calls for a fishing club by a new lakeside. Each morning for a week, the old man drives Mary Fortune in his mulberry-colored Cadillac to watch the excavation. Everything in the surroundings speaks to Mr. Fortune's feelings of entrepreneurial know-how. He especially enjoys the bulldozer digging a huge hole where the old pasture that Pitts managed to clear of bitterweed used to be. The machine's shovel-blade feeds Mr. Fortune's hunger for superiority over his son-in-law. With his whole being swelling in an atmosphere of mastery, Mr. Fortune uses these morning inspection tours to teach Mary Fortune how to rule others through ownership of property. He insinuates his malice into the girl with the keen, unrelenting determination of the evil *logismos*. Mr. Fortune's pleasure in disenfranchising people is real, but the privilege conferred by title-deed is a demonic delusion gratifying his ego.

The reader's anagogical eye can discern that the demons are playing the falsifier false and that the chewing up of the soil is ruinous and disgusting. The bulldozer gorges itself on the red soil and then, "with the sound of a deep sustained nausea" (*CW* 525), spits up the particles. The blade makes the natural red clay of Georgia hemorrhage over the corrugated hole. The site is a perilous pit. The hollow yawns a warning of the abyss that oppression is creating in the family, a chasm that is swallowing them up. Like the moist, sloping cavity, power is slippery. Both Mr. Fortune and Mary Fortune are physically at risk of falling down the embankment of the pit that has the very conical shape of Dante's Inferno. The geometry of their physical positions this morning further reveals the deceptions of power. From the moment Mr. Fortune wakes, Mary Fortune is on top of him and pulling the reins. She bestrides his chest in bed, ordering him to hurry so that they can see the concrete mixer at the construction site. At the lakeside, he sits on the car bumper, and "she sat on the hood with her bare feet on his shoulders" (*CW* 528). When she wants to shift the direction of their verbal tilts, she stamps his shoulders with her feet to impel him. He clearly is under her foot.

There is more to this tableau of delusory power. The anagogical eye detects a three-part eyesore: Mary Fortune straddling the Cadillac hood with Mr. Fortune sitting below on the bumper. The interlocking shapes compose a craniofacial disfigurement right out of hell. Female and male faces enclosing the car grill reproduce Dante's Cerberus, the three-headed dog with blood-red eyes and greasy black beards in canto 6 of the *In-*

ferno. Cerberus's job is to flog the souls being punished for gluttony as they wallow in filth and are pelted by fiery rain. As voracious eating fills Dante's scene in Satan's underworld, ravenous greed fills O'Connor's picture in the upper reaches of the devil's territory. The bulldozer "systematically ate a square red hole in what had once been a cow pasture" and then stuffs the clay in its "big disembodied gullet" (*CW* 525). As Mr. Fortune relishes this gorging, he battens on his power to humiliate Pitts by selling the land and corrupting his granddaughter. Dante's devil-dog reifies the inner forces of evil gripping the characters and announces O'Connor's censure of the old man's bingeing on wrath and self-will. She adds machinery to the mythic hell-fiend's nature to update its cultural office in Georgia's burgeoning backwoods. On the Fortune place, the ugly demonic beast dehumanizes as it feeds on its victims.

As we have seen many times in O'Connor's writing, the demonic flow intimately affects the needs of the human body. In "A View of the Woods," everyone feels deprived. They hunger, eat, and remain starved. Mary Fortune at nine is already "'stout'" (*CW* 536) from trying to comfort herself and control her own life, but the girl cannot reclaim her body and spirit from her family's dominance, which has the tenacious hold of evil behind it. She understandably looks at the bulldozer with "complete absorption" (*CW* 525) while it ingests and spits up soil. The mechanical rhythm replicates her repeated efforts to satisfy her appetite for freedom only to be sickened by restraint. When the bulldozer threatens to go beyond the stake, the roaring girl lurches after the machine, again like a dog on a leash. Whereas her eyes seek freedom, Mr. Fortune's eyes crave possession. He stares "sometimes for hours" (*CW* 525) without ever reaching the bottom of his avarice. And it seems unlikely that Mr. Fortune will ever feel satisfied. Having substituted wealth for power and power for human companionship, the isolated old man lives in vanity. His vanity is the emptiness portrayed in Ecclesiastes 4:8 in the solitary individual "who has no one" and feels "no end to all his toil" because "his eyes are never satisfied with riches." This pit is the snare into which the demons have thrown Mr. Fortune.

One week before the story begins, Mr. Fortune confides in Mary Fortune that he is negotiating to sell the lot in front of the house so that a developer named Tilman can construct a gas station. This deal is no typical bit of devilry, because this section is no ordinary parcel of land. This property lies at the front door of the house, and the new gas station would imprison the Pittses by depriving them of "'the lawn'" (*CW* 532). Pitts grazes his calves on the expanse, and everyone enjoys the liberating view of the pine trees that rise across the road. Mr. Fortune, a master of timing, tells the family about his plan at high noon (Satan's appointed hour), during dinner. The planned obliteration of their view of the woods is intolerable to the family, who experience the decision as an evil blight on their lives. The unpalatable fare dished out by the old man sickens everyone and stirs the Cerberus instinct in Pitts, and the drama of punishment in Dante's second circle replays itself in the Georgia backwoods. Like the guardian dog in hell, Pitts goes berserk with rage. He blames his daughter for the sale of the lawn, summons her to the woods, and beats her with Cerberus's calculation.

Soon a self-sustaining frenzy of abusive power runs its course. Pitts's impotence speaks to Mr. Fortune's impotence; then spite begets spite; and wrath speeds the male conflict to a mortal confrontation between the old man and the young girl. Mr. Fortune closes the deal at Tilman's, at which moment Mary Fortune fights for her family's interest by hurling bottles and whatever else is available at Tilman and her grandfather. No one gets away with making the old man look bad. The girl's public tantrum outrages Mr. Fortune. As with Pitts, the affronted ego closes its mind to anything but its own power. The Cerberus in the old man takes over. Mr. Fortune dumps the girl in his Cadillac to discipline the "hellion" (*CW* 543) once and for all. Since Pitts by his flogging has endowed the girl's body with the value of ownership, his rival Mr. Fortune competes for rank by borrowing the satanic violence that he thinks the child respects. Mr. Fortune brings Mary Fortune to the exact lonely spot where Pitts beats her to reclaim his investment in Mary Fortune's obedience.

But Mr. Fortune's demons outsmart him. They serve the old blackguard only to get him, and they are in league with the demons roiling Mary Fortune. She has learned to send a mannequin to the post. "'Nobody's ever beat me in my life,'" she snaps to her grandfather after he sees Pitts whip her, "'and if anybody did, I'd kill him'" (*CW* 541). By splitting her wounded body from her scarred psyche, Mary Fortune keeps her life intact. Her denial of her father's stropping compels the girl to examine her lowly status as victim and thereby toughens her resolve against abuse from any other source. She blinds herself to one devil and sees the other clearly. She repeats her death threat to her grandfather when he removes his belt to reprove her for her rampage at Tilman's. The instant his belt slaps her ankles, the blow throws a switch located in the girl's guarded humanness, and her wrathful demon, waiting for nine years to show its full power, overtakes her. In a flash she is on top of the old man, pummeling his chest. The Cerberus in Mary Fortune also comes alive. Nothing is more pronounced than her mouth with its vociferous appetite for revenge against Mr. Fortune and the absent male who initiated the beatings. She bites the side of Mr. Fortune's jaw. When he begs for mercy, she gnaws more deeply as the demon in Dante's hell would respond to the beseeching shades. With glee, Mary Fortune's fury affirms it demonic affiliation: "'I'm PURE Pitts'" (*CW* 545). But once more, power proves to be a slippery delusion. Another stunning reversal occurs when Mary Fortune loosens her grip and the old man rolls over, mounts the girl, and grabs her neck. A more precise demon than the girl's scattershot rage takes over. The narrator counts with the old man as he "once" pounds the child's head against a rock and then brings down her skull "twice more" (*CW* 545). He kills her without remorse. Having gotten all that it wants out of the old man's heart, the logismos summarily flows out of its aged—and now useless—victim. Mr. Fortune takes "two steps" (*CW* 546) and dies of a convulsive heart attack.

The ending of "A View of the Woods" is an accumulation of three demonic scenes engraved on one another. In the foreground, the deserted spot in the woods erupts into a double homicide. Behind the blood-stained earth is the hellish picture of gluttonous demons devouring each other, and within this picture is a revelation of the wrathful sinners receiving the spiritual torment of their own brutality. These interwoven scenes mark an anagogical movement from the dark Georgia woods to the dismal wood of Dante's circle of gluttony (the third ring in upper hell) and down further to the circle of violence (the seventh circle in lower hell). Cerberus of the upper region intrudes his flesh-eating bulk in each of these scenes. Just before Mr. Fortune dies, he desperately looks around for help and sees only "one huge yellow monster which sat to the side, as stationary as he was, gorging itself on clay" (*CW* 546). His demons have managed to damage the battered man's optic nerve to distort his perception, for the masticating figure is really Mary Fortune's corpse. Mr. Fortune's visual fallacy holds more for the anagogical reader than the old man ever saw with ordinary sight. Mary Fortune's tenement of clay and Cerberus unite to open the jaws of hell before Mr. Fortune. In this ugly permutation, Mr. Fortune finds his own "conquered image" (*CW* 545). He who intends to give a moral lesson gets back what he sends out, and he receives the lesson on his body, which now becomes the body of his knowledge of his doom. As a basis for the relationship between grandfather and granddaughter—between all persons—power amounts to a gnawing on the humanness of the other. Possession ends in death, which is the fixed goal of the logismoi. As Abba Poemen says: "Violence makes both small and great to be overthrown" (*Sayings*, Poemen 179 [192]).

The fact that Mr. Fortune in the shame of his soul cannot recognize Mary Fortune brings out the effect of his avarice. His greed renders everyone invisible to him except as they serve his wealth. Money is his only real power and identity, and it blinds. The yellow of the chewing monster emblematizes the way that Dante's violent usurers (canto 17) are recognizable only by the escutcheons on their moneybags. Usury is another way of understanding O'Connor's exposing of Mr. Fortune's evil. Usury is a sin against human industry and identity insofar as it reproduces only the material it begins with—in "A View of the Woods," clay produces clay, a lifeless parody of human productivity. Dante puts the violent against nature along the outer margin of hell's seventh circle, where they sit despondently in burning soil, trying to fend off a rain of fire. A purse (one is yellow, like O'Connor's machine) hangs on the neck of each, and the eyes of these shades feast on their moneybags. The torrid heat of Dante's seventh circle sizzles in "A View of the Woods" to vivify what it is like to live under demonic rule. After Mr. Fortune and Mary Fortune leave the courthouse with the sale papers ready for Tilman's signature, the sky darkens with "a hot sluggish tide" that thickens the air, "the kind felt when a tornado is possible" (*CW* 541). Eager to avoid the squall, the old man rushes to get the whipping of Mary Fortune over before the "downpour" (*CW* 544).

If only the old codger had as good a country sense of emotional climate as he has of physical weather, he might have been able to duck the oncoming gale; but the eye of the turbulence lies within, and there is no escaping the cyclonic waves of his own making. First, he and Tilman are buffeted by the flying objects hurled by Mary Fortune. Shortly afterward in the woods, "a pack of small demons" (*CW* 545) bombards Mr. Fortune in the form of Mary Fortune's fists, feet, and teeth. All of these swirling body parts have been sought by Mr. Fortune's controlling will; and now they, the objects of his own willful satisfaction, play the demon on him. Mary Fortune is the old man's retribution, his inner wrath returning to make him dance under a "rain of blows" pounding his stomach. Like those damned in Dante's *Inferno* who squirm in a burning tempest, Mr. Fortune rolls on the ground "like a man on fire" (*CW* 545). The red Georgia clay in which the two now are caught in a bizarre mud-wrestle redescribes the burning, engulfing ground in Dante's hell, the ultimate blazing desert.

The forecast of hell for the old man is a foreboding of life without love, and love is the law of O'Connor's universe. By Mr. Fortune's abuse of his love for Mary Fortune, he engenders his doom. The girl, however, has a different fate. O'Connor does not quiver over the child's daring and death; in a letter, O'Connor says that the girl is "saved" (*HB* 190). After nine years of power overwhelming her innocence, she ends triumphantly victimized. She dispossesses the tyrant of all he owns and any reward for his treachery. What remains at the end of "A View of the Woods" is the tract of woodland, which endures in sacred reserve. As the final scene begins, the long, slender pines "appeared to be gathered there to witness anything that would take place" (*CW* 544). The trees alone, O'Connor notes, "are pure enough" to put the carnage into moral perspective (*HB* 190). To put it most graphically, I would say that the Georgia pines compose the geography of solitude. The final scene lacks all reference points except that of the creator of it all, and that single focus is the ultimate solitude. The grove is purged of all the human claims imposed on it. The trees escape the old man's exploitation, Pitts's need to possess it, and the family's desire for its beauty. As Mr. Fortune tries in his mind to evade the mayhem, he sees "the gaunt trees . . . marching across the water" (*CW* 546). The sight of striding trees recalls Jesus' healing in Mark 8:24 of the blind man of Bethsaida, who gradually recovers his sight but cannot yet distinguish things clearly: he sees men as walking trees. "A View of the Woods" shows a similar recovery of vision. At last, Mr. Fortune's optic nerve, damaged by demonic pressure, is restored by divine justice so that he sees his personal evil in punching down Mary Fortune, who is perceived as the monster to his side. The setting of evergreens indicates a judgment rooted in the foundation of all time, a prospective justice that overcomes the destruction wrought by the demons pitched in ceaseless battle against love.

At the end, O'Connor includes the element of water—which is not in the biblical scene of sight recovered—in Mr. Fortune's view. Tears could account for the water he sees; and certainly, the bloodbath calls for weeping; but given the demons' tenacious pressure on the old man's heart and eyes, hallucination more probably explains the liquid. The delusion seems to be a materialization of the lake that was planned for the new fishing club, now conjured up as the demons' snide mockery of their victim's greedy scheme. There is no recreation to be enjoyed in this body of water, for the old man "could not swim" and "had not bought the boat" (*CW* 546). This water is about to swallow him in the destructive flood of his evil. If threatening, the water is also revivifying insofar as the view of the woods in their stark solitude beyond Mary Fortune's crushed skull also contains the *penthos* of godly sorrow for agony endured and salvation lost. The flow of compunction is the source of mercy and life, without which earth and human relations are nothing but an arid desert, a land of hunger and thirst—nothing but the Fortune tract—a dismal place where humans and beasts are doomed to death.

The grim fate of Mr. Fortune and Mary Fortune Pitts would not have surprised the desert mothers and fathers. They record numerous accounts of solitaries ravaged by unleashed demonic energy. Two such stories preternaturally apply to O'Connor's writing. Both come from John Cassian, who probed the disasters in the desert. The first casualty concerns an old man named Hero. For fifty years in the desert, Hero toiled in the solitary life with greater fervor than that of the ascetics around him. His fasting was so rigorous, his aloneness so relentless, that even the Easter liturgy did not bring him to assemble in church for the meal with the brethren. The reason for his refusal was that to take the small share of food would give the impression that he departed from "what he had chosen to do" (*Conferences* II, 5 [65]). Therein lies the fault: not in fasting and not merely in the pride that Hero derives from abstinence but in the man's preference to be guided by his own ideas instead of yielding to the counsel and respect of his brothers and the rules of his predecessors. As Cassian explains, this presumption of the priority of Hero's own ideas of virtue and of will led to his being fooled: "He showed the utmost veneration for the angel of Satan, welcoming him as if he were actually an angel of light" (*Conferences* II, 5 [65]). Bondage to the dark messenger entangled Hero in a web of mortal delusions. Believing that the merit of his virtues would keep him from harm, Hero tried to experience freedom from danger and "threw himself headlong into a well, whose depths no eye could penetrate" (*Conferences* II, 5 [65]). Rescued by his brothers, Hero died two days later. To the very end, Hero clung to his cherished illusions, never recognizing that he was the sport of devilish craft (*Conferences* II, 5 [65]).

The bearing of this desert calamity on O'Connor's fiction will be more poignant if we consider Cassian's other example of diabolical deception in solitude. The second misadventure tells of a son who was nearly killed because his father was taken in by a pretext of holiness. The father, a solitary, had for so long seen before him a devil shining like an angel and granting revelations that the man was fooled into thinking the devil to be an angel of justice. Eventually, the solitary was captivated, at which point the demonic spell turned murderous. The messenger ordered the man to sacrifice his son so that he, the father, "might equal the merit of Abraham the patriarch." The father would have killed the son had the son not noticed his father sharpening a knife and preparing chains for the slaughter, after which the son fled in terror (Cassian, *Conferences* II, 7 [66]). The father's failure to recognize evil perverted his impassioned commitment to virtue. From the countless fallen around them, the desert-dwellers knew that the way to virtue was laid with subtle demonic traps. After surveying the fatalities, Cassian could find no other cause for the downfalls than lacking a "discerning eye" (*Conferences* II, 3 [63]). This discovery brought Cassian to set a great value on the talent that O'Connor prized as the capacity to identify "the Devil . . . as the Devil" (*HB* 360). Being able to recognize what is true and from God or what is false and from Satan is the habit of being that protects one's other habits from disintegrating into ends in themselves.

If the call for clear-eyed discernment seems appropriate only for those seeking God, and if the two fourth-century vignettes sound like fantastical misfortunes of already strange figures, we have only to turn to "The Lame Shall Enter First" to find the same ill fortune in twentieth-century, unbelieving, suburban American life. Here, amid Little League baseball games, IQ scores, and psychology textbooks, a man who seeks to help others is duped by the devil, who plays on his victim's altruism. This freethinker's delusions replicate and go beyond the sinister shocks in Cassian's desert calamities. Like the old man Hero, O'Connor's hero, named Sheppard, believes in the impeccable virtue of his practice. That false confidence disposes Sheppard, as it did Hero, to see Satan's messenger as the source of life. The masterly demon eventually pushes Sheppard to the edge of a moral pit. Sheppard is spared death, but his son is not. Unlike the son in the Cassian account, O'Connor's boy falls victim to his father's lack of discernment. O'Connor's Isaac does not survive beyond the age of ten to become the father of Jacob.

Death not only concludes "The Lame Shall Enter First"; death precedes the action. A year or so before the story begins, Sheppard's wife died. She was young; she was "'good and generous'" (*CW* 612); and her presence is sorely missed by her husband and son. Grief over the young woman's death is all the more in the air of the male household because Sheppard refuses to mourn. He also prohibits his son from showing his pain of loss. Tears are sorely needed. *Catanyxis* strikes deep in both survivors, who have yet to experience the release of penthos. Norton, the son, is ready to cry and does. The simple mention of "'your mother'" makes tears roll down his face until, that is, his father ridicules the child for crying. Sheppard must check his son's raw sorrow, because Norton's tears are yet another wound of love that he, the young widower, cannot bear. Without the balm and freedom brought by tears, Sheppard sits "helpless and miserable, like a man lashed by some elemental force of nature" (*CW* 597). Sheppard, a meticulous moralist, has premature white hair and bears the worry lines of an internalizer on his face, so rigid these days because of his resolve not to shed tears over the woman he dearly loved and also because he does not heed the wailing of the son he loves. This uncon-summated mourning blocks energy vital to Sheppard's spirit and disposes him to illusions of mastery over truth, pain, and evil. These illusions are sure signs of the demonic grip on his soul.

The forces of delusion fill the vacuum left by the young wife and mother. We never learn her name. A name would limit her identity; and in Sheppard and Norton's world, she was the unifying love who made life full. Because she is still their reference point as the source of life, her absence creates their desert. Their aloneness is all the more desolate because father and son, standing apart, have no access to each other's destitution. Instead, Sheppard's panic over the boy's tears sharpens the overwhelming fear of abandonment in his son. With little Norton, the chasm feels impassable insofar as his gestures toward solace are futile. He eats, has become stocky, and feels empty inside. He sells seeds and fills four jars with nickels and dimes, which he frequently computes without ever feeling that he himself counts. Sheppard tries to cope with loss by counseling boys at the reformatory. While he may be carried along for a time by his Saturday satisfactions, when that excitement inevitably comes to an end, then his inner emptiness widens.

In trying to make sense of his bereavement, Sheppard becomes a monk in the way in which he adopts a practice to foster his belief that social work will save him. He no longer uses the bedroom he shared with his wife but sleeps in an "ascetic-looking iron bed . . . on the bare floor" (*CW* 605). Showing no interest in women, he accepts the celibacy forced on him by widowhood. He is strict. He denies himself pleasure. And at the reformatory, he has another cell, "a narrow closet with one window and a small table and two chairs in it" (*CW* 599). In this austere compartment that reflects his cold, depressing, and antiseptic ascesis, Sheppard turns his isolation into a ministry that combines priestly absolution with a big brother's pep talk about becoming a productive member of society. But unlike the abba—whose reaching out in prayer or action to others is anchored in love—Sheppard's altruism arises from self-concern and pride. Sheppard admits no doubts, has no needs, has no religion. He judges himself to be charitable. From daily experience, however, it is clear that with someone who is practicing charity well, especially through what they say and how they listen, that the person is responding in a new, deep, open way. These are the very qualities that we immediately pick up in the *Sayings* of the desert ascetics, whose selfless concern for others has kept them fresh in wisdom for over 1,600 years. Sheppard presents a different example. He listens to promulgate his set attitude, and his counseling amounts to the imposition of himself on the younger person. Being full of himself passes for wisdom. "'There are a lot of things about yourself,'" Sheppard says to Rufus Johnson, his latest project, "'that I think I can explain to you.'" Among Sheppard's more vacuous explanations to Johnson, who has a clubfoot, is that his "mischief was compensation for the foot" (*CW* 600).

Sheppard meets his match in Johnson. At fourteen, Johnson is a career criminal in the making. He breaks into houses, steals, destroys, and lies. He is also a racist and an unscrupulous nihilist. Bully is too tame a word for this teenager. Hitler, whose haircut and stance Johnson emulates, comes closer and yet does not do the boy full justice. O'Connor refers to Johnson as "one of Tarwater's terrible cousins" (*HB* 456) and thereby invites us to see him, as we see Tarwater in *The Violent Bear It Away*, as a killer under the power of his demons who is responsible for the death of a trusting and needy younger boy. Just as alarming as the reappearance of a teenage killer under demonic control is O'Connor's offhanded postulate that numerous such young malevolent creatures are on the loose. Her remark, suitably, is made in a letter to John Hawkes, who had been on the lookout for members of this gang swarming O'Connor's universe (*HB* 456).

If Sheppard cannot discern the devil, Hawkes and other demon-watchers should easily spot their subject in "The Lame Shall Enter First." His entry into the house of sorrow affords free access; Sheppard gives him the housekey. Rain slashes the windowpanes and the gutters rattle to announce his arrival. It is afternoon, but the rooms grow dark. Amid the gloom, the young jailbird "in a wet black suit" stands "like an irate drenched crow" (*CW* 603) with eyes darting ravenously for its usual pickings. Once inside, Johnson virtually courts recognition as an evil presence. His first act is a dance of strange bodily gyrations. Some uncontrollable inner disorder sends him into a mocking pretense of feminine sexuality. Without missing a beat, Johnson barges into the closed bedroom used by Sheppard's wife to make a toilet with the dead woman's comb and brush, sweeping his hair aside in Hitlerian style; he then puts on her corset with dangling supporters that sway to the rhythm of his prurient instincts. This is cross-dressing that defiles both genders in life and death. The aim of this demonic seduction is to torment little Norton with an obscenely hermaphroditic phantom of his mother. Shaming the dead comes as naturally to demons as does their ability to conjoin or change genders and shapes. Whatever the gambit, the demonic seeks always to control. To claim domination, Johnson snaps his fingers and stamps his feet. Then comes a victory dance in advance of battle in the form of a frolic to the kitchen with the whooping of a usurper who takes no prisoners.

If there are any doubts left about Johnson's moral ties, his subsequent actions dispel them. The intruder flamboyantly displays a pride and anger that the ancient solitaries recognized as the most dangerous passions. When Sheppard excuses Johnson's senseless vandalism as the result of his move from the country to the city, Johnson rises above sociological cant to insist on the serious source of his conduct. "'Satan,'" Johnson boasts, "'He has me in his power'" (*CW* 600). The black radiance in the eyes of Satan's subject may come and go, but the pride of loyalty and the gleeful contempt of those who miss that allegiance are permanent. So deep runs his diabolical abhorrence of others and of the world that, at fourteen, Johnson speaks, when he deigns to talk, exclusively in the acidic language of opprobrium. For the sake of his pride, Johnson must contradict, disagree, and deceive. We can discern the power generating these hostilities in its somatic effects, which range from his tongue, through the sinews of his body, and down into his club foot, which is made "monstrous" (*CW* 599) by his brutality. Wrath turns his entire body into pride's weapon: "'If I kick somebody *once* with this,'" Johnson tells Norton as he wiggles his big black shoe, "'it learns them not to mess with me'" (*CW* 603). Whereas Sheppard sentimentalizes Rufus's foot, O'Connor links it to his moral responsibility by showing that Johnson's swollen foot is an extension of his swelled head: "The leather parted from it [the thick shoe] in one place and the end of an empty sock protruded like a grey tongue from a severed head" (*CW* 600). What makes the club foot frightful is not its shape but that it replicates the head, a head warped by pride into the source of sin. The poetic conceit linking Johnson's head and foot would not seem strained to the ancient hermits. What is terrible about Johnson's club foot to O'Connor is precisely what appalled the desert elders about evil: sin cripples one to love, to express one's gift, and to grow humanly.

In addition to pride and anger, the other five sources of evil are equally present in Johnson. His arrival is an act of covetousness expressed by his mock-erotic dance; but his real lust is for power, which makes him envy Norton's independence from his control. To gratify this urge, Johnson reduces Norton to a waiter who must serve the gluttonous führer as he slothfully reclines on Norton's bed. With all seven strains of evil flowing in his nature, Johnson is a thoroughbred among O'Connor's villains. To make his genealogy most perfect, O'Connor takes Johnson's ancestry back even further than the medieval reckoning of evil to the fourth-century recognition of the eighth deadly passion of *acedia*. The elders felt that the demon of acedia sapped strength and joy from the soul. The mark of that inner depletion appears in Johnson's face. His forehead is "cold and dry like rusty iron" to the touch (*CW* 619); his mouth is "set in a thin icy line" (*CW* 621). Three times, the narrator describes the teenager's facial expression as "glum" (*CW* 610, 611, 619); and Johnson reacts "glumly" (*CW* 621) to the clerk at the shoe store. Johnson's insufferable gloom is another form of crippling. Acedia disables the spirit, impairs the inner life from evolving, and has shriveled up Johnson's capacity for delight: "It was part of Johnson's make-up never to show enthusiasm" (*CW* 606). It is also in his constitution to abandon all hope. When Sheppard speaks of Johnson's being an astronaut, the boy says: "'when I die I'm going to hell'" (*CW* 611). Even more daunting than the toughness that Johnson presents to the world is the despondency brought about by acedia. The eighth deadly sin of acedia hobbles the boy's soul at fourteen by making him believe that he is beyond forgiveness.

Johnson's despair of salvation would be a sure sign to the desert-dwellers of the boy's being Satan's prisoner. "For this is what the evil one generally does," says the clear-eyed John of Lycopolis, "when he [Satan] overcomes someone he makes him lose his judgement, that afterwards he should no longer be able to raise himself up" (*Lives*, John of Lycopolis 36 [57]). Such despondency has centrifugal force, binding others to the same hopelessness. Through Johnson's torment, O'Connor shows the inner workings of fatalism. Gloom feeds on gloom until dejection feels indomitable and irresistibly coercive. As the story unfolds, despair disables Johnson's conscience by crushing any possibility of contrition. Deprived of the hope of being delivered from his sinful state, Johnson eagerly gives himself over as an ally to the cause of evil. In this service, he calculates how to destroy Sheppard and Norton. In the rawest terms, that demonic assault on Sheppard and Norton is the story. As is expected from a trafficker in double-dealing, the demonic in Johnson advances by tactics suited to his victims' desires. Whether Johnson casts spells or disenchants, his two-pronged pitchfork of persuasion and revocation works to devastate. Since Sheppard knows that he is good and has "'the truth'" (*CW* 612), Johnson slashes through Sheppard's moral pretensions by showing him to be a dupe. Johnson's parting shot shows how incisive the demon's perception can be and how his knowledge can impale. As the police cart Johnson back to jail, he trumpets: "'The devil has you in his power'" (*CW* 628). Hatred has its own sharp intelligence; but in expressing what he knows, Johnson shows more genius than talent, for he speaks (sometimes hisses) and lives in rabid fragments.

Because Norton is more trusting than his father, the child is more exposed to Johnson's deceit. Norton's neediness whets Johnson's appetite to annihilate Norton's hope to find his mother along with his life. In one stroke, Johnson also can destroy Sheppard by taking away his son.

Scheming is so integrally a part of Johnson's nature that O'Connor never has to take the reader inside the delinquent's mind: his actions are his character. The operation of the evil thought-flow, the logismos, that appears in *The Violent Bear It Away* recurs in "The Lame Shall Enter First." Once again, the enemy comes on to his victim as a friend. The lonesome Norton now has a companion with whom he can swim and have lunch at the Y. He no longer stands alone receiving his father's criticism. The night Johnson arrives, he turns to Norton in supportive outrage over Sheppard's self-righteousness: "'God, kid . . . how do you stand it? . . . He thinks he's Jesus Christ!'" (*CW* 609). And so the amiable trickster waxes until he kills Norton with kindness.

Such affectionate brushings initiate the dire movement of the logismos. The evil flow then gains entry into Norton's mind at the point of the boy's grief over his mother's death. Norton cannot make human sense of his mother's disappearance and death. His father tries to help, searches the bottom of his inner void, and squeezes out some sympathy: "'She doesn't exist.'" The words fail, and Sheppard feels their inadequacy: "'That's all I have to give you,' he said in a softer, exasperated tone, 'the truth'" (*CW* 612). Johnson has other truths about existence, which he eagerly provides to fill in the gaps left by Sheppard. The logismos speaks of good and evil, virtue and sin, salvation and damnation. These notions ease Norton's bafflement by making available a moral universe that connects him to the life of his mother beyond his father's void. But this new world spins to satanic sorcery. Johnson makes the dead woman present to the child by explaining that she is "'on high'" (*CW* 612). Naturally, Norton wants to find her. And, naturally, Johnson will show Norton how to reach on high. The possibility of having access to the invisible world of his mother opens Norton's heart to the logismos. Once inside Norton's accepting consciousness, the evil flow fills the child with death-seeking goadings that Johnson disguises as a call to life with his mother. When the two go to the ballpark for a Little League baseball game, Johnson can be seen with his hand on Norton's shoulder and his "head bent toward the younger boy's ear" (*CW* 613). That hand and that voice, like the bootleg working in Tarwater, slide down into the child to seize his soul with malignant probings.

As the evil flow sinks into Norton's soul, the logismos shifts the bearing of the child's inner life. Before, when Sheppard's self-centered truths set the limits, Norton's world was a dark closet of abandonment; but now, with Johnson's heaven and hell expanding the boundaries of his yearning, Norton begins to feel a divinely composed sense of self that is part of a vast plan. The pain of mourning disposes the child to a spiritual sense of life. Johnson's absorbing picture of hell makes Norton anxious over his mother's fate, which might include the chance that she is burning in eternal darkness. "'Is she there?'" he asks his father. Lurching toward Sheppard, Norton pleads and kicks: "'Is she there burning up?'" "'Is she on fire?'" (*CW* 611). The unhealed wound of love has gone deep into the child. At ten, Norton expresses a rudimentary penthos. With all his heart and body, like Mrs. Greenleaf wailing over victims of disaster, Norton mourns for the possible loss of his mother's salvation. Having been stabbed in the heart and shocked by catanyxis, the child suffers because what joy gives—eternal life—may be lost for his mother. In learning about the effect of sin, then, Norton through his grief seeks the source of happiness and thereby learns about God. He is so young, so alone, so untaught, so mentally slow; and yet, he is so morally keen.

Overtaken by the desire to join his mother, Norton hangs himself in the attic. Even readers living at the end of a century deluged by violence and familiar with the murder of Bishop in *The Violent Bear It Away* will find Norton's suicide sickening. Like Bishop, Norton is victimized by his father and a befriending older male; both children are further dehumanized by being destroyed not for who they are but for what they represent in power plays between the older males. But unlike Bishop, who resists death with everything he has, Norton succumbs to the idea that he is unworthy to live. The logismos succeeds in clotting Norton's heart by cloaking death as new life. Norton's death is another death in the desert. The story leaves the solitary child dangling from the ceiling beam in the wilderness of death's shadows, which are cast by the demons driving his tormentors.

The reader, too, is left suspended. Such youthful despair is unfathomable, and yet one senses in Norton's body "launched . . . into space" (*CW* 632) an innocent, affirming ascesis that might also claim holiness. At the very least, the child's suicide is an attempt at snatching the truth for himself. In so striving, Norton in death claims an inner self that his father devalued and reclaims that true self from the false, brutalizing control of Johnson. Perhaps the scandal of Norton is O'Connor's recognition that there can be bodily integrity and purity of heart among the weakest of the weak. Without the aid of doctrine or ritual, Norton expresses his faith. He acts decisively to count, to be somebody. Counting in the O'Connor world comes not from growing up to be an astronaut but lies in what she calls integrity and what Thomas Merton calls the "true self" (*Waters* 349). The true self, in which the divine dwells, lies beyond the reach of the logismos because the true self remains secure in God. Norton makes contact with his inmost being by means of the natural progress of his desire. Throughout the story, he has one aim: to find love. Mourning is his desert. Solitude is the condition of his search, the power of which is immense. It guides all the child's choices and unifies them into one intention. In the end, Norton's will wills God to the degree that his body becomes a prayer of hope in things unseen. With singleness of attention, which the desert solitaries call purity of heart, Norton dies a witness to his faith in love as felt in his hoped-for union with his mother in everlasting life. His ascesis is a kind of shedding, a leaving behind, of everything human.

At the end of "The Lame Shall Enter First," there is another call to the shattering encounter with the divine that is registered in yet another wound of love crafted movingly through O'Connor's poetics of solitude. Consummate poet of the body that she is, O'Connor grounds the unseen in the thick of flesh and blood. This action centers on the bleak aloneness in which Sheppard is left after the police take Johnson away. Once again, the logismos initiates the inner movement by dealing a heart-smashing blow. Accused by Johnson of being in the devil's power by playing Jesus, Sheppard tries to explain away his culpability: "'I did more for him than I did for my own child'" (*CW* 631), he murmurs to himself. This time, however, the pat on the back hammers home the falsifier's falsity, for the exoneration exposes the truth he does not want to see. A spark of awareness activates his conscience: "He had stuffed his own emptiness with good works like a glutton" (*CW* 632). These words have life. The stale maxims of social science give way to the fresh language of morals and, more precisely, of sin, which Sheppard disavows. These are also words of conversion. If they take root, they can change Sheppard's life. For now these words serve as an ascetic lash that strips away the delusions holding him back from Norton. A sense of neglecting his son jolts Sheppard out of his chair and sends him running to embrace his real son. The logismos, in trying to shut Sheppard's heart, inadvertently splits it with the liberating trauma of his seeing his personal evil. Drawn to that inner exposure, Sheppard moves with awful speed from arrogance, through wounded lament, to honesty.

This development translates itself into Sheppard's decisive struggle with temptation, the warfare that defines the solitary's life. His choices are clear: one is seductive, the other is harrowing. Sheppard could continue to deny abusing Norton; and that decision would mean a triumph for his demons. Or he could confront his responsibility; and that choice would open the way to victory for himself and for virtue. Being put to this test is Sheppard's saving gift. "Without temptation no-one can be saved," says Anthony (*Sayings*, Anthony the Great 5 [2]). "Take away temptations and no-one will be saved," the gentle Evagrius emphasizes (*Sayings*, Evagrius 5 [64]). Sheppard's trial of temptations occurs the night before Norton's new dawn. Sheppard goes to embrace Norton and say "that he loved him" (*CW* 632). Now he runs to Norton's empty room and then to the attic. Now he stares at Norton's hanging body. The corpse stuns him and seems to defeat his decision to confess his love. At this point, Sheppard, too, is at the end of his rope; but O'Connor does not strand him in unavailing dread (as Sheppard had abandoned Norton). O'Connor delivers Sheppard instead to the desert of the heart for the same reason that Israel finds itself in the desert and that the primitive solitaries fled to the desert: to approach the truth in oneself that leads to God. The desert directive in scripture is exacted by God of those who seek God; and in O'Connor's world, the call also comes to those who deny God: "I will now allure her [Israel], and bring her into the wilderness, and speak tenderly to her" (Hosea 2:14). Sheppard's bereaved helplessness, then, affords a transfixing possibility. If he opens his heart to the desert call, he can draw strength from his dread; and by feeling through his desolation, Sheppard can once again feel love. Where one can love in O'Connor's world, especially in the place where the worse happens— the desert—God begins to be.

For the desert's promise to be fulfilled in Sheppard, he will have to leave the judging and saving to God. This letting go of pride liberates. Spared from squandering moral energy on futile side issues, Sheppard is freed to fight the battle of his life. He must wage war from the great inescapable sadness—his desert—in which he finds himself. The battle entails mourning his wife and son as well as facing down the chimerical excitements of self-indulgently helping others. In the throes of separation from his family, he will perhaps catch the reassurances from the desert warriors who found wisdom in their losses. "Go, cast your weakness before God and you shall find rest," urges Abba Agathon (*Sayings*, Agathon 21 [23]). The elders' fund of experience also taught them the value of facing death squarely, as Sheppard now must: "Always keep your death in mind and do not forget the eternal judgement, then there will be no fault in your soul" (*Sayings*, Evagrius 4 [64]). These voices seem to reach those who need to hear them. They require a way of listening that allows more of the meaning to come out and that might also make the experience of solitary struggle less frightening. Now that the painkillers of denial and helping Johnson have worn off, Sheppard certainly needs help in confronting the triple anguish of his wife's death, his son's suicide, and the fact that he too will die.

In the final tableau of "The Lame Shall Enter First," Sheppard seems ready to take in the elders' counsel. He makes a beginning. He is besieged and contrite. As he looks within and down, he stares into the vanity-steeped "pit" (*CW* 632) of his bogus good works. As he looks without and up, he sees Norton's hanging body. It is hard to suppose that his losses would not be more than enough to make him cry, but his eyes are dry. "Nevertheless," writes Irénée Hausherr, the authority on penthos, "it can happen that the heart stubbornly refuses to the eyes the soft rain of tears." Citing the great ascetic Saint Basil, Hausherr attributes the heart's dry rebuff to "previous negligence" (75). Habitual failure to let his sorrow flow or even to respect Norton's tears would account for Sheppard's dry eyes. The first recourse for dry eyes, as previously shown, is the pierced heart. Sheppard experiences the blow in stages. In the aftermath of Johnson's final, devastating truths, Sheppard "bent slightly like a man who has been shot but continues to stand" (*CW* 631). Then, when he goes into his house and reflects on his misdirected benevolence, the impact deepens as Sheppard feels his "heart constricted with a repulsion for himself" (*CW* 632). That self-scrutiny opens into the wound of love when he sees Norton. The boy's dead body unseals Sheppard's eyes to the saving grace of shock that promises tears. In penthos, Norton, who readily cries, is father to his father.

Sheppard may single out a smart delinquent for his charity, but Ruby Turpin in "Revelation" makes no exception in helping others. Her nature is to give. So expansive is her generosity that she will lend a hand whether those in need are "white or black, trash or decent" (*CW* 642). As a churchgoing Christian, she could do no less: "To help anybody out that needed it was her philosophy of life" (*CW* 642). As Ruby sees it, her love of neighbor justifies her salvation. Despite her righteousness, Ruby is on firm biblical ground in linking her response to the needs of others with being "'saved'" (*CW* 652). The love of neighbor expresses friendship with God. The Mosaic Law sets forth the relation, and the life of Jesus fleshes out the bond. In modeling their lives on the Gospel, the desert solitaries identified their quest with the love of neighbor. To read the *Sayings* and the *Lives* is to enter a world of gentle concerns for others, all expressed amid the roughest rocks and ugliest storms of the ancient desert. The hermits' good will brought prayer into action. When the plague struck Alexandria, Anthony left his cell to comfort the dying. Austere in their solitude, the ascetics gave legendary desert hospitality a special grace in their "receiving Christ" in visitors (*Sayings*, Cassian 1 [113]). Strangers were greeted with a large-hearted "welcome" and sent away "in peace" (Ward, *Daily Readings* 43). In stark contrast to the Roman rulers who aimed to dominate the ancient world, the hermits strove to found communities through reconciliation. They dared to hope that such friendship might extend to the larger world. That world—so enormous, chaotic, and hostile—was for the elders transformable into something personal and secure in the Lord's peace.

The ancient texts shower us with comments about concern for others. The various sayings are themselves gifts of spirit directed toward the welfare of listeners. One saying hardly suffices to convey the prodigious silent love in which the elders met others, but a plain admonition from Amma Theodora suggests how solitude brought the hermits to grasp from within the need of others. This desert mother's counsel goes to the heart of "Revelation." The insight arises as Amma Theodora is spelling out the virtues that are required of all those who seek to impart wisdom. A person who instructs, Theodora says, should "be a stranger to the desire for domination, vain-glory, and pride; one should not be able to fool him by flattery, nor blind him by gifts, nor conquer him by stomach, nor dominate him by anger; but he should be patient, gentle and humble as far as possible; he must be tested and without partisanship, full of concern, and a lover of souls" (*Sayings,* Theodora 5 [83–84]). Being a lover of souls puts charity at the center of spiritual life, and Theodora obviously gestures toward an ideal. In drawing her exemplary profile of the lover of souls, the amma uncannily describes just how Ruby Turpin—who believes that she, as one who is saved, can give lessons in manners and morals—falls short of her claims.

As with the desert teachers, Ruby is tried by means of demonic attacks on her virtues. Ruby's virtues lie in the tight coils of the southern class and race system that prevailed before the civil rights movement legally changed America. For Ruby, hierarchy is inevitable. In her mind, whether trash overtakes decent people, blacks come before whites, or those who dip snuff and lounge on sidewalks drinking root beer gain more respect than do hardworking people, divisions of graded ranks prevail. Arbitrary categories become her absolutes, and so a shift in privilege nevertheless leaves intact the structure of power. Ruby's sense of degree and position is so worked into her consciousness that she reminds God that however creation turns, "'there'll still be a top and bottom!'" (*CW* 653). O'Connor wastes no time enmeshing Ruby in the clash between her social classifications and her avowed charity toward all. The outbreak occurs not in the streets or the legislature but in the physician's office. A very small room occupied by southerners (all white) of differing ages and economic status in a middle Georgia farming town in the early 1960s (as civil rights were taking hold), with its occupants all under the democratizing strain of illness, has to be tense.

When the manners police—in the form of Ruby Turpin—enters, the quarters are further compressed into a walled interrogation chamber; and then the disruption becomes truly hellish. Ruby arrives with her husband Claud, whose infected ulcer on his leg requires medical attention. Two empty spaces are available for the Turpins, but there is not enough room for Ruby's emotional demands. By Ruby's rights, the drowsy blond boy on the sofa should make room for her. Wordlessly, Ruby commands attention as she fills the entire room with her annoyance. Her mute displeasure utters a hostile inner jabber that all can hear. A person "may seem to be silent," says the keen Abba Poemen, but if the person's "heart is condemning others he is babbling ceaselessly" (*Sayings*, Poemen 27 [171]). Ruby's disapproval is the first objection from a pack of hostilities that she unkennels. The rest are carefully sheltered behind a screen of deportment for release as needed. The group's failure immediately to recognize Ruby's silent demands provokes Ruby. Her "little bright black eyes" (*CW* 633) summarily cut the strangers down to size. When she does speak, her words announce her control by ordering Claud to take the chair. Ruby, all 180 pounds of her, however, will stand above the others in reproving aloneness, an isolation caused by her hostility.

Only a well-dressed lady with gray hair escapes Ruby's judging black eyes; and that exception serves Ruby's darker, not charitable, purposes. Having declared war on the room, its inhabitants, the doctor (who at five dollars a visit could afford a bigger waiting room), and the world, Ruby makes an alliance with the respectable woman to take potshots at the others. The tactic has two objectives; both are demonic. The affronts diminish others while spinning the illusion of Ruby's upholding of propriety. Although the charity by which Ruby defines herself demands concern and reconciliation, her disordered passions drive her to disturb, divide, and rule the roost. All of Ruby's antipathy swells up from an imagined slight from a sleepy boy too sick to slide over to accommodate her. But it is Ruby who is neglectful toward others in a preemptive way, thus indicating that she is fighting a battle beyond the insubstantial discourtesy in the room.

O'Connor wants the reader to know that Ruby's essential struggle lies deep within herself, where she is grappling with brutal adversaries genteelly manipulating her distress through manners. The turmoil of a person aspiring to goodness but resorting to harm was understood by the desert elders as another battle in the ceaseless war against Satan. The opening scene of "Revelation" illustrates what the desert teachers saw as the rebellious soul "not bearing anything and doing its own will" (*Sayings*, Isaiah 7 [70]). By persistently imposing her personal dictates on others, Ruby demonstrates the truth of the ancients' insight that "our own wills become the demons," an admonition that cannot be repeated too often for O'Connor's headstrong country people, who must learn that it is "these [our own wills] which attack us in order that we may fulfill them" (*Sayings*, Poemen 67 [176]).

If Ruby is in the dark about the working of her wills, she knows well enough about how segregationist culture operates to use its prejudices to appease the demons menacing her. To see how the wars of race and manners collide in the waiting room, one needs to skip ahead briefly to that evening when Ruby is going to sleep. Some people read before retiring, others might relax with a nightcap, and some may pray to collect themselves. (O'Connor herself read from Thomas Aquinas's *Summa Theologiæ* and said compline to prepare for the night.) Ruby's version of night prayer is a conversation with Jesus about who she would have "chosen to be if she couldn't have been herself" (*CW* 636). Her will is the fulcrum of the exchange. She draws close to Jesus by presenting her personal options to tell Jesus what to do with them. In a word, Ruby acts as a ventriloquist to Jesus' dummy. Jesus the puppet pipes back Ruby's choices of being "'a nigger or white-trash'" (*CW* 636). Although both alternatives are unworthy of Ruby, she will defer to Jesus, who is made into a racist, by allowing Jesus to make her a "neat clean respectable Negro woman, herself but black" (*CW* 636). In this way, she can be proud of being humble. Apart from revealing Ruby's own deep dissatisfaction with who she is, the rumbling night prayer exposes the gloom in which her spirit is mired. Ruby must conjugate who she is not to accept herself.

Such a delusional exercise in virtue is part of Ruby's self-torment. In grappling with her demons of self-hatred, she empowers them through pride and so ends up further away from the virtue she seeks. O'Connor does not take this spiritual habit lightly. As Ruby falls asleep, blacks and other people, all neatly stratified, are "all crammed in together in a box car, being ridden off to be put in a gas oven" (*CW* 636). The political demons take the good woman unawares. They sneak up on Ruby's self-doubt to lead her to a dream of class and racial oppression that ends in mass extermination. Her inner antagonism identifies her soul as belonging to a generation very much marked by the blood politics and savagery running from World War II through the early 1960s. Ruby's self-dealing categories of human worth lull her into collusion with the loathsome evils of totalitarianism. O'Connor, who sees social history at its spiritual vortex, reminds her readers once more that the demons are never far removed from the horrors of every age.

However momentous the issues behind her protagonist's struggle, the battlefield in O'Connor fiction is always down-home, whether at a bus stop, in the woods, or, as here, in a doctor's office. With a recognition of the phantasmal roiling in Ruby's mind, one can return to the waiting room to see how mental violence leads to armed assault. That chain of injury results from Ruby's easy movement from being a rural magistrate of behavior to a backcountry provocateur. Because judgmental hierarchy is in the way she sees others, the transition comes about without Ruby knowing how she affects people. On this occasion, her visual assessment begins with footwear and works up to personal worth: red and gray suede fits the smart lady; Girl Scout shoes suit her dumpy daughter from Wellesley; tennis shoes are to be expected on the old lady; and the lank-faced mother of the slouching boy wears bedroom slippers of black and gold straw that match her trashy presence.

To Ruby, who stands in sensible and tasteful black pumps, such visual appraisals are entirely natural; but for a person seeking to love others, crotchety sartorial edicts are potentially harmful. In their desire to love unconditionally, the desert fathers and mothers detected in ordinary behavior such as Ruby's critical glances the casual disapprovals that deepened into serious habits of disparagements. Judging others brings evil to the person judged and the person judging. The injury to the person criticized is a clear affront to God. The danger that comes to the person condemning another was of particular importance to the solitaries, because it was likely to go unnoticed. In his discourse "On Refusal to Judge Our Neighbor," Dorotheos of Gaza spells out how the judgmental mind "begins to forget about it own sins and to talk idly about his neighbor, speaking evil against him, despising him, and from this he falls into the very thing he condemns" (6 [131]). For the desert teachers, the will to judge is an appetite that grows insatiable if it is not restrained. This association accounts for the images of voracious gratification that surround the theme in the ancient texts. Knowing how the instinct to criticize others dehumanized him, Abba Xanthias says: "A dog is better than I am, for he has love and he does not judge" (*Sayings,* Xanthias 3 [159]). Judging others consumes the dignity of those run down as it devours the humanness of the person doing the condemning.

The rugged eloquence of Dorotheos and Xanthias gives readers access to Ruby's interior life. Her soul has the bent that Dorotheos saw formed by small things that lead to a perilous habit; and as Dorotheos foretold, Ruby has forgotten her personal sins in carelessly faulting others. In particular, Abba Xanthias's extreme image of animality, with its stinging admission of self-debasement, fits right into "Revelation." Although unthinkable to Ruby, the monstrous image comes to her as she, already grown stout on satisfying her stomach for faultfinding, hungers for more satisfaction and shifts from running down the people around her to attacking her absent black workers. A casual comment on the weather triggers Ruby's resentment: "'It's good weather for cotton if you can get the niggers to pick it'" (*CW* 638). Basking in the prestige of instigator, Ruby feels free to express the racist pride that she covers with self-seeking neighborliness: "'I sure am tired of buttering up niggers, but you got to love em if you want em to work for you'" (*CW* 639). This slur prompts the white woman in slippers to secure at the expense of blacks a social solidarity she otherwise lacks: "'They ought to send all of them niggers back to Africa'" (*CW* 640). As the poor woman adds deportation to Ruby's night prayer of internment, a moment in the waiting room condenses the injustice of centuries. In a flash, we see that the outside world, as the desert elders recognized, is not simply outside; it is what we are made of.

Suddenly, what Ruby has made of the room springs to infernal life with direct personal animus now aimed back at Ruby. Mary Grace, the daughter of the proper woman, has had all she can take of Ruby's sinister attacks; infuriated, Mary Grace flings a book that hits Ruby over the left eye and sinks her fingers in Ruby's neck. All hell breaks loose as the deranged passions in Mary Grace bring the demonic beast hidden in Ruby out in the open. Lunging at Ruby, Mary Grace whispers in a low, penetrating voice: "'Go back to hell where you came from, you old wart hog'" (*CW* 646). The evocation of a broad, flat-faced pig with large tusks curving up over the conical warts in the cheeks between its eyes hits Ruby like the berserk onslaught of the wild animal itself. Ruby may be stunned by the inconceivable charge, but the revolting beast conveys the ignominious truth of Ruby's words and actions. No critical ingenuity is needed to see how the image suits Ruby. She hogs the crowded room of strangers, who experience her furies as intrusions from a punishing underworld. She backbites at blacks, snorts at poor whites, grovels before rich whites, and bristles at Mary Grace. Ruby's insatiable taste for rash censure resembles the appetite of a hell-hog. And with her usual anatomical exactness, O'Connor now adds the scar on Ruby's throat to mark the disfiguring damage caused by Ruby's vocal detractions and the cut above the left eye to indicate the wounds inflicted by Ruby's slashing glances at her neighbors. The lesions left by Mary Grace on Ruby's "good skin" (*CW*

635) publicly expose Ruby as the "falsifier" whose "very life is a lie," one whom Dorotheos of Gaza says "is not a simple but a two-faced" woman (9 [162]). O'Connor exposes both faces. Behind Ruby's cherished visage of refined neighborliness lurks the ruby-red, growling, minatory countenance of the woman who scorns her neighbors. The warthog is her demon exposed.

Ruby's bodily injuries are, in the end, the hurts that can help. The desert mothers and fathers saw the body as integral to moral growth, and that possibility lies in the facial and neck wounds that Ruby bears. If the lacerations sink into her consciousness to teach her soul about her boarish evil, Ruby can learn how to become the good woman she claims to be. This inner schooling brings "Revelation" to a close and runs from around midday to sundown. For Ruby, it is her afternoon of tribulation and no small amazement, especially when the sun sets behind the trees on the Turpin place to make bright a vision of her vice. At the end, Ruby's struggle is to struggle over being called an ugly hell-hog. She is alone in fighting her demons. Her moral desire to exorcise the beast and see herself as attractively virtuous is genuine and salutary. As there are very few inner struggles that the desert-dwellers did not carefully examine in light of the search for virtue, so one can get to Ruby's heart by sympathetically seeing her trial through her aspiration to be a person for and with others.

Dorotheos of Gaza, whose work in a desert infirmary made him a master psychologist, is especially helpful here. Dorotheos speaks encouragingly to a heart such as Ruby's that is stirred up to rashness by thoughts set on malice. Her failures to overcome her heedlessness are human and a part of the spiritual combat that Dorotheos warmly addressed. Typically, Dorotheos's concern is to check the small before it becomes the large: "Even if you are a little troubled and you desire promptly to get rid of it, since it is still small, you can do so by remaining silent with prayer on your lips and by one good heartfelt act of humility" (8 [150]). As a Christian, Ruby would presumably be disposed to reflection and humble generosity, but neither characteristic is her way of dealing with inner disturbances. She confronts the troubling image of her evil with the same hotheadedness with which she meets strangers. She obsesses the charge of being a razorback hog and lingers all afternoon on the harm done to her by Mary Grace. Ruby's self-sorrow follows the pattern that Dorotheos perceived as the spirit's fall into recklessness: "But if you dwell on it and inflame your heart and torment yourself with thoughts about why he [the enemy] said this to me, and what do I have to say to him, you are blowing on the embers and adding fuel and causing smoke!" Soon one begins "to let fly at others," and rancor bears malice. "This is how you get into a rage" (8 [150]).

This is how Ruby's inner world ignites into a "final surge of fury" (*CW* 653): taking figments of her mind as moral reality, she dwells on her injuries and wages war against herself, those around her at home, and God. Lying in bed, she weeps. Hers are not the godly tears of penthos or tears of remorse but the weepy frets over her appearance. Alert to the beguilements of snickering demons within, Amma Syncletica reminds us that such tears as fall from Ruby's eyes are a grief "that comes from the enemy, full of mockery" (*Sayings,* Syncletica 27 [235]). The adversary's derisions assail Ruby whenever she appeals for a restoration of her good image, which is whenever she sees someone on her farm. In response to her petitions, her husband Claud mechanically kisses Ruby, and the black workers compliment her; but Ruby feels cheated. She is swindled, of course, by her own insincere requests. Even with the dark protuberance of defeat over her left eye looking "like a miniature tornado cloud" (*CW* 651) about to erupt over her face, Ruby still is determined to prove that as long as she draws breath, she intends to work her will and that she has the power to do so when it matters to her.

In sounding Ruby's distress, O'Connor uncovers an inner disorder that the desert teachers recognized as the outcome of unchecked vanity. They called the stubborn pursuit of vainglory a "mania for self-justification" (or *dikaioma*). The condition was seen as a torment by "the most savage demons" mocking the proud person, and the outcome was "fatal" as the willful need for personal vindication "draws a man into hell" (qtd. in Hausherr 92). Ruby is mocked by her demons twice over. She feels the stings of ridicule that result from her determination to prove herself right without any sense of the spiritual death toward which her vanity takes her. Ruby's face bears the signposts of the hell to which the demons are taking her. The redness of wrath swells through her body to bring out the traces of warthog in her. It is Ruby's will, righteous and ironbound, that is driving her back into the hell from which Mary Grace saw Ruby's demon escape. All these forces converge when Ruby marches down to the pigpen "with the look of a woman going single-handed, weaponless, into battle" (*CW* 651) to hose down a sow and seven shoats. Ruby is alone and in the solitude to which O'Connor brings her heroine for the truth she must know about herself. Gaining that understanding involves warfare to the end. In this contest, Ruby's vanity and her true opponent are finally revealed. We see that her enemy all along has been God. She now interrogates God: "'What do you send me a message like that for?'" (*CW* 652).

Her offensive culminates in a manic outburst of contempt for God: "'Who do you think you are?'" (*CW* 653).

Precisely because Ruby's questions are honest in their barefaced irreverence, O'Connor finds them worthy of an answer. Given Ruby's colossal arrogance before God, one holds one's breath in anticipation over what will happen to Ruby. But always the artist to amaze, O'Connor on this occasion astounds by allowing the reader a sigh of relief, a long deep release of gladness through high jinks. Instead of falling in on Ruby, the sky opens up into a magnificent, carefree procession to heaven. In a fiction noted for violence bearing away the kingdom of God, the spectacle surprises with its restraint and gentleness. Ruby's foolish pride turns not into dust but bursts into horseplay. The merry racket of the enormous throng of human spirits "rumbling toward heaven" (*CW* 654) graphically answers Ruby's question about why God sends the message that she is a warthog from hell. Mary Grace's assault is to alert Ruby to the spiritual death, the hell, toward which she was heading and to redirect Ruby's will so that she can take her place among the redeemed—albeit holding up the rear, with her dignified stiffness as something of a drag on the free-spirited cavalcade. The story ends as God smiles on Ruby. O'Connor's theology of pranks is sheer desert humor. When Abba Anthony asks how to deal with demonic attacks, an inspired voice says to him, perhaps with a knowing smile: "'Humility'" (*Sayings*, Anthony the Great 7 [2]). Humility is not only "victorious over the demons," says Amma Theodora (*Sayings*, Theodora 6 [84]); humility "is a great work, and a work of God" (Ward, *Daily Readings* 32).

The great work of God that is humility lays bare the revelation of "Revelation." Besides correcting Ruby's rash heart and her turmoil, humility is God's beaming leniency and quiet forbearance of Ruby in all her laughable sinfulness. Ruby's daredevil anger is not used by God to fuel a corresponding revenge but to elicit a cheerful acceptance of Ruby's weaknesses. On God's side, there is a generosity, a control of violence, that may not rival the humble self-emptying of the Incarnation but does manifest the self-lowering that Ruby needs to incorporate into her life with others. The revelation invites Ruby to share in the divinely human comedy. If she finds the jaunty vision preposterous by her prim notion of decorum, Ruby can also feel the stripping away of her false dignity as enhancing. She will, of course, need to cultivate a sense of humor, which she noticeably lacks, to appreciate the rollicking crowd and accept her starchy self. She who feels ready to give the world "a friendly smile" (*CW* 635) might turn her amicable expression inward. If she does, then out of her rage would come blessed laughter; and her isolating prejudice would open into the new communal life celebrated in the celestial parade. Out of this life with others will rise Ruby's life with God. The ascetic effect of the vision that exposes Ruby's evil is not to frighten but to encourage her to change.

The ancient hermits have words that speak directly to Ruby's need to change: "Just as one cannot build a ship unless one has some nails," says Amma Syncletica, "so it is impossible to be saved without humility" (*Sayings*, Syncletica 26 [235]). Humility is salvation. The nails of humility will hold Ruby's virtues together and fasten them to God. Moreover, humility will relieve Ruby of the interior humiliations of exerting unrelenting pressure on her spirit. The words of another elder serve to explain Ruby's torment: "We have put the light burden on one side, that is to say, self-accusation, and we have loaded ourselves with a heavy one, that is to say, self-justification" (*Sayings*, John the Dwarf 21 [90]). Unburdened of vindicating herself, Ruby can draw good from her weaknesses, failures, and fears. There is nothing so humbling and democratic, nothing so heartwarming as the sight of all the respectable country landowners, with their faces altered from having their virtues burned away, strutting behind rousing freaks and raving screwballs with unalloyed smiles leading the pack heavenward. Surprised by her sin and shorn of pretenses, Ruby Turpin is saved by God's humor.

8 The Power of Exile

A brother asked Abba Poemen, "How should I behave in the place where I live?" The old man said, "Have the mentality of an exile in the place where you live, do not desire to be listened to and you will have peace."

—Poemen, *The Sayings of the Desert Fathers*

Let yourself be despised, cast your own will behind your back, and you will be free from care and at peace.

—Sisoes, *The Sayings of the Desert Fathers*

SOLITUDE, AS HAS BEEN SHOWN, for O'Connor's searchers is the founding experience of a new relation with God. By encountering their loneliness, her solitaries approach a still more unfathomable loneliness, for human loneliness in the O'Connor world touches on divine loneliness. Solitude constitutes a part of the likeness of God in which the human person is created. This aspect of divine life emerges in O'Connor's fiction in moments of self-abandonment in her protagonists. From this surrender, the solitary can hope to draw light—as does Mrs. Flood following her blind guide, Hazel Motes, in *Wise Blood* toward the point of light—to illumine the path to union. Along the way, the lone searcher can also hope to receive strength to battle the demonic forces set on opposing any progress toward God. Ordeal by ordeal, this divinely supported courage carries the solitary across the chasm of alienation to reach God. The desert mothers and fathers saw exile as the catalyst for this crossing, and they looked to the nearby desert as the condition for a new heroism. The desert's nature, of course, is to keep from yielding its secrets. Its very starkness suggests that discovery and growth are delicate at best. Still, the hints of new vitality were enough to sustain the ancient questers in their outcast state. From exile there can pour forth a peacefulness that is strong enough to gather people from far and near into its calming flow.

Three stories in *Everything That Rises Must Converge* show with valedictory exuberance the power of exile. "The Enduring Chill" does so by cutting close to the autobiographical bone in portraying an aspiring writer forced home at age twenty-five by a medical crisis that leads to chronic illness and cultural deprivation. The tyro artist survives, and so too does the AWOL sailor in "Parker's Back," also in his twenties, who meets with expatriation in all the many places in which he tries to anchor his nomadic desires. This roamer's survival takes the form of being cast adrift with a startling tattoo of Christ on his back that makes him a pariah deportee bearing the Spirit. The last of these stories, "Judgment Day," chronicles O'Connor's exile of a southerner in the East; and the story's setting east of New York City touches on the Christian East of the old men of the desert. This immigrant too is an old man, a *geron*, who crosses from the twenty-fourth hour in alien New York to the twenty-fifth hour at home in his true country. In exilic death, he prevails.

All three stories reveal the power of exile in the desert where no such strength was suspected. And yet, while there is power, perhaps the desert finally has no secrets. Instead, it is the irreducible emptiness that makes the solitary aware of the need for divine aid. In showing how God's help enters the exile's life, these stories not only tell a story but also fix a vision of grace. Each exile sees that God is with him. All end with the hope of restoration, but the endings are touched with rue. Remorse now occasions a new heroism of sorrow. Disease brings the young writer to a heartpiercing sense of guilt for past wrongs that accomplishes an inchoate *penthos* without tears. Then, wretchedness forces the tattooed Christbearer to cry like an infant, and his weeping initiates him into abject suffering for all that he carries on his back. Finally, in the agony of dying, O'Connor's geron, by forgiving himself and his assailant, becomes a hero of penthos.

A consideration of the wisdom that her solitaries acquire in exile serves as the conclusion to this study of O'Connor's poetics of solitude. In observing the condition in which O'Connor leaves her questers, one sees that the hermit life in her fiction is expressly a lay life. These characters wear no clerical habit; they look like the people living around them and are in the thick of things. Although their trials resemble those of the desert mothers and fathers, the place of the hermit in our time has shifted since the fourth century. Then, the desert-dwellers set out to transcend

the human. Many sought lofty spiritual realms. O'Connor's hermits have
no such aims. Her solitaries never lose contact with the world. They seek
no strange contemplative powers. Their gift of solitude is to recover in
ordinary human life the essential self that provides a relation with God.

"The Enduring Chill" concerns chronic illness and protracted dying.
Published in the July 1958 *Harper's Bazaar,* the story is actually a long
time coming, if one considers that the predicament parallels O'Connor's
own unwilling return in December 1950 to the "Georgia wilderness" (*HB*
77). In coping over seven years with failing health in the "place where
there's no company" (*HB* 163), O'Connor realized the possibilities that
the ancient hermits saw in sickness dealt with through faith. "If illness
weighs us down," says Amma Syncletica, "let us not be sorrowful as
though, because of the illness and the prostration of our bodies we could
not sing, for all these things are for our good, for the purification of our
desires" (*Sayings,* Syncletica 8 [232]). Oppressed by ill health, O'Connor
did find her voice; and in "The Enduring Chill," she brings the ailing
writer Asbury Porter Fox to his Georgia desert for comparable discover-
ies. It is a measure of O'Connor's refusal to exploit her sickness that what
she has to say artistically about sickness should come to the reader in
the grandeur of humor, the peculiar humor of desert life. The comedy of
this story arises from Asbury's solitary struggle to live with the Holy
Ghost, who, for O'Connor, is "full of surprises" (*HB* 293). Against God's
self-communication she sets Asbury's self-ignorance. Put another way,
the creative power by which God brings the world into being searches
out a feckless writer who cannot bring his few words to life. The incongruity is the source of blessed laughter.

Comedy in its Dantesque form also signifies a journey to God (which
makes the comedy divine), and the humor of "The Enduring Chill" attends Asbury's appointed encounter in Timberboro, Georgia. His is a journey to God by means of ascesis in the desert. Stricken with undulant fever
and on fire with resentment, Asbury must return home. Home is "this
collapsing country junction" (*CW* 548) that is synonymous with exile.
For Mrs. Fox, Asbury's indefatigably cheerful mother, the two new fronts
on the town's rundown stores betoken improvement; but for Asbury, the
place is the desert. In fairness to Timberboro, Asbury's view of the local
desert is really a view from the desert of his inner world. Wherever he
goes is bare and hostile because the intolerable death he sees around him
externalizes the emptiness he inhabits within himself.

In casting about for a fertile place to live and work as a writer, Asbury follows the beaten path (one that O'Connor herself took in 1949) to New York City. His expedition to the American cultural center amounts to a wandering into the marginal isolation that only the metropolis of millions can impose. "The insufferableness of life at home" (*CW* 560) pales next to the bitterness Asbury experiences in the place of his romantic desire. New York loneliness is cold with shame, a loneliness that tells Asbury he is a fool, an outcast, and a loser. He gave up a white, two-story farmhouse with a wide porch set on the crest of a Georgia hill for a warren of two damp rooms and a toilet in a closet in a five-story New York walk-up with garbage in the hallway. The dream of writing dissolves into the dreariness of selling books part-time in a bookstore. New York also dashes Asbury's hope for intellectual fellowship. He is friendless except for Goetz, who means well but whose spiritual journey in Buddhism leaves him cold, detached, and mistaken about Asbury's serious illness. The city of illusion exists for Asbury far beyond the city of fact. For all the hurting disenchantments, however, he still prefers loneliness in a freezing flat, shivering under two blankets and an overcoat lined with the *New York Times*, to the warm but stifling comforts of home. That persistence at least speaks for Asbury's capacity for determined self-sacrifice, a disposition that will help him face what lies ahead.

Asbury cannot do for art what the ancient solitaries did for their faith and leave the city for the desert. The hermits believed in God and consciously sought to be near God. Asbury's world is different from that of the primitive hermits. His situation is far more precarious. Asbury is neither a Christian nor a Buddhist. A resolute atheist, he "had never been a sniveler after the ineffable" (*CW* 568). There is honesty in his hauteur; and in his own way, Asbury repeatedly expresses, however obliquely, the basic spiritual prompting of the desert: Asbury seeks freedom. "'We've got to think free,'" he urges a black worker on his mother's farm, "'if we want to live free!'" (*CW* 559). His words in the context of encouraging the workers to drink unpasteurized milk are pretentious, but they convey the meek thirst of his soul. He explains in his secret letter to his mother that he flees to New York "'to find freedom, to liberate my imagination'" (*CW* 554). In his desire to write and search for a context, Asbury seeks to cast off the domination of alien impulses. It is the unexpected benefit of hostile New York that brings Asbury to the poverty that prepares him for the truth of his own exhortation. In the New York desert, he begins to learn the truth of his heart.

Everything about Asbury is a matter of simple schooling and beginnings—his failed beginning as a writer and his averse beginning as a person of God. At age twenty-five, he is still called "boy" by the narrator

(*CW* 572); and the story limits him to the elementary lesson in his future education as a solitary. At the end, he reaches the point of *catanyxis* that embeds a new attitude in his soul. This instruction remains preparative, suspending the novice in the instant of reception, which marks the catanyctic moment unfolding. Deep down, in that place where stirs his desire to be free, Asbury even acknowledges the force of detention and death. He experiences himself in Georgia as living in the "desert" (*CW* 561), the desert felt in its primal hardship and transforming power. Strange as it seems to the high modernist mind in Asbury—which savors the intellectual complexities of Joyce and Kafka and cherishes the illuminations of Frazer's *The Golden Bough*—the plain farmhouse on the hillcrest proves to be the source of inspiration that Asbury has been looking for but calls by the name of art and intelligence. If time and the muses have forgotten the distant hills on the outskirts of Timberboro, God has not abandoned the place. As deserts go, the Fox dairy farm may be emotionally unbearable to Asbury; but to anyone with unjaundiced eyes, the locale is well-favored. From the front porch, where Asbury relaxes in the morning, he can look at the lawn down the hill to trees and a red road that runs a quarter of a mile between two pastures, one with the dry cows and the other with the milk herd.

Asbury's bedroom upstairs in the farmhouse is a space apart from everything. The room is large and airy. A faded blue rug hints of color, and newly laundered white curtains freshen the entire atmosphere. On the wall, is a picture of a woman chained to a rock. There are an antique bed with an ornamental headboard, several chairs, and a comfortable rocker. When the rocker is removed for a visiting priest, the spareness of the room comes through. So too does the room *démeublé* expose Asbury's true self. A writer by aspiration, Asbury is a hermit in hiding; and the design of the enclosure holds the plan for his true work. His room "with its severe wall stains had a certain cell-like quality" (*CW* 564) that enforces the spiritual work he is called to undertake in this desert. One cannot live, of course, in any place with impunity. This room in particular has powerful forces that will mold Asbury in its own image and inhabit his sensibility. These four walls combine country openness and comfort with monastic enclosure and austerity.

The most distinct feature of Asbury's cell is not of human making. It is the water stain on the gray walls that descends from the top molding and spreads through ceiling leaks directly over the bed. The Georgia desert has a concealed source of moisture that forms "a fierce bird with spread wings" and icicles, one in its beak and others hanging from its wings and tail (*CW* 555). The discolored blemishes have strangely escaped

Mrs. Fox's fastidious housekeeping and have remained on the wall since Asbury was a child. Such a chance design in wet plaster expresses O'Connor's response to Asbury's and the modern world's anxiety about the transcendent and fragile human body. The fresco celebrates the tangible yet unnoticed presence of the divine spirit in places of human neglect and indifference. The bird-shaped stain watches over Asbury. Its presence suggests that flesh destined to decay could be transformed into something free and new, something like the accidental spoiled smudges poised for flight into the eternal. Sick in the Georgia desert, Asbury has before and above him the sheltering Spirit of God. This bird and the room are all he needs to get well. In the life to which Asbury is called, everything else is extraneous. In ancient lore, a certain hermit, as needy of help as is Asbury, asked an abba for a word. The old man said to the confused hermit: "'Go, sit in your cell, and your cell will teach you everything'" (*Sayings*, Moses 6 [139]). "The Enduring Chill" settles Asbury in his cell to show him through the fierce bird-stain who the teacher is and what the master will teach—in fine, it shows him everything.

The Spirit of God is the teacher who introduces Asbury to the curriculum of everything by introducing the writer to the alphabet of the heart. This primary education comes about through four elders who provide for Asbury's diseased body and aching soul. Mrs. Fox acts in her maternal capacity as a desert amma of limited faith and boundless bedside attention, and there are three older men who serve as abbas. Each nurtures Asbury in an aspect of renunciation. The timely appearance of these elders proves that the fierce bird is as active in helping Asbury as it is forceful in emblazing its power into his wracked body. The new knowledge taught by the bird and its human advocates is depicted, like a visual aid in a classroom, in the wooden fruit carved across the headboard of Asbury's bed. This design of abundance commemorates the harvest identified with the Pentecostal gifts that Asbury receives in his cell. The "fierce bird with the icicle in its beak" (*CW* 568) will plant the hard seeds of ascesis that yield the flower of renunciation.

Asbury's first lesson concerns illness, something O'Connor knows well and the condition that the early hermits, with their exposed bodies in the harsh wastes, confronted continually. For all the physical pain that attended solitary life in the ancient desert, suffering in the ancient texts comes through with a different tone than it does in twentieth-century life. The modern person is given to regard illness as a metaphor and therefore is prone to protest about the malady and, more agonizingly, what it signifies. What sickness now implies is cultural repudiation, personal punishment, or scientific failure, all of which increase the fear and isolation that accompany illness. The desert elders conceptualized disease differently. Their search for God overrode every other concern and fostered an obedient resignation to physical life as it was given. This submission integrated illness and pain into the ancient ascetics' spiritual labor. Desert life cultivated a factual, at times cold, presentation of illness, a stance reflected, as shown, with impressive sanity and emotional balance in O'Connor's frank statements about her disease.

Among the elders, Dorotheos of Gaza gives the most extensive first-hand desert commentary on sickness. He himself suffered constant ill health and founded an infirmary for his sick brethren, but his *Discourses* is serenely uncommunicative about his tribulation and is impartially forbearing to the pain of others. When he mentions "'my bodily weakness,'" physical debility becomes the condition for developing humility ("Introduction" 28). Ascetic detachment can seem superhuman in coping with sickness (and perhaps too harsh to the modern sensibility). One deathbed moment in Dorotheos's *Discourses* illustrates such spiritual stoicism. A brother in the terminal stages of tuberculosis, coughing constantly and vomiting blood, seeks pardon for his sins from an old hermit, and the aged abba replies: "'Have no fear, brother, but rather let your soul rejoice and exult for joy in the Lord. . . . You will have more pain but it will have an end'" ("Introduction" 43). This reaction is realism sanctified—the tonic key in which sympathy was expressed among the solitaries. In showing their concern for others, the hermits were not stingy, nor were the demands on the hermits' charity few. Late antiquity was a time of plagues and massacres, during which the desert-dwellers were deeply involved in the care of victims; and throughout the work of the sick, their spirituality brought the ascetics to see the healing power of faith over the gravest physical afflictions. Invariably, the charisma of curing pointed toward the salvation over evil. "God, heal your creature," Abba Poemen says over a child whose face is turned backward, "that he be not ruled by the enemy" (*Sayings*, Poemen 7 [166]). All the accounts show the location of healing beyond the holy person in the Spirit that each elder bears.

The Spirit's assistants in "The Enduring Chill" steer Asbury to the same source of restoration. Even Mrs. Fox, who attributes much of her son's problems to his artistic pursuits, is on to a certain truth in that she senses a crisis in her son's inner world. Without discounting his protracted fever and weight loss, one can see that Asbury is also laid low and held prisoner by his demons: his refusal to acknowledge his mother's aid, his contempt for the "asinine" (*CW* 556) country doctor, and his hostility toward the visiting priest's instruction to pray. Asbury will not take yes for an answer. He wills to die. He is alone, captive to his wills and fighting a sickness of the soul as well as bodily fever and chills. The hidden letter accusing his mother of pinioning his artistic wings divulges the actual disabler as Asbury himself: "'I have no imagination. I have no talent. I can't create'" (CW 554). These are not honest admissions of shortcomings but self-lacerations intended to blame his mother for his failure. Asbury has enslaved himself in faintheartedness and abstractions, especially in those modern dogmas of unbelief that glamorize his terror. The hermits would recognize Asbury's self-induced despair as brought about by the demon of *acedia*. He feels that the end is at hand; and Asbury, whose gratification lies in impotence and destruction, welcomes extinction as it closes in. "'I'm going to die'" (CW 569), he declares three times to Morgan and Randall, the two black workers who come to cheer him up. Asbury's deathbed pronouncement typifies how his purposive desire becomes his demon. Having convinced himself that death is an agency of his will, he can then glorify the pride he wins in annihilating himself.

Although sunk in despondency, immobilized by sickness, and stranded in artistic defeat, Asbury can nevertheless find a way to the freedom he seeks. Liberty and the healing of his spirit begin in his stricken body, which is the school of his reformation and his work in progress. Undulant fever from its onset teaches Asbury that he cannot control his health and should not use sickness to push others around, which is subtly harmful to himself because his private mandates disregard the rights of others. On this score, the hermits offer Asbury sound advice: "When there is someone who takes care of you, you are not to give him orders" (*Sayings*, Sisoes 29 [218]). Honest dependency can protect the soul.

Humor has a way of cutting through Asbury's defenses. To do the job, O'Connor commissions a physician with a smiling manner who seems to have stepped out of *The Lives of the Desert Fathers*. In the fourth century, Abba Anthony heard that there was a person who was his equal in the city. The man "was a doctor by profession" who was generous to the poor and was a man of faith (*Sayings*, Anthony the Great 24 [6]). O'Connor's healer is Doctor Block, whose arrival Mrs. Fox announces "as if she had captured this angel on the rooftop and brought him in for her little boy" (CW 556). This round, cherubic-faced messenger is certainly generous in putting up with Asbury's arrogance. Block's spirituality expresses itself in humility before the body's complexity. He acknowledges that "'most things are beyond me'" (CW 557). His humility protects him from Asbury's insults and yields the accurate diagnosis of Asbury's infection. Clear-eyed and patient, Abba Block is "the enemy of death" (CW 562) who battles the real adversary.

More than medical accuracy is needed to disencumber Asbury of his demons. He must experience that rough, sudden spasm of anguish that wrenches deep in his soul a determination to seek the freedom he desires. Asbury awaits catanyxis. Two additional enemies of death prepare Asbury for the catanyctic moment. These emissaries are priests who fight the powers that destroy the spirit. The instruction given by these two ordained "elders" (the ancient term for a sacral officer) bears directly on Asbury's hidden life of desert solitude. The first old envoy is Ignatius Vogle of the Society of Jesus. He is a fleeting New York acquaintance whose remembered presence comes back to Asbury at home as he lies in bed stung by the idea of dying in the desert. At a certain moment, the feeling that death is near softens his voice to "almost a sob" (*CW* 549). On the verge of tears and thinking back to an incident in New York, Asbury cannot draw solace from his friend Goetz, who said after the Buddhist lecture that "'no one is saved'" (*CW* 550). The statement arouses Asbury's curiosity; and in words that catch the spirit and phrasing of the ancient formula, "Abba, give me a word so that I may be saved" (*Sayings*, Euprepius 7 [62]), Asbury turns to Vogle and says: "'And what do you say to that?'" The old priest says: "'There is . . . a real probability of the New Man, assisted, of course . . . by the Third Person of the Trinity'" (*CW* 550). This is the only time that Vogle speaks, but his words bring everything into focus.

The Jesuit's one sentence has the force of a desert saying. His spare words are uncompromising in the faith from which they issue, and the words are generous in the glimpse they give of eternity. And like the desert utterances, Abba Ignatius's saying condenses a complex theology, from which one feature in particular speaks directly to Asbury's search for meaning. Vogle's hope for the new person, as other readers have noted, comes from Saint Paul's letter to the Colossians, in which Paul aims to change the Colossians' minds by reminding them that their belief in Jesus has clothed them with "the new self, which is being renewed in knowledge according to the image of its creator" (Colossians 3:10). For the sick and solitary Asbury, it matters that for Paul the practice accomplishing this new nature is that of mortification. Ascesis shapes the entire Pauline exposition of the true Christian life in this celebrated passage (Colossians 3:1–15). The believer puts "to death" (3:5) whatever is evil in oneself. By stripping "off the old self" (3:9), one gradually becomes "clothed . . . with the new self" (3:10). In a parallel exhortation to the Corinthians, Paul movingly applies ascesis to the enduring human anxiety over sickness and death: "For this perishable body must put on imperishability, and this mortal body must put on immortality" (1 Corinthians 15:53).

The possibility of developing this new person in himself has been Asbury's aim all along, although he calls this imperishable self by negative and cultural names. To his great surprise, even to his embarrassment, Asbury is already encompassed by this likely change. With death before him, Asbury must grapple with his demons of pride, anger, and sloth. A few basic lessons are all that he needs to redirect his ascetic temperament toward the new meaning he desires. Father Finn from Purgatory, the last elder, offers a spiritual primer. Massive and gawky like Block, but without the physician's playfulness and yet with his own blunt humor, Finn barges into Asbury's sickroom and gets down to business. Blind in one eye and deaf in one ear, Finn is impervious to Asbury's pretensions. The more the obnoxious Asbury waxes with his high-modernist importunings about Joyce and the myth of the dying god, the more Finn takes on "a martial tone" (*CW* 566) to strike down the demons inciting Asbury. Asbury may repeatedly debase himself by exploiting his illness to manipulate others, but tenacious Abba Finn nevertheless addresses the life in Asbury by treating him with a stern dignity that Asbury has never before experienced: "'But you're not dead yet!' said the priest, 'and how do you expect to meet God face to face when you've never spoken to Him?'" (*CW* 566). For Finn, only prayer, the solitary's mighty weapon, overcomes the enemies that Asbury must combat.

The need to speak to God bears intimately on the solitude enclosing Asbury. Conversing with God for the ancient hermits is more than reciting words and outward performance, more even than homage to the one Lord. Alone, amid the scraps of the desert waste, the elders urgently felt the necessity for a relationship with the absolute; it was through ascesis that the hermits came to see prayer as the integrating energy of human life. Prayer is their loving response to the divine initiative of love that calls to one's innermost being. Although the lone wolf of Timberboro denies a desire to know God, his self-dissatisfactions prove otherwise. The habit of approaching God through his soul, rather than through myth or symbol, will teach Asbury how to live and how to die through the habit of self-scrutiny. Rooting out the evil within himself will open the fearful young man to divine support. That aid through prayer will permit Asbury to live in the world as it is, without the compulsion to distort his perception as a defense against the unresolved interior conflicts with his mother, art, hometown, and God. We know from those proficient in seeking God that communication demands serious exertion and ardor. When a brother asked Abba Anthony to pray for him, the old man said: "I will have no mercy upon you, nor will God have any, if you yourself do not make an effort and if you do not pray to God" (*Sayings*, Anthony the Great 16 [4]). Abba Finn is on hand to revive the strict Antonian edict to jar Asbury out of sloth: "'If you do not pray daily, you are neglecting your immortal soul.'" And again, in Anthony's very voice, Finn declares: "'Nothing is overcome without prayer'" (*CW* 566). Prayer can strengthen Asbury's soul at the same time that it softens his heart, which needs unclogging to free up the goodness hampered in it by his demons.

The elders' guidance culminates the next evening with Doctor Block's telling Asbury: "'You ain't going to die'" (*CW* 571). The good news from the laboratory actually disheartens Asbury because it robs him of the drama of his existence; he utters a "low moan and then was quiet" (*CW* 572). The probability of death gave him intensity and became a safety valve promising release from his pain and isolation; but now that he learns that he will live, Asbury is at the center of an aloneness that he cannot count on death to dissolve. He can no longer take bitter solace in the dark of his demons' embraces. Suddenly, all the emotional work spent in letting go of life has to reverse itself; and it is in the solitude burdened by chronic illness that Asbury must bring life to fruition. This terrible disclosure at the end of "The Enduring Chill" redounds on Asbury in a different way than do the upheavals experienced by O'Connor's other solitaries. O'Connor knows that emotions are always fresh and that God's intrusion into human life is never predictable; and so she does not repeat herself. There is no gunshot, no blazing fire, no goring bull, no corpse wrapped in barbed wire. Readers look for dismemberment but find physical resuscitation. Where we expect explosion, there is a transition. Asbury himself seeks relief but experiences confrontation. Instead of vestigial life sliding away from him, new life slips into him—a mere hint of the profundity with which his life has become suffused. Nothing less than the Holy Spirit of God is entering Asbury.

The charisma of the Spirit pervades desert writing as the great consolation given to those who follow the way of solitude. The gift bestowed by the Spirit of truth follows repentance, which cleanses the soul of impurity or distraction from the heart's single attention to God: "When it [repentance] has completely purified them [the souls], it sends them to the Holy Spirit which endlessly pours out on them softness and sweetness" (qtd. in Hausherr 143). Those seeking to be consoled must give themselves up to penthos, for sorrow disposes the soul to divine comfort. Two brief sentences in the story's last paragraph capture Asbury's ascetic transition to this state of readiness. Together they bear out Vogle's hope for the new person: "The old life in him was exhausted. He awaited the coming of new" (*CW* 572). Old habits fail Asbury. For the first time in his life, Asbury's impersonations and illusions are torn away from him. In their place, a spark of purpose and destiny stirs in him as a delicate chill grazes over him in the tender brushing of a "warm ripple" (*CW* 572). Asbury's awareness of his faults makes him vulnerable to sorrow, which opens him to the Spirit's refreshment. Catanyxis inaugurates the new life awaiting him.

The ancient writers believed that "*catanyxis* comes from on high, from the divine dew of the Spirit" (Hausherr 145). O'Connor's theology of grace derives from an identical poetics of vitalizing deliquescence. The Spirit is the Paraclete, and this winged intercessor of God has hovered over Asbury as the water stain and finally descends on Asbury as a melting fierce bird. Catanyxis occurs as Asbury's "breath came short" (*CW* 572). The aftershocks from this blow alter Asbury's interior world, and their current comes to the reader as through minute examination of Asbury's vision. His eyes, the sun, and the dissolving timberline register Asbury's contemplation of inaccessible light. As he prepares for "some awful vision" (*CW* 572), everything softens. His eyes pale. He blanches. The blinding, roseate sun pours as liquid through the wall of dark trees to dissolve their pitchy solidity. And more melting occurs: the bird-stain moistens. Water that has been stopped up for years begins to thaw and filters into the inner world. The divine dew that the ancient desert-dwellers hoped would refresh them in their desert now gently falls on solitary Asbury in his desert-racked misery with God's consoling, if terrifying, life.

The poetics of Asbury's solitude, this liquefying, is atmospheric, something akin to the kinetic mood of his soul as the divine dew seeps new life into the currents of Asbury's spirit. In thinking about O'Connor, I would never have anticipated using the word *gossamer* to explain anything she writes about, and yet gossamer stays in mind as the right word to capture the floatings that lave Asbury. Graceful ripples first wash over him soothingly and then swirl as a wind that clears his impaired sight. Once his vision is "shocked clean" (*CW* 572), Asbury sees keenly with eyes lit by both longing and remorse. As pride brings about Asbury's affliction, so humility points toward recovery. His new knowledge is not only that he has a low-down cow's disease but, as O'Connor's explains in a letter of 28 December 1957, "that he knows nothing" (*HB* 261). This is not to say that Asbury is stupid or insensate. On the contrary, the mind held in a state of unknowing is cleansed of preconceptions and therefore alive to those ineffabilities that Asbury once discounted as foolish. In fine, this realization signals Asbury's bowing before truth. In knowing that he is ignorant, Asbury gains the new knowledge of humility. And that is where, as O'Connor says in the same letter, she leaves him: "That really is what he is frozen in—humility" (*HB* 261). Asbury's awareness of his faults is the boundary between shock and new life—which is to say, the desert. By bringing Asbury to see his emptiness, O'Connor reaffirms the basic desert teaching, attributed to Anthony and developed by Dorotheos, that "'before anything else we need humility'" (2 [94]). Meekness fosters growth as an organic force required to sustain life and promote well-being: "As the breath which comes out of his nostrils, so does a man need humility and the fear of God" (*Sayings*, Poemen 49 [173]). Against this background of self-abasement, the elders perceived a social consequence that was also important to their search for God: "For this is humility: to see yourself to be the same as the rest" (*Sayings*, Motius 1 [148]).

These desert insights into humility map out what lies ahead for Asbury. A snob such as he, who must spend the rest of his life among those he looks down on, will find through humility a fellow feeling with others that will ease his solitude in his desert. Rapport with his mother, sister, and the black workers will teach him, as does his drinking unpasteurized milk, that he is not the source of wisdom. By admitting his folly, Asbury will gradually learn to attribute all virtuous actions to God. Unexpected grace accrues from the ceaseless habit of humility. "In point of fact," Dorotheos says, "there is nothing more powerful than lowliness" (2 [96]). Asbury quickly learns the power of humility. It comes as a plummeting terror felt in his infected blood and frail bones.

After humility comes faith, which cultivates endurance. That is the pattern of desert spirituality and the movement of "The Enduring Chill." The hermit writer in O'Connor so finely intuits the constitutive elements of the interior search that, in the end, Asbury's story recaptures both in figural detail and spiritual scope the patristic understanding of the Spirit's presence in ascetic life. The hermits held fast to Jesus' promise to send the Paraclete, his advocate, to console his apostles over his impending death. "When the Spirit of truth comes," Jesus says, "he will guide you into all the truth" (John 16:13). Abba Ammonas describes this promised guidance to souls lost in grief as an effluence. First there is the charisma of repentance that "calls all souls and washes them from their impurity," and then the spirit of repentance "sends them to the Holy Spirit which endlessly pours out on them softness and sweetness" (qtd. in Hausherr 143).

Since the bedridden Asbury cannot be sent anywhere, the Paraclete comes to him. And although *sweetness* is no more in O'Connor's lexicon than is *gossamer*, O'Connor does have the fierce bird surround Asbury with gentleness. On the horizon of the farm, the soft dying day eases the air of strain as its warm light fills Asbury's world with tenderness. Ammonas's sweetness becomes O'Connor's affable instruction. She leaves

Asbury alone with the Spirit, whose friendship betokens the compunction and strength Asbury must develop. The watermark points the way to inner growth as the atmosphere becomes porous, fluid, infinitely renewable. The bird-stain enters Asbury's life by changing from a solid to a liquid state; thawing sets the Paraclete into vital motion. This change presages the process of interior freedom. Asbury's heart must melt hard feelings into tenderness. Then he will be able to weep and, through tears, like the warming bird-stain, come to new life. By freezing Asbury in humility, O'Connor dramatizes penthos near melting into tears. Those nascent tears will bring out the hidden workings of Asbury's new relationship with the Paraclete. If Asbury is called to weep, his story is not one to weep over. Rather, "The Enduring Chill" calls for rejoicing. The shock of joy after so much pain, the prospect of solitude after so much society, signals spiritual restoration. After all, Asbury's world would be incomplete if he did not end by not renouncing it, by changing from blind indulgence to clear-eyed self-scrutiny.

"Parker's Back" begins with a backcountry tableau of a married couple outside the house they have rented to make a life together. Sarah Ruth Cates is sitting on the front porch snapping beans. Her husband O. E. Parker sits on a step glumly observing his wife from some distance. Although Parker is where he lives, he is not at home at home. He is sick of home, disgusted by Sarah Ruth, and longs to be elsewhere. Parker's route to this dead-end marriage is a love-map with many years in its making and myriad sidetracks pursued. Now age twenty-eight, Parker began a vague search at fourteen when wanderlust seized him at a fair. In a sideshow tent, he saw onstage a man tattooed all over his body. The designs gleamed with figures of humans, animals, and flowers. As the performer moved, his body brought a universe to life. The spectacle stunned the teenager. The tattoos held the wonder he lacked in himself and etched a world that relieved his deep loneliness. He was hooked on the spot as a tattoo fancier. The "peculiar unease" (*CW* 658) Parker experienced at the fair was the call to live with those splendors that he knew were on earth and could also be in him.

Parker's hunt for that place where glories thrive is inevitably a matter of tattoos. Besides the strong sexual appeal that these body pictures have for the women Parker seeks, tattoos express his need to stabilize his uprootedness. At different locales, when the needles puncture his skin, otherwise unreal cities and groundless ports reify into a living part of his being. The act of linking his body to the world's body offers momentary respite from Parker's perpetual moving about. Parker sails through places and jobs like a moon through a homeless sky. Obscurity surrounds his actual wanderings as secrecy shrouds his full name. This opacity makes O. E. Parker's passages less an experience of places than of the inner disturbances they stir up. All we know for sure is that "everywhere he went he picked up more tattoos" (*CW* 659) and no lasting satisfaction. The drift takes its toll. By remaining in constant motion, he never has to look at himself except in narcissistic admiration. Although young and healthy, Parker within is really a dying man whose eyes look everywhere for healing without knowing what is destroying him. He grumbles, curses, grovels, brawls, and sobs without gaining any insight into his trials and geographical triangulations.

For an understanding of Parker's warring inner life, one can turn to Augustine, an ancient writer O'Connor admired who was torn like Parker by his sexual desires and came to a radical change through the example of the desert solitaries. In his celebrated exploration of memory, Augustine writes: "men go out and gaze in astonishment at high mountains, the huge waves of the sea, the broad reaches of rivers, the ocean that encircles the world, or the stars in their courses. But they pay no attention to themselves" (8 [216]). For Augustine, this flight away from one's self reenacts the fall of the human soul; and to run away from oneself is to drive oneself further from God, who lies within one's inmost being. And so it is with Parker. The marvel he seeks by fleeing around the world lies within himself—the very self he shuns. Moreover, the roaming of his unquiet heart is for the divine, though he gives no thought to God.

To his mother, teachers, the U. S. Navy, and his wife, Parker is an unruly hedonist hell-bent on pleasing his will and senses at any cost. But O'Connor takes Parker the heathen more seriously (Coles 90–93). She sees him battling principalities and powers, engaged in the essential combat of solitude. Parker's very failure to grasp his predicament marks his struggle and indicates the hold his chaotic passions have over him. The demons' skill is to delude him into a snare of false allurements that take him away from the wonder he seeks. These provocations also keep him in flight from human relations. He is a solitary who never stops, never settles in any place. His goal may be self-gratification, but his balky divagations express the double dimension of journey and the need for rootedness that defines desert life. Parker's share of the desert world also comes through in what he does not seek. He has no interest in wealth and prestige, and so temporal goods and power do not block his search. Underneath his bluff machismo there is a contrary conviction lying so deep that Parker holds no communication with it. He knows only an insatiable ache that yields disconnected tattoos pressing down as fevered, clashing fantasies: "It was as if the panther and the lion and the serpents and the eagles and the hawks had penetrated his skin and lived inside him in a raging warfare" (*CW* 659). All the signals that matter to Parker come through tattoos (Farnham 114–16; Westarp 103–4). They encode his inner strife with the message that he is mired in habits that obstruct his finding the wonder he seeks.

As Augustine says and O'Connor shows, only a great external power can break the habits that subject a person to his or her demons. In the case of O. E. Parker, O'Connor's toughest renegade, divine intervention takes the form of theophany, as fearful and dazzling in "Parker's Back" as it is in the book of Exodus. God appears visibly to Parker not once but twice, first *to* him and then *in* him. The initial appearance recapitulates the calling of Moses. While baling hay—but preoccupied with getting a tattoo for his back—Parker crashes the tractor into a tree that bursts into flame: "He could feel the hot breath of the burning tree on his face" (*CW* 665). His feet and head also get the message from the fervid spirit. In Scripture, God ordered Moses to remove his sandals because he stood on holy ground (Exodus 3:5); but with Parker, compliance requires more assertive action, and so the fire devours his shoes. The theophanic blast propels hotfoot Parker fifty miles to the city to get the blistering presence of God felt in the accident burned into his back. The burning tree does to Parker what the burning bush did for Moses: it conveys divine holiness through an attraction that instills fear. This dread is in the interest of freedom, for Moses is the prophet without equal in liberating those in captivity.

O'Connor's fusing of the Mosaic call with Parker's pursuit of freedom adds something new to her desert poetics. Moses, Israel's liberator, held a special place in the minds of the early hermits. For the Christian desert-dwellers, as for the Israelites, Moses was a desert man set apart under God's election and charismatically empowered to bring a people to God. The freedom he accomplished was gained through power forged in exile. Moses has been preeminently the man of law, which guides Jews and Christians in understanding the will of God. Obedience to divine will was the hallmark of the hermits' renewal of the covenant. Abba Anthony saw Moses as the mediator of the divine law and word. When presented with an enigmatic passage from Leviticus, Anthony cries in a loud voice: "God, send Moses, to make me understand this saying" (*Sayings*, Anthony the Great 26 [7]). When the solitaries felt the divine likeness in their brethren, they observed their faces shining with the reflected glory of Moses. "We see this in the stories describing the visages of some of the greatest elders," writes Burton-Christie; "they were seen to reflect the light of the great biblical exemplars" (290).

Moses' prominence in patristic writing receives its crowning exposition in Gregory of Nyssa's fourth-century treatise *The Life of Moses*. A brief comment on this crucial formulation of Christian spirituality will explain its bearings not only on Parker's call but also on the sweep of O'Connor's poetics of solitude. In Gregory's reflection, the Mosaic charisma exemplifies the practice and goal of ascetic life. Moses' withdrawal from active participation in worldly affairs prepares for his reception of God's instruction and service to others. Emphasis quite naturally falls on the desert as the ground of Moses' calling and moral development. By means of desert hardship, the prophet gains the hearing of the people; then, as the people progress toward Canaan, the desert dramatically portrays how God restores the exiles' capacity to reflect the divine nature. For Gregory, the marvel of this similitude of God is bound to the austerity of desert life. In effect, Moses leads his people through a ceaseless ascetic transformation into the likeness of God. Gregory goes on to seek out the spiritual understanding that corresponds to history. By these scriptural signs, the ancient hermits identified themselves as part of the historic people of God.

Gregory's spiritual interpretation of history corresponds to O'Connor's anagogical and ascetic reading of our age. O'Connor sees the present need to establish a relation with God and through her fiction commends asceticism as a way of finding our true selves and healing our inner wounds. O. E. Parker seems a most unlikely figure through whom to recommend self-denial, but O'Connor perceives in Parker's headstrong hedonism a desire for spiritual discovery that expresses the hidden longing in his counterparts. She makes the lost soul Parker the guide to direct an equally bewildered age back to its sacred origin. And with an incongruity that befits her choice of moral lamp, O'Connor has Parker light the way through the Mosaic glory blazing on his back. There is no end to surprises in this desert as the dullest of men comes to wear the brightest countenance. As in the Exodus story, fire translates the essence of divinity in "Parker's Back." The process takes hold when Parker's tractor crashes and "the hot breath of the burning tree" scorches his face (*CW* 665). Once this intense heat strikes Parker, its current takes him over. Without knowing what hit him, and yet sensing that the burning sensation countenances no defiance, the singed Parker speeds his truck to the city for a tattoo, the only balm for the burning ache. Gradually, the fire sweeping across Parker's face spreads into his will to melt its ironclad bond to personal gratification, and he chooses as "a suitable design" (*CW*

665) "the haloed head of a flat stern Byzantine Christ with all-demand-ing eyes," the sight of which parches his throat, which is "too dry to speak" (*CW* 667). The tattoo is meant to stoke Sarah Ruth's sexual in-terest but instead inflames another desire in Parker the seducer. Work-ing with what God finds in Parker—namely, his love of tattoos—the di-vine fire does to Parker what the flame has done repeatedly in sacred history: God's fire terrifies and consumes to purify Parker.

Fire expresses yet another quality of ascetic practice. For Amma Syn-cletica, citing Hebrews 12:24, this discipline interiorizes the fire of the theophanies: "Our God is a consuming fire" (*Sayings*, Syncletica 1 [231]). For those who receive and embrace the fire of the Spirit, the practice of self-purification becomes synonymous with the desert call: "You cannot be a monk unless you become like a consuming fire" (*Sayings*, Joseph of Panephysis 6 [103]). Renunciation consumes the solitary's life in worship to God. The experience entails living with physical and spiritual terror, for "man purifies his soul in the fear of God, and the fear of God burns up his body" (*Sayings*, Macarius the Great 12 [130]).

O'Connor gives unmistakable indications that Parker is living un-der the sign of ascetic fire. By the time he arrives at the tattooist's shop, he "was already losing flesh" and is so preoccupied with needing a tat-too that is "better even than the Bible" that he "began to lose sleep" (*CW* 664). It is not simply Sarah Ruth's indifferent cooking that causes Park-er's physical losses, nor is it anxiety that deprives him of rest. A stark discipline is taking hold in him as he wrestles with his nagging demons. The site of his struggle is his heart, the locus of ascetic conversion. Its palpitations control him. At the tattooist's shop, Parker finally stops running. He sits down to thumb through the book with pictures of God. In doing so, his heart alone, not his feet, propels him backward and for-ward: "Parker's heart began to beat faster and faster until it appeared to be roaring inside him like a great generator" (*CW* 667). His heart senses the proximity of God, whose energy creates the wonder Parker has been seeking all his life. He searches for wonderment, sexual excitement, and freedom; he finds God, the source of it all. At the sight of the Byzantine Christ, Parker's heart stops or—as O'Connor typically represents divine contact as a penetrating, edged instrument—it "appeared to cut off" (*CW* 667). The eyes in the face of glory pierce Parker. In fact, the full face stabs Parker. Christ himself is the catanyxis, delivering a blow that resuscitates Parker's stopped heart. The fearless daredevil sits "trembling; his heart began slowly to beat again as if it were being brought back to life by a subtle power." There "was absolute silence" (*CW* 667), the silence of solitude in which Christ reads Parker's inmost being.

As only God looks to the heart (1 Samuel 16:17; James 2:9), the icon's sharp eyes alone penetrate Parker's true self, reaching to whom he really is and what he truly wants. Then the eyes draw obedience out of the man who has heeded only personal whim. Wordlessly, Parker acquiesces to have the intricate Byzantine Christ tattooed into his back. Tattooing involves the burning and coloring of flesh, which become part of the consuming fire controlling Parker's destiny. In sacred matters, purification comes first. Parker must wash his back. The rest of the expiation is beyond his control. Christ is indelibly scorched into Parker's skin in such a way that healing scars form the likeness of Christ. After two days under the deft tattooist's hot stippling, Parker is in the hand of God, the artist whose craft glows forth when the tattoo is finished. Christ's face glitters with a radiance that stimulates the damaged optic nerve of the morally blind Parker. Parker wants to ignore the image; but when forced to look into two mirrors, he cannot miss the rays from the "all-demanding" eyes that are "enclosed in silence" (*CW* 670). Christ's eyes insist that Parker confront the divine image singed into his flesh. The Greek word for tattoo is *stigma,* meaning brand or hot iron. Parker is stigmatized in accordance with the fourth-century penal practice of being marked as defamed by domination and with the subsequent mystical understanding of being honored with stigmata corresponding to Christ's wounds. This ineradicable divine likeness issues the call to self-scrutiny, which will force Parker's demons into the light of awareness.

Reluctant to face either Christ or his demons, Parker buys a pint of whiskey, swills it down, and flees to revel with his cronies in a pool hall. But everything has changed; evasions and denials do not work. The icon stares, as George Kilcourse richly explains, with the force of Christ's own ascesis, a *kenosis* or self-emptying of his divinity (Philippians 2). This "uncongenial" figure, to use Kilcourse's term, manifesting Christ's voluntary human poverty and anguish left by kenotic transformation (Kilcourse 35–46), throws Parker's old partners in sin off balance. Like Satan, his servants readily identify the sacred. Stunned by the icon's heart-reading eyes, the carousers slap, mock, abuse, and finally in a rage throw Parker out. Parker's lifelong brawling takes a turn, and his interior combat becomes externalized. Former friends expose themselves to be enemies; and Parker, who had once scorned Christ, now fights to defend him. The melee reveals what Augustine meant by the tenacity of evil habits. Like all demonic assaults, the pool hall row inflicts physical pain that can teach Parker the lesson about himself that hedonist indulgence had obscured. Grumbling, cursing, delinquency, drunkenness, and debauchery come back to him stripped of their alluring guises to be unveiled in their bare-knuckled destructiveness. Dumped in the back alley, Parker sits battered in a strangely satisfying solitude, "examining his soul" (*CW* 672). He may be alone, but he is not desolate; he may be mauled, but he is not diminished. The dregs of defeat hold the particles of Parker's conversion. Having traveled the spectrum from anger to grief to submission, Parker has begun his spiritual education. Without an elder to guide him, Parker will have to learn with his body the hard lessons of intimacy with God.

The next instructive assault comes quickly. Acting as though he is "still in charge" (*CW* 672), Parker dashes home for the sexual favors that the tattoo should bring from Sarah Ruth. When she sees the Christ, however, she throws a temper tantrum. Another wife might be satisfied to beat her husband for staying out all night, but Sarah Ruth thrashes Parker to condemn him and all that the face of Christ stands for: "'He don't *look*,' Sarah Ruth said. 'He's a spirit. No man shall see his face.'" After screaming, "'Idolatry!'" (*CW* 674), she flogs Parker with a broom across his shoulders, which are already cut and enflamed with the fresh lesions of Christ's face. Sarah Ruth's fiery scourge sums up the fraudulence of her religion. She is entirely convinced that flesh is evil, God is utterly remote, and salvation is available only to the few who could attain her hidden spiritual knowledge; and she is, for O'Connor, totally wrong. In denying Christ's humanity, Sarah Ruth attacks the basis for the Christianity that she vehemently professes. She replaces the Incarnation with her stingy idea of God. In worshiping her private truth, she is the idolater. Moreover, her self-denials, which suit her scrawny body and small heart, are in the interests of pride. Such self-righteousness exemplifies false asceticism in that Sarah Ruth denies herself to despise the physical world.

As a reviler, Sarah Ruth nevertheless performs a spiritual service for Parker by bringing into the open the demons that have been distorting his search for wonder. In denying the genuine humanity of Christ, she rejects the dignity of flesh. Such hatred of the body is hardly new in the history of religion. It took a particularly florid expression in the mid-third century with the prophet Mani, whose preoccupation with the nature of evil brought about a dualism between absolute evil and absolute good. Goodness, for Mani, is only the spirit. The Christ of the Manichee is the passive crucified Jesus and nothing more; he is certainly not God's Logos in wholly human form. Manichean Christianity is the church of mind. Augustine had studiously fought it; the desert mothers and fathers battled the reduction of goodness to mere spirit; and O'Connor wages war against "the Manichean spirit of the times" that has "infected" our age and widened the "disjunction between sensibility and belief" (*MM* 33).

O'Connor commissions O. E. Parker, her staunchest sensualist, to combat the foes of the body. O'Connor pays Parker the deeply painful honor of burning into his back the patron under whose aegis Parker will wage war. Humility will arm him for combat, and sorrow will remold Parker's body through tears to fit the icon of Christ. The future of Parker's transformation into solitary warrior is already clear to the onlooker's eye and ear. Parker's sexual urgency gives way to sobbing as his self-indulgence dissolves into a lament for the world. As Elijah mourns under a broom tree for the idolatry of Israel (1 Kings 19:4), Parker leans against the pecan tree crying from the injuries inflicted by the idolatries of our time. Parker now feels the cultural demons for the harmful illusions they are. And so he changes at the story's end. He is weeping in a new solitude that opens his way to God. The dazzling Christ marks and adopts Parker as a son of light who, wrestling with the demons of darkness, shines with the promise of the supreme day of light.

Both God's understanding of Parker and Parker's new understanding of himself are rooted in asceticism. The old vessel he made for himself is shattered. Released from the compulsion to seduce, Parker can now submit to Christ, who bestows esteem through deference. Parker's homage, however, will not be a subjugation but a means to interior progress. Parker will get into trouble along the way. (How could he not?) But God will get him out of trouble again. Parker's resignation to sorrow makes all the difference in battling the adversary. As Sarah Ruth's eyes harden with triumph in beating him, Parker's eyes soften with surrender. And yet while he bends in defeat, one senses that the lines have been laid out for a successful outcome against the enemy. The plan is in the tattoo on his back that precipitates the flow of tears from his eyes. The man of selfish instinct has been called not only to be a man for others but to be the man of penthos, the solitary whose heart, stabbed by God, streams with a compassionate grief over the possible loss of salvation. Conversion demands renunciation, for disciplining the will turns the heart to God. This process brings about an increasing transformation into the likeness of God.

From Scripture, it is known that the human search for God, which arises from the natural human desire to know what God looks like, has a crucial impediment. Because of human sin, the face of God is mortally fearful. God does not permit Moses a direct experience of the divine countenance. When responding to Moses' prayer to see God's glory, God says: "you shall see my back, but my face shall not be seen" (Exodus 33:23). God's reply is definitive, and yet God's words do not remove the human desire to see the face of God. In human encounters, face-to-face contact stirs interior recognition in the heart, and humanity naturally seeks this awakening with the divine. Asceticism provides for Gregory of Nyssa in *The Life of Moses* a way of reconciling the human desire to behold God with God's decision to remain hidden even when manifestly present. By uniting Moses' burning need to see God with the aim of desert life, Gregory finds the directive for the ascetic seeker: "And to the one asking about eternal life he [God] proposes the same thing, for he says *Come, follow me*. Now, he who follows sees the back" (251 [119]).

Gregory's ascetic reading of Moses' life leads us directly to O'Connor's anagogical presentation of Parker as a reluctant, shriven solitary crying like a baby against a pecan tree. Here she shows her unwilling age how to fulfill the human longing to encounter God face-to-face: Behold Parker's back. Never has O'Connor been more daring than in "Parker's Back" in disclosing the concealed God. Nor has she been anywhere more pointed. "'Look at it!'" Parker cries to Sarah Ruth and the rest of the world. And again, he is crying in anguish: "'*Look* at it!'" (*CW* 674). At the end of the story, written near her own death, O'Connor is most direct: Follow Parker's back.

To follow Parker's back is not just a story of drawing near to God and of God's self-disclosing. "Parker's Back," O'Connor's final bidding from her final solitude, tells of rebellious unbelief in a way that reassures readers that the church is not just for believers but also for strivers, even loathsome ones. O'Connor's solicitude goes far beyond ordinary sympathy for those she described to John Hawkes on 13 September 1959 as caught in "the conflict between an attraction for the Holy and the disbelief in it that we breathe in with the air of the times" (*HB* 349). Hers is a compunction, a mourning for the possibility of lost eternal life, whether her own or that of others. Few ever had a greater understanding of such compassion than did the desert mothers and fathers; they were specialists in penthos. Although many writers have expressed anguished concern for our age, no one has felt and given life to the very special urgency of godly sorrow for our time as has O'Connor. Penthos is the spiritual passion underlying her writing that bursts forth like the tattooed Christ in her final work—a passion whose result is an exceptionally significant art. As in Parker's struggle with his unbelief, the encounter with God for O'Connor is one of shocking intimacy; but that intimacy brings her man of sorrows even closer into mystery. The initial light of the burning tree ignited by Parker's tractor yields to the baffling shadow of the pecan tree against which Parker leans, sobbing in pain. Once again, God's revelation in O'Connor's world takes the form of unknowability; but this time, grace abounds to the chief of sinners.

"Judgment Day" tells of a southern man forced in old age to die in New York City. The condition of estrangement is O'Connor's tried and true subject; and among her numerous displaced persons, the old man has been consistently the most forlorn, and most intriguing, for O'Connor. Her first published story, "The Geranium" (1946), takes up the old southerner exiled in the East, and she recasts his plight several times during the course of her career. The elderly outcast hovers in O'Connor's imagination as the classic embattled wanderer whose journey to God she must get just right. All her versions of the old sojourner's struggle profit from O'Connor's fine rendering of descriptive detail; all delineate the aged castaway with clear-eyed dignity; and all have a sharp narrative design. But the final recounting in "Judgment Day" has a felt intensity and supplementary inner vibration that its predecessors have merely in latency. The story may be regarded as a testament of the old hero's finest hour, a consummation of all his strivings and strayings, the fulfillment of his bravest responses to a sequence of eternity-making circumstances.

The source of this new and culminating power lies in O'Connor's assimilation of desert asceticism into her art. There is so much more— more evil and more resistance to evil—surrounding the old man's loneliness in "Judgment Day" than is found in the social dislocations of the earlier texts. The pains of reclusion in the preceding versions are in the final account recharged with the courageous faith of a bereft man who consciously embraces the trial of solitude not as social rejection but as the condition of eternal life. With greater agony comes greater consolation. The hero's struggle in "Judgment Day" is no longer just a matter of getting his old body back where it belongs. Rather, the test of courage for the aged warrior is to get his entire menaced being to rest with God. Whereas the opponents in the previous accounts are time, the strange place, and alien mores, the enemies in "Judgment Day" are the old man's own worst evils incandescently brought back to life in a murderous attack. But the demons that cleave tenaciously to the old man's heart are at last expelled. "Judgment Day," in sum, is forged in the crucible of solitude, which produces the epitomizing example of O'Connor's desert poetics.

Ascesis filters into the basic aspects of the story's narrative to pare the structural coordinates of time and place to a potent minimum. The action takes up one hour or so on a cold winter morning in New York. A mere trickling of sand in the hourglass condenses the long flow of T. C. Tanner's hard life. While precise unity of time is common among O'Connor's stories, the brevity of the narrative present of "Judgment Day" calls special attention to her technique because the length of the antecedent past is by far the longest in O'Connor's fiction—longer even than the sweep of past life in her two novels. "Judgment Day" reaches back thirty years through Tanner's memory and thereby telescopes the farthest backward glance into the shortest present to give us a glimpse into the timeless future. Little wonder, then, that this temporal confluence creates a sense of summing up in urgency, since the story was completed several months before O'Connor died, while she was severely weakened by infections and medication (*CW* 1256). Her distillation of T. C. Tanner's prolonged, vexatious life into his last hour abridges clock time to soul time.

As with time, so it is with place. Tanner's hour marks the juncture connecting his spiritual pilgrimage with a geographical journey. The physical adventure stretches back 1,100 miles to Corinth, Georgia, from which Tanner came and to which he struggles to return. That distance contracts in the story to his daughter's cramped fourth-floor apartment in a tenement. Poor health further restricts Tanner to a chair by a window facing a brick wall. The picture that lingers is of a Georgia woodsman caught in an Edward Hopper scene of New York decay and vacancy. Being caught in an urban coop is especially racking for an old-timer who is accustomed to the freedom of his local fishing stream and trees. Although this small area makes Tanner feel jailed in an unlawful exile, there is another side to his confinement. O'Connor puts her dying old man in a cell for reflection and solitude, where he must grapple with his demons to get back home. Home burial for Tanner is an anguishing necessity. Having his body put in native ground means dying in the Lord. Corinth is his entry into peace. From the beginning to the end of "Judgment Day," the old anchorite has only his cell, and his New York cell is all that he needs to reach his goal. One hour in his cell brings Tanner to render an account of his actions over a lifetime. "Go, sit in your cell," says Abba Moses, "and your cell will teach you everything" (*Sayings*, Moses 6 [139]). Nearly 1,600 years later, O'Connor vivifies this essential counsel for spiritual growth in a dank hallway leading to a grim apartment in freezing New York. The city is Tanner's desert, and he knows it. In a postcard to his friend Coleman Parrum, Tanner describes the Yankee waste as "NO KIND OF PLACE" (*CW* 676).

As Abba Moses predicts, Tanner's cell schools him in finding peace with God. The lesson comes through his daughter's reneging on her promise to bury him in Georgia and a brutal neighbor, a black man who revives racist demons in himself that Tanner thought he had conquered.

Tanner's thirty-year glance into his past tells us how prepared he is for these adversaries. The period runs roughly from the early 1930s to the early 1960s. These were fateful decades in American social history that thrust their evils into the piney woods of middle Georgia. Tanner was born and bred in the Old South that for him had none of its legendary social or moral securities. The bygone order, in fact, was a lingering agony for Tanner. The poverty of the Great Depression became his permanent economic privation; he witnessed the bloodthirsty arrogance and devastation of World War II, to which he lost two sons; he was caught up in the maelstrom of postwar cultural changes that deepened his social displacement; and in old age, he grappled with the civil rights movement that altered everything he understood about his relations with others and the world. Add to these hardships a chronic kidney condition and banishment in the East, and one can say that T. C. Tanner's life is warfare on many fronts from beginning to end.

The demons inciting injustice and violence in Tanner's outer world also cause strife in his inner world. As a defense against indignity, he is proud to the point of doing himself in; and his basic instincts have persistently been to dominate others, to destroy, and to inflict grave injury. Notwithstanding his propensity for violence, Tanner is also a man of faith. Since childhood, the most powerful restraint on his evil impulses is "the fear of hell" (*CW* 681). Because there is no letup in his demonic urge to destroy, the fear of losing God does not lessen in Tanner as he matures. In fact, a lifetime of poverty and dislocation has sharpened Tanner's need to rest with God and therefore has strengthened his spiritual arsenal. By the time Tanner arrives in New York, his prolonged engagement with evil has made him a seasoned veteran in the war against Satan. None of this remarkable inner life, of course, is seen or felt by those around Tanner. Sitting in the chair by the window near the end of his long pilgrimage, O'Connor's last warring old southerner lives among us unrecognized for the spiritual combatant that he is.

While anonymity suits Tanner's eremitical struggle, it would not violate his integrity to reflect on the remarkable inner work this plain man undertakes in captivity. In fact, it would be true to O'Connor's art to go beyond the dismissive social view to see how the old man's burdens are his destiny. O'Connor wants her readers to understand that a man of low social status who spends most of his life on land that is not his own and, worse, ends up as a stranger in a strange land, after many false starts, still toils and stumbles because of his fierce conflicting wills; and yet, in the shadow of inner emptiness, the old man's deepest endowments come to fruition. To see Tanner's spiritual flowering in his winter life is to appreciate the special meaning that accrues to the epithet "old man" in "Judgment Day." Antiquity had a term to honor as well as describe particular virtues in old age. In patristic writing, a male who was mature in years and spirit was a *geron,* the Greek word for old man. Geron is also the name accorded the solitaries who were acknowledged as persons bearing spiritual gifts in how they live and what they say. The collection of *The Sayings of Old Men* is a *gerontikon.* O'Connor is too down-home to use such words, but one can profit from thinking of T. C. Tanner as a modern geron and of "Judgment Day" as O'Connor's "Gerontion." Inevitably, the 1919 poem of that name by T. S. Eliot, who spoke to O'Connor's sensibility, comes to mind; and the association points up the differences in how Eliot and O'Connor saw growing old in the arid wastes of modern life and in the ways in which asceticism informs the art of both. Eliot's weary speaker is "Swaddled with darkness" amid "windy straits" and finds more of his inner deadness in the "wilderness" he inhabits (21–22). Spring depletes him further. "In depraved May" Eliot's old man feels himself to be "A dull head among windy spaces" (21–22).

O'Connor's landscape is equally harsh, but nature's bluster affects Tanner in a strikingly different way. Winter, O'Connor's season of God's will, replenishes him. Alongside Eliot's blanched and fretted European, who picks his way through "Rocks" and "merds" (21) with profitless cerebrations, O'Connor's backwoods geron is sanguinely vital. Tanner can be counted on to be playful and neighborly—dangerously so. He is committed to the world that Eliot's grouser despises. Tanner acts. He gets up and goes. He loves. His heart goes to beloved Corinth friends in friendship with God. Self-scrutiny and his will surrendered to God serve as a magnetic compass directing Tanner homeward. O'Connor's geron is a winter man who remains exposed to the will of God. Clearly, the desert tests but does not daunt Tanner. He knows New York is "this no-place" (*CW* 685) emitting air "fit for cats and garbage" (*CW* 676); and yet, like Anthony the Great, Tanner understands the desert as the call to partake joyously in all that God has created.

Tanner's struggle to accept God's call comes to light as he looks back on his past. His review is a rustic version of Augustine's journey through memory. Plainly described, these reconsidered years for Tanner are, as the past was for Augustine, desert years. The life of O'Connor's geron has been nomadic. He has wandered through a series of lonely, alien places and circumstances that have brought him into deeper geographical and personal zones of emptiness. All but Tanner's last days are spent in the Georgia backwoods, and even that paltry ground is not his own. At one time, Tanner did own a small piece of land that he lost through some unspecified misfortune. Bad luck stays with him. Widowed, with his daughter up North, Tanner squats on property owned by people in Florida. This patch of land is nearly worthless and yet suitable for Tanner. He and his friend Coleman Parrum build a shack and run a liquor still on the place. When Doctor Foley, a local black entrepreneur, buys the land and demands that Tanner cut him in on the bootlegging operation, Tanner in demonstration of poor white pride leaves for New York. The city proves sorrier than where he squatted, and his captivity is more painful than the domination he would have felt working for Foley. Forsaken as New York is, the urban shambles are not Tanner's last desert. There is the torturous and fatal passage through the tenement's hallway that leads finally, after all the other desert places he has traveled, to the starkest place of all. The desert Tanner discovers is the desert of his own soul. Because this territory is held in sin, it is understandable that the old man's looking back on his thirty-year exodus gleams with wicked memories along with flashes of regret and deliverance.

To enter Tanner's recollection is to pass into the vanished world formerly inhabited by Anthony the Great. Once inside Tanner's loneliness, one discovers for the first and last time in O'Connor's fiction her treatment of friendship, that special form of love that the ancient solitaries celebrate, that Augustine honors in his *Confessions*, and that richly permeates O'Connor's letters. Friends sustained the hermit novelist by expanding the confines of her anchoritic life. On her side, O'Connor was a steadfast friend who in correspondence as well in direct contact gave from the deepest part of herself. The bond of friendship in "Judgment Day" involves Tanner's love for Coleman Parrum, his black partner in Corinth, with whom he shares a shack. Fate shunts both to hardship and impermanence. They live apart from society on unoccupied land without right, title, or payment of rent. The grace of their thirty-year companionship strengthens Tanner to deal with his loneliness and his murderous will. Tanner's tie to Coleman is indissoluble. It stabilizes Tanner and gives new meaning to his solitude. Lived out in Tanner's love for Coleman, God's will is no longer a matter of demands placed on Tanner. Rather, God's will becomes the essential adventure that Tanner undertakes in loving partnership. Grounded on mutual support even though separated when the story takes place, Tanner makes his way to God by means of his anticipated reunion in Georgia with Coleman. The trees, the streams, and the friend in Corinth seem all the sunnier for having been evoked through the misty chill of the New York winter.

O'Connor's personal correspondence reveals how friendship is bound up with her faith in God; but her representing of the love between male friends in "Judgment Day" as a path to God is entirely new to her fiction. Clearly, O'Connor is taking risks here. Besides the provocation that inheres in celebrating the love of a white man for a black man in the South during the years leading up to the 1960s (or in any time, really), the subject requires O'Connor to overcome her innate reluctance to portray aspects of her personal life. Friendship is a protected issue for her. But the nearness of death, which opens up her characters' hearts, also frees O'Connor to be more than usually vulnerable; and so in "Judgment Day," she exposes to view the foundation and inner workings of the human bond of friendship that in unaccountable and very intimate ways give humans courage.

Friendship in "Judgment Day" centers on a far grittier daily existence than anything O'Connor experienced on her mother's comfortable farm and fine house in Milledgeville. Tanner and Coleman's predicament is the most abject condition recorded in O'Connor's writing, and hers is a world in which scarcity is the norm. The poverty shared by Tanner and Coleman is so grinding that it makes the subsistent lot of Mason Tarwater and his great-nephew in *The Violent Bear It Away* superabundant by comparison. Powderhead at least yields corn and has a name. The place where Tanner and Coleman settle has no name because it has no monetary worth. Nevertheless, this unfit place is home. Their shelter is a shack in which Coleman sleeps on a pallet at the foot of Tanner's bed. As the hierarchical arrangement indicates, Coleman is bound ("'paroled'" [*CW* 680]) to Tanner; but the legal agreement belies the true covenant between them. Tanner is fettered to indigence, which binds them together in equality. Both have hit bottom. Both are hermits. Coleman cooks, cuts firewood, and empties slop. Tanner, once from plain people, has been reduced to settling in with a disreputable black drifter.

Lowliness makes Tanner susceptible to Foley's power, and the infamy of Tanner's living with a black man outrages his daughter; but the old man's loss of public esteem recommends him and his black cohort to O'Connor. Together, they exemplify a life that is opposed to racism and pride. Their reliance on each other fosters a recognition that what they receive in friendship comes from God. True friendship draws on God's friendship, as shown first in the giving of God's son and then in Jesus' giving of himself for others. This ideal of self-donation lays out the lines along which O'Connor develops friendship in "Judgment Day." Neither gain, nor kinship, nor business, nor personal desire unite Tanner and Coleman. Certainly, survival on the most primitive terms keeps them together. And yet amid the stinking decay and sweat, of which there is a great deal in their bodies and their habitat, the dynamic of their friendship is spiritual, decidedly rooted in the fear of God and fleshed out in a desert practice born of an appreciation that, as only O'Connor's desert humor could describe it, "clownishness and captivity had been their common lot" (CW 683).

By now, one expects to find features of eremitical spirituality in O'Connor's fiction, but one could not have anticipated the fine degree to which the desert differentiates the bond between Tanner and Coleman. As with O'Connor's other strivers, her *geron*, without knowing about the desert-dwellers, gives tangible form to the ancient ascetics' instructions for friendship. Any discussion of the desert teaching about friendship must acknowledge at the outset that an ambivalence shades the presentation of brotherly love. In the *Sayings*, reticence and indirection surround the subject of intense personal relationships. The motive was not animosity toward same-sex relations or disgust with the body but concern over erotic attachment in general: personal entanglements would have gotten in the way of their struggle to control sexual needs along with other bodily desires. Friendship, however, is a different matter. There is a considerable emphasis in patristic writing on warm, committed feeling among the hermits. *The Lives of the Desert Fathers* repeatedly honors friendship. Moreover, *The Lausiac History*, a central text, is itself a gift of stories of anchorites given in love by Palladius to Lausus, who aspired to emulate the hermits; and with Palladius, there is no hesitation in cherishing a sister or brother as a helper or a guide on "the journey which leads to the Kingdom of God" ("Foreword" 17). That aim of drawing near to God, which is the center of ascetic life, forges the bond uniting friends. In *Christian Friendship in the Fourth Century*, Carolinne White stresses that "the Christian ideal of friendship is intimately bound up with the ascetic ideal" (221); and both are all that O'Connor wishes for her protagonists.

Besides Augustine's writings, the most sustained commemoration of friendship in patristic sources comes in Cassian's imaginary interviews with various ascetics, collected as his *Conferences*. Cassian is remarkable not only for his insights but also for his honesty in acknowledging physical feelings among members of the same sex. Conference 16, "On Friendship" (frequently omitted from selections of Cassian's writing when homophobia set in), in particular sets out the spiritual ideals shaping relations among the solitaries and provides a basis for understanding how imaginatively "Judgment Day" assimilates the ancient precepts for brotherly love. Although an admiring apologist of the Egyptian hermits, Cassian is realistic about the pitfalls awaiting anyone pursuing the life of the spirit, and friendship for him epitomizes the larger strictures along with the consolations of desert solitude. Above all, Cassian understands how friendship can further the Christian's progress toward salvation.

The overarching motive between friends for Cassian is renunciation. The goal among friends is freedom in pursuit of holiness. As self-denial separates the solitary from the social world, so in the desert it joins one solitary with another: "The first foundation . . . of true friendship consists in contempt for worldly substance and scorn for all things that we possess" ("On Friendship" 451). Cassian then applies the principle of detachment from material things to the emotional attachments of the inner world, where friendship thrives. Above all, one must not cling to one's private will, to which the demons cling. Brotherly love requires one "to prune his own wishes" so as not to "prefer his own opinions to those of his neighbour" (452). Letting go of personal desires promotes a recognition that "the blessing of love and peace" must come before whatever is useful or necessary (452). For this concord to prosper, one must give up anger, the demon that divides friends and cools love.

Cassian brings all these teachings into focus by citing as the last basis for friendship the founding experience of desert life: keeping death before one's eyes. In relation to death, Cassian's reflections on friendship are more than usually astute, for he is afraid neither of mutual tenderness nor the body's end. Far from being morbid and self-involved, facing death squarely saturates friendship with a gentle acknowledgment of what is trivial before the commandment and judgment of God. The person who feels death's immanence will not allow grievances, small or large, to linger in the heart and will repress "all the motions of lusts and sins of all kinds" ("On Friendship" 452). Cassian rounds out his commentary with a question posed in a gentleness born of his insights into solitude: "Lastly, how can he retain even the least vexation with his brother, who realizes that he is presently to depart from this world?" (452).

"Judgment Day" answers Cassian's question. Certainly, in the teeth of death, T. C. Tanner does not hold on to any annoyance that came between him and Coleman, and there was much to overcome. Their first encounter is a battle of nerves. At the time, Tanner is the foreman of a sawmill employing six black laborers, a sorry crew that does not show up on Monday and is hard to keep in line when they do come to work. Tanner "managed them with a very sharp penknife" (*CW* 681), with which he also whittles wood. The knife's constant violent motions get the men to work and cover up Tanner's trembling hands that result from his kidney condition. One day, Coleman drifts onto the scene and is ignored; but when he comes the next day, Tanner must deal with him because Coleman is a challenge to Tanner's precarious power over the black men. Coleman is twice Tanner's size, and he is drunk. Leaning against a tree, Coleman the idler insolently looks down on his black brothers who bother to work at the mill under this scrawny white man. Coleman is a cool boozer who shows by his stance that the smaller white boss is not "so big" (*CW* 682) as he acts. His challenge to white male authority introduces grave risks all around. Murder is in the air. In his astute close reading of "Judgment Day," Ralph Wood reminds us that a white man could easily get away with killing a black man in the South at the time ("Obedience" 171n.10). Aware of his impunity, Tanner brags about putting his penknife into a worker's gut if pushed to it, but he knows that this big, haughty black stranger could with "pleasure" (*CW* 683) grab the weapon and turn it back on him.

This cagey, deadly racial sparring takes an unexpected turn as the men size each other up. Both are wary and yet drawn to the other. An "invisible power working on the wood" in Tanner's nimble hands produces two rims of spectacles that he wires together into fake eyeglasses for Coleman's bloodshot "muddy liquor-swollen eyes" (*CW* 683), which sorely need help. Alcohol has impaired his sight but not his heart and sense of humor. Tanner's frank gesture of playful optics softens the tough black man and opens his inner eye. In a blink, a vision of their vulnerabilities flashes to dispel the hostility between them. Coleman recognizes Tanner's fear of being showed up as a bungler and as impotent before his workers, and Tanner takes in Coleman's tacit admission of his own bungling. The poseurs of toughness sense the authentic loneliness they share. They are lost solitaries whose hard paths have crossed.

At this juncture, black and white stand before each other divested of facades. Such psychological nakedness can be held in view only briefly. Macho banter quickly clothes their exposure, and humor seals for life their mutual recognition. Coleman smilingly defers to Tanner's status as a white man who owns up to the stronger black stranger's gracious acceptance of this puny white man's vanity. Neither is in control. The unseen power uniting a proud hothead with a drunkard is love born of humor and humility. Humility in particular permits black drifter and white weakling to see that they are not each other's enemy, but that both are captive to evil impulses of a mightier power. That gleam of self-scrutiny shifts their contest away from race to their common foe, Satan, who manipulates them through their inner demons of pride and wrath. The meekness bringing Coleman and Tanner together summons the friends to combat their adversary. Their ordnance is what Cassian calls the "similarity of virtue" ("On Friendship" 451) that anchors friendship. Coleman and Tanner are so good for each other that their alliance flourishes for thirty years, during which time black and white, bear and monkey, meld into union.

After three decades of reading each other's heart, Coleman and Tanner exchange outer shapes while inwardly becoming more themselves. Coleman has shriveled into "a stinking skin full of bones" (*CW* 679) and is as soused as ever on stump liquor. Tanner, on the other hand, has taken on Coleman's old ursine body and is as ready as ever to kill. When Doctor Foley comes, Tanner's first thought is to protect himself from Foley's control by shooting the "brown porpoise-shaped" (*CW* 680) proprietor. Fear of losing eternal life, certainly not of the law, keeps Tanner from murdering the landowner; Tanner is unwilling to go "to hell for killing a nigger" (*CW* 684). He may live with and love a black man, but he will not run his still for a sharp black conniver. We sense in Tanner's instinctive wrath the demon of pride staking a claim that supersedes Foley's title on this territory. Tanner decides to save face by going north to live with his daughter. The old man does not mean to do himself in, but pride invariably coils back on the vulnerability it pretends to protect. Pride drives Tanner to the devil's lair in New York.

If the wilderness of middle Georgia makes Tanner, then the desert of New York City unmakes him. New York deprives the old man of everything except his love for Coleman and his desire to rest with God. The alien city dispossesses him of the overgrown paths and stream that are his native land, while comparable destructive forces in his body, those of sickness and aging, reduce Tanner to immobility and reliance on his daughter's care. These physical hardships are the stern discipline of his exile. The demonic denizens of the desert, unerringly drawn to weakness, unleash their attack on their worthy victim. First, Tanner feels the pang of filial betrayal when overhearing that his daughter will renege on her promise to bury him in Corinth. Then the remains of his dignity and body become a target of neighborly hatred. The African-American actor who has recently moved into the adjacent apartment loathes Tanner for his cordial entreaties. The black city-dweller is too accustomed to personal and racial estrangement to accept friendliness. Alienation suits the actor, and enmity gives him something to say and do. He seethes hostility when Tanner greets him with the affectionate southernism "'Preacher'" (*CW* 683). Besides having no sense of humor and no use for neighbors, the actor does not believe in God or, as he says, any of "'that crap'" (*CW* 690). Tanner's being white and old qualifies him for the worthless heap. On first encountering Tanner's amicability, the actor, groomed in a flashy city version of Doctor Foley's power attire, knocks Tanner down, causing a concussion and a stroke.

The actor's response conforms to the conduct expected in the devil's territory. Where Satan reigns, gratuitous brutality signals strength. The hermits, accustomed to the sudden demonic assaults, learned otherwise. They came to see violence as a weakness resulting from the failure to recognize one's own capacity for evil. As O'Connor shows in Coleman's first meeting with Tanner, beneath violence lies spiritual frailty; and the weak for Cassian are "harmful and cannot bear wrongs" ("On Friendship" 458). Cassian's words on the inner infirmity that works against friendly relations are so wise that one would do well to hear him out in full. For Cassian, the spiritually weak are "quick and ready to offer reproaches and sow the seeds of quarrels, while they themselves cannot bear to be touched by the shadow of the very slightest wrong, and while they are riding roughshod over us and flinging about wanton charges, they are not able to bear even the slightest and most trivial ones themselves" (458). Cassian's desert psychology goes to the heart of O'Connor's portrait of the actor. Because he is too weak to be befriended, the most simple appeal to neighborly assistance causes him to commit the most vile injury. When Tanner lifts his hand to ask for help after stumbling down the stairs, the actor beats the old man to death and desecrates his corpse.

Tanner's death in the desert caps a series of deprivations and demonic assaults. His death is raw and persecutory. With calculated precision, the actor wrenches Tanner's head and limbs between the bars of the banister. He then obliterates the old man's face with his black hat, creating an execution-style black hood. This is killing as vengeance against love. A laughingstock locked in the heathen's rage, Tanner dies as a sacrifice to devils. His murder is rich in implications to satisfy the current need to account for human conduct by the oppressions causing it. The conflicts in "Judgment Day" emerge from harsh and unjust exercise of power, and the black actor sums up in one fatal moment the race relations in America that remain unchecked by self-examination and uncleansed by neighborly love. These powerful social forces, however, come to the reader without any call for legal redress. The laws of society are beside the point that O'Connor aims to make. Like the ancient hermits who rejected the late Roman culture that rejected them, O'Connor turns her back on the violent way of the modern age, which in the name of law has destroyed millions of people and has no use for faith.

Justice for O'Connor lies elsewhere. If one wants to see how critical of society O'Connor can be, one has to follow the route she takes to a juridical order that dispenses justice by enforcing observance to a moral universe guided by divine integrity and interposed by mercy. In every story, O'Connor uses the malefactor as entrée to this higher order, and each time she amazes by turning the tables on the adversaries of God. In "Judgment Day," the black actor is the agent of retribution in pummeling Tanner with the forces of his own past wrathful and racist demons; but then O'Connor tricks the trickster with retaliation. Rather than stopping the old wayfarer, the actor accelerates Tanner's final passage. O'Connor transforms the dark hallway where violence has made its home into the desert of expiation that Tanner successfully crosses. Tanner is on his way home.

To get home, Tanner's must traverse the hallway of the tenement. The narrow, crooked corridor is "dank-smelling and empty" and carpeted with "moldy" linoleum (*CW* 693). The residue of a dingy waste is tangible. Its slovenly jumble, however, merely hints at the dread of the passageway. Tanner has entered a mystical terrain where the essential features are not temperature and odor but modulations of the heart and will in their relationship to God, who is the goal of the old man's journey. O'Connor's geron must negotiate the deepest desert of all, his soul. In this interior geography, what counts is how Tanner confronts the demons who beset his heart. Like the ancient hermits, Tanner sees the forces blocking his way to God not as indomitable powers but as outer and inner weaknesses he must overcome. He resists the outer demon of betrayal in his daughter by putting all his physical energy into getting home, and he entrusts the same total resource to combating the demons of pride and wrath in the actor. The source of Tanner's strength is self-scrutiny. He sees that he was wrong to leave Georgia and that pride, not Doctor Foley, drove him out. He confesses the harm of his own willfulness. Despair in New York also teaches him the lesson of loneliness, and he testifies that if he had known that New York meant enslavement, he "would have been a nigger's white nigger any day" (*CW* 685). By taking the worst implications of "nigger" into himself, the old white man purges "nigger" of its racial sting to denote the moral status of accepted surrender. Tanner's being a "nigger" means yielding not to injustice but giving himself over to God and to Coleman's friendship.

As meekness keeps Coleman free in Corinth and spares him from the trap set by pride, so Tanner's new humility in New York frees him from racism and self-importance. Being the boss, he understands, is a demonic illusion that caused pain to others and himself. Having admitted his dependency on Coleman, Tanner can see that Coleman is also wiser in staying put and accepting his lot as black, poor, drunk, and free of illusions of self-sufficiency. Coleman, to use words he would never need, does not cling to his ego. His "I" is not cultivated or pandered to. Coleman is a desert-dweller who accepts hardship as the will of God, whose law shapes Coleman's soul. Coleman is a hero of obedience who teaches by his very being. Small wonder that Coleman is a cherished friend. Tanner comes to Coleman's wisdom as he sets out for Corinth to join his friend, who can be trusted to get Tanner's body where it belongs. Proper interment for the old man is the material provision for the life awaiting after death. His heart and mind are united in getting home, but he will need a greater resource to get there. To avail her geron of that aid, O'Connor sees to it that the trip is physically impossible for Tanner to complete on his own. His impaired body lumbers a few feet before he collapses. Never has Tanner's existence been more precarious, and he knows it. His cares are greater than ever. No sooner does he gain enough muscular control than his balance gives way, sending the tremor inward to strike his self-confidence: "A sensation of terror and defeat swept over him" (*CW* 693). After falling down the steps, Tanner is so weak that he must strain to open his eyes and lift his hand for help. Everything goes into preserving himself from physical defeat, and he fails physically because the black actor is on hand to kill him.

Tanner's state at the end of "Judgment Day" is that of crushing privation. The hardships endured in Georgia are mild next to the destitution that finally overtakes his body and leaves his soul the patrimony of insecurity. When Thomas Merton says that the "life of the hermit is a life of material and physical poverty without visible support" (*Questions* 187), the modern monk depicts the emptiness that O'Connor brings her solitary geron to experience. For both Merton and O'Connor, this emptiness is requisite for the fullness of life. With Tanner's body broken and his mind fixed on judgment day, he knows that the final form of his being means nothing less than his resurrection. Usually one to allow such an unutterable reality to remain in mystery, O'Connor in a letter plainly explains that "a resurrection of the body . . . will be flesh and spirit united in peace, in the way they were in Christ" (*HB* 100). The locus of this perfecting growth is Tanner's dying body, which manifests the condition of his soul's learning, agony, and reward.

As penthos delivers Tanner to the fullness of his life, and as his destiny brings O'Connor's fiction to a close, so one can use the last leg of his interior journey to reflect on how O'Connor's poetics of solitude is both a mode and an accomplishment, an orientation and a fulfillment. One way to look back on O'Connor's encompassing artistry is through Seamus Heaney's 1995 Nobel Lecture, entitled "Crediting Poetry." In accepting the prize, Heaney credited poetry for making possible an exploration of "the wideness of the world" through which he comes to terms with the anguish and atrocities he witnessed in his native Northern Ireland. The "wideness of language" opened the ground for Heaney "to make space . . . for the marvelous as well as for the murderous" in his poetry (449, 458). Heaney's expressed salute to lyric poetry describes the implicit tribute that O'Connor pays to fiction. Again, in honoring the power of language, Heaney's words also gauge O'Connor's moral expanse. From the beginning of her career, killing and wonder have shaped the patterning of her explorations. So interconnected are violence and the supernatural that murder frequently catalyzes saving grace. And Heaney's range finder of poetic intensity is much the same as O'Connor's instrument for determining the breadth and depth of her purview. As we have seen, O'Connor's power springs from the allusive, ascetically charged extension of her words. The spirituality forged in solitary struggle with evil marks her stories as a huge act of faith in fiction and in God. That trust in the poetics of fiction comes through with a joyful clarity at the end of "Judgment Day." Here, O'Connor distills the murderous and the marvelous into an epitomizing moment as Tanner passes through the final cavern of darkness to reach God.

The instant Tanner feels his body overwhelmed by defeat, he throws himself on God for support: "'The Lord is my shepherd,' he muttered, 'I shall not want'" (*CW* 693). His confession, uttered in the psalm of helplessness, welcomes divine help in crossing the final desert, his darkest valley, to the house where Tanner hopes to dwell. At this point, O'Connor draws a curtain across the old man's grief, and readers see and subsequently remember him in vital joy. From within, his heart's need keeps his direction fixed. This singleness of desire has always been crucial in the solitary's finding a way through the unmarked desert. Abba Anthony says: "Whatever you find in your heart to do in following God, that do, and remain within yourself in Him" (Ward, "Foreword" xxvi). Anthony's pragmatic advice—the essence of desert spirituality—accounts for the personal integrity Tanner achieves in exilic solitude. A proud heart is humbled before his maker. His open heart holds the power to receive soul-shaking truths about himself. He sees the devil in himself, accepts blame, and suffers assaults with a humility that makes the victory his. He bears poverty and keeps death before him to feel its force in his blood and tendons. The pain of mortality makes of the old man's body not only the discipline of his life on earth but also the condition of his resurrection to eternal life.

Resurrection comes to Tanner twice in dreams of reunion in Corinth. This repeated hope endows the word *judgment* in the story's title with an additional desert richness. As Tanner imagines his body coming to rest at home, he intuits the essential value of his life: his profound love for Coleman Parrum intimately links him to God. Tanner's life and death, as Anthony says, are with his neighbor (*Sayings*, Anthony the Great 9 [3]), for human bonds are the basis of humanity's wholeness with God. This resonant homage to the love between Tanner and Coleman stands out in O'Connor's writing, because elsewhere in her fiction, frustration and annoyance mark human relations; but in her story of human friendship, as in O'Connor's personal relations, encouragement and comfort are the rule among the old Georgians. With her old men there is concern not for self but for others, which indicates that the divine dwells in their friendship.

In Tanner's reverie, this loving care felt for a friend's physical well-being bursts into geriatric hoopla. Fun, trickery, and delight greet his body's return. These are visceral pleasures, for Tanner's struggle always has been physical. Grace comes by means of the 6:03 A.M. train bringing Tanner in a pine box to Corinth. He knows for sure that Coleman, red-eyed on bootleg liquor and reliable on love, will be at the station as he has been present for Tanner for many years. Coleman will have the good sense to get a mule and wagon to tote the corpse to the grave. And Hooten, the stationmaster friend to the two friends, will lend a hand. The whoopee in the reunion is familiar. Having watched Ruby Turpin's ragtag hallelujah parade ramble heavenward in "Revelation," one can readily picture the procession's sequel in "Judgment Day." Two tattered, age-bent old hicks, wedding hilarity with solemnity, plod to the trudging gait of the borrowed mule that hauls their prodigal friend to the burial ground that surely is not their own. The only thing that is their own is their loyal love. That fidelity makes of their labor a true rite of Christian burial. The earthiness and the piety of the motley cortège, the levity of its grandeur, are celestial—and preposterous, and rightly so. As clownishness is their shared lot, merriment with cheers all around is their fit mode. After all, the bonds of friendship based on exilic poverty and practiced in trust to God have in them a grain of folly.

Faced with the world to come, the work of folly is the supreme wisdom of faith. Faith brings the train south, and faith protects Tanner in solitude. Friendship in "Judgment Day" thrives on faith to widen aloneness into community. Burial cannot be done alone. Being dependent makes Tanner grateful for others: first to his daughter, who ultimately does ship his body to Corinth; and then to Coleman and Hooten, who certainly receive the body and get it into the dirt. Faith takes the geron out of the turmoil of the world and beyond the range of demonic forces to friends who band together as a small, inconspicuous colony of the kingdom in the desert of exile. To toast the occasion, these friends will have a delight that is waiting at Coleman's still to cap their intoxication over setting Tanner right for everlasting life. The last of Tanner's tricks (pushing through the coffin) is to inaugurate the festivities: "'Judgment Day! Judgment Day. You idiots didn't know it was Judgment Day, did you?'" (*CW* 694). Now they know.

Tanner's epiphany marks the high point of his inner journey and of all the spiritual passages in O'Connor's fiction. The geron's illumination of rest in fellowship reaches all the way back through O'Connor's stories and novels to redress the devil's most blatant subversions of friendship among humans. T. Fawcett Meeks, archlackey of the fiend, tells young Tarwater in *The Violent Bear It Away:* "'And that's the way it ought to be in this world—nobody owing nobody nothing'" (*CW* 362). For Meeks, the best course in Satan's jurisdiction is seeking to love no one and to be loved by none. Tanner's home burial reverses the demon's wisdom. In the old man's dream, everybody owes everybody everything. As Tanner passes from mortal view, here in Corinth one sees a coming together as a community for the purpose of rejoicing in the life of God. Paradoxically, Tanner struggles in solitude and dies in unity. His movement and fate sum up the power of exile and aloneness. The act of withdrawal operates to restore the values that have been reversed. O'Connor's killers, despots, and self-regarding heathens, after all, have souls to think about; and though they comply with social hypocrisies and violence, their determining choices are unworldly.

The goal of friendship for the ancient solitaries is peace. Peace is realized for Tanner. *Hesychia,* or rest, involves receiving others, as Coleman and Hooten welcome Tanner, and reaching out to others, as Tanner does to his friends, to his assailant, and to God for help. Hesychia is inseparable from prayer, which Tanner draws upon in muttering: "'The Lord is my shepherd'" (*CW* 693). His coming together with friends shows that he does not want. The reuniting of lost friends, O'Connor knows from her reclusion, is better honored with smiles than with tears. Tears, nevertheless, have their place, and tears are part of Tanner's preparation for joy. When his daughter says that she will bury him in New York, Tanner is beside himself in grief, because salvation is all that matters to him. He tries but cannot contain the rush of sorrow. The betrayal stabs his heart. Grief swells up: "tears ran down his cheeks; he wiped each one furtively on his shoulder" (*CW* 678). Mourning for the possible loss of salvation, Tanner weeps the true tears of penthos. To lament this loss allows the old man to confront his personal evil and seek pardon for his sins. Repentance does not stop the flow of tears, but its does change their direction.

In the desert elders' experience, tears led to life. Compunction affords the opportunity to review in solitary contemplation what Tanner has lived through in passionate action. He rushes from extremes of anger and pride to the extreme of surrender. Between those extremes a vast distance is traversed and put into perspective through penthos. Moreover, "only weeping leads to blessed laughter" (qtd. in Hausherr 11–12). Sure enough, godly sorrow brings Tanner from murder, both the one he was tempted to commit and the one he suffered, to the marvel of hearty humor. Having undergone the new ascesis of imposed rather than chosen renunciation, Tanner achieves the new penthos. The old man's acute grief, mixed with smiles, expresses O'Connor's modern ascetic piety. With evidence from the heart and an eye on the unseen and believing that the murderous can yield the marvelous, Flannery O'Connor has made the story of T. C. Tanner and her other solitaries as much a prayer as a work of fiction.

Works Cited

Arendt, Hannah. *On Violence*. New York: Harvest, 1970.

Asals, Frederick. *Flannery O'Connor: The Imagination of Extremity*. Athens: University of Georgia Press, 1982.

Athanasius. *The Life of Anthony and the Letter to Marcellinus*. Trans. Robert C. Gregg. New York: Paulist, 1980.

Augustine. *Confessions*. Trans. R. S. Pine-Coffin. Baltimore: Penguin, 1961.

Bacht, Heinrich. "Logismos." *Dictionnaire de Spiritualité*. Vol. 9. Paris: Beauchesne, 1976. 956–58.

Bacon, Jon Lance. *Flannery O'Connor and Cold War Culture*. New York: Cambridge University Press, 1993.

Balthasar, Hans Urs von. *Prayer*. Trans. Graham Harrison. San Francisco: Ignatius, 1986.

Brinkmeyer, Robert H., Jr. "Asceticism and the Imaginative Vision of Flannery O'Connor." In *Flannery O'Connor: New Perspectives*. Ed. Sura P. Rath and Mary Neff Shaw. Athens: University of Georgia Press, 1996. 169–82.

Brown, Peter. *The Body and Society: Men, Women, and Sexual Renunciation in Early Christianity*. New York: Columbia University Press, 1988.

———. *The Making of Late Antiquity*. Cambridge, Mass.: Harvard University Press, 1978.

———. *The World of Late Antiquity*. New York: Norton, 1989.

Burns, Marian. "O'Connor's Unfinished Novel." *Flannery O'Connor Bulletin* 11 (1982): 76–93.

Burton-Christie, Douglas. *The Word in the Desert: Scripture and the Quest for Holiness in Early Christian Monasticism*. New York: Oxford University Press, 1993.

Butler, Alban. *The Lives of the Fathers, Martyrs, and Other Principal Saints*. 4 vols. Baltimore: Metropolitan Press, 1845.

Bynum, Caroline Walker. *Holy Feast and Holy Fast: The Religious Significance of Food to Medieval Women*. Berkeley: University of California Press, 1987.

Cassian. John. *Conferences*. Trans. Colm Luibheid. New York: Paulist, 1985.

———. "On Friendship." In *Nicene and Post-Nicene Fathers of the Christian Church*. 2d ser. Vol. 11. Grand Rapids, Mich.: Eerdmans, 1973. 450–60.

Chitty, Derwas J. *The Desert a City*. Crestwood, N.Y.: St. Vladimir's, 1966.

Coles, Robert. *Flannery O'Connor's South*. Baton Rouge: Louisiana State University Press, 1980.

Dante Alighieri. *The Divine Comedy*. Trans. Charles S. Singleton. 6 vols. Bollingen Ser. 80. Princeton, N.J.: Princeton University Press, 1977.

Delbanco, Andrew. *The Death of Satan: How Americans Have Lost the Sense of Evil*. New York: Farrar, 1995.

DeLillo, Don. *Great Jones Street*. New York: Vintage, 1973.

———. *Underworld*. New York: Scribner, 1997.

———. *White Noise*. New York: Penguin, 1985.

Desmond, John F. *At the Crossroads: Ethical and Religious Themes in the Writings of Walker Percy*. Troy, N.Y.: Whitston, 1997.

———. "The Lessons of History: Flannery O'Connor's 'Everything That Rises Must Converge.'" *Flannery O'Connor Bulletin* 1 (1972): 39–45.

———. *Risen Sons: Flannery O'Connor's Vision of History*. Athens: University of Georgia Press, 1987.

Di Renzo, Anthony. *American Gargoyles: Flannery O'Connor and the Medieval Grotesque*. Carbondale: Southern Illinois University Press, 1993.

Dorotheos of Gaza. *Discourses and Sayings*. Trans. Eric P. Wheeler. Kalamazoo, Mich.: Cistercian, 1977.

Early Fathers from the Philokalia. Trans. E. Kadloubovsky and G. E. H. Palmer. London: Faber, 1981.

Eliot, T. S. *The Complete Poems and Plays, 1909–1950*. New York: Harcourt, 1952.

Elliott, Alison Goddard. *Roads to Paradise: Reading the Lives of the Early Saints*. Hanover, N.H.: University Press of New England, 1987.

Evagrius Ponticus. *The Praktikos and Chapters on Prayer*. Trans. John Eudes Bamberger. Spencer, Mass.: Cistercian, 1978.

Evans, Robert C. "Poe, O'Connor, and the Mystery of The Misfit." *Flannery O'Connor Bulletin* 25 (1996–97): 1–12.

Farnham, James F. "Further Evidence for the Sources of 'Parker's Back.'" *Flannery O'Connor Bulletin* 12 (1983): 114–16.

Feeley, Kathleen. *Flannery O'Connor: Voice of the Peacock*. New York: Fordham University Press, 1982.

Fitzgerald, Robert. "Introduction." In *Everything That Rises Must Converge*, by Flannery O'Connor. New York: Farrar, 1965. vii–xxxiv.

Fitzgerald, Sally. "An Interview with Sally Fitzgerald," by Susan Elizabeth Howe. *Literature and Belief* 17 (1997): 1–20.

Frost, Robert. *The Poetry of Robert Frost*. Ed. Edward Connery Lathem. New York: Holt, 1967.

Geertz, Clifford. *The Interpretation of Cultures*. New York: Basic Books, 1973.

Gentry, Marshall Bruce. *Flannery O'Connor's Religion of the Grotesque.* Jackson: University Press of Mississippi, 1986.

———. "The Hand of the Writer in 'The Comforts of Home.'" *Flannery O'Connor Bulletin* 20 (1991): 61–72.

Gregory of Nyssa. *The Life of Moses.* Trans. Abraham J. Malherbe and Everett Ferguson. New York: Paulist, 1978.

Han, Jae-Nam. "O'Connor's Thomism and the 'Death of God' in *Wise Blood.*" *Literature and Belief* 17 (1997): 115–27.

Hausherr, Irénée. *Penthos: The Doctrine of Compunction in the Christian East.* Trans. Anselm Hufstader. Kalamazoo, Mich.: Cistercian, 1982.

Hawthorne, Nathaniel. *The Scarlet Letter.* Ed. Sculley Bradley, Richmond Croom Beatty, and E. Hudson Long. New York: Norton, 1962.

Heaney, Seamus. *Opened Ground: Poems, 1966–1996.* London: Faber, 1998.

Hendin, Josephine. *The World of Flannery O'Connor.* Bloomington: Indiana University Press, 1970.

Jung, C. G. *Modern Man in Search of a Soul.* Trans. W. S. Dell and Cary F. Baynes. New York: Harvest, 1962.

Kilcourse, George. "'Parker's Back': 'Not Totally Congenial' Icons of Christ." *Literature and Belief* 17 (1997): 34–46.

Kinney, Arthur F. *Flannery O'Connor's Library: Resources of Being.* Athens: University of Georgia Press, 1985.

Lawrence, D. H. *Studies in Classic American Literature.* New York: Viking, 1961.

The Lives of Simeon Stylites. Trans. Robert Doran. Kalamazoo, Mich.: Cistercian, 1992.

The Lives of the Desert Fathers. Trans. Norman Russell. London: Mowbray, 1980.

Meek, Kristen. "Flannery O'Connor's 'Greenleaf' and the Holy Hunt of the Unicorn." *Flannery O'Connor Bulletin* 19 (1990): 30–37.

Merton, Thomas. *Disputed Questions.* New York: Farrar, 1976.

———. *The Seven Storey Mountain.* New York: Harcourt, 1976.

———. *Thoughts in Solitude.* New York: Farrar, 1976.

———. *The Waters of Siloe.* New York: Harcourt, 1949.

———. *The Wisdom of the Desert.* New York: New Directions, 1960.

Nash, Roderick. *Wilderness and the American Mind.* 3d ed. New Haven, Conn.: Yale University Press, 1982.

The New Oxford Annotated Bible with the Apocrypha. Revised Standard Version. Ed. Herbert G. May and Bruce M. Metzger. New York: Oxford University Press, 1973.

Niland, Kurt R., and Robert C. Evans. "*A Memoir of Mary Ann* and 'Everything That Rises Must Converge.'" *Flannery O'Connor Bulletin* 22 (1993–94): 53–73.

O'Connor, Flannery. *Everything That Rises Must Converge.* New York: Farrar, 1965.

———. *Flannery O'Connor: Collected Works.* Ed. Sally Fitzgerald. New York: Library of America, 1988.

———. *The Habit of Being: Letters of Flannery O'Connor.* Ed. Sally Fitzgerald. New York: Farrar, 1979.

———. *Mystery and Manners: Occasional Prose.* Ed. Sally and Robert Fitzgerald. New York: Farrar, 1969.

Olschner, Leonard M. "Annotations on History and Society in Flannery O'Connor's 'The Displaced Person.'" *Flannery O'Connor Bulletin* 16 (1987): 62–78.

Palladius. *The Lausiac History.* Trans. Robert T. Meyer. Westminster, Md.: Newman, 1965.

Paphnutius. *Histories of the Monks of Upper Egypt and the Life of Onnophrius.* Trans. Tim Vivian. Kalamazoo, Mich.: Cistercian, 1993.

Percy, Walker. *Lancelot.* New York: Ivy, 1977.

———. *The Moviegoer.* New York: Ivy, 1961.

———. *The Thanatos Syndrome.* New York: Ivy, 1987.

The Sayings of the Desert Fathers: The Alphabetical Collection. Rev. ed. Trans. Benedicta Ward. Kalamazoo, Mich.: Cistercian, 1984.

Schaub, Thomas Hill. *American Fiction in the Cold War.* Madison: University Wisconsin Press, 1991.

Sexton, Mark S. "'Blessed Insurance': An Examination of Flannery O'Connor's 'Greenleaf.'" *Flannery O'Connor Bulletin* 19 (1990): 38–43.

A Short Breviary. Ed. Monks of St. John's Abbey. 5th ed. Collegeville, Minn.: Liturgical, 1951.

Smith, Marcus A. J. "Another Desert: Hazel Motes's Missing Years." *Flannery O'Connor Bulletin* 18 (1989): 55–58.

Spaltro, Kathleen. "When We Dead Awaken: Flannery O'Connor's Debt to Lupus." *Flannery O'Connor Bulletin* 20 (1991): 33–44.

Stewart, Columba. *Cassian the Monk.* New York: Oxford University Press, 1998.

Teilhard de Chardin, Pierre. *The Prayer of the Universe.* Trans. René Hague. New York: Perennial Library, 1973.

Thomas Aquinas. *Summa Theologiae: A Concise Translation.* Ed. Timothy McDermott. Westminster, Md.: Christian Classics, 1989.

Torchia, Joseph. "Inside Flannery O'Connor." *Flannery O'Connor Bulletin* 25 (1996–97): 81–102.

Waddell, Helen. *The Desert Fathers.* Ann Arbor: University of Michigan Press, 1957.

Walker, Sue. "The Being of Illness: The Language of Being Ill." *Flannery O'Connor Bulletin* 25 (1996–97): 33–58.

Ward, Benedicta. "Foreword." In *The Sayings of the Desert Fathers: The Alphabetical Collection.* Rev. ed. Trans. Benedicta Ward. Kalamazoo, Mich.: Cistercian, 1984. xvii–xxvii.

———. *Harlots of the Desert: A Study of Repentance in Early Monastic Sources.* Kalamazoo, Mich.: Cistercian, 1987.

Ward, Benedicta, ed. and trans. *Daily Readings with the Desert Fathers.* Springfield, Ill.: Templegate, 1990.

Westarp, Karl-Heinz. "Teilhard de Chardin's Impact on Flannery O'Connor:

A Reading of 'Parker's Back.'" *Flannery O'Connor Bulletin* 12 (1983): 93–113.

White, Carolinne. *Christian Friendship in the Fourth Century.* Cambridge: Cambridge University Press, 1992.

Williams, George H. *Wilderness and Paradise in Christian Thought.* New York: Harper, 1962.

Wood, Ralph C. *The Comedy of Redemption: Christian Faith and Comic Vision in Four American Novelists.* Notre Dame, Ind.: University of Notre Dame Press, 1988.

———. "Flannery O'Connor, H. L. Mencken, and the Southern Agrarians: A Dispute over Religion More Than Region." *Flannery O'Connor Bulletin* 20 (1991): 1–21.

———. "'Obedience to the Unenforceable': Mystery, Manners, and Masks in 'Judgment day.'" *Flannery O'Connor Bulletin* 25 (1996–97): 153–74.

Index

RICHARD GIANNONE is a professor of English at Fordham University and the author of *Music in Willa Cather's Fiction, Vonnegut: A Preface to His Novels,* and *Flannery O'Connor and the Mystery of Love.*

Typeset in 9.5/12.5 Trump Mediaeval
Composed by Jim Proefrock
at the University of Illinois Press
Manufactured by Maple-Vail
Book Manufacturing Group

University of Illinois Press
1325 South Oak Street
Champaign, IL 61820-6903
www.press.uillinois.edu